Albert Cornelius Perkins

Exercises at the Centennial Celebration of the Founding of Phillips Exeter Academy, New Hampshire, June 20 and 21, 1883

June 20 and 21, 1883

Albert Cornelius Perkins

Exercises at the Centennial Celebration of the Founding of Phillips Exeter Academy, New Hampshire, June 20 and 21, 1883
June 20 and 21, 1883

ISBN/EAN: 9783337061951

Printed in Europe, USA, Canada, Australia, Japan

Cover: Foto ©ninafisch / pixelio.de

More available books at **www.hansebooks.com**

EXERCISES

AT THE

CENTENNIAL CELEBRATION

OF THE FOUNDING OF

PHILLIPS EXETER ACADEMY,

NEW HAMPSHIRE,

JUNE 20 AND 21, 1883.

EXETER, N. H.:
WILLIAM B. MORRILL, PRINTER.
News=Letter Press.
1884.

INTRODUCTORY.

Phillips Exeter Academy is one of the few American schools which can boast of having attained the age of a century. Its founder, Hon. JOHN PHILLIPS, LL. D., who was himself for some years a successful teacher, had the wise foresight to launch and give direction to the school in his lifetime. During eighty-four of its hundred years, it had only two principals, the one for fifty, the other for thirty-four years. Dr. BENJAMIN ABBOT, the former of these, elevated the infant seminary to the highest rank, and won for himself a position as an educator of youth scarcely second to that of the most eminent masters of the great public schools in England. Dr. GIDEON L. SOULE, his successor, had already been a professor in the Academy for sixteen years, and upon being advanced to the principalship, fully maintained the authority and dignity of the office, and the well earned credit and standing of the school.

Among the many brilliant names upon the roll of instructors in the Academy, are those of RICHARD HILDRETH, for fourteen years, and JOSEPH G. HOYT, for eighteen years, who gained here, as they did subsequently in other fields of effort, the highest repute for learning and ability. Of the Academy to-day, it is enough to say that two of its professors, Messrs. WENTWORTH and CILLEY, have served for a quarter of a century each, with usefulness and distinction in no way inferior to those of the ablest of their predecessors, and that its methods, its traditions and its prestige have been fully preserved, while the continually increasing requirements of successive years have been abundantly met.

The general catalogue of Phillips Exeter Academy reveals some extraordinary facts. Beyond dispute the galaxy of great names which it contains is unequalled in the annals of any school in the country, within the like period. The wide diffusion of its more than five thousand Alumni is not less remarkable. Among them are found representatives from every state and territory of our own country, and from each of the four quarters of the globe.

In respect to its religious character this school is entirely free from sectarianism. The Founder provided that the Principal should be a member of a Calvinistic church, and that the Trustees and Instructors should be Protestants. Every student is required to be present at the daily devotional exercises in the Chapel, and to attend some church, regularly, on the Christian Sabbath. But no denomination controls the school, and the students, or their parents or guardians for them, have the power to choose what form of religious worship and church they will attend. The morals of all pupils are sedulously inquired into, and no boy whose influence threatens to be injurious is suffered to remain in the Academy.

The standard of scholarship of Exeter has always been of the highest. Students are expected to keep well up with their classes, and to do their work faithfully, in order to retain their connection with the school. There is no room in it for the idle or the incompetent. To have gone through the course of Exeter carries with it the assurance that the work has been thoroughly done.

In the discipline of the school as much freedom is allowed the pupils as is consistent with safety. This course has been found most efficacious in encouraging them to cultivate self-reliance, a sense of honor and true manly qualities.

As the one-hundredth anniversary of the foundation of Phillips Exeter Academy drew near, the friends of the institution assumed, with one voice, that the interesting and important event was to be celebrated by suitable memorial exercises. Meetings of those especially interested were accordingly called, at which it was determined that the celebration should be held at the close of the summer term, on June 20 and 21, 1883.

It was also decided that the exercises should consist of a Reunion of the Alumni, to be held on the evening of the former day; of an Oration and a Poem, to be delivered in the forenoon of the second day; and of Addresses by the presiding officer and distinguished guests, after the public dinner to be served in the afternoon of the second day.

A general Committee was appointed by the Trustees to take charge of the Centennial Observances, consisting of Messrs. CHARLES H. BELL and JOHN C. PHILLIPS of their own Board, GEORGE A. WENTWORTH of the Faculty, and PRENTISS CUMMINGS of Boston, Mass., and ARTEMAS H. HOLMES of New York, N. Y., of the Alumni.

Invitations were given to Hon. GEORGE BANCROFT, LL. D., of Washington, D. C., to preside at the dinner; to Rev. HORATIO STEBBINS, D. D., of San Francisco, California, to deliver the Oration; to EDWARD HALE, A. B., of Cambridge. Massachusetts, to recite the Poem; and to the Principal, ALBERT C. PERKINS, Ph. D., to make the Address of Welcome to the Alumni.

Each of the gentlemen named accepted the part assigned him.

It is only necessary to add that the gathering of the Alumni was fully equal to the most sanguine expectation. that the occasion was full of enjoyment to them, and highly satisfactory to every friend of Phillips Exeter Academy.

NOTE. It is proper to state that most of the Addresses are printed from the stenographer's report, without revision by their authors.

WEDNESDAY EVENING.

On the evening of Wednesday, June 30, the meeting of the Alumni was held in the Academy hall. ALBERT C. PERKINS, Ph. D., the Principal of the Academy, presided, and delivered the following

ADDRESS OF WELCOME.

I do not know who it was that first took from Lucretius the phrase *alma mater* and applied it to a school of learning. The readiness with which men have accepted and adopted it is proof that no other name more fitting or more significant could be found. The personality of such a parent is indeed somewhat intangible. No artist can draw her lineaments or define her stature. But her character, her guiding influence, her capacity to encourage and help her children, her love and solicitude for them while they are under the roof-tree, her watchful anxiety for them when they have let go her hand and have bidden her good bye are all solid realities that are felt in the lives of thousands of men. Many elements go to make up the qualities of our cherishing mother. All that lingers in the atmosphere and constitutes the *genius loci* is a part of her. The aim of the founders, the influence of early instructors, the way in which that influence has been perpetuated, the achievements of generations of men who were trained under her, the aroma exhaled from story and tradition, the name and fame of preacher, statesman, lawyer, teacher, historian, poet, healer, man of art, man of business, all are united in filling our conception of the traits assigned to this beloved mother. I can easily believe that you, who come back here to-day, are glad to recognize this close and tender relationship. I can assure you that all that this relationship implies is bound up in the welcome extended to each and every one of you. Some of you were here in the early years of the century. You have heard the story of the school from the lips of men who personally knew John Phillips; you thus link us to the day a hundred years ago, when for Phillips Exeter Academy it was "time for school to begin." You remember Dr. Abbot in the prime of his manhood, and you are able to reproduce, as no one else can, the spirit of those days of hope and promise, as well as of fulfilment. We look upon you, and with renewed sense of the truth of the words we say: The glory of children are their fathers.

Others of you, the great body of the Alumni who are now in the active business of life, bearing the brunt of affairs, were here under the instruction of Dr. Soule. Ten years ago he was here to welcome me. The shadows of advancing years touched him gently, and brought out a sweetness, rare even in the ripest old age. A father wrapt in the interests of a son could not extend to him counsel more kind and considerate than that which I received from him. My acquaintance with him of six years enables me to imagine somewhat of the cordial paternal cheer with which he would have greeted you and bidden you to this feast, if his eye could have seen this day. Let the memory of him, as it abides here in freshness and beauty, be the best greeting we can give to you.

A thousand busy men are living who have joined our school within the last ten years. These, more than anybody and everybody else, are the school of to-day. They come from colleges, from professional schools, from the first steps of the slippery steep on which they are feeling that the work of life has fully begun. The "shades of the prison house" have not yet wholly closed around them. We hear the ringing tones of their voices, the confident word of hope, and feel the rush of that enthusiasm that keeps the world forever young. Our festival would be a lonesome place without them; and with no cold or formal words we summon them. The fathers shall see the same boys in them that were here of another generation. Perhaps too they will feel that the bond which unites us most firmly is the survival of something of the boyish spirit, and that in a gathering like this we can take liberties with Shakespeare and say:

"One touch of boyhood makes the whole world kin."

We gladly salute those not of our household, sons of other schools, benefactors, helpers in the work of training men. The "common bond" surrounds us and includes within it all who, like our founders, have set "virtue and piety" and "sound learning" as the imperishable jewels of the soul.

"There are few spectacles more striking or more affecting than that which a great historical place of education presents on a solemn public day." So said Macaulay at Glasgow when the famous University had reached the end of four centuries. So say we at the end of our first century, as we have turned towards the four winds in quest of the children of the Academy, as we have seen them coming from the ends of the earth and gathering around us with their wealth of honors and precious influences, their record of the impress they have stamped upon the history of their time.

But, after all that can be said, the warmest welcome you will receive must be one not uttered in words. A sentiment pervades the air; it finds expression in the thrill that darts through the clasped hands of old friends, in the gleam that lights the faces of those who come home again to find that sweetness of which they have been able to sing, but not to taste, in the message which the voice of nature shall speak to them as they walk over this ground and pass beneath these trees. It was under the sway of emotions, kindled by thoughts like these, at the commemoration day of a great university, that once in his life the matchless tongue of Edmund Burke faltered and became mute.

It is well that in an age like this, so busy, so practical, so secular, there remains one pious pilgrimage holding a firm place in the affections of the best men—the pilgrimage which the scholar makes to the scene of his early struggles and victories. There he finds what to him comes nearest to the fountain of perpetual youth; there he slakes his thirst with never-failing draughts; there he learns to adjust himself to the world around him; there he clarifies his vision, dimmed it may be by ambition, or greed, or disappointing failure; there, let us ever devoutly pray, he shall never cease to hear the greeting of a fond mother for her returning child. Our salutation is at the end, not of a year, but of a century. It is full of the memory of what that long period has accomplished for the school, for the country and for the world. We expect to hear much, we ought to hear much of all this; but still in an age of progress so wonderful, we do not feel afraid to set our growing school before the eyes of men, to point to her sons girdling the earth with sources of light, enriching literature, science, art, politics, religion, and ask What century plant has produced a fairer flower?

I am now permitted to present to you one of the most highly honored of the sons of the Academy—one who was here early in the present century, a pupil of Dr. Abbot, a life-long friend of Dr. Soule, widely known as a friend of sound and liberal learning—Professor Packard, of Bowdoin College.

ADDRESS OF PROF. ALPHEUS S. PACKARD, D. D.

I entered the Academy, June, 1811, having been admitted on the "Phillips Foundation." I found at Capt. Halliburton's, where those on the "Foundation" boarded, among others, Jared Sparks, John Gorham Palfrey, and Charles Briggs, all on their last term in the Academy before entering Harvard. Those in this position are often called "charity students." They were none the worse for that, none the worse for themselves, nor for the Academy. Not one of us, I am sure, has ever been ashamed of the appellation. Could the record of the "Phillips Foundation" be examined it would, I think, afford an argument in the question recently raised regarding the value of such charities.

I recall with peculiar interest the assistant, then on his' last term of service, Nathan Lord, in subsequent years President of Dartmouth.

At the opening of the next academic year, September or October, 1811, a lad was admitted on the "Foundation" to one of the places made vacant by the entrances to college, the son of a prominent clergyman of Massachusetts, George Bancroft. We were fellow foundationers, fellow boarders, and a part of the time classmates during that year. I had advantage of my comrade in one respect, and I acknowledge in one respect only, which, however, I have held ever since ; I was a year or more older. The record has it, that I entered at twelve, he at eleven. He entered Harvard, myself at Bowdoin. Our paths have been widely divergent. It is nearly sixty-seven years since we had speech of each other, and, I may say, that among special attractions to this celebration has been the hope of meeting my school-mate of seventy-one years ago.

I do not, I trust, violate the propriety of the occasion by referring to a scene of our academic life. Older Alumni remember the exercise in declamation Wednesday afternoons in the Academy Hall. On one of those occasions, Bancroft in a dialogue personated an old man, a father, in breeches, long hose, shoes with buckles, and a bob-wig. His personation was done to the life. The Principal, Mr. Abbot, Prof. Hildreth the assistant, and Henry W. Fuller, had seats on the floor near the entrance. From the side benches near them, I noticed the dignified Principal shaking his sides with laughter at the spectacle on the stage at the farther end of the hall, of the little old man, with emphatic pointing of his forefinger, expostulating in sharp, high-strung tones of displeasure.

It is a tradition, that a German master as he entered his school-room was accustomed to doff his hat, reverentially, to his pupils. When asked the meaning of that act he replied, "because among my boys may be future syndics and burgomasters of the city;" thus obeying the precept of Juvenal, "Reverentia maxima debetur puero." Those who were in the small circle at Capt. Halliburton's in my day thought little of the future that awaited them; one to hold a marked position in the ministry of a church in Baltimore, then to establish wide and lasting reputation by contributions to American history in the lives of Washington and Franklin, and in volumes of the diplomatic correspondence of their country, and lastly to become Professor and then President of Harvard; another after a ministry in a historic church of Boston, to hold a professorship in Harvard and a seat in Congress, and to win a name as the accomplished and faithful historian of New England; and that Worcester boy of eleven! whatever his promise in academic or college days, no soothsayer could have predicted, nor any phantasy of his own suggested, what awaited him in coming years, of honors and responsibilities in the Cabinet at Washington, of foreign embassies at the courts of St. James and Berlin, nor of that which, more than any position in civil life, will bear his name to future generations,—that a labor of fifty or more years in libraries and archives of his own and foreign lands would make him the standard historian of the United States. Let me add, that I question whether any event has touched his heart more than the invitation to preside on this occasion. While thus honored himself, he needs no assurance that the Alumni feel that his acceptance of the chair honors them.

The idea by such an occasion as this is naturally suggested, how important such an institution is to the country! The famous schools of England, Eton, Harrow on the Hill, Charter House, Rugby, how have they contributed to the stability and fame of England! When the Marquis of Wellesley was drawing near his end, in remembrance of his school-days, he enjoined that his body should be laid in the chapel of Eton; and his more renowned brother, the Iron Duke, when he revisited the same school of his early life, and was reminded of the achievements of his life in its prime, exclaimed, "It was at Eton that Waterloo was won;" and in our time that same school sent to Oxford, then to Parliament, and lastly to the position he now holds as one of the ablest, if not the ablest and most cultured of the prime ministers of England, William E. Gladstone. The names I just now mentioned on the "Phillips Foundation" of my day, and I will add those of the twin-brothers, William Bourne Oliver and Oliver William Bourne Peabody, valued names in this town, of Jonathan P. Cushing, who afterwards left an honored remembrance as President of Hampden Sidney College in Virginia, and I must add, that of Gideon Lane Soule, who came on the "Foundation" a year after me, whose eminent service of fifty years was duly commemorated when he retired from office,—these names alone would give character and reputation to any institution. Let me remind the members of the Academy now present, that it is an inspiration to recall the remembrance of eminent men who have frequented the walks, and sat in the halls, under the eminent teachers of this great school.

We ought to be thankful for the endowment of memory. We may wish to forget many things, but who would forget the precious reminiscences this occasion revives? To us, who have reached "the snowy summits of our years," it is a compensation for some of the infirmities of advanced age, that while the present leaves dim traces on the memory—the past, by the constitution of our nature, is yet distinct and fresh. We can look back and down to far distant vales yet bathed in the sunlight of early days. I beg to add a tribute of grateful acknowledgement for what I owe to this venerable Institution; to the unsurpassed dignity, the friendly oversight, spirit of firm yet gentle command, and high tone of scholarship, which were, and have been, maintained from its birth to its centennial day.

Dr. Perkins said: There is one of our sons living in a neighboring town whom I have found through an experience of many years, to be a most remarkable neighbor,—one who is always seeking to do favors and never asking them. It is due to him, very largely, that we are able to look on the representations of the faces of so many of the Alumni and trustees and teachers of the school as adorn these walls; and, if pictured lips could ever speak, I am sure they would utter his name every time he steps within this chapel. I call upon this honored benefactor to address you now—Ex-Governor Prescott.

ADDRESS OF HON. BENJAMIN F. PRESCOTT.

Mr. Chairman: I will not attempt to reply to your flattering introduction, because in so doing I should be obliged to refer to my own work, which might have the appearance of egotism, a quality of character which I have always supposed I did not possess. This gallery of portraits, medallions, and marble busts, with the exception of two or three, may be owing to my personal efforts. The photographs and other works of art are due to the efforts of others. My only regrets are that many more are not upon the walls that rightfully belong here, and which I hope will soon adorn the collection. The group represents, so far as it goes, the faces of those who have been closely identified with the Academy. Its influence upon the pupils, I hope, is salutary. If it is, I am amply paid for my labor. But sir, I will pass this matter altogether. In order to keep within the time allotted for this occasion, I have put upon paper certain facts I wish to set forth, and which, if trusting to an *ex tempore* address, I might omit. The facts and figures may be new, and perhaps of interest to the Alumni and the public who have looked forward with great interest to this memorable occasion.

Mr. President:—We are coming together after an absence of many years, to exchange congratulations around the shrine of this ancient, revered, and renowned institution. We esteem it a precious privilege to be present when its record of an hundred years may be properly set forth in song and speech, by the eminent men who have been designated to take part in the exercises.

And now at the beginning of these centennial festivities we are more than ever impressed with the magnitude of its success, and the grandeur of its history.

The Founder, the distinguished patron of learning in his time, builded greater than he knew, and the result of his munificent donation here has accomplished more for the good of mankind than he ever expected or anticipated. The founding of this seminary of learning by Mr. Phillips was a bold step at the time it was done, for the Revolution was not over, and it was uncertain when peace would be declared between the colonies and Great Britain. But a good cause never waits for uncertainties.

This was the first charter to a literary institution granted by the state. The General Assembly was in session in this town. It was its second session. It met on the second Wednesday of March in the fifth year of the declared independence of the United States. On Tuesday, April 3, 1781, the liberal charter was granted. The instrument had been well considered and matured by Mr. Phillips and his friends. The first Constitution of the then young state was not adopted until October 31, 1783. Thus the charter of this venerable institution antedates the fundamental law of the state by more than two and one-half years. The treaty of peace between the United States and Great Britain was signed November 3, 1783, hence our *alma mater* is older than the declared independence of the United States, and nearly ten years the senior of the Constitution of the Republic. The institution then is entitled to respect by age, if for nothing higher or better.

Through wise counsels the Academy was set in motion on a broad and liberal policy, and its doors were opened to the youth of the land, with no other requirements, except that they present satisfactory evidences of good character and minds susceptible of development. The Academy has been remarkably fortunate in its board of trust and instructors. During its long and eventful history, it has had but thirty-six trustees by election, while seven are necessary to constitute a full board. Many of this number have served from twenty-five to forty years each. The same fact is true in reference to its principals. From 1783 to 1788 it was experimental, and was under the management of William Woodbridge. Dr. Benjamin Abbot, the Nestor of American instructors if not the world's, commenced his career as principal in 1788, and held and fully maintained that responsible position for *fifty* years, when, in 1838, he retired full of honor, commanding the respect and love of all who knew him. He was dignified, courteous, watchful, and kind. Dr. Gideon L. Soule began his labors in the Academy in 1822, as an instructor in the ancient languages, and served with distinguished ability in that chair until 1838, a period of sixteen years, when he was unanimously elected principal to succeed Dr. Abbot, and he served in that position thirty-five years, making fifty one years of continuous service, the combined service of the two being 101 years, and the principalship, eighty-five years, a fact not known in the history of this or any other country. He, too, retired like his predecessor, beloved by all, and commanding universal respect. At the retirement of Dr. Soule, in 1873, the present principal, Dr. Albert C. Perkins, commenced his duties as governor of the school, and took upon his shoulders the mantle that had been so gracefully worn by his predecessor. He has served a decade, having had more than a *thousand* pupils under his management. The school has materially increased in numbers under his wise administration, and he, too, lays aside the mantle untarnished, which he received from his illustrious predecessors. May it always rest upon equally worthy shoulders.

What a remakable history! What other school in the whole world can present the record of having run a completed century with one preceptor and three principals, and under two of the latter eighty-five years?

The world may ask for a statement of our record, whether the result in the past century has been sufficient to warrant its support and patronage in the future. I have prepared a brief and incomplete summary, in no instance exceeding the figures, and in most instances falling far short of the number in each division, owing to the want of data to make a perfect exhibit.

It appears that the whole number of pupils who have had their names entered upon the records is 5,278, of which number over 1,200 have been graduates of colleges, and upwards of 100 are now in colleges, not yet graduated. From this number we have had five Ministers Plenipotentiary to the courts of the most powerful and prominent nations, seven Cabinet ministers in the administration of our own government, eight Senators, and twenty Representatives in the Congress of the United States; twelve Governors of states, one Associate Justice of the United States Supreme Court, four Chief Justices of the Supreme Courts of states, sixteen Associate Justices of the Supreme Courts of states, four Justices of the Circuit Courts of the United States. Attorney Generals of states, 3; presidents of colleges, 9; professors in colleges, 52; clergymen, 180; teachers, 245; attorneys at law, 510; physicians, 262; authors, 32; editors, 25; journalists, 20; eminent historians, 4; merchants, 260; captains in the mercantile marine, 33; major-generals in the army, 3; rear admirals in the navy, 2; and scores of officers in both departments of the service. In fact there is scarcely a branch of business which is not represented by men who received their early, and in many instances only education here. If any institution can show a better record, let it do so on its hundredth anniversary.

Some may ask for names. I will designate a few without classification. Lewis Cass, Daniel Webster, Leverett Saltonstall, Edward Everett, George Bancroft, Jared Sparks, John A. Dix, Joseph Stevens Buckminster, Joseph Greene Cogswell, John G. Palfrey, Gideon L. Soule, William B. O. Peabody, Francis Bowen, Alpheus Crosby, John P. Hale, Jeffries Wyman. In this short list we find the most accomplished diplomats, statesmen, divines, historians, authors, teachers, scholars, and legislators this country has known, whose names and fame reach beyond the limits of the republic, and are well known and honored in lands beyond the sea. Time forbids my going farther.

There has been but one purpose here, and that has been to establish the pupils firmly in the elementary principles of the languages taught and the sciences incorporated in the curriculum. With the foundation well laid and thoroughly understood, the future development is made easy. Manliness and self-reliance are taught and made conspicuous, both of which are of the utmost importance.

The work here is done without ostentation or unnecessary show. The school has stood in the front rank of the classical institutions of the country because it has been governed by one purpose, to thoroughly instruct the pupils in the branches taught.

Unnecessary, unimportant and harsh rules and regulations were never adopted for the government of the boys, but they were expected to maintain the dignified bearing of gentlemen, and bring honor to themselves and the school.

The institution has been conservative and at the same time progressive. It has never caught up the radical notions of the day, but has stood for a full, rounded and well developed education, symmetrical in every part, without cramping or narrowing one faculty for the benefit of the others. It is well known to the colleges and universities of the country, and its course has always received their approval and endorsement. In fact it has been large enough to establish a curriculum which the colleges have accepted, as it antedates most of them; and with such eminent instructors, a course of preparatory studies was arranged that met the requirements of any college.

I have alluded to the principals. I should be dirclict to duty if I failed to mention some of those who have aided in the instruction and management of the Academy, to whom much of its prosperity and success is due. These principals have been supported by such distinguished scholars as Daniel Dana, Nicholas Emery, Samuel D. Parker, Joseph Stevens Buckminster, Ashur Ware, Francis Bowen, Ebenezer Adams, Hosea Hildreth, Alexander H. Everett, the Peabodys, Nathan Lord, James Walker, Joseph Gibson Hoyt, Paul A. Chadbourne, George A. Wentworth, Bradbury L. Cilley. Hosea Hildreth served as instructor fourteen years, Joseph G. Hoyt eighteen, George A. Wentworth twenty-five, and Bradbury L. Cilley, twenty-four years.

No school can fail when directed even in part by such men, and the standard of scholarship under such instruction cannot be low.

It was a fortunate circumstance that the Academy was located in this town, noted for the urbanity and culture of its citizens during its entire history. The influence of the men and women here has aided much in moulding the character of the boys who had the good fortune of their society.

Mr. President—the past is secure, the future of the institution is full of promise. Its past hundred years have been a marvelous success. It has had unbroken prosperity. It has done its full share in directing the rise and development of our common country. It has seen hundreds of colleges, and thousands of high schools and academies spring up all over the land, and many of them with princely endowments; still its members have steadily increased. It has never been jealous of the success of others, and has endeavored to build up all educational institutions and enterprises, rather than pull down. With such a record it starts off on its second century. We cannot foretell its work in the future, but judging from the past, which is our only safe criterion, we predict for it a prosperity and influence even greater and wider than in the past. It needs larger endowments and fuller equipment to keep abreast with the demand of the age, and we trust that those who have watched its history, and known of its work, will place in the hands of the corporation, which has always sacredly cared for the funds, such additional endowments as will bring corresponding prosperity and influence to our beloved *alma mater*.

Dr. Perkins said: There is another institution very much like this of ours, beyond the valley of the Merrimack. You know there are student contests which are apt to wax the warmest between brothers. Sometimes our boys, when they come face to face with the boys of Andover, have their interests excited a little more than they do at other times. It is not because they feel they are so far apart, but because they are so near together. We have the good fortune to have with us, this evening, the Principal of Phillips Academy at Andover, my college friend, whom I have known since my school days, and I take great pleasure in presenting to you at this time, Dr. Bancroft.

ADDRESS OF CECIL F. P. BANCROFT, Ph. D.

It gives me great pleasure to take part in any celebration like this which commemorates the virtues and the deeds and the great worth of the Phillips family. Every student of Andover must take a profound interest in everything which in any way contributes to the better appreciation of what that family has done for the country and for the world. Wendell Phillips, in one of his speeches, speaking of the family, says "they have been at Andover, hence, elsewhere in America." I meet often, and always with a thrill of emotion, an esteemed friend and neighbor, Samuel Phillips, the son of Samuel Phillips, who was the son of Colonel John Phillips, who was the son of Lieutenant Governor Samuel Phillips, who was the son of the Hon. Samuel Phillips, one of the founders of the school at Andover, a brother of your Dr. John Phillips, who was the joint founder with his brother at Andover and sole founder here at Exeter; and he, in turn, was the son of the Rev. Samuel Phillips of Andover, who was the son of Mr. Samuel of Salem, who was the son of the Rev. Samuel of Rowley, who was the son of the Rev. George of Watertown, who came to this country in 1630 with Sir Richard Saltonstall, with Simon Bradstreet and Gov. John Winthrop, and was the peer of these great men. The institutions at Exeter and Andover are the result of the sagacity and the liberality of the same persons of the same family; they were planted in the same interests; they have labored on the same foundations   As I said, Dr. John Phillips, some years before the planting of this school, united with his elder brother in laying the foundations of the school at Andover. When Samuel Phillips died John Phillips became the president of the board of trustees. Although he gave the larger part of his fortune to this school, he was the contributor of the largest part of the quick capital of the school at Andover, his brother contributing lands and other properties for the founding of the Academy; and in his will he left a handsome legacy which has been employed ever since, for the most part, in sustaining students of limited means and of great promise.

The two institutions have, furthermore, been based upon the same chartered privileges, for the most part, although deriving their powers from different States. The principles enunciated in their charters are almost identical, whole paragraphs being copied from the one instrument into the other, the same idea prevailing, that learning and religion, that the teaching of young men how to live as they ought in the world, is the high end for which wealth should be employed, for which the country should aspire and through which alone the country can live. The same persons have often served on the boards of trustees of the two schools. There has been a marked conformity in respect to instruction. Dr. Abbot was fitted for college at Andover, Dr. Soule prepared himself in part for his work here by teaching school in the Andover Academy. Dr. Perkins was prepared for college, likewise, at Andover; and, in turn, three Principals of Phillips Andover Academy fitted for college at Exeter. There has been an interchange of teaching all along the line in other positions in the schools. There has been, furthermore, a generous rivalry in the work proposed by each of the schools and carried forward by each, each doing its own work. Only thirty miles apart, but never coming in collision, each rejoices in the prosperity of the other, each is helped by the prosperity of the other, so that every aid given to the school here is helpful to the school there, and every aid given to the school there is counted for a new foundation here. And I am pleased to hear that one of our own sons, one of your trustees, has signalized this celebration, as he did ours five years ago, by a gift of $25,000.*

But, I think, we cannot emphasize too much, on an occasion like this, the fact that the great work proposed for such a school as this goes forward upon the power of ideas rather than through the power of situation, of endowments, of those accessories which at times seem to us so dazzling and so necessary. Other schools are richer than this, other schools are older than this; can we find one better than this? There are some principles which, it seems to me, account for the great prestige and power of such a school as this. In the first place, it was not planned for a local interest; it was planned for mankind. It comtemplated, not a local patronage, but it contemplated the world; and it contemplated not ordinary boys, but, throughout its deeds of trust and its acts of incorporation and the voluminous correspondence which we have, partly in print and largely in manuscript, it will be found that the founders of this school provided for youth of excelling genius, of remarkable abilities, of unusual promise. They never contemplated the rank and file; they always aspired to teach here the best minds that could be assembled, irrespective of those conditions which have prevailed elsewhere and which did prevail, perhaps, up to that very hour. The instruction here has been carried forward by the best men that could be commanded,— men the peers of the highest presidents and professors in the land, men of undoubted learning, men of undoubted zeal,

---

*John C. Phillips, Esq., of Boston.

men of undoubted capacity, men of singular devotion in the work of teaching.

And, again, behind it all have been those lofty views of life and of duty, those roots of faith which have pervaded every endeavor on the part of those men whom we properly call the pious founders of the school; especially these lofty views of what it is to live, of what it is to labor for others, of what it is to support the state, what public spirit means, what learning is designed to answer in all its highest and noblest uses; so that no boy can come within the sphere of such ideas without receiving that first impulse towards generous culture, that outlook towards a future and towards others which sanctifies his every aim.

These schools are sometimes called the Etons and Winchesters and the Rugbys and the Harrows of our land. I had the privilege, a few years ago, of catching a swift glimpse of those great schools, and I was impressed with three things: first, that the chapel was the center of English school life; second, that great foundations were necessary for the accomplishment of the highest ranges of educational work; and, third, that no school can permanently prosper which does not keep in view at every point the genius of the time, the requirements of the age in which it labors. And so you will find everywhere in these great schools religious faith, you will find the evidences of princely gifts, you will find new buildings, new laboratories, new appliances of the physical sciences and the modern languages coming up as time requires, and taking their places side by side with the old trinity of education. Is this the Eton of America? Oh, it will be when, in the ages, possibly the generations—if possible, let it be in the decades—to come, missions shall stand beneath these foundations, when the Principals of the Phillips Exeter Academy shall have the same consideration, enjoy the same emoluments and have the same commanding power as the Bishop of a Church, as the President of Harvard College, as the Senators whom we send to Congress, as the

Governors of our states. The large foundations must come, the great ideas must be maintained, the gifts and graces which come from the teaching of God must be present to quicken and vivify the whole. Then with men, then with money, then with all this history, with all this precious past, there can be no doubt that this Academy shall be, indeed, the Eton of the land.

And now I come officially to bring you the salutations of eleven thousand pupils of 105 years, and to express the wish that this school may flourish forever.

Dr. Perkins said: There is one gentleman present with us this evening who enjoys a peculiar distinction. I think it belongs to no one else in the world. He was here, friends, a pupil under Mr. Wentworth and Mr. Cilley, and he has a son here under the same instructors. If I am wrong in the statement that this man is peculiar in that, I should like to be corrected; otherwise I will call upon him to whom I have referred, Mr. Charles H. Pennypacker.

ADDRESS OF MR. CHARLES H. PENNYPACKER.

Mr. President, and Ladies and Gentlemen: I plead guilty to the rather embarrassing allusion made in my introduction upon this occasion; but I may say in answer to it that this institution is at all times, and has been within my recollection, worthy of so atrocious a crime. I well remembered the circumstances under which I came to this place from the State of Pennsylvania; I remembered distinctly the reception which I met, and, having these circumstances and that experience before my eyes and in my memory when I had a candidate to present for admission to an Academy in this country, I could think of no place more fitting than Exeter, New Hampshire. It was not only a place to educate the mind, not only a place for excellent mental discipline, but it also abounded in all those attributes of character which go to make up the gentleman. I remembered the teachings of Dr. Soule. They extended beyond the recitation room. They went out into the daily walks of the every-day life of the student in Exeter; and when he left here, be it to go to Pennsylvania, to any Southern state or any other state, he took with him such pleasant memories that he could not but be the better for having been here. Therefore it was that I presented my son to this institution, and I trust that neither the institution nor myself will ever regret the operation.

My friends, it has been said in your hearing that Exeter has done well in the past. Her history has been made; the record is before you. What shall we do in the present? What shall we do for the future? That is the problem which is now presented to us upon this anniversary. It makes no difference what may have been the glories of the past hundred years; if we do not keep abreast of the times, if we are not keenly alive to every new word and every new work, we will lag in this struggle and Exeter may, perchance, follow the example of some other institutions. Throughout the past twenty years, year by year, her Alumni have been increasing in number, and upon every glorious battle-field of our civil war, I might say, her sons have been found, either upon the one side or the other, and they battled none the less bravely because of their experience here; and in every relation of life, no matter what it may be, whether it be the law, whether it be divinity, whether it be the medical profession or whether it be the every-day business of life, they have shown themselves worthy of this training; and I trust, therefore, that we shall take fresh courage for the future, especially in the light of the experience that we have already heard, when the utterances of some seventy years have come down to us, when we find that good physical health has been at all times and under all circumstances upon the very best understanding with scholastic training. When we remember these things, we really think there is a good chance for the boys of Exeter.

———

Dr. Perkins said: I don't know how many of you are familiar with the town of Peterborough in New Hampshire, but I am sure it would be a pretty severe imputation on your general intelligence if I were to intimate you didn't know some of the honored sons of that town who have been here in this school. The names of the Smiths, and of the Morisons, and of the Holmeses, will occur to many of you. I now call on one of them to speak to us, the Hon. Nathaniel Holmes.

ADDRESS OF HON. NATHANIEL HOLMES.

It is a pleasure for me to answer for my native town, which I see by your catalogue sent four students to this Academy in the second year of its foundation and in the first year after the peace of 1783, though I see at least one here present who might more fitly do it. My own recollections of Exeter go back to the old Academy of fifty years ago; with the new, living so far away for the most part, I have had no very near acquaintance. But my two years at Phillips Exeter Academy, from 1831 to 1833, remain quite fresh among the most agreeable memories of my life. I was soon initiated and sat down to hard study. There was for me some novelty in the old town. One of the things that first attracted my attention was the harbor, half water, half mud-flat, and that famous single schooner moored to its solitary wharf far down the ebbing tide. I believe I saw it again this blessed day. In fact, I had first arrived here three or four weeks before the term was to begin, and, having a strong desire to see the great ocean, I took the stage along the coast to Boston and had some glimpses of it, and thence found my way home on foot to the farm in Peterborough. My father set me to hauling mill-logs until the time came to start again. I began to think I might as well have staid in Exeter.

There is no need that I dwell on particulars known to many, if not all, here present. Of course, Dr. Benjamin Abbot was the Principal and had charge of the large Latin room. I see him again upon the wall, in his picture, natural as life, sitting there among the immortal. And George J. Abbot, and for some time Henry French, was monitor and wielded a beneficent authority over the younger men; and there was the Greek room under Prof. Soule; him, too, I see again upon the opposite wall sitting familiar among the worthies of the past; and the English room under Prof. Joseph H. Abbot. If memory serves me, some few for, whom digging at Greek roots and mathematics was rather tough work, perhaps, did sometimes have the audacity to speak of "Gid." Soule and "Joe." Abbot; but of the venerable Principal there was, I think, no abridgment of the entire reverence due to the majesty of his name and presence and his gracious manner. Then there was the hall above, where the young orators began, with fear and trembling, to learn the art of "winged words," and the mysterious "F. S. T." with its "Golden Branch," then (as I suppose it is still) the prime object of youthful ambition among all. An election into that fraternity was the first sign to the young hopeful that the vague wandering of his uncertain ark on a wide sea of troubles was at length nearing land. Such as had a strong predeliction for future greatness could now and then slip into the Court House, near by, and listen to the eloquence of George Sullivan, Ichabod Bartlett, the elder Atherton and Mark Farley. The still small voice of the Rev. Mr. Hurd spoke the words of wisdom in the little church adjoining; he was an elegant speaker, but his doctrine was for me, even at that day, a little too orthodox to carry my whole sympathies with him.

I sometimes think that the whole of education consists in learning to read and write and cipher; but most of us have to learn, as years advance, that, at this day of the world, to read means to know the language of all the sciences and about one-half the tongues of all the earth, living and dead; that to write means to write books that will pay or will live—he is a rare man whose books will both pay and live—and to cipher—it might dizzy the arithmetic of memory to say what, short of the entire geometry of the heavens and the earth.

It is said we live in an age of transition—transition into what? into science and the unknowable? into agnosticism?—this last seems to me to be a new classical substitute for the plain old Anglo-Saxon term "knownothingism"—into Pantheism, perhaps, or (as Carlyle preferred to call it) Pottheism; and what this may mean I never found anybody that knew or could define. For my part, as yet I see no end to knowledge or the capacity of the human mind for learning and knowing. Indeed, it is one of the wonders of our time (as it seems to me) that the most advanced science finds itself, *nolens volens*, penetrating into a purely metaphysical realm, approaching, as it were, the judicial palace of the Supreme Thought, not, indeed, by the direct high road of pure reason and the front gate, but through the by-ways and back-alleys, the narrow passages, "the crannies and offices of man," groping darkly for an entrance by the back door. If neither Aristotle nor Kant nor Hegel has given us a perfect theory of the universe, God, nature and man inclusive, why then it simply remains for somebody else to do it better. "Attempt it not!" exclaims Thomas Carlyle. But we may rest assured that there will be no ceasing of the attempt until the thing is done. For myself I am much inclined to say, with Bacon and King Solomon of old, "That it is the wisdom of God to conceal the mysteries of the universe as in innocent play with children, and the glory of man to find them out."

Dr. Perkins said: If you will look over the names on our general catalogue from 1840 to 1850, you will pause very often to dwell on familiar names,—names that have become distinguished for service done in the various professions or in business. Upon a gentleman bearing one of such names I shall now call,—the Rev. Augustus Woodbury, of Providence, Rhode Island.

ADDRESS OF REV. AUGUSTUS WOODBURY.

Gentlemen of the Alumni, Ladies and Gentlemen: It has always been a source of regret to me that I never have had any sons to send to this Academy to follow in the footsteps of their father; and the remarks of our friend from Pennsylvania have added another pang to these feelings of regret. When we look back upon the past and take account of what has been done, and look forward to the future with hope, believing that there are still greater things to come from this institution, it certainly seems to go without saying that we congratulate ourselves and congratulate each other that we have reached this hundredth anniversary. We are glad that we have lived to see this day. It is an occasion for recalling the associations of the past, for gathering up the scattered threads of friendships to weave a new bond of union; to bid each other "God Speed" as we separate, never, perhaps, to meet again on this side of the grave, remembering our obligations to those who have so faithfully instructed us, and making it our ambition to be worthy of their instruction. As our venerable friend who has just taken his seat has said, and I take it is the expression of the sentiment of all of you here present, to me, at least, it is,— that among the pleasantest of the past days of my life were the days I spent in Exeter. We had our rivalries, our contests, our struggles with each other, but we had our enjoyments and our satisfactions. And it is a delight, now, to recall both of these, for, in these boyhood's experiences, we may well believe that all things work together for good, if they are rightly taken and rightly used. The character of a school depends, of course, upon the character of its students, the character of the Alumni whom it sends forth, the character of its instructors and the character of its instruction. The students, I apprehend, will speak for themselves, as they have already spoken. It would not become me to speak of the character of the Alumni. We have had a long list of distinguished men who have received their preparatory training in this school; but, of the character of the instruction and of the character of the instructors I can well speak for a single moment. I came to Exeter about six years after Dr. Abbot had ceased to be Principal, but his venerable form was still a familiar object upon the streets. And I remember how kind and courteous he always was to the students, and how bright the day seemed to us after we had received his passing salutation. Mr. Soule was Principal. He was assisted by Messrs. Hoyt and Swan, and the obligation which I, in common with all who came under their instruction owed to those faithful men, can never be cancelled. Mr. Soule, indeed, was the object of our veneration; Mr. Hoyt was the object of our love. I think I may safely say that I have never known any man before or since his time who was able to engage so closely to himself the affections of his pupils, and any one who so fully secured their complete esteem. It was my good fortune to know him quite intimately in after life, after I had left the school; he was at my home and I was at his.

And, as for the character of the instruction, it was not simply a place for preparatory training—and I think, in that regard, it was incomparable,—but it was also a place for the discipline of manners, of morals and of character. In my day, and I think it is true of the present day, Exeter was no place for a lazy boy or a selfish boy, or a boy with low ambitions, or a boy of vulgar disposition; and if any boy of that character happened to find himself here, he also found it necessary either to correct his habits or to take himself away. There was this discipline which has shown itself in the years that followed after. And I think at that time, too,—and I presume they do now,—the instructors had a very happy method of taking the nonsense out of a boy. Boys, as you all know, and men too, for that matter, sometimes have a certain feeling of self-assurance and self-conceit; but I think that the admonitions that were received by us at that time,— I do not intend to give myself away,—the admonitions that were received by us at that time, were very effectual in making us at least more modest than we should have been without them. And I have often wished, when I have seen boys at public exhibitions, and even men at public exhibitions, that they might have received some such discipline as I received in my boyhood.

And, speaking of these exhibitions, it was the custom then not to have an exhibition very often. They had not then come into vogue. Nowadays, scarcely a primary school can finish its term without having a questionable exercise of this kind; but, in those days, public exhibitions were somewhat rare, and their rarity gave them a certain glory. It was the custom then,—it was in the old Academy,—for the young of the town to do their part in decorating the walls, and ladies it was a labor, I think, of two or three weeks. It was the duty of those boys who took part in the exhibition, to invite certain young ladies from the town, and to see that they were escorted to the place and escorted home again. I confess that it was with some misgiving as to whether it would be consistent or not with allegiance to the girls we left behind us, but we tried to do that duty as we tried to do all our other duties in the best way we could. And I have no doubt that from those happy occasions have resulted some of the unions in after life which have been so fruitful of blessings and happiness.

And, then, the Golden Branch, to which Judge Holmes has referred. I scarcely know what to say about that; the contests we had there, the debates that we engaged in, the electioneering that went on, the canvassing for office that began as soon as the presiding officer's term had begun, and continued through his term in order to prepare for his successor. Now, Mr. President and gentlemen, I have known something of political canvasses in New Hampshire, when the "Independent Democrat" was alive and was contesting with the "New Hampshire Patriot" for the political supremacy of this state, and I have known something of political canvassing in Massachusetts and Rhode Island, but I confess that I have never gone through a political canvass since that time which was equal to those which we had in the old room at the east end of the old Academy. Governor Prescott has given us the names of a long list of those statesmen and governors, senators and representatives, etc., and I have no doubt their success in politics has been due to their experience in the Golden Branch. I sometimes wonder whether our fellow alumnus, Gov. Butler, was not a member of the Golden Branch. On one of those particular occasions, I recollect it now, though I have not thought of the matter from that time, scarcely, till this, a very serious question was in dispute. It was impossible for us to settle it; it went on for several weeks, when the thought occurred to me that possibly the member of Congress from the district to which I belonged might help us. And, so, in my boyish innocence, I sat down and wrote a letter to him, stating the question and asking him to give us his counsel. He helped us very courteously indeed. He acknowledged the receipt of the note, he expressed his interest in the question which we were discussing, and he concluded with quoting these lines of Virgil:

"Non nostrum inter vos tantas componere lites."

I should think not! Experienced politician as he was, having long parliamentary practice in Congress, it was altogether too much for him. And I defy any man to have settled the questions which came up in those days in the Golden Branch.

But I must not indulge, Mr. President. My time was limited to ten minutes, and I presume it has about expired. It has seemed to me sometimes in thinking of this institution and how much those who have had the benefit of her instructions have loved her, how she has been the object of their affections from the moment they set foot across her threshhold, as students and Alumni of this Academy,—it has seemed to me like the case of the old Hebrews, who, wherever they went, however far away from their native land they wandered, carried in their hearts the affection for their sacred city. They made their annual visits for the purpose of laying on its shrine their offerings. They came back from journeyings to rebuild the temple of their adoration; they thought of it by day, they dreamed of it by night, and when they prayed they opened their windows towards Jerusalem. The Alumni of Phillips Exeter Academy carry the institution with them wherever they may go, however far they may wander.

> Where'er I roam, whatever realms to see
> My heart untravelled fondly turns to thee.

They come here to make their offerings; and when the old Academy was burned, by their liberal contributions and willing gifts they built this elegant and commodious edifice, and so they carry in their hearts, from the beginning unto the end, the interest of this sacred shrine of their youth. And everyone of us, I think, would repeat the fervent and impassioned words of the Hebrew Psalmist, "if I forget thee, oh, Alma Mater of my youth, let my right hand forget her cunning; if I do not remember thee, let my tongue cleave to the roof of my mouth."

Dr. Perkins said : I fancy that when we come to examine the register that will be laid before the Alumni to-morow for their signatures, we shall find that the number of visitors here who have been in the school since 1870 will be greater than the number of all others. I shall call now upon our last speaker, who will represent these younger men, the Rev. Richard Montague, of Providence, Rhode Island.

ADDRESS OF REV. RICHARD MONTAGUE.

Mr. President : Unless my memory fails me there was, when I was here twelve years ago, a rule somewhat to this effect, the repeal of which I have never learned : That students who were living in private families must dwell in families that are authorized to board them by the Faculty of the school; and that if the families in which they were dwelling should chance, at any time, to notice that they were out after ten o'clock, they should forfeit all other privileges. Having been assigned to most estimable hosts this day by the authorities of this honored institution, and noticing that I am out beyond the regular time, and, fearing that they, perhaps, may be getting a little anxious, I think a mere word is all that a representative of the younger graduates may be expected to utter. In fact I am reminded of the story of the boy who with his brother, was expected by his pious father regularly, every morning, before he could go out to play, to repeat a passage of Scripture. And he was extremely anxious every morning to play, so that he managed nearly every time to repeat the required verse from Scripture. But, one morning, when he was especially eager to get out, having overheard his brother say that "he would rather be a door keeper in the house of the Lord than to sit in the tents of wickedness forever," he simply said to his father, "so say I," and was off. After all these words of congratulation on the honorable history of our honored Academy, might it not be enough for me if I should simply add. "so say I ?" But, yet, perhaps, those of my associates who are here, if no others, would expect a single word of testimony touching what this Academy has done for us. . It was my privilege to be here but a year, and yet, in that year I think two lessons were very powerful on me. We young men are governed by our ideals, and our future and our usefulness in the world depend upon the character of the ideals which inspire and move us. I received two ideals touching scholarship and life work in general which are summed up in two words,—thoroughness and persistence. As I look down into the faces of some of my honored instructors who were here then and are still working in this institution, there comes back to me most vividly the meaning of the word thoroughness. I never dared face my Greek Professor, great as was his kindness and encouraging as were his manner and his words, unless I had the thorough mastery of the passage of Greek in hand. And I hardly need to add that I didn't dare to go to the board to put on a theorem in Geometry unless I knew what I was about. For myself, I am very thankful for that lesson.. It is an ideal that is worth years of striving to get.

The other ideal that impressed me strongly was the necessity of persistence in work. I don't know of anything that could illustrate it better, in my recollections of my life here, than this one instance. New England, so far as I recollect, has not been very much troubled with earthquakes; but, in the days of the old Academy Hall, in '71, we did have a little earthquake in Exeter. We were reciting at the time to Dr. Soule, of precious memory, and suddenly there came a movement altogether strange and indescribable. It seemed as if the floor was going up; it seemed as if the supporting columns in the hall were going to fall; it seemed as though the roof would be lifted away from us, and we were, as it were, tossed in a ship by the waves. We knew not what was going to happen next. The Doctor stood it better than we did, but, at last, even he rose from his seat and looked out of the window. Then he saw that Abbot Hall was still standing and the trees were growing as they had been growing the day before, and, resuming his seat, he said calmly, "Foster, construe that next sentence." I have ever felt since, that no matter what earthquakes of opposition might assail the purpose, or what temptation to the pleasures of ease might allure, our motto should be persistent application to the work in hand. And that seems to me a lesson which it was well worth learning.

I can fancy that these honored teachers who have been so influential upon the characters and lives of the hundreds of students who have gone out from this Academy, and who have gone out from this world to their better rest, may in their older days have found much pleasure by turning over the old catalogues of the students whom they used to teach. It seems to me that if the aged parent can delight in recalling the careers of his children now in the prime of life and in enthusiastic work in the world, so the teacher, who has perhaps laid aside his active work and who is now in the declining years of his life, can have great pleasure in tracing the history of his successful pupils.

I don't see that the Professors who are here now and who were here when I was, are one day older then they were twelve years ago. But, I suppose sometime, if the world only lasts long enough, they will be a little older, and, if they ever should be, it strikes me that it would be an exceeding great pleasure to them could they look over the record of us younger men and be able to say, honestly, "they have done good work in the world;" and, if we have done good work in the world, I am sure they can each say honestly, "that work was largely done through my instruction, through my inspiring influence, through the ideals that I implanted in their young minds." May every one of us younger graduates, give them the opportunity to say it truthfully.

Dr. Perkins said: Now, with the very strongest wishes for a good bright day to-morrow, we will separate.

THURSDAY FORENOON.

The exercises were continued at half-past ten o'clock in the forenoon of Thursday, June 21, when the Centennial Oration and Poem were delivered in the presence of an audience that filled the great tent in the common opposite the Academy.

CENTENNIAL ORATION BY REV. HORATIO STEBBINS, D. D.

Mr. Bancroft, Gentlemen of the Board of Trustees and Friends of the Academy: Wherever on the earth stand the monuments of human struggle, self-sacrifice and devotion, there it is good for the living, as they move forward in the ever-flowing procession of generations, to pause in their march and pay venerating respect, gratitude and admiration: —a hundred years of the Academy justify the occasion.

We pay distinguished honors to the Founder, whose benefactions have trimmed the lamp of learning here and sent its mild and steady beams afar; we cherish grateful regards for all those who have, by word or deed or fostering care, strengthened the foundations of the Academy, reared its walls anew, or as masters of the mind have ministered to its intellectual and moral life, and sent its influence abroad wide as the beams of the sun. We confess our debt to an institution which has a vested earthly immortality in the mind of man, and on which time and death cast no contempt!

The rise and development of institutions, of whatever name, are the rational and intelligent expression of man's individual helplessness, attesting that he has, and can have, no isolated completeness or perfection. No creature receives so great benefits from his kind as man, or is so dependent on his kind. The horse or the dog, withdrawn from his fellows of the species, shows no perceptible depreciation, and fills out the figure of his being. If brought in contact with man, the animal surpasses his companions of the tribe, and by his dependence wins a better destiny than is vouchsafed to him through communion with his own race. But man thus withdrawn is an arrested development, a frost-bitten infancy, in which even the opening buds of speech are cut down. It is a profound saying of Spinoza that "Nothing is more useful to man than his fellow man; no more excellent way can be desired by men for the preservation of their being, than a concord of all men in all things, such that the minds and bodies of all make up, as it were, one mind, and one body, and that all together strive to the utmost of their power to preserve their being, and all seek together the common good of all."

This union and dependence of men is through identity of nature and the diffusion of that Almighty Spirit which is the inspiration of all. Human society is of the nature of an endowment, a perpetual fund, from which every man receives benefits that he cannot acquire for himself. Herein is the power of social order, civilization and history. This makes laws, manners, and religions, and that continuity of thought and action we call the life of the race. If the animals were thus united, if they were as dependent on one another and capable of such a common bond of good, they could drive out man from the earth, and hold the world. But having no such dependence, and no such power of mutual help, divine order, a common mind, a public opinion are impossible. The great outward social fact, expressing the unity and oneness of man's inner nature, is, that society does more for every man than he can pay for, secures to him the great privileges and immunities of existence, so that whether he will or no he has nothing that he has not received. There is no money that a man gets so much for as he does for his taxes, and when he has paid all his bills, they do not cover the full cost of all that he has had. Nor is this the result of a mutual partnership where every man pays his own share, but it is the very condition and nature of man in society that bear these fruits as a tree bears apples or a vine bears grapes. There is an inherent tendency of beneficence in things human, and man by the fact of his nature and his association with his fellows on the plain of that nature, receives great and enduring good, the foregleams of his destiny. This tendency is the key-note of all good in the world of men and things, and all man's active beneficence and public spirit, and a hint taken from the great human theme, to augment and glorify man's estate. Thus all the good that adorns the earth, the charities and humanities of the human world, "out from the heart of Nature rolled."

The distinguished and supreme expression of the mutual dependence and helpfulness of men is in Education; and perhaps the most adequate conception of human life and human society is that in which they are represented as a school. It was the vital power of that thought which made Lessing's little pamphlet, *The Education of the Human Race*, one of the most fruitful seeds that was ever cast upon the furrows of the world. For this reason the founders of great schools are justly regarded as the benefactors of mankind. Anticipating man's destiny, hastening to proclaim it, believing in their fellow men of unborn generations, having, it may be, honorable desires for posthumous fame and corporate immortality, or inspired with reverent passion to promote the great Intent, they have established perpetual fountains of living waters in the eternal heights of the mind. They have recognized the unity and identity of human nature, and that, "through the ages one increasing purpose runs," and, for the promotion of that "purpose," they have set enduring privileges and opportunities, to be enjoyed with no sense of debt, but gratitude—that happy debt from which the noble mind would never be discharged, as the wise receive the benefactions of the common world. The world is a school, with endowments so opulent, and priviliges so great that no man can fully discharge his obligation; and a school is a little world founded on the same plan. The historic fact illustrates the great principle, that education cherished either in great founded schools, or by illustrious public opinion, recognizes the essential value of man's intellectual and moral nature, and of his dependence on his fellow men for the development of that nature. Christianity was the embodiment of the great principle, and lent its humanizing power to promote it. Charlemagne, the genius of the middle age, conceived of education as the foster child of religion; and the founders of the Republic identified it with the welfare of the State, whose existence was justified by its sympathy with the nature and destiny of man.

If human experience has taught anything, if man in action has displayed the wants and tendencies of his own being, this is manifest: that all his higher interest must be provided for, and the nobler his nature the more he wants. The supply of his highest wants requires vast resources, sustained by constant care, and continually refreshed by new accessions of living power. In whatever domain the *laissez faire* theory may be true, it is not true when we come to man as man, in his highest relations. Man cannot be let alone or left to chance. Great provisions must be made for him: not to guard him as a child and perpetuate his feebleness, but to inspire him, as a free, self-directing, responsible being. For this, individuals, touched with exalted enthusiasm of human good, while as yet an infinitely small portion of humanity discern it, establish their estates in eternal foundations, and prophetic statesmen strike the rock of public opinion, and it pours out rivers of water! This is our expression of that supreme bond, that binds man to man, and man to God.

One of the noblest objects of human contemplation, is a man of great motives, looking upon the the world with steady, strong wisdom and pure feeling, devoted to the supreme purpose of human good. Standing in the calm inaccessible heights of moral greatness, the passions of the hour do not disturb him. The weakness, the ignorance, the folly, the pride, the ingratitude of men, lie beneath his feet as clouds beneath some sunlit mountain glory. He believes in himself, and in the world, and in the Maker, because he walks and sees in eternal light. He has such a sense of the grandness of human things, that humility and gratitude move his breast. If he has great material powers, he is beset continually with the thoughtlessness of the public and the ingratitude of states. And there are those around him who speak contemptuously of the public, and blaspheme that human society whose foundations are the ever-proceeding spirit of God. But the consummate man, of great purposes of good, understands the prejudices and passions of the hour, and sees and feels and knows that the good he proposes is perpetual, and will stand above these at length, as the sun in his mid-day splendor stands above the morning mists that hung around his rising. Always great in his moral consciousness, he is not defeated by indifference or neglect, but confident that good can never be lost, he entrusts it to his fellow men and the generations that come after him.

Such a man, from the scanty records preserved of him, was our Founder, John Phillips. Early in the history of the country, while yet this Commonwealth of New Hampshire lay upon the borders of the wilderness, amidst narrow and provincial views, hemmed in by sharp necessity to a frugality which, however friendly it might be to the severer virtues, gave little opportunity to expansive sympathies, our Founder conceived a plan of enduring good on principles so vital, yet so liberal, that no collision has arisen in a hundred years between the stipulations of his bequests and the rising intelligence and changing forms of the modern age! And if no collision for a hundred years, then none forever.

I am not anxious to prove him no wiser than he knew. I cheerfully accord him a place among those noble minds that have been the instruments of ideas above themselves. There are two things, however, pertaining to common sense and right reason, that a wise man of material and moral power must consider if he would do well. He must ask himself: What can I do that will supply a perpetual human want? And how can I do it so that it will be adapted, or will adapt itself to the changing circumstances of society and men? Here truth culminates in paradox, and all things truly great and permanent are mutable. That which admits no change may exist, but it cannot be said to live. All great principles set forth in idea or purpose ever enter into new combinations and bear fresh fruits. The enlightened Founder of institutions must be without caprice, or whim, believing in the present order of things, but believing in it as no finality, and not mistaking his self-will for his last will and testament. I applaud the name and memory of our Founder, a man of simple tastes and simple habits, who, trained to theology when theology cherished that zeal which is peculiar to narrowness of view, was too modest to become a teacher of religion, and devoting himself to the palaver of a country trader, thus gathered an honest fortune which he set apart as the perpetual foundation of a great school, with magnanimity of thought and feeling, under which the Academy has been adapted to the ever wider circles of thought and intelligence, as naturally as corn grows or lilies bloom. I applaud him for that simplicity of mind and purpose, which, whether consciously or unconsciously, led him to establish this foundation not for this or for that, but for the mind and heart of man! The restriction which confides the administration of the trust and the instruction of the Academy to Protestants, cannot be considered an invidious distinction against that branch of the Christian church which from high ecclesiastical motives as the custodian of truth, enrolls the modern methods of education upon its syllabus of errors.

Our school, founded on so enlightened principles, for the cultivation of those studies which were included in the general scheme of a liberal education a century ago, has expanded, under the fostering care of wise and good men in the administration of its affairs, and of a line of distinguished masters and teacher, by natural impulse within, with the awakened and ever widening sympathies of learning.

Although vague generalizations are to be avoided, it may be said with propriety, that the present is a period of transition in education; and there are some who say that it is more than this, a period of intellectual and moral transition, in which the general field of human life and experience is transferred from the literary to the scientific side. Without assenting to such a view as the final result of the modern spirit, the area of education has been vastly increased within the last half century, and the relative rank of the subjects of education has been modified, at least to the extent of recognizing individual aptitudes, and no longer requiring all to adopt the same methods as the only instruments of culture or learning.

There is an opinion held by educational men, and widely diffused among those who claim to have only a common sense view of the subject, that what are called liberal studies are not well adapted to the practical duties and industries of life. The opinion has given a new impulse to what is called technical or professional education, in distinction from that general discipline, the object of which is knowledge and mental power. New subjects have been enrolled on the lists of education, and natural science, which has conquered new empires in these modern years, has opened fields of industry that were unknown to former generations, and given to the common vocations of men the intellectual rank of special professions. The more man knows of the world around him the more it responds to his intelligence, and the mind in things replies to the mind in man. It is not within the scope of this occasion to discuss the relative value of studies, either as a means of culture in its widest sense, or as a preparation for special vocation. It is only necessary to keep in view the distinction between liberal education and professional education. The test of the one is the discipline of the man, putting him in the widest relations with humanity as a general preparation for life in whatever sphere he may be called to act. The test of the other is an immediate special utility. The first may not be ascetic or unpractical: the second may not be indifferent to utility of the highest kind. For all general purposes this broad distinction is sufficient to give us an idea of the place the Academy holds in relation to the spirit of the time.

There has been a great impulse given to popular education throughout the country in the lifetime of the present generation. It is forever honorable to the sagacity and sincerity of the founders of the Republic that they associated the common school with the welfare of the state. The civilization of our era moving westward across the continent, has borne the mighty theme aloft, like a song of victory, to the shores of the other ocean; and it may be said with the sobriety of history that the education of New England, and the civil law of New York have become the public opinion of the country. The idea of a nation of men voluntarily taxing themselves in the round sum of a hundred millions of dollars per annum for education, that all may have a little, inspires admiration and respect. There are those, however, who believe that the common school system of the country is a failure. I do not belong to that class. Their opinions, it seems to me, are formed on principles of touchy æsthetics, rather than on fine intellectual and moral sympathies. The common school may be mechanical, and it may be a coarse machine, and the education it gives very crude. It does not accomplish what it ought to accomplish. But in this respect it does not differ from free institutions in general, laws, manners and religion. The common school is no more a failure than popular liberty, constitutional law, or the Christian religion are failures. It seems to be one of the unavoidable conditions of all human things that good does not do as much good as we sometimes think it ought to do. While this may seem discouraging to those inclined to take melancholy views of human affairs, to others, cheered by a mightier hope, it may suggest that our earthly horizons are not wide enough for the longer levers of the divine intent to swing in. The truth is, a people are educated by having the care of education, and by being interested in it.

We do not teach an ox to browse by tying him up in the stall. Good comes only by seizing the instrumentalities through which it comes. A few years ago I was travelling in the mountains and valleys of the western coast, when I came to a place, which after the manner of new countries, was called a city, to distinguish it from the wilderness. While resting there by the wayside, talking with a man who represented the local intelligence and spirit, two riders came up in half Spanish saddles, broad brimmed hats, shirt sleeves and outside boots, and their faces had a fine bronze that does not belong to academic groves. They had come in from a distance to talk with the local citizen there, about the schoolhouse and the school which they were going to establish in the borders of the woods. Their business done, the intelligence and counsel which they needed got, they sprang into their saddles and were off. As they went, I remarked to the sensible man whose advice they had sought: How these men are educated by having the care of education! The little shanty stands there, not a poetic building, but like other simple things in human life, it cannot be seen truly unless poetically. There from a few homes, inspired by the common affections of human nature, widely separated in a yet wild and unsubdued country, a dozen or twenty children frugally but neatly clad, find their way, plucking gentle daises and flaming eschscholtzias as they go, as a tribute of childhood feeling to the teacher whose gentle manners have won their love! Those sunburnt riders understand and appreciate education far better than the bishops at the council of Nicæa understood and appreciated the Christian religion.

There is an idea of education in the general mind of the country, crude, vague and dim it may be, like a universe yet in nebulous mist, but an idea that amounts almost to a religion. The public opinion which provides even the most elementary education for all, however short it may come of the fulfilment of its idea, is a pledge and promise of unspeakable good. It is the acknowledgment of a great human bond arising in identity of nature and destiny. This public opinion has received a great impulse from the rapid development of the arts of life, demanding schools of special discipline and knowledge. There is an increasing conviction that let whoever will sow the seed, intelligence will reap the harvest. And there is a deeper conviction in noble minds, strong as the "ground swell" of the sea or the momentum of a planet, compared with which all other opinions are the temporary accidents of time and circumstance, that the true ground and justification of education, is the man himself, his nature and being. The ultimate reason of all human discipline is the worth and grandeur of intellectual and moral being. On any other ground our senses are a brood of chattering apes, and the brilliant utilities of our modern civilization are a "scouring of barbarian pots and kettles."

It is claimed by some that public education supported by the State should include the whole field of human studies from the grammar school to the university. It was a favorite idea of Channing that the public lands should be set apart for the education of the people. The public has not proved itself thus far a very safe trustee of school funds. States and cities in the Union that have been endowed with more than regal splendor have squandered or lost their patrimony. The act of Congress of 1862, giving to the States a vast domain, afforded a new opportunity to establish what is called "the higher education" under the care of the State. The brilliant imagination of the illustrious founder of English polemical idealism has been fulfilled, and the name of Berkeley has been given to the site of a modern State University, that fronts the western ocean. There has also been a movement in some quarters to establish a National University, to be sustained by the General Government as the crown of the public school system of the country.

The general interest in education, vague, dark, groping though it may be, a wise man will interpret as the first and indispensable condition of all moral and intellectual supply, a consciousness of want. The misery of ignorance is, that it wants nothing. The man who would be a benefactor of learning, or the institution that would have an honorable rank and influence, must discern and seize this tendency of the time.

For all practical purposes it may be said that opinion is divided in regard to the higher education, whether it shall be entrusted to the State or to the institutions founded by private munificence. The question naturally settles itself. There is some confusion in the common mind concerning what constitutes the higher education, of which we hear so much. That education only which looks upon man imaginatively, kindles his mental power, inspires his reason, and binds his will in the happy freedom of self-control can be called the higher education. It may not be technical or professional, but human. It may not be unpractical but it must be ideal. The truth that fronts the sun, undazzled in that insufferable light, is, that man is greater than anything he does, and treating him prosaically and practically only, is like applying the surveyor's chain to sunrise, or undertaking to find the square acres of the beauty of the world! But the

State, as State, can regard education chiefly from the point of utility. A high and noble utility it may be, but a utility that must fall short of the grandeur of intellectual and moral being. The higher education transcends state reasons. Naturally the question settles itself, and the technical or professional education falls into the hands of the commonwealth, and liberal education is committed to institutions founded, not for State but human reasons.

The spirit of the Academy then is that of wide and true sympathy with the progress of the time. As a preparatory school it anticipates the ever-enlarging area of human studies, and chooses such as have not only utility, but fitness also for the purpose of education. Any subject worthy to be made a part of the education of the young must be such as a lad can master, and by mastering feed that hungering power of attention which constitutes the difference between a mental treadmill and mental activity. The subjects of science should be within the reach of thought and observation, without prolonged or abstruse experiment. Literature and history should be presented as the temple of the world, in the vestibule of which a youth may stand with uncovered head. And Language, that "Manual of Humanity" should be adorned and enlarged, as no other study is capable of being, by comment and illustration, until the dry paradigm buds and blooms, the dwelling-place of memory and imagination. These are the views and the subjects of education which should engage the care and attention of a great founded school; not ascetic and regardless of the useful, neither practical nor professional to the exclusion of the ideal.

To this end, great funds established in former generations, and cherished and strengthened by living men in succeeding time, should be administered not secretly as a private trust with which nobody has any business, but with wise regard to the right of society to know something of that in which it is most deeply interested, and which was dedicated to human good. Endowments demand perpetual vigilance not only for their protection, but for their use and adaptation to changing wants. Funds incapable of being adapted to the new circumstances of new generations, are a public nuisance.

In a great school, a community of youth, the subject of discipline must always be one of supreme importance. It is a subject, too, which the public, and especially parents, ought to understand. It is commonly supposed that a youth on leaving home for school or college encounters peculiar temptations and exposures. It may be reasonably doubted, however, whether he encounters any greater trials than he would anywhere else. Leaving home is a crisis always: the momentous crisis of freedom, responsibility and self-control. Parents should understand the general fact, and lay it well to heart, that a youth carries with him the tone of thought, feeling and manners that he has imbibed in his father's house, and that school and college are entitled to some allowance on that account. The temptations of a community of studies are not more severe for youth than the temptations of the general world of affairs. The guarantee of conduct is industry, and the wisest discipline is that which encourages industry, and associates it indissolubly with all noble learning. Regulations that cannot be enforced are worse than none; and take care lest you incur the folly of undertaking to decide when a boy becomes a young man.

It is affirmed by some, that the increasing wealth of the country tends to make our great schools the resort of much idleness, extravagance and luxury. It is a subject about which there is doubtless much vague impression, and more vague exaggeration. But it is true that idle and expensive habits brought from home are a bad influence in a place of learning, introducing an element of difficulty into the discipline, and setting up a standard of social superiority, where the only true tests are manliness of character and an earnest mind. There can be no doubt that it is the duty of a great funded school, to crowd the vices of self-indulgent extravagance into narrow quarters, to give them no standing, and to curtail their baleful influence by giving all its moral force in favor of simple manners, industrious scholarship, and upright manhood. A great funded school, established by the wise and good, while it makes no discrimination and allows no standards but character and mind, should ever be the friend of the poor; and on any other ground it has no right to be. It has been said that next to a good man in adversity, the object most pleasing to heaven is a good man successful in a great cause. That profound wisdom might be paraphrased and applied to youth in the pursuit of noble studies. If there is an object that kindles our admiration and inspires our love, it is a youth born into hard necessity, his mind warmed by the gentle heat that hatched the world, imagination tinging his morning horizon, and who never dreams that he is poor so happy is he in the wealth of his unworn heart. If there is another object of intellectual and moral beauty that wins and fixes our admiring regards, it is a youth nurtured in affluence, surrounded by the temptations of self indulgent ease, but chastened and admonished by wise paternal counsels and example, rising above the allurements of sense, the sight of the eyes and the pride of life, and finding in industry, in intellectual labors and accomplishments, the field of true honor, and the moral dignity of self-respect! It is one glory of the Academy that it has done something to diffuse such impressions of true human worth among men.

My own conviction is, that an important and indispensable element in the administration of a great school, is the personal influence of masters and teachers. Presence, bearing, insight, character, sympathy, are the invisible, indefinable powers of intellectual and moral guidance. A mind that has great influence, must, like the sun, send out rays of light, and rays of heat, and there must be atmosphere to diffuse them. This light and heat and atmosphere are as essential to the intellectual and moral world, as they are to mountain, meadow or sea. The consummate master of youth supplies in himself many of the restraints and protections of home, and his mind is like a climate upon a landscape.

The Academy has been singularly happy in a distinguished line of Masters, and in the influence they had on the minds of succeeding generations. The late Gideon L. Soule is impressed upon my mind and memory, as the eminent figure and representative of a great Master and Teacher of youth. When I sat in these seats, I formed a youthful opinion of him, as one of the best teachers of the Greek and Latin Classics, that American scholarship had produced. My mature judgment confirms the boyhood opinion. His gifts and acquirements as a Master, were not less distinguished, than those that belonged to him as a Teacher. Nature had endowed him with a noble frame, the most felicitous expression of the dignity and courtesy that were in him. As he walked across the Campus, or stood erect, or sat in his seat in the class room, he was a model of refinement and of that repose that belongs to strength. Never have I seen a man who could so see into and see through a youth! What penetration! What genial sagacity! What sympathy! What dark rebuke! What wise reproof! What cheerful encouragement! He multiplied his influence as in the miracle of the loaves and the fishes, and while there was enough for all, what he had left was more than he had at the beginning, for he grew wiser and better every day! Coming from afar and standing here again at this distance of time I lay upon his grave this tribute of an indebted mind!

Gentlemen of the Board of Trustees: The occasion is propitious! The sons of the Academy sent out over all the earth, return to pay revering honors; and hovering gratitudes from afar flutter gently down to rest at her feet! Heaven, in appointing you to this care and duty, has made you the instruments of Almighty Wisdom and Purpose to raise Human Society to moral beauty and glory! May the purpose of Heaven be fulfilled in you, and under your care may the

Academy still diffuse its blessings upon the human world!

Distinguished guests and friends of learning, whose presence here attests the universal sympathies of the mind, will please to receive our salutations!

Mr. Bancroft: I assume not too much, but voice a sentiment of all hearts, when in the name of this great concourse, I offer you their sincere, revering and grateful regards!

POEM BY EDWARD HALE, A. B.

A happy time!—these years that bear
The nineteenth century toward its close—
A happy time! and happy those
Who in its blessings have their share.
For when before, within our ken,
Did eager progress, and research
In all things new, such homage pay
To all things old? and when did men
With minds more worn in reason's fray
Find sweeter rest for all their needs
In memory of their fathers' creeds?
Yes, even the æsthete's neutral soul,
Which once had found in new and old
Naught save a weary tale twice told,
Now sees the sunflower's leaves unroll
As never since the world was young,
And, though faith wane in God and man,
Finds lasting comfort in Queen Anne.

Yet even now I hardly hope
Without offense to sing of one
Whose life 'tis said is already run,
Whose name her sons a few years later
Will know no more as—Alma Mater.

As to her name, perhaps 'tis fair
That one should draw the line somewhere,
And Alma Mater, although not Greek,
Is nearly as old, is quite antique.
But she herself? Is it true as they say
That like her name she has had her day?
That even when at her best estate
She was only a myth that is out of date?

A myth? I'll grant it—but tell me, then,
What it is in the old town here
That brings us back to its streets again?
Are the rivers, the Fresh and the Salt, more clear
Than other streams that we hold less dear?
Are the wild flowers out by the Ledge more sweet,
The moss more soft to the lingering feet?
Are the banks of the Eddy the only spot
Where the pines and the seawinds ever meet
To whisper their secret and tell it not?
Is it these alone or something more
That stirs our memories o'er and o'er,
That calls to our hearts and bids us come—
Come as men to their boyhood's home—
Come as brothers to meet with brother—
Come as sons to a foster mother?

Yes, call her a myth if you must and will,
But call her, if honest, a mother still;
And greet her now while yet she stands,
A mother's love in her smiling tears,
Waiting to welcome with outstretched hands
Her wandering sons of a hundred years.

Her eyes are bright with a happy pride
As she sees us coming side by side
From farm and workshop, near and far,

From trade and pulpit, bench and bar;
And her thought goes back to the time again
When we were boys who come as men.

To say that then in the old-time days
She taught us well, were scanty praise
If teaching mean the steady ramming
Of grammar and prosody, roots and rules
Into the heads of would-be fools,
And, just at the close of the last long year,
Of finer points a judicious cramming
To help one enter his college "clear."
"And didn't we do it?" Often, yes;
And the boisterous joy in that first success
Is fresh to-day. But more than that,
A nobler debt we've owed to her
Since first in the chapel there we sat
Waiting uneasy with restless stir
To have laid down the time-worn rule
We thought a part of every school.

But after the prayer, we hear: "Young men,
"The Academy has no rule until
"It is broken. And now"—You know what then,
And how we followed in mute surprise
The lead of the master's hands and eyes
As we clapped again and again once more,
Until at last, with fingers sore
And beating hearts, he let us go,
Proudly resolving, yet humbly too,
That as we were done by so we'd do,
That trusted thus we would be true.—
'Twas our first day only; yet even then
As the bell up yonder began to ring
We might have heard its legend sing:
"They come as boys, but they go as men."

For some 'tis long ago, that day;
Yet not so long that we need to fear
That the mother will think us strangers here.
Through all the years that have passed away
She has followed our steps as best she might
Keeping us always at least in sight;
Though in public life, perhaps, of late
She has felt her zeal somewhat abate;
For things that she used to think were fixed,—
Truth and policy,—now seem mixed,
And are held, so far as she can see,
As questions, decidedly, of degree.

No, not as strangers she bids us come.
Strangers? Ah, but she knows too well
The tale that the missing faces tell,
And the bright eyes dim, as one by one
She counts those over whose work is done.
Still she looks in the crowd for those
With whom for more than fourscore years
She shared her labors, her joys, her fears,
Who won for her all else above
The respect of her children, her children's love:
Still she looks for some younger son
Whose task was ended ere well begun;
Still she looks, and not all in vain;
For Love and Memory teach her how
To welcome them still with the living now.

So may her children see her there
A century hence, as young, as fair,
And greet her then as again she stands
Waiting to welcome with outstretched hands,
A mother's love in her smiling tears,
The sons of twice a hundred years.

THURSDAY AFTERNOON.

At one o'clock P. M., a procession, consisting of the Invited Guests, Trustees, Officers, Alumni and Students of the Academy, was formed in Court Square under the direction of RUSSELL STURGIS, Jr., Esq., of Boston, Chief Marshal, and marched to the second tent, where dinner was served.

At the conclusion of the dinner, the Hon. GEORGE BANCROFT, President of the day, rose and addressed the assembly.

ADDRESS OF HON. GEORGE BANCROFT, LL. D.

Sons of Phillips Exeter Academy: After invoking the blessing of heaven our first thought to-day is for our country, of which Phillips Exeter Academy is the contemporary. It was incorporated in the year which saw the surrender of Cornwallis; it was organized while the statesmen of America and England were concerting peace between the two nations; it was opened during the ratification of the treaty which conducted the people of the United States to its place among the nations of the earth. Exeter Academy came into life simultaneously with our republic, and rests on the principle that the freedom of the people and the culture of the people must flourish together.

The Founder, whose ancestors for three generations out of four had been ministers of the gospel, was himself trained to that office, but wanting power of voice, and having natural skill as a man of business, he devoted himself to secular pursuits, yet ever with this ruling thought: "a part of my income is required of me for the more immediate service of God ;" and so by thrift and frugality he was able, in his own lifetime, to scatter most liberal gifts in many directions, and to found this Academy, which was of his own design as well as his own endowment, and by a two-fold title bears his name.

For the place of the Academy he selected Exeter, in the temperate zone of New Hampshire, and then occupied exclusively by a race of men who inherited the right to freedom and activity of mind from the best ancestry, and retained the inexpensive habits of rural life.

The Founder belonged to that class of Christians which has made itself famous in the world's history by its battling for civil freedom ; and by its constant zeal for public education wherever it obtained the rule, alike in Geneva and in Prussia, in Scotland and in New England. It was his will that the preceptor of the Academy should be a Calvinist, as if to inscribe on its walls that in theology the first principle is the absolute sovereignty of God ; that in morals the first aspiration should be for purity of will. For the instructors there was no limitation but that they should be Protestants, and in that day the people of New England almost to a man were Protestants : otherwise the doors of the Academy were thrown wide open to persons "from every quarter" of this land, and indeed of the world.

The constitution of the Academy was wisely framed and partook of the best characteristics of the best English schools. As in Eton, there were scholars on the foundation around whom gathered the young volunteers; and it is the rule that no one can harbor pupils but after approval and under supervision.

In the first five years of the school "the unwearied exertions" of Woodbridge, its earliest Preceptor, were baffled by his want of health. In 1788, the year in which the people of the United States adopted their Constitution, Exeter Academy found its great chief in Benjamin Abbot, on whom Heaven bestowed length of days and fixedness of purpose. He found it languishing in the feebleness of childhood; it rose at his coming into health and beauty, and during his more than fifty years, the Academy in each year gained steadily in character and in efficiency. He was a good scholar and gave thorough instruction in Latin and in Greek; as a ruler of young men he was not to be surpassed. In all the long period of his service he was never known to use a word or a tone that needed to be recalled or softened. He never reproved one scholar in the presence of another. In the time that I was under his care I cannot recall from any pupil a saying about him that was not full of respect. To-day, though it is seventy years since I passed from his care, my heart warms with affection as I recall his name.

To Gideon Lane Soule his most able successor, all who knew him ascribe a like character. You have to-day heard his just praise from one who knew him well and spoke of him with the eloquence of united judgment and affection. These two men, Abbot and Soule, filled up almost the whole of this first century in the life of the Academy.

In this age the Academy, by the progress of human culture is forced in its studies to take a wider range: the sciences knock at the door. The culture of the body is to be cared for: for why should not a scholar have health and the perfect development of his system. Remember that Pythagoras was famed among men for his physical power; and that the very best, most graceful and eloquent writer of prose in any language ever spoken among men, Plato, bore away the prize in the athletic games of Greece. Ever after your school days, continue to love nature and find joy in being in her presence. Let the winds of heaven play around you freely; breathe for two or three hours a day air which you never inhale but once. In reckoning the time to which heaven limits your life, these hours will not be counted.

To-day very great numbers of us come together in this home of our early life, one in feeling; dividing ourselves only according to our years. As we cast our eyes along the hundred arches on which stand the Exeter classes of each completed year, we turn from the last erected which rise in all their freshness and beauty to those which the waves of time have been beating into ruins. Among the many who have dropped from them before us we recall the name of Richard Hildreth the historian, son of the distinguished man who in my day was the head of the English department of the school.

John Gorham Palfrey, among most numerous competitors, has excelled everyone as the historian of New England. Jared Sparks filled a long life with most valuable contributions to the history of our country. Joseph Stevens Buckminster imparted to Boston that happy impulse which bore the town onward to its great intellectual development. John P. Hale is remembered for his services in behalf of a suffering race. John A. Dix passed nearly his whole life in the public service. Edward Everett, was among his contemporaries, swiftest in the capacity to acquire knowledge, the master of beautiful, and clear, and eloquent speech, the pure-minded patriot and statesman, the model of unshaken fidelity in friendship, a man who lived for others more than for himself. The name of Lewis Cass is written with honor in every department of the public service; and as we turn still farther back, to an arch from which time has carried away all who stood upon it to the shores of eternity, we recall the memory of Daniel Webster, the charming companion in social life, the man who knew the way to the hearts of the farmers of New England, ever the champion of Union, one who, when he uttered with impassioned earnestness his own deepest and sincerest convictions, spoke so well, that the country names him as the greatest orator of his age.

But in the presence of this crowd of aspiring young men, the past, with all its broken arches disappears from my eyes, and I see only the great high road of humanity on which you are travelling. Press on then to advance the welfare of your country; to feel and to act for mankind. If you come to excel in knowledge do not lie down with it on a couch to take pleasant dreams, but have the courage of your opinions, and plead for truth. If you acquire wealth, remember in the employ of your wealth the great rule of life of the Founder of this Academy. If you are in public life, bend your ear and listen reverently to the counsels of lowly humanity. While your service to your fellow men must not be limited to place, remember the ever varying wants of this Academy, and with the benevolence and affection of sons, enable her to meet every new condition of her being. With these admonitions we, your elder brothers, cheer you on to action, happiness and glory.

Yet do not in reply, say to the aged, that we are passing away. To a good world belong age and youth, and to us who are to go before you let your words be, "ever and forever, live joyfully and hopefully move on."

President Bancroft said: Our first tribute must be .
"The Memory of the Founder,"
and I call on the Rev. Dr. Peabody, ex-president of Harvard University to speak on that theme.

ADDRESS OF REV. ANDREW P. PEABODY, D. D.

Mr. President, you call on me, I suppose, because in my official term, with reference to the Academy, I come nearest to the Founder. I have been for forty years on this board of trust,—not quite far back enough for me to have known the Founder, but I was for a year or two a co-trustee with Dr. Abbot and well remember traditions that I had from him with reference to the Founder. But you have eloquently commemorated him and have left very little for me to say. I thank you that you have made my office on this occasion so nearly a sinecure.

President Bancroft: Not so; when a man gives you a text, you should preach on it.

Dr. Peabody: You remind me of my profession, and I will preach. Our Founder was of clerical ancestry, and clerical ancestry has been the ancestry of a very large proportion of the philanthropists, the public benefactors, the lights and guides of our New England community. If I were going to talk long, I could give you a good many names, and this name of Phillips, as you know, from the very first, has been illustrious. And on our present board of trust the honor of the name is perpetuated; and perpetuated, too, in the same tone of liberal and cordial benefaction of which the founder gave the example, an example, the following of which by our Phillips is one of the prime grounds for thankfulness on this present occasion. Our Founder belonged to a class of men, not a few of whom were living in my early days, who spared that they might give. In these days of abounding wealth we have public benefactors, and noble public benefactors, but they, for the most part, give from the fullness, the exuberance of their wealth. I knew in my time not a few men who were rigidly and pinchingly frugal that they might have the means for large and broad munificence. All the traditions of our Founder show that he was a man of that class, a man whose domestic habits, probably, would have been as inexpensive as those of his comparatively poor fellow citizens; a man who, probably, never wasted a cent or spent a cent in self-indulgence, but had all along this great plan maturing, and did not leave it to mature at his death and to blossom out in his will, but he was a liberal giver in his lifetime. Taking his benefactions to our Academy, to the sister institution at Andover and to Dartmouth College, he was the greatest public benefactor, as regard pecuniary amount, in the whole of the last century. His benefactions in his lifetime far exceeded the property that he left at his death, and with scanty provision for those whom he left behind him of his own name and kindred, almost everything that remained at his death went to one or the other of these favored institutions. His forecast, his liberality, his lengthened vision, the breadth of the provisions that he made for the administration of the Academy, all follow in line with his pecuniary munificence, and have led me to regard him, as I have no doubt he is regarded by all who hear me, as a man standing almost by himself in his time and in our New England community, a man deserving of perpetual honor, and whose name, I trust, a century hence will be held in the same veneration and receive like eulogies to those which we pay to his memory to-day.

President Bancroft said: I know you want our occupations a little diversified, and so I will ask leave to read you a part of a letter to a widow's son:

"I find him to be be a promising youth, and forward scholar for his age, and his age is short of ten years. His talents bid fair for distinguished usefulness could he be favored with the means of obtaining an education. I am informed that he is remarkably steady in his habits, and of a studious turn of mind, and of a fair moral character."

This letter was written in 1827 at Deerfield, N. H. It is addressed to the President and board of Trustees of Phillips

Exeter Academy, and at whose request was it made? At the request of widow Charlotte Butler. "I have examined Benjamin Butler, her son, and find him to be a promising youth and forward scholar." Now, you see this letter was written in the year of our Lord, 1827, so that that makes the way for the next sentiment I am going to offer you,

"The Academy of the Past."

And I request you,—Exeter makes nothing of turning out a Governor to a State.—I request you to listen to what may be said by the gentleman whom the great majority of the people of Massachusetts have raised to the Executive chair of that State—Benjamin Franklin Butler.

ADDRESS OF HON. BENJAMIN F. BUTLER, LL. D.

Mr. President, Pupils of Exeter Academy, Ladies and Gentlemen:—The introduction given by your President has almost taken from me the power of expression. With kindness, with reverence, he has brought back to my mind that mother whose exertions brought me here more than half a century ago,—the first mother sending me to the second mother for that education I could not get at home. As I love and reverence her more than anything else on earth, next my love, gratitude and reverence go forth to Phillips Exeter Academy, from which I received all of that foundation of education which has served me through life. So young in years that I could not call her Alma Mater, but rather, altrix, nursing mother, Exeter took me in her arms, and under the guidance of that good and great man;—methinks in my mind's eye I see him, all that was venerable and all that was sacred to the young boy whom he took in his hand, when the kind clergyman presented me to him, and, laying his hand upon my head, said, "My boy, you can do anything that any man can do in this world, if you will work." And that injunction I have ever remembered, and I came here, my friends, to bring back whatever I may have won by reason of the teachings of this school and to lay it at the feet of the dear Academy, as among the first fruits, humble and simple though they may be; and all that I have, and all that I may be, whatever that may be, belongs to our common mother, and I lay it upon her altar as the offering of my life.

I came here also as a representative of a class for which your Founder made provision, the class of young men who have their own way to make in the world, the class of young men, nay of young boys, who, poor in everything else, were happy in an unworn heart, and felt themselves equal to the battle of the world and ready to fight it out against all odds under all circumstances and anywhere. And you, my young friends, now with your greater advantages, with the opening of science,—for very little of scientific instruction was given to us then,—with the lightning flashing illumination upon your studies, with the steam to take you home to your parents at any moment, so that you are hardly away from home while here, with all the events of the world laid every day upon your table for your instruction outside of your classics, what ought you not to do for yourselves and the country in the future? And with what gifts hereafter may you not come, higher, nobler, better, purer, everything that is great, to lay on the altar of your dear nursing mother, Exeter Academy?

I speak, I trust, with a grateful feeling that comes to each and all of her sons. If we have forgotten the benefactor, the Founder, it is because to all of us, the older ones as well, I trust, as the younger, the Academy has become a living, breathing thing, which we look at and remember as the nurse of our youth, the pride of our younger years, and the dear remembrance of our older and maturer thought, when through the lapse of time our old associates fall away one by one, till now of my class but three remain on earth to my knowledge, and two of them are here. Then what is left to us as we go down the hill of life, our work having been done for better or for worse? When those that started with us fall away, what is left to us but the memory of friendships? What is there else of solace? The young world has grown up and passes by us; the old world has passed from us, leaving bright memories that cluster in the heart like the rich grapes upon the fruitful vine, warmed in the sun of friendship. My young friends who are about to graduate from this school to go into others, in a preparatory course of education, my still younger friends who are to stay here, let me give you a thought which used to trouble me when I was here, and which undoubtedly has flitted across the mind of more than one of you. Why should I strive, what is there left for me to do? No new worlds to discover; no great thing to do; all the discoveries of science are perfected; the great Newton has settled the heavens; Humboldt has settled the earth; Lavoisier and Gay Lussac have settled the materials of the earth in chemistry; Homer, Milton, Virgil, have ended all that there is in poetry,—what is there for me to do? Now, be honest with yourselves, my young friends, as I am honest with you, haven't you had that thought run through your minds more than once? Brush it away if it ever had place there. Remember that the light of science is just dawning. The best way to govern men is yet undiscovered. More than that, because more necessary, the best way to feed them is unknown. Civilization has its object in these two things: to govern and feed in the best way the largest number of men to the square acre; and if you will find any book of philosophy, if you will find any book of political economy that will tell you that, you will have done what I have failed to do, having overlooked it perhaps in the later years of a busy life. Nay, my friends, I feel as if I were treading on dangerous ground here, but still I must go on; I am so unfortunate as to believe that the best way not only of governing and feeding men on earth, but of directing their course onward and upward to the heaven above us, is yet open to a little investigation. Let me say to you one word further. In my judgment, while I do not underrate classical learning, having but very little of it, and what little I have I shall not undertake to exploit here, for I have not studied a book of quotations day before yesterday in order to have some here; and if I had, so far as the Latin tongue is concerned, I should not know how to pronounce it. For instance, when you and I were boys we were told that Cæsar said, "Veni, vidi, vici," and we read with admiration the orations of Cicero, but now we are told by the highest and best authority that what Cæsar did say was, "Wane, wede, witche," and that no such man as Cicero exists, and that he has left behind him one "Kikero." Even the dead languages change. What must we expect of the living language? Therefore, more literary culture for the scholar, for the literary man, for the author, for the poet, for the historian; nothing is so necessary; and what sort of historians the teaching of Exeter makes, we happen to know. But to-day has come a sterner age, with its sterner duties, and hereafter science and mechanical skill are to govern the world in peace or war. In war, the whole struggle now is to find out how much thickness of iron will withstand a given weight of shot; not to find out who those brave men are that have lived since Agamemnon,—only the question of engineering. Would you not, my young friends, have been quite as willing to have been the engineer of the Brooklyn bridge, that great triumph of engineering, as to have been Sir Humphrey Davy, or even, if we may make comparisons, to have been any of the first poets of any and every age? Therefore, to practical education, such as you will get here, those that must be practical men, who are to go into the business of life, who are to govern the country, who are to make its prosperity, its wealth, its glory and its honor, will have to look. For let me tell you this truth, and ask you to take it with you,—the mechanical engineer has his hand on the throttle of the universe to make it proceed hereafter.

President Bancroft said: We see how all things are connected, the Academy with the Universities, and with the Universities the schools for the professions, and with the schools for the professions, in great degree, also, the shaping of the Government of the country. I give you now, as a sentiment,

"The Work of the Academy,"

And I call on my honored friend, the President of Harvard University, to speak to us on that point.

ADDRESS OF PRESIDENT CHARLES W. ELIOT, LL. D.

Mr. President, Ladies and Gentlemen:—I am, I believe, the first speaker to address you who is not an Exeter boy. A Boston Latin school boy must needs feel diffident before those distinguished graduates of Exeter Academy. But I know the Academy from a different point of view from yours. I know it by a long line of excellent scholars which the Academy has sent year after year to the University. I know it by a large band of distinguished professors whom we have drawn from among Exeter boys. I know it from many of the best friends of my life, men of intellectual life, who were bred here. I know it as a national school, a school of national, and not of local, resort. I have observed that boys come to Harvard University from this institution, from all States of the Union, and I rejoice in this nationality of its repute. It is a source of strength to our country, for thus are created. strong, intimate bonds of union. I know it is a democratic institution, where the rich and the poor sit opposite each other on the same benches. But, not knowing from personal experience, I asked a distinguished graduate of the school last evening, who is prevented from being here to-day, what it was that he felt that he owed to Exeter. He said: "I was a boy. I had lived on a farm and as a mill hand at Manchester. I went to Exeter"—he hesitated, and then broke out with a certain strong feeling which moved him. Said he, "Exeter was the dawn of the intellectual life to me." What a memorable gift! what a sunrise was that,—the dawn of the intellectual life! There is no sunrise like it, except the rise of the Sun of Righteousness. And he went on to say: "Another thing I owe to Exeter, I got there my first lesson in manners." "What was it?" said I. "I was a scrubby little boy," said he, "and I met Dr. Soule in the street and he touched his hat to me,—he always touched his hat to the boys,—and it set me to inquiring how such an unparalelled emergency was to be met." He soon learned to meet it and he is one of the most cultivated gentlemen and accomplished scholars of our day.

Let me say a few words about the future of the school. You are met here to celebrate its past, but you mean to prepare for it, I have no doubt, a better future. The Academy has many needs. It needs to have its curriculum enlarged. It needs, as his Excellency the Governor of Massachusetts has well said, to have provision made for the study of science; it needs laboratories. I have been looking about its buildings to-day. It needs better dormitories; it needs a gymnasium; for, let me assure you, that the intellectual and spiritual life are best built upon a sound physical life. And, while I desire to express my adhesion to much that his Excellency has said, let me also add that I believe that the students of this Academy should look to it for something higher than either literary or scientific training. The mechanical engineer has, indeed, his hand upon the throttle-valve of the engine of modern society, but he is not the power, and the power is not in the valve. What drives the steam engine? Not the engineer, but the life-giving sun which elaborated centuries ago the coal that is put under the boilers. What is it that you must learn here which will always be above all literature and all science, powerful though science may become? You must learn the eternal worth of character; you must learn that the ultimate powers of the human race lie in its undying instincts and passions; you must learn that above all material things, is man—the thoughtful, passionate and emotional being, the intellectual, and religious man. Here lies the source of the power of educated men—they have refined and strengthened their minds and their souls. And, believe me, the supreme powers of this universe are not mechanical or material; they are hope and fear and love.

President Bancroft said: A good word ought to be spoken for Exeter,—lovely spot, beautiful charming river, with tide water to bathe in, excellent streams to freeze up and skate upon in winter, good walks and drives in summer, good coasting and sleigh riding in winter. So I will give you as the next sentiment,

"The Home of the Academy;"

and I ask my most valued friend Dr. Hitchcock, who knows Exeter by heart and loves it well, to say a word upon that theme.

ADDRESS OF REV. ROSWELL D. HITCHCOCK, D. D.

Mr. President, Ladies and Gentlemen: I have some slight claim to be heard in response to the sentiment to which you have just listened. The claim is not of one born into the family, but of one most kindly adopted, much more than a proselyte of the gate. Thirty-eight years ago I came here and was here for seven years. It was my good fortune to know the man, who, I supposed, was the first Principal of the Academy, Dr. Abbot, till my ignorance was corrected this afternoon. He had finished his well-rounded service and was sitting on the verandah, waiting for the sun to go down. Dr. Soule was in the fulness of his strength. But Exeter had other notables, one of whom I rejoice to greet now, sitting at my left (the venerable Dr. William Perry); not the "old man eloquent," but more, immeasurably more,— the man of deeds and not words, though words were not wanting when the truth needed to be made intelligent in regard to any matter that called for the testimony of a medical expert; a man to whom many lives before me are indebted for their lengthened days to behold this auspicious hour. Long may his shadow hallow this beautiful place.

I am here to-day in gratitude for the many kindnesses which I received during these seven years,—from the people of my official charge, so many of whom have passed on before me to what we call the "land of silence;" kindness from the people of the town, whom I carry in my grateful memory; and, perhaps, I may be pardoned for saying gratitude, especially, to the boys of the Academy who always treated me so kindly, and whose stout shoulders are now bearing the burdens both of church and state all the way from the Atlantic to the Pacific.

The home of Phillips Exeter Academy:—Its material home needs no orator any more than Sir Christopher Wren needed a monument. Exeter has not the strength of the hills,—the strength of the hills is some way north of us,— but it has the witchery and the beauty of the plain, the beauty which pursues us along the dusty path of life, the beauty which haunts us in our dreams. Exeter is fortunate in its physical home. It has, as we have been reminded here to-day by the first great historian of our country and of our time, it has a home also in the history of the continent. It drew breath with the Constitution; it inaugurated Dr. Abbot when the government was set in operation, and its life will continue till the government and the continent and the globe shall end.

There is a home of the Academy, of which we have been reminded also to-day, in the hearts of its Alumni. The President of Harvard has said many wise things but, nothing wiser, ever, in my humble judgment, than this, "That when an institution ceases to beg it has ceased to grow." We applaud the scholarship of the past, but, Mr. President and gentlemen, we cannot forget that the Latin dictionary was that of Ainsworth and the Greek dictionary was that of Schrevelius with Latin definitions, and between the Ainsworth of your day and the Andrews, and the Freund and how many more I don't know, of to-day, is a vast difference; and the difference between the Schrevelius of your day and the lexicon which has just come from the press of the Harpers measures also an immense stretch. The classical scholarship of the country is widely different at this moment from what it was. It is at once more microscopic and telescopic. We understand the Greek particles as our fathers and grandfathers did not understand them, and we understand the relations of these languages to all the languages of the globe as they could not be understood by those who went before us. The past is of small account when it stops. It is only as the past moves on into the future that it has significance and worth. We praise Exeter for what it has been; we demand of it more in the time to come, even in the knowledge of the three languages indicated in the gift of the original founder, English, Greek and Latin,—we demand of it in the future a much wider and richer curriculum. In order to do this there must be money. We can build universities, now, on the prairie. I remember the tradition very well, when the king of Prussia started his

University of Berlin, it was said it can have no history; there are Heidelberg, and all the old universities; Berlin can have no history. The answer was, "I know it has no past, but it shall have a future." We can make institutions now with the money that shall command the men. But better than wholly new institutions are old institutions with new blood put into their arteries. I remember very well, a few years ago, in conversing with Henry J. Raymond, the editor of the *Times*, he said somewhat sadly, "The New York *Herald* has the advantage of me in spite of all that I can do, in its years; it will always be older than the *Times*." Exeter and Andover will always be older than what may be done, always; and the best place to put money is where men began to put it the longest while ago, for the same general ends, with a wider scope of vision and with more clear and earnest purposes; and, though I am not in conference with the Trustees of this institution and do not speak at their bidding, I should feel that I had failed in my duty as a preacher, bound to have some sort of respect to my text, whether it is regarded as inspired or not, if I failed to bespeak for Exeter Academy larger endowments for the time to come, that it may do a larger and a nobler work.

Mr. Bancroft said: Exeter Academy is not without its benefactors; we hope the race of them will be continuous and marked by generosity. The sentiment that I give you next is in behalf of Exeter Academy,

"Our Benefactors;"

and I call to respond to this sentiment on the Hon. George S. Hale.

ADDRESS OF HON. GEORGE S. HALE.

Mr. President, and Ladies and Gentlemen: Our benefactors, for whom you ask me to speak, were men of deeds rather than of words, who showed their merits in their lives and in their actions more than by any graces of speech. And I cannot but feel that I should better represent them by a golden silence than by the most silver speech. But I cannot deny myself the pleasure of paying to them my tribute; I cannot deny myself the pleasure of making the acknowledgement which we all feel for them, if, indeed, that be necessary on this spot, on this occasion or at this time. For everything around us seems to me to speak for them and of them. That modest and unostentatious, but tasteful building, [pointing towards the Academy Hall] the product of their liberty, decorated by the assiduous labors and the taste of one of them with the counterfeit presentments of their living features; that small but useful library, for which, a few years ago, one of their number, alas, no longer living, placed in my hands a sum equal to the amount to which the salary of Benjamin Abbot was raised in the third year of his service, these constantly speak for them. But, more than anything else, those 5,000 Alumni who have risen during all these years, "rank behind rank in surges bright," and now scattered from the Atlantic to the Pacific and among the isles of the sea, have come back to us from the Gulf of California, from the mountains of Nevada, and some of whom are on this side the earth or "where half the convex world intrudes between,"—all these proclaim the debt they owe to the modest but generous givers, and they do not need any words which I can add for them to-day.

The catalogue is a long one—from our Founder, for whom I might add to the epitaph which has been suggested for him and say that, "Dying without issue he made posterity— he made us his foster children," and left to the succession of benefactors whom he stimulated to benevolence his example, and to his own kindred the generous spirit which in one generation after another has prompted them to hold up the lengthening chain which unites the cautious liberality of age to the prompt generosity of youth, and to recognize the obligation which the nobility of descent imposed down, gentlemen, to his namesake, whose voice would more fitly have responded to this sentiment, if his modesty had not been equal to his liberality. This catalogue is too long for me to characterize them in detail. We have long known that the Academy has' a history of its own, and I am grateful to the benefactor (Hon. Charles H. Bell) who has given to us an outward and visible sign of that history and done some measure of justice to these men. But our benefactions are not only in gifts. The faithful sons, now honorable men who have gone out from the Academy, who have won their honors by her help, and have prayed towards this Mecca and returned to it, and now have laid their honors, as they have to-day, at her feet,—historians, statesmen, teachers and divines, the wise counsellors and healers of men,—these are her benefactors. And those men, too, who have filled up the century with the service of instruction,—his Excellency will pardon me, since I am out of his jurisdiction, if I venture to differ a little from him, for, as a lawyer, he knows that he must hear the other side—I ask the Alumni of Phillips Exeter Academy whose fame they would prefer to-day, whose influence they would rather have exercised, that of Benjamin Abbot or of the engineer of the Brooklyn Bridge. The first result of that great feat of engineering was the slaughter of innocent men and women. Thousands of witnesses to the glory of the teacher have lived, and among them many still live to-day and bear testimony to his success. I am not content to accept the triumph of the engineer, I prefer the triumph of the teacher who twined the strands of character and fixed the butresses of duty to sustain human hearts and souls on their passage through useful lives to the reward of the just.

I need not add to the deserved eulogies so often bestowed on the two Principals who nearly filled the century with their labors. I cannot recapitulate the list of honored assistants. I must acknowledge the faithful services of their successor

(Dr. Perkins), not surpassed in zeal, assiduity and fidelity and conscientiousness, for the last decade. But these benefactors are not alone. When Moses' hands were heavy, they took a stone and put it under him and he sat thereon and Aaron and Hur stayed up his hands, the one on the one side and the other on the other side and his hands were steady until the going down of the sun. Among the teachers who have assisted the Principals whom we praise, there are two who have shared these labors for a quarter of the century which we commemorate. I have watched their service during a tenth of that century and I am happy to pay to them the tribute which they deserve. To them is largely due the success of the institution. I have used Scriptural names, but names which are honored in the history of New Hampshire are as good for this purpose, and I am glad to speak of George Albert Wentworth and Bradbury Longfellow Cilley,—the Aaron and the Hur who have stayed the hands of Moses during a quarter of a century; every one of you knows their services and feels that they are our benefactors.

But this is the past; the century is ended, the century of which we are proud, the century which should continue to be, as we hold it now, our glory, but which we make our shame if we do not ourselves bear up the honor, if we do not ourselves take up the lengthening chain, if we do not ourselves show that we are worthy of the benefits that we have received. The gratitude which at this moment I feel most keenly, I confess, is the gratitude I anticipate feeling to you, the gratitude for future favors, the gratitude for the gifts you are to make. "*Qui sentit commodum*," if his Excellency will pardon me for a Latin quotation, "*sentire debet et onus*,"—"He who has shared the advantage ought also to share the burden." You and I and all the five thousand, half the host whom these eminent Greek leaders Xenophon and Cilley lead yearly up to the sea in yonder halls, have shared the advantage, and it is the duty of those of us who live to share the burden for the future; to remember that the gift is a debt and that you, that *we* cannot accept it without dishonor if we do not return it. Another quotation, since quotations are not inappropriate to this place, from some of the books you study: When Æneas saw the Phrygian Penates in his dream, they said to him as they left him, "*Idem venturos tollemus ad astra nepotes,*"—"We, the same always and forever, will bear your future descendants, by our guidance and our help, to the stars." Be that your duty, and be all of you benefactors of the Academy!

Mr. Bancroft said: Dr. Abbot always used to tell the scholars whom he saw eight or ten years after they left the Academy, "Oh, the Academy as it was when you were there is nothing at all to the Academy as it is now." So, then, I shall, in the spirit of Dr. Abbot offer you the next sentiment,

"The Academy as It Is;"

and I ask Mr Charles G. Fall to speak to that sentiment.

ADDRESS OF MR. CHARLES G. FALL.

Mr. President:—

"You would scarce expect one of my age
To appear in public on this stage."

But, sir, I suppose I ought not to find fault with that youth which is the sole qualification for my standing here to speak on behalf of the younger graduates. The President of Harvard University has told us of the lesson in manners taught by Dr. Soule. I was here, sir, under Dr. Soule, and it recalled to my mind an instance, which is one of the most marvelous I have ever seen, of the power which personal magnetism and dignity exercise over other persons. At five o'clock we boys used to kick football. During the summer months Dr.

Soule had a recitation which was finished at half-past five; and, on one occasion, we were kicking across the path that led from the front door of the old Academy to his house, and, as he walked down the steps we forgot his presence and almost impeded his progress. As he came along the first word we heard was, "Boys!" It rang like a clarion note; it called a halt as much as if some General had ordered a "Halt!" while his troops were running on a battlefield.

On returning here for the first time, how the events of those days when we were here come back to us! We, sir, were here, some of us, in the days of the war. We were here in 1860 and 1861. The present Secretary of War, whom we hoped to have had the pleasure of hearing here to-day, was here at that time, and his father was President. A nephew of Major Anderson was likewise a student, and when Lewis Cass, a graduate of the Academy, resigned from a Cabinet which refused to reprovision Fort Sumter, you may be sure, sir, that the guns of Sumter re-echoed among these granite hills. Those, sir, were days when Garrison and Phillips and Seward and Greeley and Bryant and Chase were the leaders of public opinion; and the boys of those days, sir, like the boys of the Revolution, were filled with patriotic ardor. How well do some of us remember forming in a procession and marching down to the old church where the girls of the village presented us with a flag and with a motto plaited in evergreen to place over the portals of the Academy. I can see it now, "*Ducit Amor Patriæ.*" How long it stood there till it grew faded and sunburnt, stood there like the famous inscription of the Areopagus, "To the Unknown God."

And there is another instance which occurs to me which so well illustrates the spirit of the times that I will venture to narrate it. It was a boyish freak which in the light of to-day might deserve suspension, but those were other days and other times, and, according to the old adage, "circumstances alter cases." In the spring of 1861 every village had its flag-raising.

On one of these occasions in one of the neighboring villages, some gray-haired old sinner had expressed disunion sentiments and had insulted the flag. For this cause, in those times, sir, men were sometimes tarred and feathered. It was a graduate of this Academy who uttered those memorable words, "If any man haul down the American flag, shoot him on the spot!" As soon as the story was told in the Academy, some Paul Revere, I wish I knew his name, suggested that we ought to make the old gentleman a visit. No sooner said than done; and, at midnight, some thirty or forty boys, from thirteen to fifteen or sixteen years old, started out for a six or seven miles' tramp. When we reached his house some of the leaders woke him up and told him our errand. After a little parleying he came down stairs followed by his wife and family. We told him what we had heard, which he did not deny. We told him what we desired, which at first he refused to do; but, when he saw our numbers and visions of the feathers flitted through his mind, he somewhat relented. The advice of his wife, a true daughter of New Hampshire, completed the conquest, and there, sir, in his own hallway, surrounded by his family, his idols and his household gods, we made him revoke the insult, and, kneeling down upon the folds of the dear old flag, he raised it to his lips and kissed it, not once but again and again. Then, after cautioning him against the dangers' which beset the backslider, we politely bade him good night. Surely, sir, the boys of '61 were lineal descendants of the men who brewed the tea in Boston harbor.

Here, sir, is the Rugby of America. The spirit of its discipline is self-control; the essence of its instruction is self-development. While the love of knowledge is the object sought to be promoted, the perfection of its culture is manliness. Love of truth is the golden tenet of its religious creed. Not Calvin but Channing, not Edwards but Emerson, not Swinburne but Longfellow, not Calhoun but Webster, are the apostles of our faith. This revered home

of learning, fellow graduates, was once our home. These
classic groves once were our Academy. Through them, in
boyhood's days, have walked, as we all so well know,
America's greatest constitutional advocate, the monarch of
the American bar; one of our most polished statesmen, who
was, likewise, a Secretary of State and a Foreign Minister;
one of our bravest statesmen, who was a nominee for the
Presidency; our most profound historian, the Gibbon of the
nineteenth century; and senators, soldiers, governors, orators, reformers, philanthropists, cabinet members, foreign
ministers, judges, lawyers, physicians, preachers, teachers,
authors, editors, college presidents, merchant princes, men
of science and of learning. The catalogue, we have been
told, of a hundred years, contains the names of more than
5,000 graduates, the true nobility of the land, the pillars of
society and the state. These men whose names are familiar
to us and which we love to repeat, as the child loves to repeat
its catechism,—Webster, Cass, Everett, Dix, Buckminster,
Palfrey, Sparks, Walker, Fitch, Hale. Butler, Wyman, Bancroft,—these are our elder brothers. It is fitting that on such
a day as this, in the spirit of our favorite poet's deep-toned
psalm of life, we drink inspiration from their noble lives.
Would that the eye of grand John Phillips could to-day
survey this scene; would that some other philanthropist, in
emulation of his action, would enlarge the boundaries of this
land of promise for their own children to survey at another
centennial.

Some of the distinguished speakers have brought stones to
throw upon the cairns erected to the memory of Dr. Abbot
and Dr. Soule. While we heartily join with them in burning
frankincense upon these pious altars, the younger graduates,
whom I have the honor to represent, ask you to join with us
in celebrating the praises of the living. And, were it
becoming at this time and in this presence, to suggest a
sentiment expressive of our feelings, it would be this,
" Gratitude to the living instructors of Phillips Academy."

The company then rose, and joined in singing, under the lead of Prof. Oscar Faulhaber,

THE ACADEMY SONG.

BY REV. HENRY WARE, D. D.

From highways and byways of manhood we come,
And gather, like children, about our old home;
We return from life's weariness, tumult and pain,
Rejoiced in our hearts to be schoolboys again.

The Senator comes from the hall of debate,
The Governor steps from the high chair of State,
The Judge leaves the bench to the law's wise delay,
Rejoiced to be schoolboys again for a day.

The Parson his pulpit has left unsupplied,
The Doctor has put his old sulky aside,
The Lawyer his client has turned from the door,
And all are at Exeter,—schoolboys once more.

Oh, glad to our eyes are these dear scenes displayed,
The halls where we studied, the fields where we played,
There is change—there is change—but we will not deplore,
Enough that we feel ourselves schoolboys once more.

And when to the harsh scenes of life we return,
Our hearts with the glow of this meeting shall burn;
Its calm light shall cheer till earth's schooltime is o'er,
And prepare us in Heaven for one meeting more.

THURSDAY EVENING.

In the evening of Thursday a Promenade Concert was given in the great tent, by Reeves' excellent Band, of Providence, Rhode Island. A large and brilliant company were present, who were highly gratified with the choice music, and the opportunity for social intercourse.

This concluded the Centennial Exercises of 1883.

By invitation of the Committee of Arrangements Prof. EDWARD R. SILL contributed

A HYMN OF HOPE,

FOR THE 100TH ANNIVERSARY OF PHILLIPS EXETER ACADEMY.

Has, then, our boyhood vanished,
    And rosy morning fled?
Are faith and ardor banished,
    Is daring courage dead?
Still runs the olden river
    By meadow, hill and wood,—
Where are the hearts that ever
    Beat high with royal blood?

The golden dreams we cherished
    Pacing the ancient town,—
Have they but bloomed and perished,
    And flown like thistle down?
Nay, still the air is haunted
    With mystery as of old;
Each blossom is enchanted,
    And every leaflet's fold.

Not one fair hope we harkened,
    But still to youth returns;
Not one clear light hath darkened,—
    Still for some breast it burns:
Thought age by age is lying
    Beneath the gathering mold,
Life's dawn-light is undying,
    Its dreams grow never old.

As the great faithful planet
    Goes plunging on its track,
Thought still shall bravely man it,
    And steer through storm and wrack;
While but three souls are toiling
    Who would give all for right,
Whom gold nor fame is spoiling,
    Whose prayer is but for light;

While there are found a handful
    Of spirits vowed to truth, .
Clear-eyed, courageous, manful,
    And comrades as in youth;
Out of the darkness sunward,
    Out of the night to day,
While all the worlds swing onward,
    Life shall not lose its way.

When to the man-soul lonely
    The loving gods came down,
Earth gave the mantle only,
    Free mind the immortal crown.
Wild force with cloud-wraith stature
    Unscaled shall tower in vain,
And the fierce Afreet, Nature,
    Obey the sceptred brain.

O heart of man immortal,
    Beat on in love and cheer!
Somewhere the cloudy portal
    Of all thy prayers shall clear.
The fair earth's mighty measure
    Of life, untouched by rime,
Through star-dust and through azure
    Rolls on to endless time.

> The power that motes inherit,
>   That bud and crystal find,
> Hath not forgotten spirit,
>   Nor left the soul behind.
> O'er Time's dumb forces fleeting
>   This victory we begin,
> Dear eye-beams and the beating
>   Of heart with heart shall win.

DR. ABBOT IN 1847.

The Committee of Arrangements have received from Prof. SYLVESTER WATERHOUSE of Washington University, Missouri, the following interesting account of an interview which he had with the venerable Dr. BENJAMIN ABBOT in 1847, with permission to publish it if they should see fit.

Dr. Abbot was then about 85 years old. His venerable figure was seldom seen on the street, but his name was like a living presence. The personal qualities which, through 50 years of service, had won so wide a fame for Phillips Exeter Academy were well known to all the students. Stories of his high-bred courtesy and moral dignity of character, of his effective discipline and noble ardor in the work of instruction, were among the most cherished traditions of the Academy. An earnest desire to see so distinguished a teacher induced me to call on Dr. Abbot. He received me with cordiality and expressed the gratification which the visits of students afforded him.

"I have given," said he with a smile, "the best energies of my life to the education of youth, and it is but natural that I should not be indifferent to the regard of young folks."

Some inquiries with reference to my own objects in life served to introduce the theme which seemed to absorb all his thoughts. He explained at length his own theory of education and spoke of the progress of the Academy since it first came under his control in 1788. Alluding to the choice of a profession, he said,—

"I have always been accustomed to advise young men to take good care of their health, perfect themselves in their studies, acquire as much practical knowledge and general information as possible, and then let circumstances and the bent of their genius dictate what vocation they should follow."

It was suggested that some teachers recommend an early choice of a calling and the pursuit of the special studies which tend to promote professional success.

"No, no," he replied with great earnestness, "I do not believe that is best. I have always counseled the youth under my charge first to complete their general studies and then to follow the guidance of their natural tastes in the selection of a profession. A long observation of the careers of young men confirms the wisdom of this course."

A transition from this subject to the great men who had once been under his tuition was very natural to a teacher proud of the success of his pupils. The incidents which Dr. Abbot related about schoolboys who have since become illustrious were extremely interesting.

"Lewis Cass," he said, "was a very wild boy. One day his father, Major Cass, came to me and asked me if I would take his son.

" 'Certainly, but why do you ask?

" 'Oh! the youngster is headstrong and hard to manage. I am an officer and can govern soldiers, but that boy is too much for me.

" 'What does he do?

"'Plays truant, runs away from his work, steals off without my permission to go a gunning, fishing, and swimming, and is full of all kinds of pranks.'

"'Well, send him to me and I'll see what I can do with him.'

"The boy was placed under my charge. Several months later I met his father and asked him how his son was getting along. 'Well, sir,' said he, 'if Lewis was half as afraid of the Almighty as he is of you, I should never have any more trouble with him.'"

In relating this incident, Dr. Abbot fairly shook with the laughter which the recollection of Major Cass's answer excited.

It is scarcely necessary to add that controlled by the preceptor's extraordinary power of discipline, the strong motive energies which led young Cass into all sorts of boyish mischief were directed to nobler objects. The results of the wise management which quickened the ambition and roused into action the faculties of a powerful nature are recorded in American history. It was, however, intimated that at Exeter the future statesman evinced more talent for practical affairs than for the details of scholarship.

In speaking of the school-boy traits of Daniel Webster, Dr. Abbot mentioned an unexpected fact. He said that "Young Webster showed an insuperable aversion to declamation. As 'the boy is father to the man,' it might have been supposed that the lad who was destined to be pre-eminent in oratory would have exhibited an early fondness for declamation, but no persuasions could overcome his natural diffidence."

Dr. Abbot remarked that "there was a popular misapprehension with regard to Webster's scholarship. It was generally believed that Webster was a dull and unsuccessful pupil, but such was not the fact. His mind rarely seemed to be occupied with his studies. His large, lustrous, thoughtful eyes were gazing about the room, or looking out of the window; but, at recitation, the pupil who appeared not to be engaged in studious preparation always acquitted himself well. He often showed a far better grasp of the subject than those who were more familiar with the minor points of scholarship."

While Dr. Abbot was telling these anecdotes, his tones became more earnest and his eyes lighted up with a glow which these agreeable recollections kindled. It was quite obvious that age had not yet wholly quenched the fires of earlier manhood.

Heartily thanking him for his courtesies and for the rare pleasure which his conversation had afforded, I bade the venerable teacher good-bye.

The next time I saw him, he was lying in his coffin. An expression of sweet and childlike serenity rested upon his features, as though the divine hand had set upon his face the seal of a happy and well spent life.

CATALOGUE

OF

PHILLIPS EXETER ACADEMY.

1783–1883.

OF THE

OFFICERS AND STUDENTS

OF

PHILLIPS EXETER ACADEMY,

1783–1883.

BOSTON:
J. S. CUSHING & COMPANY.
1883.

PHILLIPS EXETER ACADEMY.

Trustees.

1781	HON. JOHN PHILLIPS, LL.D..............................	1795
1781	HON. SAMUEL PHILLIPS, LL.D.	1802
1781	THOMAS ODIORNE	1794
1781	HON. JOHN PICKERING, LL.D............................	1802
1781	REV. DAVID McCLURE...................................	1787
1781	REV. BENJAMIN THURSTON	1801
1781	DANIEL TILTON	1783
1783	WILLIAM WOODBRIDGE, A.M., *ex officio*	1788
1787	HON. PAINE WINGATE, A.M.	1800
1791	BENJAMIN ABBOT, A.M., *ex officio*	1838
1794	HON. OLIVER PEABODY, A.M.	1828
1795	HON. JOHN TAYLOR GILMAN, LL.D.....................	1827
1801	REV. JOSEPH BUCKMINSTER, D.D........................	1812
1802	REV. JESSE APPLETON, D.D.............................	1803
1802	HON. JOHN PHILLIPS...................................	1820
1809	REV. DANIEL DANA, D.D................................	1843
1809	HON. NATHANIEL APPLETON HAVEN...................	1830
1812	REV. JACOB ABBOT, A.M.	1834
1821	REV. NATHAN PARKER, D.D.	1833
1828	HON. JEREMIAH SMITH, LL.D...........................	1842
1831	SAMUEL HALE, A.M.	1869
1834	SAMUEL DANA BELL, A.M.	1838
1835	HON. DANIEL WEBSTER, LL.D.	1852
1835	REV. CHARLES BURROUGHS, D.D........................	1867
1838	BENJAMIN ABBOT, LL.D................................	1844
1838	GIDEON LANE SOULE, A.M., *ex officio*	1873
1842	HON. JAMES BELL, A.B.................................	1852
1843	REV. ANDREW PRESTON PEABODY, A.M.	
1844	DAVID WOOD GORHAM, A.B., M.D.......................	1873
1853	HON. AMOS TUCK, A.M................................	1879
1853	FRANCIS BOWEN, A.M.	1875
1868	HON. JEREMIAH SMITH, A.M............................	1874
1870	HON. GEORGE SILSBEE HALE, A.B......................	
1873	ALBERT CORNELIUS PERKINS, A.M., *ex officio*..........	1883
1874	WILLIAM HENRY GORHAM, M.D.........................	1879
1874	JOSEPH BURBEEN WALKER, A.M.	
1875	REV. PHILLIPS BROOKS, D.D............................	1880
1879	NICHOLAS EMERY SOULE, A.M., M.D...................	
1879	HON. CHARLES HENRY BELL, A.M......................	
1881	JOHN CHARLES PHILLIPS, A.B..........................	

Treasurers.

1781	THOMAS ODIORNE............................	1793
1793	HON. JOHN TAYLOR GILMAN, LL.D............	1806
1806	HON. OLIVER PEABODY.......................	1828
1828	HON. JEREMIAH SMITH, LL.D.................	1842
1842	HON. JOHN KELLY, A.M.	1855
1855	JOSEPH TAYLOR GILMAN.....................	1862
1862	S. CLARKE BUZELL	1880
1880	CHARLES BURLEY	

Principals.

1783	WILLIAM WOODBRIDGE, A.B., *Preceptor*	1788
1788	BENJAMIN ABBOT, LL.D......................	1838
1838	GIDEON LANE SOULE, LL.D...................	1873
1873	ALBERT CORNELIUS PERKINS, Ph.D............	1883

Instructors.

1808	EBENEZER ADAMS, A.M., *Prof. Math. and Nat. Phil.*.........	1809
1811	HOSEA HILDRETH, A.M., *Prof. Math. and Nat. Phil.*.........	1825
1817	REV. ISAAC HURD, A.M., *Theological Instructor*	1839
1822	GIDEON LANE SOULE, A.M., *Prof. Ant. Languages*	1838
1825	JOHN PARKER CLEAVELAND, A.B., *Prof. Math. and Nat. Phil.*	1826
1826	CHARLES C. P. GALE, A.B., *Prof. Math. and Nat. Phil.*.....	1827
1827	JOSEPH HALE ABBOT, A.M., *Prof. Math. and Nat. Phil.*......	1833
1833	FRANCIS BOWEN, A.B., *Prof. Math. and Nat. Phil.*	1835
1835	WILLIAM HENRY SHACKFORD, A.B., *Prof. Math. and Nat. Phil.*	1842
1836	HENRY FRENCH, A.B., *Instructor in Languages*	1840
1840	NEHEMIAH CLEAVELAND, A.M., *Prof. Ant. Languages*.......	1841
1841	JOSEPH GIBSON HOYT, A.M., *Prof. Mathematics*.............	1859
1842	RICHARD WENMAN SWAN, A.B., *Prof. Ant. Languages*......	1851
1851	PAUL ANSEL CHADBOURNE, A.M., *Prof. Ant. Languages*	1852
1852	THEODORE TEBBETS, A.B., *Prof. Ant. Languages*	1853
1853	HENRY STEDMAN NOURSE, A.B., *Prof. Ant. Languages*	1855
1855	GEORGE CARLETON SAWYER, A.B., *Prof. Ant. Languages*....	1858
1858	GEORGE ALBERT WENTWORTH, A.B., *Prof. Mathematics*....	
1859	BRADBURY LONGFELLOW CILLEY, A.B., *Prof. Ant. Languages*	
1875	ROBERT FRANKLIN PENNELL, *Prof. Latin*...................	1882

Assistant Instructors.

1784	JOSEPH WILLARD, A.B.	1785
1785	SALMON CHASE, A.B.	1786
1786	JOSEPH DANA, A.B.	1789
1789	DANIEL DANA, A.B.	1791
1791	JOHN PHILLIPS RIPLEY, A.B.	1791
1792	RUFUS ANDERSON, A.B.	1792
1792	ABIEL ABBOT, A.B.	1793
1793	CHARLES COFFIN, A.B.	1794
1794	JOSEPH PERKINS, A.B.	1795
1795	TIMOTHY WINN, A.B.	1796
1796	PETER OXENBRIDGE THACHER, A.B.	1797
1797	NICHOLAS EMERY, A.B.	1797
1797	GEORGE WINGATE, A.B.	1797
1797	WILLIAM CRAIG, A.B.	1799
1799	SAMUEL DUNN PARKER, A.B.	1800
1799	HORATIO GATES BURNAP, A.B.	1803
1801	JOSEPH STEVENS BUCKMINSTER, A.B.	1803
1803	SAMUEL WILLARD, A.B.	1804
1804	JOHN STICKNEY, A.B.	1805
1804	ASHUR WARE, A.B.	1805
1805	MARTIN LUTHER HURLBUT, A.B.	1805
1805	NATHAN HALE, A.B.	1807
1806	JAAZANIAH CROSBY, A.B.	1807
1806	ALEXANDER HILL EVERETT, A.B.	1807
1807	NATHANIEL APPLETON HAVEN, Jr., A.B.	1808
1808	REUBEN WASHBURN, A.B.	1809
1809	NATHANIEL WHITMAN, A.B.	1810
1810	NATHAN LORD, A.B.	1811
1810	JONAS WHEELER, A.B.	1811
1811	HENRY HOLTON FULLER, A.B.	1812
1812	HENRY WARE, A.B.	1814
1814	JAMES WALKER, A.B.	1815
1815	GEORGE GOLDTHWAITE INGERSOLL, A.B.	1816
1816	WILLIAM BOURNE OLIVER PEABODY, A.B.	1817
1817	OLIVER WILLIAM BOURNE PEABODY, A.B.	1818
1818	GIDEON LANE SOULE, A.B.	1819
1819	SAMUEL TAYLOR GILMAN, A.B.	1820
1820	CHARLES LANE FOLSOM, A.B.	1822
1856	JACOB ABBOT CRAM	1857
1857	WILLIAM FRANCIS BENNETT JACKSON	1857
1860	ORLANDO MARCELLUS FERNALD	1861
1861	PAYSON MERRILL	1862
1870	WILLIAM HARRINGTON PUTNAM, A.M.	1871
1871	ROBERT FRANKLIN PENNELL, A.B.	1875
1874	OSCAR FAULHABER, Ph.D.	
1875	FREDERIC TIMOTHY FULLER, A.B.	1878
1878	JAMES ARTHUR TUFTS, A.B.	
1883	GEORGE LYMAN KITTREDGE, A.B.	

EXPLANATION.

THE first line of the catalogue gives the name of the student, his age at entering the school, and the name of the city or town from which he came to Exeter. The second line gives his occupation, his college, college degrees, etc., and his residence, or, when not living, the place known as having been his home. In some instances, where the occupation is in one place and the residence in another, both places are given, — the former in parentheses. But where a person, after having passed many years in one place, retires from active occupation and makes his home in another, the first place is indicated by brackets. An asterisk against a name signifies that the person is not living; and the date of death, when known, is given at the right hand of the upper line.

ABBREVIATIONS.

Bost. Univ.	for	Boston University.
B.U.	"	Brown University.
C.U.	"	Colby University.
H.U.	"	Harvard University.
Mad. Univ.	"	Madison University.
Roch. Univ.	"	Rochester University.
Wes. Univ.	"	Wesleyan University.
Univ. Mich.	"	University of Michigan.
Univ. Vt.	"	University of Vermont.
Amh. Coll.	"	Amherst College.
Bowd. Coll.	"	Bowdoin College.
Dart. Coll.	"	Dartmouth College.
Trin. Coll.	"	Trinity College.
Will. Coll.	"	Williams College.
Coll. of N.J.	"	College of New Jersey.

1883.

Trustees.

REV. ANDREW PRESTON PEABODY, D.D., PRESIDENT.
HON. GEORGE SILSBEE HALE, A.B.
ALBERT CORNELIUS PERKINS, PH.D., *ex officio.*
JOSEPH BURBEEN WALKER, A.M.
NICHOLAS EMERY SOULE, A.M., M.D.
HON. CHARLES HENRY BELL, LL.D.
JOHN CHARLES PHILLIPS, A.B.

Instructors.

ALBERT C. PERKINS, PH.D., PRINCIPAL, *Odlin Professor of English*
GEORGE A. WENTWORTH, A.M., *Professor of Mathematics.*
BRADBURY L. CILLEY, A.M., *Professor of Ancient Languages.*
OSCAR FAULHABER, PH.D., *Instructor in French and in German.*
JAMES ARTHUR TUFTS, A.B., *Instructor in Latin and in English.*
GEORGE LYMAN KITTREDGE, A.B., *Instructor.*

STUDENTS.

1783.

*William Brooks . . . . Exeter.
*Mele Clap . . . . Exeter.
*Peter Coffin . . . . Exeter.
*John Dean . . . . Exeter 1854
  Merchant.   Newburyport, Mass.
*Samuel L. Dexter . . . . Newburyport, Mass. 1807
                                        "   "
*Benjamin Dow . . . . Hampton Falls.
*Thomas Folsom . . . . Exeter.
                                          Portland, Me.
*Nathaniel Folsom . . . . Exeter.
*Benjamin Ives Gilman . . . . Exeter 1833
  Merchant.   Marietta, O.
*Thomas Gilman . . . . Exeter.
*Samuel Gilman . . . . Exeter 1796
*William Gilman . . . . Exeter.
*John S. Gilman . . . . Exeter.
*Daniel Gilman . . . . Exeter 1804
  Merchant.   Boston, Mass.
*William Hale . . . . Exeter.
*Samuel Hobart . . . . Exeter.
*Dudley Hobart . . . . Exeter.
*Parker Hopkinson . . . . Exeter.
*Daniel Jones . . . . Exeter.
*John Kimball . . . . Exeter 1849
  Farmer.   "
*Eliphalet Ladd . . . . Exeter.
  Shipbuilder.   Portsmouth.
*Stephen Lamson . . . . Exeter.
  Hotel-keeper.   "
*Joseph Lamson . . . . Exeter 1831
  Dart. Coll. 1790; Merchant.
*Gilman Leavitt . . . . Brentwood.
*William Lyman . . . . York, Me. 1822
  Physician.   "   "
*Hawley Marshall . . . . Brentwood.
*Jacob Moulton . . . . Hampton.
*Joseph Moulton . . . . Hampton.
*George Odiorne . . . . Exeter 1846
  Merchant.   Boston, Mass.
*John Odiorne . . . . Exeter 1824

*Thomas Odiorne . . . . Exeter 1851
   Dart. Coll. 1791, A.M.; Manufacturer.   Boston, Mass.
*Ebenezer Odiorne . . . . Exeter 1817
   Manufacturer.   Malden, Mass.
*Benjamin Page . . . . Exeter.
*John J. Parker . . . . Exeter.
*Samuel Parker . . . . Exeter.
*Joseph Parsons . . . . Rye 1813
   Lumber Dealer.   Washington, D.C.
*John W. Parsons . . . . Rye.
*Paul Rawlings . . . . Somersworth 1824
      Newington.
*Isaac Robbins . . . . Plymouth, Mass.
   Merchant.   Alexandria, Va.
*Ephraim Robinson . . . . Exeter 1809
   Farmer and Shipbuilder.   "
*Joseph Sawyer . . . . Exeter.
*William Sawyer . . . . Exeter.
*Samuel Sherburne . . . . Portsmouth.
*John Sherburne . . . . Portsmouth.
*Benjamin Smith . . . . Exeter.
*John Sullivan . . . . Durham 1819
   H.U. 1790; Lawyer.   Baton Rouge, La.
*James Sullivan . . . . Durham 1796
   H.U. 1790; Lawyer.   Georgetown, S.C.
*George Sullivan . . . . Durham 1838
   H.U. 1790; M.C.; Lawyer.   Exeter.
*<i>Nathaniel Thayer</i> . . . . Hampton 1840
   H.U. 1789; A.M.; Clergyman.   Lancaster, Mass.
*<i>James Thurston</i> . . . . Exeter 1835
   Clergyman.   "
*William Thurston . . . . Exeter 1822
   Dart. Coll. 1792; A.M.; Lawyer.   Boston, Mass.
*Daniel Tilton . . . . Exeter 1830
   H.U. 1790; Lawyer; Judge Supr. Ct.   Miss. Ter.
*John S. Tilton . . . . Exeter.
*Henry Tilton . . . . Exeter.
*Moses Wells . . . . Hampton Falls.
*Daniel Williams . . . . Exeter.
   Barber.   "

56

1784.

*Nathaniel Adams . . . . Exeter.
*Josiah Bartlett . . . . Kingston 1838
   M.D.; Physician; M.C.; Gov. N.H.   "
*Nathaniel Boardman . . . . Exeter.
*William Brewster . . . . Portsmouth.
*Samuel Brooks . . . . Exeter.
*Thomas Cheswell . . . . Newmarket.
*Enoch Coffin . . . . Epping.
*Nathaniel Cogswell . . . . Gilmanton 1813
   Dart. Coll. 1794; A.M.; Lawyer.   Mexico.
*David Copp . . . . Wakefield 1803
   Lawyer.   New Orleans, La.
*Benjamin Dearborn . . . . Northampton.

[1784–85.] CATALOGUE.

*Jesse Dolloff . . . . Exeter.
*Benjamin Dow . . . . Epping 1835
*Richard Emery . . . . Exeter.
   Supercargo.   "
*George Ffrost . . . . Durham 1841
   Merchant.   "
*Samuel Gilman . . . . Exeter.
*Bartholemew Gilman . . . . Exeter 1853
*Bartholemew Gilman, Jr. . . . . Exeter 1823
             Ohio.
*Joseph Gilman . . . . North Yarmouth, Me.
   Physician.   Wells, Me.
*Jonathan Glover . . . . Marblehead, Mass.
                 "   "
*Salmon Gray . . . . Saco, Me. 1811
*John Hackett . . . . Exeter.
*Temple Hovey . . . . Berwick, Me. 1810
   Lawyer.   " "
*Joshua Lane . . . . Stratham.
*Woodbury Langdon . . . . Portsmouth 1822
   Capitalist.   "
*Samuel Lee . . . . Marblehead, Mass.
                 "
*Phineas Lovejoy . . . . Sanbornton.
*John McClary . . . . Epsom.
*John Mead . . . . Newmarket.
*Thomas P. Moffat . . . . Portsmouth.
*Robert Moffat . . . . Portsmouth.
*Abraham Morrill . . . . Brentwood.
*John Morison . . . . Peterborough 1794
                 "
*John Neal . . . . Londonderry.
*John Odlin . . . . Exeter 1841
*Henry Ranlett . . . . Exeter 1807
   Printer and Bookseller.   "
*James Robinson . . . . Brentwood.
*Joseph Shepard . . . . Brentwood.
*John Smith . . . . Exeter.
*Samuel Smith . . . . Peterborough 1842
   Manufacturer.   "
*John Smith . . . . Peterborough.
*John Steele . . . . Peterborough 1845
   Manufacturer.   "
*Joseph Swasey . . . . Exeter.
*Samuel Thing . . . . Brentwood.
*James Thornton . . . . Merrimack.
*Charles Walker . . . . Concord 1834
   H.U. 1789; A.M.; Lawyer.   "
*Isaac Williams . . . . Exeter.

                                         46

1785.

*Ezra Bartlett . . . . Kingston 1848
   Physician; Lawyer; Judge Ct. Com. Pleas.   Haverhill.
*Stephen Bruce . . . . Boston, Mass.

*Andrew Chauncy . . . . Portsmouth.
*Ebenezer Clark . . . . Greenland.
*Thomas Murray Clark . . . . Greenland 1795
   B.U. 1792.
*Jeremiah Clough . . . . Canterbury.
*Daniel Conner . . . . Exeter 1866
   Farmer.
*Oliver Dodge . . . . Hampton Falls.
*Benjamin Dodge . . . . Exeter 1838
*Allen Gilman . . . . Exeter 1846
   Dart. Coll. 1791; A.M.; Lawyer.   Bangor, Me.
*Ephraim Dennet Gilman . . . . Exeter 1833
*Caleb James . . . . Exeter.
*Enoch Jewett . . . . Exeter.
*Caleb Johnson . . . . Hampstead 1818
                       "
*James Leath . . . . Tobago, W. I.
*Theodore Mansfield . . . . Exeter.
*Jeremiah Mead . . . . Newmarket 1839
*Phineas Richardson . . . . Exeter.
*James Rundlett . . . . Exeter.
   Manufacturer.   Portsmouth.
*Joseph Safford . . . . Exeter.
   Chaise Maker.   "
*Peter Sanborn . . . . East Kingston . . . 1824
   Farmer.   Readfield, Me.
*John Smallcorn . . . . Portsmouth.
*John Toppan . . . . East Kingston . . . 1837
   H.U. 1790; A.M.; Merchant.   Claremont.
*James Toppan . . . . East Kingston . . . 1852
   Teacher.   Gloucester, Mass.
*Ebenezer Webster . . . . East Kingston.
*William Webster . . . . Plymouth.
*Samuel Williams . . . . Exeter.
                                      27

1786.

*Enoch Clark . . . . Greenland 1844
   Farmer.   "
*John T. Coffin . . . . Newburyport, Mass.
*Jesse Conner . . . . Exeter.
   Farmer.   Parsonsfield, Me.
*Frederick French . . . . Dunstable.
*Stephen Gilman . . . . Exeter 1849
   Shipmaster.   "
*Samuel Hill . . . . Portsmouth 1840
                                    "
*Joshua James . . . . Exeter.
*Bartholomew Kimball . . . . Exeter.
*Nathaniel Lakeman . . . . Exeter.
   Dart. Coll. 1790; M.D.; Physician. Beverly, Mass.
*Robert Moore . . . . Brentwood 1804
   Teacher.   Raymond.
*John Page . . . . Chester.

*Stephen Parsons	Parsonsfield, Me.	
*John Usher Parsons	Parsonsfield, Me.	1825
Dart. Coll. 1791; A.M.; Merchant.	" "	
*Alexander Paul	Tobago, W.I.	
*Benjamin Pickering	Greenland.	
*Peter Shade	Tobago, W.I.	
*Thomas Sparhawk	Portsmouth.	
*Joshua Wiggin	Exeter	1839
*John Wilson	Brentwood.	

19

1787.

*Elisha Bean	Brentwood.	
Business.	"	
*William Bell	Chester	1848
Farmer.	"	
*Dudley Folsom	Exeter	1836
M.D.; Physician.	Gorham, Me.	
*Amos Gale	Kingston	1824
M.D.; Physician.	"	
*Gilman Gale	Kingston.	
Merchant.	"	
*Josiah Gilman	Exeter.	
*John Taylor Gilman, Jr.	Exeter	1808
Dart. Coll. 1796; Merchant.	Boston, Mass.	
*Ebenezer Gilman	Exeter	1795
	Wells, Me.	
*William Ladd	Exeter.	
*William Mackay	Salem, Mass.	
*Eliphalet Pinkham	Hanover.	
*John Phillips Ripley	Hanover	1816
Dart. Coll. 1791; Lawyer.	Philadelphia, Pa.	
*Edward Rundlett	Exeter.	
*Zebulon Smith	Newmarket.	

14

1788.

*Thomas Adams	Stratham.	
*Benjamin Beale	Exeter.	
*Nicholas Emery	Exeter	1841
Dart. Coll. 1795; Lawyer; Judge Supr. Ct., Me.	Portland, Me.	
*David Fullington		
*James McClure	Exeter.	
*Joseph Simpson	Stratham.	
*Joseph Smith		
*Ezra Smith	Newmarket.	
*Edmund Toppan	Hampton	1849
H.U. 1796; A.M.; Lawyer.	"	
*Titus Wells		
*Philip Wilson	Martinico, W.I.	
*Nathaniel Williams	Nottingham	1804
	"	
*George Wingate	Stratham	1852
H.U. 1796; A.M.; Farmer.	"	

1789.

*Nathaniel Ambrose . . . .
*Israel Bartlett. . . . . Nottingham 1859
   Farmer.   "
*Luke Bixby . . . . Charlestown, Mass.
*Samuel Call . . . . Newburyport, Mass.
*Benjamin Clark 1840
   Dart. Coll. 1800; A.M.; Lawyer.
*Benjamin Colcord . . . . Exeter.
*Tristram Coffin . . . . Epping.
*Nathaniel Conner . . . . Exeter 1849
   Carpenter.   "
*William Currier . . . . Kingston.
*Joseph Dodge . . . . Exeter 1849
       "

*Daniel Meserve Durell . . . . Durham 1851
   Dart. Coll. 1794; M.C.; Lawyer; Ch. Just. Ct.   Dover.
   Com. Pleas, N.H.
*Andrew Emerson . . . . Durham 1835
   Farmer.   "
*John Emery . . . . Exeter 1874
       "

*Daniel Evans . . . .
*Peter Folsom . . . . Gilmanton.
*Peter Folsom . . . . Exeter . . . . ? 1817
       Kennebunk, Me.
*Thomas Folsom . . . . Exeter 1845
   Innkeeper.   "
*Daniel French . . . . Epping 1840
   Lawyer.   Chester.
*Benjamin Gale . . . . Kingston.
*Nathaniel Gould . . . .
*Andrew Hilton . . . . Exeter.
*Gilman Jewett . . . . Exeter.
*Theophilus Jones . . . . Exeter.
*Hill Judkins . . . . Brentwood.
*Thomas Kimball . . . . Exeter.
*James Lane . . . . Stratham 1833
   Farmer.   "
*Isaac Leavitt . . . . Exeter 1854
*Benjamin Leavitt . . . . Exeter.
*James Leavitt . . . . Exeter.
*Joseph Leavitt . . . . Stratham 1829
       Bangor, Me.
*Theophilus Lyford . . . . Exeter.
*Phineas Merrill . . . . Stratham.
*Charles Morrison . . . . Martinico, W. I.
*Mark Newman . . . . Ipswich, Mass. . . . 1859
   Dart. Coll. 1793; A.M.; Merchant.   Andover, Mass.
*John Ordway . . . . Haverhill, Mass.
*Joseph C. Page . . . . Salem, Mass.
*William Pidgeon . . . . Amesbury, Mass.
*John Robinson . . . .

*Josiah Sanborn
*Isaiah Sanborn . . . . Poplin.
*Caleb Shaw . . . . Brentwood.
*Benjamin Shepard . . . . Brentwood.
   Farmer.   Waterville, Me.
*Samuel Smith . . . . Exeter 1859
   Sadler.   "
*Samuel Stearns . . . . Epping 1854
   H.U. 1794; A.M.; D.D.; Clergyman.   Bedford, Mass.
*William Swasey . . . . Exeter.
*Joseph Towle . . . . Exeter.
*Josiah Wyatt . . . . Exeter.
   Ship Carpenter.   "

                                         47

1790.

*William Barker . . . . 22 . . . Stratham 1846
   Farmer.   "
*Gabriell Bernadent . . . . Guadaloupe, W.I.
*Joshua Blake . . . . 16 . . . Hampton Falls.
*Thomas Brackett . . . . Greenland 1851
   Farmer.   "
*John Burgin . . . . 22 . . . Pembroke 1846
   Merchant.   Eastport, Me.
*David Coffin . . . . 15 . . . Epping.
*Amos Coffin . . . . 27 . . . Hampton.
*Jonathan Cram . . . . 11 . . . Hampton Falls.
*John S. Creighton . . . . . . 13 . . . Exeter.
*John Darling . . . . 12 . . . Portsmouth.
*Luther Dearborn . . . . 19 . . . Wakefield.
*Jabez Dodge . . . . 12 . . . Exeter 1803
*Peter Dumesnil . . . . 19 . . . Guadaloupe, W.I.
*William Duquery . . . . 15 . . . Guadaloupe, W.I.
*Alexander Favea . . . . Guadaloupe, W.I.
*John Ffrost . . . . Durham.
*John Folsom . . . . 11 . . . Exeter.
*Benjamin Gale . . . . 18 . . . Kingston.
*Gabriel Joseph Genet . . . . . 16 . . . Martinico, W.I.
*Samuel Glidden . . . . 25 . . . Unity.
*John Hopkinson . . . . 11 . . . Exeter.
*Ebenezer Lane . . . . 19 . . . Stratham 1842
   Farmer.   Pittsfield.
*Dudley Leavitt . . . . 18 . . . Stratham.
*Isaac Lord . . . . 12 . . . Washington.
*Stephen Mead . . . . Exeter.
   Shoemaker.   "
*Daniel Lane Morrill . . . . . 18 . . . Epping 1869
   Clergyman; U.S. Sen.
*Nehemiah Ordway . . . . 19 . . . Haverhill, Mass.
*William Pickering . . . . 12 . . . Greenland 1850
   H.U. 1797; A.M.; Lawyer.   "
*Isaac Pinkham . . . . Durham.
*George Washington Prescott . . . . . Newcastle 1817
   Dart. Coll. 1795; A.M.; Lawyer.   Portsmouth.

*Nathaniel Rogers . . . . 16 . . . Newmarket.
*Joseph Fogg Rowe . . . . . . 15 . . . Kensington 1829
  Farmer.   East Kingston.
*Richard Tuck . . . . 10 . . . Manchester, Mass.
*Isaac Waldron . . . . 16 . . . Barrington.
*Jacob Weeks . . . . Greenland 1800
  Merchant.   Charleston, S.C.
*Chase Wiggin . . . . 24 . . . Stratham.
*George Williams . . . . 12 . . . Exeter.
*William Woodbridge . . . . 10 . . . Salem 1832
  Merchant.   Savannah, Ga.

1791.

William Balch . . . . 16 . . . Barrington.
*Thomas Beede . . . . 19 . . . Poplin 1848
  H.U. 1798; A.M.; Clergyman.   Farmington, Me.
Pierre Bergeron . . . . 20 . . . Hispaniola, W.I.
*Joshua Brackett . . . . 15 . . . Greenland 1816
  Physician.   Portsmouth.
*William Brown . . . . 19 . . . Hampton Falls . . . 1856
  Farmer.   " "
Benjamin Dale Bryant . . . . 20 . . . Newmarket.
*Joseph Young Burgin . . . . . 18 . . . Allenstown 1820
  Teacher.   Portsmouth.
Samuel Burley . . . . 21 . . . Ipswich, Mass.
Ichabod Canney . . . . 13 . . . Madbury.
Moses Clark . . . . 17 . . . Stratham.
David Elkins . . . . 23 . . . Gilmanton.
*Peter Lawrence Folsom . . . 19 . . . Gilmanton 1842
  Dart. Coll. 1796; A.M.; Merchant.   "
James Folsom . . . . . ,, ... 21 . . . Gilmanton.
*Joseph Smith Folsom . . . . . 18 . . . Newmarket 1804
  Merchant.   Lee.
David Foss . . . . 18 . . . Barrington.
David Foster . . . . 14 . . . Canterbury.
Pierre G. Daroterre Genet . . 18 . . . Martinico, W.I.
*John Ham . . . . 16 . . . Dover 1837
  Dart. Coll. 1797; A.M.; Lawyer.   Gilmanton.
*John Hamilton . . . . 13 . . . Berwick, Me. 1805
  H.U. 1798; A.M.   Portsmouth.
Nathan Hilton . . . . 18 . . . Newmarket.
Morris Hobbs . . . . 15 . . . Northampton, Mass.
  Carpenter.   " "
*Josiah Hook . . . . 16 . . . Salisbury, Mass.
*Moses Hook . . . . 14 . . . Salisbury, Mass. . . 1821
  H.U. 1798.
Amos Judkins . . . . : . . . . 23 . . . Kingston.
Huard Lanoiroix . . . . 20 . . . Guadaloupe, W.I.
*Thomas Leavitt . . . . 18 . . . North Hampton . . . 1800
  Business.   Hampton.
John Lovering . . . . 15 . . . Exeter.
George Nichols . . . . 13 . . . Portsmouth.
*John Noyes . . . . 27 . . . Atkinson 1841
  Dart. Coll. 1795; A.M.; M.C.; Merchant.   Putney, Vt.

[1791–92.] CATALOGUE.

*Nathaniel Adams Parker ... 10 ... Portsmouth.
Nathaniel Pease .... 23 ... Newmarket.
Edward Philbrick .... 22 ... Newmarket.
Orlando Sargent .... 22 ... Amesbury, Mass.
Christopher Sargent ...... 19 ... Amesbury, Mass.
*Henry Sheafe .... 12 ... Portsmouth 1854
  Merchant.   Boston, Mass.
Walter Smith .... 16 ... Newmarket.
*Nathan Tilton .... 18 ... East Kingston 1851
  H.U. 1796; A.M.; Clergyman.   Scarborough, Me.
*Joseph Tilton .... 17 ... East Kingston 1856
  H.U. 1797; A.M.; Lawyer.   Exeter.
John Waldron .... 15 ... Barrington.
Permot Wiggin .... 20 ... Exeter.
*Samuel Winslow .... 22 ... Epping 1833
  Farmer.
*William Henry Young .... 19 ... Gilmanton 1797
  Business.
*Jonathan Young .... 18 ... Barrington 1838
  H.U. 1798.   Acton, Me.
                                        43

1792.

Nathaniel F. Adams ..... 12 ... Exeter.
William Henry Blodgett ... 12 ... Boston, Mass.
Samuel Gilman Blodgett ... 9 ... Boston, Mass.
Charles Frederick Blodgett .. 10 ... Boston, Mass.
Thomas Boardman .... 22 ... Exeter.
George Boyd .... 14 ... Portsmouth.
  Merchant.
Samuel Brown .... 16 ... Kingston.
*John Burnham .... 19 ... Scarborough, Me... 1825
  H.U. 1798; Lawyer.   Limerick, Me.
*Lewis Cass .... 10 ... Exeter 1866
  LL.D.; Gov. Mich.; U.S. Sen.; Sec. War; Min.   Detroit, Mich.
  to France; Sec. State.
*Andrew McClary Chapman .. 18 ... Newmarket 1850
                                  Wakefield.
*Charles Coffin .... 13 ... Buxton, Me. 1851
  Dart. Coll. 1799; A.M.; Lawyer.
*Benjamin Cram .... 11 ... Exeter 1859
                               Somerville, Mass.
*Thomas Dean .... 10 ... Exeter.
*Charles Dean .... 12 ... Exeter 1829
  Sadler.   Portland, Me.
John H. Dearborn .... 10 ... Ossipee.
*Noah Emery .... 10 ... Exeter 1813
  Shipmaster.
Peter Fogg .... 12 ... Exeter.
George Folensbee .... 13 ... Salisbury, Mass.
*Samuel Folsom .... 10 ... Exeter.
*Nathan Boardman Folsom .. 12 ... Lee 1863
  Merchant.   Portsmouth.
Benjamin French .... 17 ... Epping.

John Furber . . . . 19 . . . Northwood.
Nathaniel Gilman . . . . 13 . . . Exeter.
Nathaniel C. Gilman . . . . . 12 . . . Exeter.
*Samuel Kinsman Gilman . . . 10 . . . Exeter 1795
                                                                                       "
*Warren Gilman . . . . 20 . . . Newmarket 1855
                                                   South Newmarket.
Daniel Gookin . . . . 21 . . . Boscawen.
Jonathan Longfellow . . . . . 27 . . . Newmarket.
*Benjamin Lovering . . . . . . 10 . . . Exeter.
  Shoemaker.   "
Jacob Pearson . . . . 10 . . . Exeter.
Josiah Robinson . . . . 22 . . . Wakefield.
Paul Robinson . . . . 22 . . . Newmarket.
Thomas Rowell . . . . 24 . . . Amesbury, Mass.
Joseph Sawyer . . . . 17 . . . Salisbury, Mass.
Jethro S. Searle . . . . 15 . . . Salisbury, Mass.
*William Smith . . . . 11 . . . Exeter 1855
  Painter.
*John Phillips Thurston . . . . 11 . . . North Hampton . . . 1832
  Dart. Coll. 1797; A.M.; Merchant.   New York, N.Y.
Daniel Towle . . . . 10 . . . Exeter.
*Samuel Weed . . . . 17 . . . Amesbury, Mass. . . 1857
  H.U. 1800; M.D.; Physician.   Portland, Me.
*Jonathan Whittaker . . . . . . 21 . . . Bath, Me. 1835
  H.U. 1797; A.M.; Clergyman.   New Bedford, Mass.
*John Wingate . . . . 11 . . . Stratham 1831
  Farmer.   "

1793.

*William Adams . . . . 21 . . . Washington.
  Dart. Coll. 1799.
*Stephen Bean . . . . 21 . . . Gilmanton 1825
  Dart. Coll. 1798; Merchant.   Boston, Mass.
Edward Colcord . . . . 19 . . . Exeter.
Jacob Cram . . . . 10 . . . Exeter.
Trueworthy Dearborn . . . . . 20 . . . North Hampton.
                                                     Concord.
John Dodge . . . . 20 . . . Hampton Falls.
*John Folsom . . . . 17 . . . Exeter 1847
*Stephen Goodhue . . . . 20 . . . Deerfield.
  Teacher.   Ohio.
*Benjamin Hoit . . . . 18 . . . Stratham 1800
  Farmer.   "
*Joseph Hoit . . . . 19 . . . Stratham 1849
  Farmer.   "
*Joseph Jewett Hoit . . . . . . 11 . . . Exeter 1847
  Carpenter.   "
William Hoit . . . . 10 . . . Exeter.
*Joseph Hoit . . . . 20 . . . Epping 1807
George Jones . . . . 17 . . . Newcastle.
*Joshua Lane . . . . 20 . . . Stratham 1846
  H.U. 1799; Clergyman.   New York.
*Jotham Lawrence . . . . 16 . . . Epping 1863
  Lawyer.   Exeter.

Ephraim Leavitt	23	Stratham.	
*Edward Little	20	Newbury, Mass.	1849
Dart. Coll. 1797; Lawyer.		Danville, Me.	
John Morrill	14	Salisbury, Mass.	
Thomas Coffin Norris	17	Epping.	
*Azor Orne	10	Marblehead, Mass.	
		" "	
*Daniel Osgood	16	Salisbury	1852
Dart. Coll. 1799; A.M.; Physician.		Havana.	
*Daniel Page	19	Deerfield	1819
Teacher.		So. Carolina.	
*Enoch Greenleaf Parrott	12	Greenland	1828
Merchant.		Portsmouth.	
John Light Piper	22	Stratham.	
Noah Robinson	17	Stratham.	
John Rundlett	20	Gilmanton.	
Samuel Rundlett	14	Exeter.	
Nathaniel Shaw	17	Brentwood.	
Benjamin Shaw	16	Brentwood.	
*William T. Smith	21	Deerfield	1859
Farmer and Teacher.		"	
Samuel Taylor	11	Hampton.	
*Nathaniel Upham	19	Deerfield	1829
M.C.; Merchant.		Rochester.	
Daniel Wedgewood	19	North Hampton.	
Edmund Wiggin	21	Stratham.	
Clerk.		Thomaston, Me.	
Jedidiah Witcher	21	Bedford, Mass.	
Samuel Wyatt	13	Exeter.	
Hotel Keeper.			

37

1794.

William P. Adams	9	Exeter.	
William Bagley	15	Amesbury, Mass.	
Horatio Gates Balch	16	Barrington.	
Joseph Brown	9	Exeter.	
Charles S. Bryant	21	Newmarket.	
*Samuel Phillips Chamberlain	9	Exeter	1822
Lieut. U.S. Navy.		Portsmouth.	
*George Clifford	11	Exeter	1805
*Samuel Shepard Conner	9	Exeter	1820
Yale Coll. 1806; M.C.; Lawyer.		Albany, N.Y.	
Ebenezer Currier	21	Hampton.	
*John Dane	26	Francestown.	
Clergyman.			
*Freese Dearborn	16	Hampton	1862
Farmer.		Exeter.	
Benjamin Dole	19	Salisbury, Mass.	
*John S. Durell	19	Dover	1854
Farmer.		"	
*Rufus Emerson	14	Scarborough, Me.	1859
City Official.		Portland, Me.	
*Jonathan French	16	Salisbury, Mass.	1856
H.U. 1798; A.M.; Clergyman.		North Hampton.	

*William Garland . . . . 18 . . . Rye 1820
   Merchant.   Portsmouth.
*Eliphalet Giddings . . . . . . 10 . . . Exeter.
*Tristram Gilman . . . . 14 . . . No. Yarmouth, Me. . 1828
   Dart. Coll. 1800; A.M.; Lawyer.   Wells, Me.
Joseph Gilman . . . . 19 . . . Gilmanton.
Levi Hannaford . . . . 18 . . . North Hampton.
*John A. Harper . . . . 14 . . . Sanbornton 1816
   Lawyer.   Meredith Bridge.
John Hill . . . . 27 . . . Nottingham.
Thomas Leavitt . . . . 10 . . . Exeter.
   Carriagemaker.   "
*Jacob Maine . . . . 20 . . . Rochester 1807
   H.U. 1800; M.D.; Physician.   Portsmouth.
Samuel Page . . . . 12 . . . Exeter.
William H. Page . . . . 15 . . . Exeter.
Charles Pearson . . . . 9 . . . Exeter.
*James Pearson . . . . 12 . . . Exeter 1820
Samuel Safford . . . . 12 . . . Exeter.
*Elisha Smith . . . . 16 . . . Beverly, Mass. . . . 1817
   Mariner.
*Horatio Southgate . . . . 13 . . . Scarborough, Me. . . 1864
   Farmer.   "   "
*Andrew Eliot Thayer . . . . . 10 . . . Hampton 1846
   H.U. 1803; Bookseller.   Nashua.
William Thompson . . . . . . 13 . . . Newburyport, Mass.
*Samuel Tibbetts . . . . 14 . . . Dover 1810
   H.U. 1799; Lawyer.   "
*Samuel Russell Trevett . . . . 10 . . . Marblehead, Mass. . 1822
   H.U. 1804; A.M.; M.D.; Physician.
*Samuel Holten Webster . . . . 11 . . . Danvers, Mass. . . . 1812
   Shipmaster.   Staten Island, N.Y.
John Weeks . . . . 15 . . . Wakefield.

                                                   37

1795.

*Joseph Balch . . . . 9 . . . Newburyport, Mass. 1849
   Insurance Agent.   Boston, Mass.
Daniel Brown . . . . 14 . . . Hampton Falls.
*Joseph Stevens Buckminster . . 11 . . . Portsmouth 1812
   H.U. 1800; A.M.; Clergyman.   Boston, Mass.
*James Burley . . . . 10 . . . Exeter 1850
   Bank Cashier.   "
George Clark . . . . 14 . . . Epping.
Greenleaf Clark . . . . 13 . . . Epping.
Benjamin Clark . . . . 10 . . . Stratham.
*Hector Coffin . . . . 11 . . . Newburyport, Mass. 1846
   Shipmaster.   "   "
*Jeremiah Dean . . . . 13 . . . Exeter 1799
   Mariner.   Boston, Mass.
Israel Gale . . . . 20 . . . Kingston.
Broadstreet Gilman . . . . . . 18 . . . Newmarket.
Leonard Hall . . . . 13 . . . Portsmouth.
*William Hill . . . . 12 . . . Portsmouth 1849
   Capitalist.   "

*Benjamin Hoit	13	Epping	1825
Manufacturer.		"	
Joseph Lackey	11	Newburyport, Mass.	
*John Lakeman	10	Exeter.	
*Joshua Brackett Langdon	10	Portsmouth	1810
John Hill March	18	Stratham.	
Joseph Osgood	13	Newbury, Mass.	
Chandler Peavey	23	Durham.	
John Norris Pillsbury	21	Kingston.	
William Pillsbury	18	Kingston.	
*Moses Porter	14	Saco, Me.	1819
Dart. Coll. 1798.			
John Prentiss	14	Londonderry.	
Thomas Roberts	14	Boston, Mass.	
Charles Rundlett	20	Gilmanton.	
Nathan Sanborn	18	Hawke.	
*Joseph Sewall	21	York, Me.	1859
Business.		" "	
*George Meserve Sheafe	11	Portsmouth	1804
H.U. 1800; A.M.		"	
Elijah Tuttle	21	Barrington.	
John Weeks	21	Chester.	
*Paul Wentworth	12	Dover	1855
Merchant.		Concord.	
*Charles Wentworth	12	Portsmouth.	
Bradstreet Wiggin	19	Meredith.	

34

1796.

*James Hervey Bingham	15	Leominster	1859
Dart. Coll. 1801; A.M.; Lawyer.		Washington, D.C.	
*Benjamin Greenleaf Boardman	12	Newburyport, Mass.	
Business.		" "	
*Edward Brooks	10	Medford, Mass.	1817
*Stewart Brown	17	Deerfield	1844
Teacher.		Montpelier, Vt.	
David Coffin	14	Buxton, Me.	
Joseph Conner	15	Andover.	
*William Shackford Cooper	14	Dover	1864
*Joseph Warren Dow	17	Hampton Falls	1833
H.U. 1805; A.M.; Clergyman.		Tyringham, Mass.	
*Simeon Folsom	20	Newmarket	1816
Merchant.		Exeter.	
*John Gilman	13	Exeter	1822
Shipmaster?		New Orleans, La.	
*Abraham Hilliard	18	Kensington	1855
Dart. Coll. 1800; A.M.; Lawyer.		Cambridge, Mass.	
*Silas Holman	19	Portsmouth	1807
Merchant.		"	
Eliphalet Howe	18	Epping.	
Robert Dalton Jenkins	11	Newburyport, Mass.	
Business.		" "	
Haynes Johnson	20	Keene.	
*John Ladd	21	Deerfield	1817
Teacher and Farmer.		"	

Isaac Ladd	21 . . .	Gilmanton.
Cassius Lee	16 . . .	Westmoreland, Va.
*Francis Lightfoot Lee . . . . . H.U. 1802; A.M.	13 . . .	Westmoreland, Va. . . 1850
*Hall Jackson Locke . . . . . . Teacher.	14 . . .	Rye . . . . 1836 Newcastle.
*Isaac Lyman . . . . Lawyer and Farmer.	21 . . .	York, Me. . . . . . 1824 " "
Edward Martin	14 . . .	North Yarmouth, Me.
*John McClary	11 . . .	Epsom 1821
*Samuel Morrill . . . . Apothecary.	17 . . .	Epping . . . . 1858 Concord.
*John Nelson . . . . Dart. Coll. 1803; A.M.; Lawyer.	18 . . .	Gilmanton . . . . . . 1838 Haverhill.
*John Wilkes Parsons . . . . . Physician.	17 . . .	Rye . . . . 1837 "
Joseph Parsons	22 . . .	Rye.
*Ede Robinson . . . . Teacher.	23 . . .	Deerfield . . . . . . 1809 "
*Leverett Saltonstall . . . . . . H.U. 1802; A.M.; LL.D.; M.C.	12 . . .	Haverhill, Mass. . . 1845 Salem, Mass.
*Benjamin Sanborn . . . . . . Teacher.	22 . . .	Deerfield . . . . . . 1853 "
*Thomas Sheafe, Jr.	12 . . .	Portsmouth 1798
Jonathan Smith . . . . Business.	16 . . .	Brentwood. Exeter.
William Stocker	11 . . .	Newburyport, Mass.
Augustine Washington	15 . . .	Westmoreland, Va.
Bushrod Washington	10 . . .	Westmoreland, Va.
*Daniel Webster . . . . Dart. Coll. 1801; A.M.; LL.D.; Lawyer; M.C.; U.S. Sen.; U.S. Sec. State.	14 . . .	Salisbury . . . . . . 1852 Boston, Mass.
David White	18 . . .	Boston, Mass.
*Benjamin Wiggin . . . . Hotel Keeper.	21 . . .	Exeter . . . . 1835 Wakefield.
Samuel Wiggin	14 . . .	Exeter.
Samuel Willey	21 . . .	Nottingham.

40

1797.

*Joseph Boardman . . . . Business.	16 . . .	Exeter . . . . 1857 "
Jonathan Brown	17 . . .	Hampton Falls.
*George Washington Cass . . . Farmer.	12 . . .	Exeter . . . . 1873 Muskingum Co., O.
*Charles Lee Cass . . . . Farmer.	10 . . .	Exeter . . . . 1842 Ohio.
*Peter Chadwick . . . . Clerk of Courts.	14 . . .	Deerfield . . . . . . 1847 Exeter.
*James Clark	13 . . .	Sanbornton . . . . . 1861 "
Samuel Craige	20 . . .	Trecothick.
John Craige	18 . . .	Trecothick.
Thomas Craige	14 . . .	Exeter.
Levi Dearborn	12 . . .	Rochester.

Abel Fisk	13	Wilton.
*Jonathan Footman	15	Dover.
*Job Foss	20	Barrington.
John French	22	Stratham.
*Joseph Hanson Gage	18	Dover 1823
Shipmaster.		"
Nathaniel Giddings	13	Amherst.
*Charles Gilman	10	Exeter 1857
		Norwich, Conn.
*Samuel Gilman	12	Exeter.
*Jonathan Gilman	13	Exeter 1809
		Malden, Mass.
Nicholas Gilman	14	North Yarmouth, Me.
*John Heath Goddard	13	Portsmouth 1875
*John Grant	11	Boston, Mass. . . . 1820
*Joseph Grant	10	Boston, Mass. . . . 1858
Merchant.		" "
David Greene	18	Stratham.
*James Johnson	17	Keene 1856
H.U. 1808; A.M.; Clergyman.		St. Johnsbury, Vt.
*William Johnson	19	Keene.
Business.		"
*Alexander Ladd	13	Portsmouth 1855
Merchant.		"
*Henry Lamson	10	Exeter.
*Josiah Lane	19	Stratham 1860
M.D.; Physician.		Franklin, Pa.
*John Tillon Leavitt	21	Chichester 1848
		"
John McClure	12	Exeter.
*John Merrill	15	Conway 1855
H.U. 1804; A.M.; M.D.; Physician.		Portland, Me.
*Benjamin Merrill	13	Conway 1847
H.U. 1804; A.M.; LL.D.; Lawyer.		Salem, Mass.
*Ezekiel Williams Morse	14	New Haven, Conn.
Woodbridge Odlin	10	Exeter.
*Peter Odlin	9	Exeter.
*Joseph Douglas Osborne	11	Exeter 1803
		"
Rufus Page	11	Hallowell, Me.
Samuel Page	22	Readfield, Me.
John Parsons	21	Alfred, Me.
*Samuel Page Peirson	13	Biddeford, Me. . . . 1806
*Samuel Philbrick	12	Exeter 1868
Bank Cashier.		Skowhegan, Me.
Richard King Porter	13	Biddeford, Me.
*Levi Prescott	15	Hampton Falls . . . 1850
Farmer.		" "
*George Rogers	18	Newmarket.
Pelatiah Ruker	21	Alfred, Me.
William Shannon	18	Rochester.
Moses Titcomb	13	Portland, Me.
*Samuel Walker	18	Haverhill, Mass. . . 1826
Dart. Coll. 1802; Clergyman.		Danvers, Mass.

*Seth Shackford Walker . . . . 17 . . . Dover 1859
Land Surveyor. Durham.
*William Walker . . . . 17 . . . Portsmouth 1854
South Newmarket.
Thomas West . . . . 18 . . . Haverhill, Mass.
Robert Ball Willis . . . . 18 . . . Haverhill, Mass.
Merchant. Boston, Mass.
Eleazur Young . . . . 20 . . . Barrington.

54

1798.

Nicholas Richelieu Barbottiau . 19 . . . Guadaloupe, W. I.
William Boardman . . . . . . 18 . . . Newmarket.
Jeremiah Bradbury . . . . . . 16 . . . Pepperellborough, Me.
*David Clark . . . . 16 . . . Northwood 1824
Farmer. "
*Jonathan Cook . . . . 14 . . . Wiscasset, Me.
Government Service.
*Jaazaniah Crosby . . . . 18 . . . Hebron 1864
H.U. 1804; Clergyman. Charlestown.
John Dudley . . . . 17 . . . Brentwood.
*Caleb Emery . . . . 11 . . . Sanford, Me. 1831
M.D.; Physician. Eliot, Me.
*Benjamin Hitchborn Fosdick . 13 . . . Portland, Me.
*Henry Goddard . . . . 12 . . . Portsmouth 1871
Merchant. Boston, Mass.
*William Gordon . . . . 10 . . . Amherst 1871
H.U. 1806; Lawyer. Charlestown.
*Moses Grant . . . . 12 . . . Boston, Mass. 1861
Merchant. " "
Richard Hoit . . . . 15 . . . Amesbury, Mass.
Josiah Hook . . . . 13 . . . Sandown.
John Jackson . . . . 12 . . . Portsmouth.
*Paul Jewett . . . . 18 . . . Rowley, Mass. . . . 1841
B.U. 1802; A.M.; Clergyman. Salem, Mass.
William Short Johnson . . . . 11 . . . Exeter.
*Benjamin U. Lapish . . . . . 16 . . . Durham 1810
"
*Moses Leavitt . . . . 13 . . . Chichester 1860
"
*John Leavitt . . . . 13 . . . North Hampton . . . 1820
Cambridge, Mass.
*Charles Little . . . . 16 . . . Campton 1813
Farmer and Merchant. Centre Harbor.
Jacob Longfellow . . . . 22 . . . Newmarket.
William Low . . . . 12 . . . Gloucester, Mass.
*Joseph Merrill . . . . 21 . . . Stratham 1848
Dart. Coll. 1806; Clergyman.
*Thomas Nasson . . . . 19 . . . Sanford, Me. 1825
*Henry Nutter . . . . 12 . . . Exeter.
*John Odiorne . . . . 14 . . . Salisbury, Mass. . . 1826
Shipmaster. Boston, Mass.
*William Bourne Orne . . . . 13 . . . Marblehead, Mass. . 1864
Shipmaster. Brooklyn, N.Y.
John Paine . . . . 24 . . . Parsonsfield, Me.

*Mark Wentworth Peirce ... 12	... Portsmouth 1846	
Merchant.	"	
*Jacob Sheafe 15	... Portsmouth 1848	
Merchant.	Pottsville, Pa.	
*Ebenezer Smith 16	... Durham 1869	
Merchant.	"	
William Spence 11	... Portsmouth.	
James Starr 19	... Dunstable.	
*Woodbury Storer 14	... Portland, Me. 1860	
Lawyer.	" "	
*Seth Storer 10	... Peppercllborough, Me. 1876	
Bowd. Coll. 1807; A.M.; Lawyer.	Scarborough, Me.	
*John Barnard Swett 10	... Exeter 1840	
Merchant.	Philadelphia, Pa.	
Benjamin Thurston 13	... North Hampton.	
*Henry Wadsworth 13	... Portland, Me. 1803	
Elijah Wells 18	... Rumsey.	
Edmund Stafford Young ... 16	... Brentwood.	
	41	

1799.

*Nathaniel Carter 10	... Newburyport, Mass.	
Business.	" "	
*Richard Cobb 11	... Portland, Me. 1837	
Bowd. Coll. 1806; A.M.; Merchant.	Boston, Mass.	
*Isaac Foster Coffin 12	... Portland, Me. 1861	
Bowd. Coll. 1806; A.M.; Teacher.	Jamaica Plain, Mass.	
*John Perkins Cushing 12	... Boston, Mass. 1862	
Merchant. [Canton, China.]	Watertown, Mass.	
*James Greene Dana 14	... Amherst 1841	
Editor.	Frankfort, Ky.	
Isaac Somes Davis 14	... Gloucester, Mass.	
William Edwards 14	... Portsmouth.	
Robert Fletcher 9	... Amherst.	
*Jacob Folsom 20	... Newmarket 1826	
Farmer.	Wolfborough.	
*Joseph G. Folsom 10	... Exeter 1813	
*Phillips Gilman 10	... Exeter 1838	
	Defiance, O.	
William Gordon 15	... Newbury, Mass.	
*Reuben H. Greene 16	... Dover 1877	
Merchant and Farmer.	Winslow, Me.	
*Augustine Heard 14	... Ipswich, Mass. ... 1868	
Merchant.	Boston, Mass.	
*Charles Hutchins 13	... Concord 1868	
Merchant.	"	
Joseph Jewett 13	... Portland, Me.	
James Johnson 10	... Keene.	
Moses Judkins 19	... Kingston.	
*John Ladd 17	... Epping 1845	
M.D.; Physician.	Lee.	
*Walter Langdon 10	... Portsmouth 1842	
Capitalist.	New York, N.Y.	
John Lapish 14	... Durham.	
*Moses Little 17	... Newbury, Mass. .. 1802	
Business.	Boston, Mass.	

[1799.

*Timothy Little . . . . 22 . . . Windham 1849
M.D.; Physician.   Portland, Me.
*Ebenezer Little . . . . 10 . . . Campton 1864
Farmer.   "
*Samuel Livermore . . . . . . 13 . . . Portsmouth 1833
H.U. 1804; Lawyer.   New Orleans, La.
Thomas Manning . . . . 12 . . . Portsmouth.
Shipmaster.   "
*Isaac Mansfield . . . . 12 . . . Marblehead, Mass.
     "   "
*Andrew McClary . . . . 12 . . . Epsom 1811
Farmer; Capt. U.S. Army.   Washington, D.C.
*Robert Means . . . . 13 . . . Amherst 1842
Bowd. Coll. 1807; A.M.; Lawyer.   Lowell, Mass.
John Murphy Molloy . . . . . 12 . . . Salem, Mass.
*Emperor Moseley . . . . 10 . . . Salem, Mass. 1806
Supercargo.   "   "
William Murray . . . . 13 . . . Newbury, Mass.
John Nelson . . . . 16 . . . Exeter.
*Daniel Newcomb . . . . 13 . . . Keene 1809
H.U. 1803; A.M.; M.D.; Physician.   "
*Seth Newcomb . . . . 12 . . . Keene 1811
H.U. 1804; A.M.; Lawyer.
*Henry Stearns Newcomb . . . 11 . . . Keene 1825
Dart. Coll. 1807; Lieut. U.S. Navy.
Thomas Newman . . . . 16 . . . Boston, Mass.
*John O'Brien . . . . 13 . . . Newburyport, Mass. 1865
Bowd. Coll. 1806; A.M.; Lawyer.   Brunswick, Me.
*Moses Osgood . . . . 14 . . . Newbury, Mass.
*_Amos Pettengill_ . . . . 18 . . . Salem 1830
H.U. 1805; A.M.; Clergyman.   "
Thorndike Putnam . . . . . . 12 . . . Haverhill, Mass.
*Moses Quimby . . . . 13 . . . Stroudwater, Me. . . 1859
Bowd. Coll. 1806; Lawyer and Farmer.   Westbrook, Me.
*Robert Reed . . . . 12 . . . Amherst 1857
Builder.   Manchester.
Daniel Reeves . . . . 13 . . . Charleston, S.C.
Daniel Rundlett . . . . 14 . . . Exeter.
*William F. Salter . . . . 12 . . . Portsmouth 1849
Merchant.   New York, N.Y.
*Joshua Safford . . . . 14 . . . Salem, Mass. 1869
Government Service.   "   "
Thomas Sawyer . . . . 15 . . . Newburyport, Mass.
Lawyer.
Thomas Shannon . . . . 15 . . . Moultonborough.
*Samuel Sheafe . . . . 13 . . . Portsmouth 1857
Merchant.   "
*Henry Sherburne . . . . 10 . . . Portsmouth.
Mariner.   "
*Jacob Sheafe Smith . . . . . . 13 . . . Durham 1880
H.U. 1805; A.M.   Gorham, Me.
*Valentine Smith . . . . 25 . . . Durham 1869
Lawyer.   "
James Stevens . . . . 14 . . . Bradford, Mass.
*Henry Sturgis . . . . 10 . . . Boston, Mass. 1819
Merchant.   "   "
*_Benjamin Titcomb_ . . . . . . 11 . . . Portland, Me. . . . 1829
Bowd. Coll. 1806; Clergyman.   Freeport, Me.

.Samuel Torrey	12	Boston, Mass.
John Walsh	12	Portsmouth.
*John Chandler White Business.	14	Boston, Mass. ... 1846 Mississippi.
John Williams	15	Newmarket.

60

1800.

*Ephraim Abbot H.U. 1806; A.M.; Clergyman.	20	Concord........ 1870 Westford, Mass.
*Charles Atkinson	15	Newbury, Mass. ... 1845
Joseph Bartlett	15	Lee.
*John Bliss H.U. 1808; U.S. Army.	13	Haverhill ...... 1854 Florida.
*Francis Boardman Merchant.	13	Salem, Mass. .... 1870 " "
Thomas Jones Boardman Business.	13	Newburyport, Mass. " "
Josiah Calef.	17	Kingston.
*Abiel Chandler H.U. 1806; A.M.; Merchant (Boston).	23	Fryeburg, Me. ... 1851 Walpole.
Samuel Clark	12	Portsmouth.
*Nathaniel Coffin Bookkeeper.	13	Newburyport, Mass. 1833 " "
*John Davis Editor.	21	Concord. "
*Henry Dean Business.	12	Exeter .... 1849 Portsmouth.
*Thomas Perkins Doubleday	10	Charleston, S.C.
Warren Dow		
*Samuel Goddard Merchant.	12	Portsmouth ..... 1871 Boston, Mass.
*Christopher Gore Sign Painter.	13	Boston, Mass. ... 1849 " "
*George Grant Merchant.	10	Boston, Mass..... 1849 Pittsburg, Pa.
Jonathan Greene	17	Hampton Falls.
*Nathaniel Appleton Haven H.U. 1807; A.M.; M.C.; Lawyer; Editor.	10	Portsmouth ..... 1826 "
Leonard Hunnewell	11	Portland, Me.
*James C. Marston	12	Boston, Mass.
*Daniel Melcher	13	Portsmouth.
Dennis O'Brien Mariner.	12	Newburyport, Mass. " "
*Henry Olcott Lieut. Marines, U.S.N.	12	Charlestown..... 1821 Gosport, Va.
*George Olcott Yale Coll. 1805; A.M.; Bank Cashier.	14	Charlestown..... 1864 "
*Henry Osborne Chaisemaker.	11	Exeter .... 1836 "
John Osgood	12	Newbury, Mass.
John Carr Roberts Palmer	18	Wakefield.
*Jeremiah Pearson	13	Newbury, Mass.
*Edmund Pearson Bank Cashier.	13	Exeter .... 1866 Skowhegan, Me.

*Samuel Huntington Porter . . 13 . . . Rye 1807
   Printer and Editor.   Savannah, Ga.
*John Whittingham Rogers . . 12 . . . Salem, Mass. 1872
   Merchant.   "   "
*Richard Saltonstall Rogers . . 10 . . . Salem, Mass. 1873
   Merchant.   "   "
*Nathaniel Leverett Rogers . . 14 . . . Salem, Mass. 1858
   Merchant.   "   "
*James H. Sargent . . . . 19 . . . York, Me.
*Daniel Rindge Sheafe . . . . . 14 . . . Portsmouth 1854
   Merchant.   "
*Francis Sheafe . . . . 12 . . . Portsmouth 1816
*William Parsons Sigourney . . 11 . . . Boston, Mass. . . . 1829
                                             "   "
 Sherburne Sleeper . . . . 15 . . . Kingston.
 John Smith . . . . 13 . . . Exeter.
 Daniel Smith . . . . 12 . . . Exeter.
 Ichabod Snow . . . . 18 . . . Moultonborough.
*Rufus Swasey . . . . 12 . . . Exeter 1840
                                      Boston, Mass.
*Israel Thorndike . . . . 14 . . . Beverly, Mass. . . . 1867
   Merchant.   Boston, Mass.
*George Thorndike . . . . 12 . . . Beverly, Mass. . . . 1811
   Bowd. Coll. 1806; A.M.

                                                             45

1801.

*Theodore Chase . . . . 14 . . . Portsmouth 1859
   Merchant.   Boston, Mass.
*Henry Codman . . . . 11 . . . Boston, Mass. . . . 1853
   H.U. 1808; A.M.; Lawyer.   "   "
*Joseph Green Cogswell . . . . 14 . . . Ipswich, Mass. . . . 1871
   H.U. 1806; A.M.; Ph.D.; LL.D.; Librarian. New York, N.Y.
*Josiah Quincy Guild . . . . . . 14 . . . Cambridge, Mass. . . 1861
   H.U. 1807; Business.   Milton, Fla.
*Charles Head . . . . 11 . . . Boston, Mass. . . . 1821
   Merchant.   "   "
*Charles Heard . . . . 14 . . . Ipswich, Mass.
*James Perkins Higginson . . . 10 . . . Boston, Mass. . . . 1879
   Merchant.   "   "
*Charles Lamson . . . . 11 . . . Exeter.
 John Lane . . . . 19 . . . Stratham.
 Benjamin Leavitt . . . . 14 . . . Exeter.
 Gilman Leavitt . . . . 13 . . . Brentwood.
 Jonathan Lowell . . . . 13 . . . Amesbury, Mass.
*James Cushing Merrill . . . . 16 . . . Haverhill, Mass. . . 1853
   H.U. 1807; A.M.; Lawyer.   Boston, Mass.
*Samuel Merrill . . . . 14 . . . Haverhill, Mass. . . 1869
   H.U. 1807; A.M.; Lawyer.   Andover, Mass.
 Samuel Peak . . . . 17 . . . Newtown.
*Benjamin Prince . . . . 18 . . . Newburyport, Mass. 1815
   Dart. Coll. 1807; A.M.; Lawyer.   Cincinnati, O.
*Josiah Rundlett . . . . 19 . . . Exeter 1831
                                        "
*John Salter . . . . 13 . . . Portsmouth 1858
   Shipmaster.   "

*Lucius Manlius Sargent	15	Boston, Mass.	1867
Lawyer and Author.		" "	
*Ebenezer Smith	14	Durham	1830
Yale Coll. 1809; Teacher.		Neshaminy, Pa.	
*James Perkins Sturgis	10	Boston, Mass.	1851
Merchant.		China.	
John Storer	16	Wells, Me.	
John Swasey	14	Exeter.	
*William Browne Swett	11	Exeter	1837
Merchant.		Boston, Mass.	
John Thompson	14	Durham.	
*William Thompson	15	Portsmouth	1843
Shipmaster.		"	
*Andrew Thorndike	11	Beverly, Mass.	1854
Merchant.		Boston, Mass.	
*Joseph B. Towne	14	Hopkinton.	
Merchant.		"	
Thomas Towne	12	Hopkinton.	
Merchant.		St. Louis, Mo.	
David Williams	13	Natchez, Miss.	
James C. Williams	10	Natchez, Miss.	
Daniel Woodman	19	Kingston.	

32

1802.

Caleb Adams	15	Stratham.	
*John Bishop	15	Medford, Mass.	1830
James Blair	16	Exeter.	
*George William Boyd	11	Portsmouth	1859
Bowd. Coll. 1810; A.M.; Merchant.		Portland, Me.	
William Brown	13	Portsmouth.	
*Thomas Brown	13	Portsmouth	1822
Shipmaster.		"	
Edward Codman	11	Boston, Mass.	
*Clark Dean	10	Exeter	1826
Business.		"	
John Gookin	14	North Hampton.	
Charles Greene	19	Dover	1854
Merchant.		"	
*Joseph Hamilton	13	Berwick, Me.	
*Oliver Hamilton	19	Berwick, Me.	
*William Stone Ingraham	14	Portland, Me.	1806
*George Jefferds	14	Wells, Me.	1823
Hotel Keeper.		Kennebunk, Me.	
John Lee	15	Castine, Me.	
*Dudley Little	27	Hampstead	1827
Farmer.		"	
Charles Loring	15	North Yarmouth, Me.	
*Richard Lovering	11	Exeter	1853
Shoemaker.		"	
*Augustus Magee	13	Boston, Mass.	
*Joseph Bolles Manning	15	Gloucester, Mass.	1854
H.U. 1808; A.M.; Lawyer.		Ipswich, Mass.	
*Sylvester Melcher	13	Portsmouth	1875
Merchant.		"	

CATALOGUE. [1802-3.

*James Miltimore . . . . 13 . . . Stratham 1852
   Teacher.   Charlotte Hall, Md.
*Nathaniel K. G. Oliver . . . . 14 . . . Exeter 1832
   H.U. 1809; A.M.; Teacher.   Boston, Mass.
*George Parker. . . . . 10 . . . Boston, Mass. . . . 1825
   H.U. 1812; A.M.   Baltimore, Md.
George Pickering . . . . 13 . . . Danvers, Mass.
*William Plumer . . . . 13 . . . Epping 1854
   H.U. 1809; A.M.; M.C.; Lawyer.   "
Winthrop Sargent. . . . . . . 10 . . . Gloucester, Mass.
*James Sheafe . . . . 13 . . . Portsmouth 1845
   H.U. 1808; A.M.; Capitalist.   "
*Samuel Spring . . . . 10 . . . Newburyport, Mass. 1877
   Yale Coll. 1811; A.M.; Clergyman.   Hartford, Conn.
James Tash . . . . 17 . . . New Durham.
Thomas Stow Thing . . . . . 15 . . . Brentwood.
James Weeks . . . . 13 . . . Portland, Me.
*John Cravath May Windship . 13 . . . Exeter 1814
   H.U. 1809; Lawyer.   Rapides, La.
Joseph Woodman . . . . 18 . . . Buxton, Me.

                                                                          34

1803.

*John Emery Abbot . . . . . . 10 . . . Exeter 1819
   Bowd. Coll. 1810; A.M.; Clergyman.   Salem, Mass.
David Andrew Baum . . . . . 13 . . . Demarara, W.I.
*Samuel Bond . . . . 21 . . . Augusta, Me. 1809
   Merchant.   "   "
*Jacob Tilton Chamberlain. . . 12 . . . Exeter 1811
                                                          New Orleans, La.
*Jonathan Clark . . . . 15 . . . Northwood 1864
   Business.   Gilmanton.
*David Coffin . . . . 14 . . . Newburyport, Mass. 1815
   Business.   "   "
*Moses Colby . . . . 20 . . . Exeter 1847
   M.D.; Physician.   Wakefield.
Thomas Prince Crafts . . . . . 13 . . . Middleborough, Mass.
*Jonathan Peele Dabney . . . . 11 . . . Salem, Mass. 1868
   H.U. 1811; Clergyman.   Boston, Mass.
*Nathaniel Deering. . . . . . . 12 . . . Portland, Me. 1881
   H.U. 1810; A.M.; Lawyer.   "   "
*Nicholas Bartlett Doe . . . . . 17 . . . Newmarket 1856
   Lawyer.   Saratoga, N.Y.
*Samuel White Duncan . . . . 12 . . . Haverhill, Mass. . . 1824
   H.U. 1810; A.M.; Lawyer.   "   "
*Theodore Eames . . . . 18 . . . Haverhill, Mass. . . 1846
   Yale Coll. 1800; A.M.; Teacher.   Brooklyn, N.Y.
*Henry L. Eastham . . . . . . 12 . . . Exeter 1833
   Farmer.   "
*Jeremiah Fellowes. . . . . . . 12 . . . Exeter 1865
   Bowd. Coll. 1810; Lawyer.   "
*Jeremiah Parsons Fogg . . . . 15 . . . Kensington 1821
   Lawyer.   Steubenville, O.
*Henry French . . . . 20 . . . Portsmouth.
*Nathaniel Giddings . . . . . . 12 . . . Exeter.

*Charles W. Gilman . . . . . . 10 . . . Exeter 1871
  Apothecary.   "
Charles Gordon . . . . 14 . . . Newbury, Mass.
  Business.   Boston, Mass.
George Grafton . . . . 12 . . . Salem, Mass.
*Wells Healey . . . . 14 . . . Kensington 1857
  Farmer.   Hampton Falls.
*Timothy Hilliard . . . . 17 . . . Kensington 1847
  H.U. 1809; A.M.; M.D.
*Eliphalet Ladd . . . . 12 . . . Portsmouth 1821
  Merchant.   Boston, Mass.
Daniel Lane . . . . 19 . . . Buxton, Me.
*Joseph McLellan . . . . 14 . . . Portland, Me. . . . ? 1830
  Postmaster.   Brunswick, Me.
*Archibald McPhail . . . . . . 23 . . . Wakefield.
  Teacher.
*Joshua Winslow Peirce . . . . 12 . . . Portsmouth 1873
  Shipowner and Farmer.   "
*Joseph Prescott . . . . 17 . . . Hampton Falls . . . 1809
*Edmund Quincy Sheafe . . . . 15 . . . Portsmouth 1839
  Merchant.   "
*Samuel Stevens . . . . 24 . . . Andover, Mass. . . . 1809
  H.U. 1809.   "   "
*George Washington Storer . . 14 . . . Portland, Me. 1864
  Rear Admiral, U.S.N.   Portsmouth.
*Weare Tappan . . . . 13 . . . Kingston 1868
  Dart. Coll. 1811; A.M.; Lawyer.   Bradford.
Timothy Thorndike . . . . . . 19 . . . Jaffrey.
*John Tibbets . . . . 16 . . . Dover 1819
  Shipmaster.   "
*Letsom Winship . . . . 12 . . . Exeter.

                                                          36

1804.

*Jeremiah P. Adams . . . . . . 13 . . . Exeter.
Peter Aikin . . . . 23 . . . Chester.
*Amos Blanchard . . . . 14 . . . Exeter.
Benjamin Cram . . . . 17 . . . Hampton Falls.
  Farmer.   "   "
*Israel Woodbury Davis . . . . 15 . . . Beverly, Mass. . . . 1814
  Merchant.   "   "
George Lyman Emerson . . . 13 . . . York, Me.
*Henry Folsom . . . . 11 . . . Exeter.
*George Edward Head . . . . . 11 . . . Boston, Mass. . . . 1861
  H.U. 1812; Lawyer.   "   "
Richard Tuttle Hunt . . . . . 12 . . . St. Croix, W. I.
Fitz Edward Hutchins . . . . . 12 . . . Boston, Mass.
Ralph Johnson . . . . 14 . . . Freeport, Me.
John Leighton . . . . 14 . . . Durham.
*William Augustus Leverett . . 13 . . . Portsmouth 1820
  Merchant.   Boston, Mass.
*Theodore Lyman . . . . 12 . . . Boston, Mass. . . . 1849
  H.U. 1810; A.M.   "   "
*Theodore Bland Moses . . . . 14 . . . Exeter 1871
  Business.   "

*George Washington Osborne . 13 . . . Exeter 1869
   Business.   "
George Pearce . . . . 12 . . . Gloucester, Mass.
John Pearson . . . . 11 . . . Newburyport, Mass.
   Business.   Bangor, Me.
*Clark Gayton Pickman . . . . 12 . . . Salem, Mass. 1860
                                        Boston, Mass.
John Pratt. . . . . 13 . . . Boston, Mass.
Richard W. Rogers . . . . . . 13 . . . Newmarket.
*John Rogers . . . . 17 . . . Newmarket 1837
   Business.   Exeter.
*Ichabod Rollins . . . . 14 . . . Dover 1873
   Merchant.   Portsmouth.
*Thomas Robie Sewall . . . . 12 . . . Boston, Mass. . . . 1864
   Business.   "   "
John Signorette . . . . 14 . . . Guadaloupe, W. I.
*Henry Smith . . . . 15 . . . Durham 1828
   Clergyman.   Camden, N.J.
*George Smith . . . . 14 . . . Exeter 1868
   Carriagemaker.
William Stearns . . . . 12 . . . Salem, Mass.
*Thomas Stevens . . . . 14 . . . Beverly, Mass. . . . 1868
   Lawyer.   "   "
*George Langdon Storer . . . . 14 . . . Portland, Me. 1854
                                        Buffalo, N.Y.
Josiah Thatcher . . . . 15 . . . Gorham, Me.
*George Augustus Trumbull . . 12 . . . Petersham, Mass. . . 1868
   Business.   Worcester, Mass.
Winthrop Watson . . . . 18 . . . Newmarket.

                                                   33

1805.

Samuel Avery . . . . 20 . . . Stratham.
*Horatio Bigelow . . . . 14 . . . Cambridge, Mass. . . 1824
   H.U. 1809; A.M.   Louisiana.
*Eleazer Blanchard . . . . 22 . . . Chester 1809
   Student at Dart. Coll.   "
*John Bond . . . . 15 . . . Augusta, Me. 1829
   Lawyer.   Alabama.
*Charles Browne . . . . 12 . . . Beverly, Mass. . . . 1856
   H.U. 1812; A.M.
John Alphonso Chandler . . . 14 . . . Monmouth, Me.
*William Carroll . . . . 11 . . . Hampton 1817
   H.U. 1813.
*Isaac Chapman . . . . 14 . . . Beverly, Mass. . . . 1822
   Bookkeeper.   "   "
*William Cross . . . . 14 . . . Newburyport, Mass. 1825
   Merchant.   Boston, Mass.
Jonathan Freeman Dana . . . 12 . . . Exeter.
*Samuel Fellowes . . . . 17 . . . Exeter 1828
   Mechanic.   "
Joseph Greely . . . . 21 . . . South Hampton.
*Samuel Hale . . . . 12 . . . Barrington 1869
   Bowd. Coll. 1814; A.M.; Manufacturer.   Portsmouth.
Ebenezer Hale . . . . 18 . . . Brattleborough, Vt.
Benaiah Hanson . . . . 24 . . . Windham, Me.

*John Henniker Ingraham . . .	12 . . . Portland, Me.	1868
Caleb Johnson	15 . . . Utica, N.Y.	
Joseph Kent	15 . . . Chester.	
Israel Lakeman	16 . . . Exeter.	
*George Lamson	12 . . . Exeter	1826
Bowd. Coll. 1812; A.M.; Editor.	New York, N.Y.	
Mark Lane	17 . . . Stratham.	
*William Lang	14 . . . Effingham	1875
Farmer.	Milan.	
*George Long	13 . . . Portsmouth	1819
Merchant.	Boston, Mass.	
*John Manning	16 . . . Gloucester, Mass. . .	1852
H.U. 1810; A.M.; M.D.; Physician.	Rockport, Mass.	
*John Howard March	14 . . . Greenland	1863
Merchant.	Paris, France.	
*James Odell	20 . . . Stratham	1822
M.D.; Physician.	"	
*Benjamin Pickman	15 . . . Salem, Mass.	1835
Merchant.	Boston, Mass.	
John Pierson	14 . . . Biddeford, Me. . . .	1828
*William Reed	17 . . . Easton, Mass. . . .	1812
H.U. 1811.		
*Charles Roby	23 . . . Dunstable	1826
B.U. 1810; A.M.		
*William Augustus Rogers . . .	12 . . . Salem, Mass.	1821
H.U. 1811; A.M.; Lawyer.	" "	
*Richard Rollins	17 . . . Dover	1813
Merchant.		
*John Lane Sheafe	13 . . . Portsmouth	1864
Lawyer.	New Orleans, La.	
William Sherburne	12 . . . Portsmouth.	
William B. Simpson	13 . . . North Hampton.	
*Frederic Southgate	13 . . . Scarborough, Me. . .	1812
Bowd. Coll. 1810.		
George Strong	13 . . . Randolph, Mass.	
Joseph Weld	11 . . . Plymouth.	
Thomas Wiggin	19 . . . Exeter.	
*William Young	13 . . . Newburyport, Mass.	1821
H.U. 1810.	" "	

40

1806.

*Amos Atkinson	14 . . . Newbury, Mass. . . .	1863
Merchant.	Boston, Mass.	
*John Lauris Blake	18 . . . Northwood	1857
B.U. 1812; D.D.; Clergyman; Author.	Orange, N.Y.	
Levi Blanchard	13 . . . Exeter.	
*Oliver Brooks	10 . . . Exeter	1848
Clerk Orphans' Court.	Philadelphia, Pa.	
Henry Burleigh	13 . . . Exeter.	
*Nathaniel Hazeltine Carter . .	12 . . . Concord	1830
Dart. Coll. 1811; A.M.; Editor.	New York, N.Y.	
*Samuel Luther Dana	11 . . . Exeter	1868
H.U. 1813; A.M.; LL.D.; M.D.		
*Thomas Amory Deblois	12 . . . Boston, Mass. . . .	1867
H.U. 1813; A.M.; LL.D.; Lawyer.	" "	

Godfrey Delorm . . . . 20 . . . Guadaloupe, W. I.
*James Henry Duncan . . . . . 11 . . . Haverhill, Mass. . . . 1869
   H.U. 1812; A.M.; LL.D.; M.C.
*Edward Augustus Emerson . . 13 . . . York, Me.
   Business.   Boston, Mass.
*Charles Folsom . . . . 11 . . . Exeter 1872
   H.U. 1813; A.M.; Editor and Librarian. Cambridge, Mass.
Jacob Frost . . . . 21 . . . York, Me.
*Nathaniel Gilman . . . . 12 . . . Exeter 1858
   Business.
*William Charles Gilman . . . . 11 . . . Exeter 1863
   Manufacturer.   Norwich, Conn.
*Nathaniel Batchelder Gordon . 15 . . . Exeter 1847
                                      Lawrence, Mass.
*John T. Gordon . . . . 13 . . . Exeter 1865
   Farmer.
*Ezra Haskell . . . . 24 . . . New Gloucester, Me. 1858
   Yale Coll. 1811; Teacher.   Dover.'
*Edmund Kimball . . . . 13 . . . Newburyport, Mass. 1873
   H.U. 1814; Lawyer.   Wenham, Mass.
*Samuel Ladd . . . . 13 . . . Dover.
   Printer.
Joshua Lane . . . . 18 . . . Readfield, Me.
Nathaniel Leavitt . . . . 16 . . . Brentwood.
Bradstreet Gilman Leavitt . . 15 . . . Portsmouth.
*Josiah Little . . . . 15 . . . Newbury, Mass. . . . 1860
   Bowd. Coll. 1811; A.M.; Farmer.   Newburyport, Mass.
*John Lougee . . . . 12 . . . Exeter 1866
   Cabinetmaker.
John Madison . . . . 12 . . . Portland, Me.
*Robert Neil . . . . 13 . . . Portsmouth 1837
   Accountant.
Elijah F. Page . . . . 18 . . . Hopkinton.
*Nathaniel Anthony Paine . . . 14 . . . Worcester, Mass. . . . 1819

Benjamin Pearce . . . . 15 . . . Hillsborough.
*Moses Pillsbury . . . . 18 . . . Bridgewater 1832
   Dart. Coll. 1811; Lawyer.
*Edward C. Piper . . . . 16 . . . Wakefield 1881
   Farmer.
Henry A. Ranlett . . . . 14 . . . Exeter.
*John Rollins . . . . 13 . . . Newbury, Mass. . . . 1833
   Business.   Newburyport, Mass.
*Nathaniel Rundlett . . . . . . 12 . . . Exeter 1846
   Business.
*Josiah Gilman Smith . . . . . 13 . . . Exeter 1877
   Merchant.
*Tristram Storer . . . . 13 . . . Saco, Me. 1847
   Shipmaster.
*George W. Sturgis . . . . . . 12 . . . Boston, Mass. 1826
   Merchant.
Samuel Tenney . . . . 18 . . . Byfield, Mass.
*Edward Thorndike . . . . . . 12 . . . Beverly, Mass.
   Merchant.   Boston, Mass.
*Charles Thorndike . . . . . . 10 . . . Beverly, Mass. 1833
   Merchant.   Boston, Mass.
*Elisha Fuller Wallace . . . . 14 . . . Milford 1870
   Dart. Coll. 1811; Lawyer; U. S. Consul. Cuba.

*Richard Webster 17	...	Rye	1856
Teacher.		"	
Ebenezer White 12	...	Rutland, Mass.	
*Andrew Paine Wiggin 14	...	Stratham	1846
M.D.; Physician.		Greenland.	
*Samuel Woodbury 21	...	Acworth	1819
Dart. Coll. 1811; A.M.; Clergyman.		Groton, Mass.	

46

1807.

*Henry Allen 15	...	Beverly, Mass. ...	1844
Farmer.		Illinois.	
*Zachariah Allen 11	...	Providence, R.I. ..	1882
B.U. 1813; A.M.; LL.D.		" "	
*Abraham Andrews 20	...	Winsor, Conn. ...	1869
Dart. Coll. 1811; A.M.; Teacher.			
*Barnabas Bates 20	...	Boston, Mass. ...	1853
Clergyman and Editor.		New York, N.Y.	
Peter Bazin 13	...	Boston, Mass.	
*Thomas Peter Bidau 15	...	Paris, France.	
Elias Blanchard 10	...	Exeter.	
Joseph Blunt 11	...	Newburyport, Mass.	
Business.		New York, N.Y.	
*Charles Briggs 17	...	Halifax, Mass. ...	1873
H.U. 1815; A.M.; Clergyman.		Roxbury, Mass.	
Alexander S. Chadbourne. .. 14	...	Portsmouth.	
Joseph Cutts 11	...	Kittery, Me.	
*John Davis 15	...	Beverly, Mass. ...	1838
Farmer.		Wenham, Mass.	
*Henry Elijah Dix 14	...	Boston, Mass.....	1822
H.U. 1813.			
*Edward Everett 13	...	Boston, Mass.....	1865
H.U. 1811; LL.D.; Ph.D.; Clergyman; Prof. H.U.; M.C.; U.S. Sen.; Gov. Mass.; Sec. State; U.S. Min. to England; Pres. H.U.		" "	
John Gale 16	...	Exeter.	
*Benjamin Ives Gilman 12	...	Marietta, O.	1866
B.U. 1813; A.M.; Business.		Monticello, O.	
John Goddard 10	...	Charlestown, Mass.	
*John Heath 14	...	Brookline, Mass. ..	1835
*Winthrop Hilton 12	...	Deerfield	1869
Bowd. Coll. 1814; A.M.; Farmer.		"	
*Stephen Farrar Jones 21	...	New Ipswich.	
Yale Coll. 1812; Teacher.		Beaufort, S.C.	
Ephraim K. Lamson 10	...	Exeter.	
Henry Marston 12	...	Boston, Mass.	
*Andrew Williams Miltimore.. 15	...	Stratham	1865
Shipmaster.		Newburyport, Mass.	
*Thomas Handyside Perkins, Jr. 11	...	Boston, Mass. ...	1850
Merchant.		" "	
*William King Porter 11	...	Topsham, Me. ...	1839
Bowd. Coll. 1814; Lawyer.		Turner, Me.	
*George Prince 15	...	Salem, Mass	1810
		" "	
*William Henry Robbins ... 12	...	Hallowell, Me. ...	1849
Bowd. Coll. 1814; Lawyer.		Scheraw, S.C.	

*William Robinson . . . . 12 . . . Exeter 1865
   Merchant.   Augusta, Ga.
*Charles Sheafe . . . . 16 . . . Portsmouth 1816
   Capitalist.   "
*John Sherburne Sleeper . . . . 13 . . . Exeter 1878
   Editor.   Boston, Mass.
James Smith . . . . 17 . . . Newmarket.
*Edwin Smith . . . . 16 . . . Wiscasset, Me. . . . 1875
   H.U. 1811; Lawyer.   Warren, Me.
*Alfred Smith . . . . 15 . . . Durham 1876
   Merchant.   "
*Tasker Hazard Swett . . . . . 12 . . . Exeter 1841
   Merchant.   Boston, Mass.
John Tayloe . . . . 14 . . . Richmond, Va.
*Benjamin Ogle Tayloe . . . 11 . . . Richmond, Va. . . . 1868
   H.U. 1815; A.M.   Washington, D.C.
David Tukesbury . . . . 26 . . . Amesbury, Mass.
*Augustus Thorndike . . . . . 10 . . . Beverly, Mass. . . . 1858
   H.U. 1816; A.M.
*William Thorndike . . . . . . 12 . . . Beverly, Mass. . . . 1835
   H.U. 1813; A.M.; Lawyer.   "   "
*George W. Weeks . . . . . . 16 . . . Greenland.
   Farmer.   "
Warren White . . . . 16 . . . Brookline, Mass.
Samuel Wiggin . . . . 17 . . . Stratham.

                                                      42

1808.

John Adams . . . . 10 . . . Exeter.
Charles Wentworth Apthorp . 12 . . . Medford, Mass.
Noah Barker . . . . 19 . . . Stratham.
   Teacher.   "
*David Barker . . . . 12 . . . Rochester 1834
   H.U. 1815; A.M.; M.C.; Lawyer.   "
Joseph Baxter . . . . 11 . . . Boston, Mass.
   H.U. 1815; M.D.
Thomas Boardman . . . . . . 12 . . . Exeter.
Achille Bonhomme . . . . . . 14 . . . France.
Americus Brown . . . . 15 . . . Deer Isle, Me.
*Isaac Lyman Buckminster . . 12 . . . Portsmouth 1825
   H.U. 1815; A.M.   Norton, Mass.
Effingham Capron . . . . 17 . . . Uxbridge, Mass.
Nathaniel G. Dana . . . . . . 11 . . . Exeter.
*John Dearborn . . . . 20 . . . North Hampton . . . 1832
   Business.   Lynn, Mass.
Robert Gordon . . . . 23 . . . Bedford.
*Micajah Hawkes . . . . 21 . . . Lynn, Mass. 1863
   M.D.
*Charles Keating . . . . 13 . . . Boston, Mass. . . . 1817
   H.U. 1814.   Cambridge, Mass.
*Oliver Keating . . . . 11 . . . Boston, Mass.
George Kent . . . . 12 . . . Concord.
   Dart. Coll. 1814; Lawyer.   Washington, D.C.
*Thomas Leavitt . . . . 14 . . . North Hampton . . . 1860
   Hotel-keeper.   Hampton.
Nathan Leonard . . . . 20 . " . . Middleborough, Mass.

*Edward S. Manning . . . . . 12 . . . Portsmouth.
Shipmaster. "
Benjamin Ogle . . . . 11 . . . Annapolis, Md.
*Richard Elvin Orne . . . . . 12 . . . Salem, Mass. 1860
Bowd. Coll. 1815; Shipmaster. " "
* *William Bourne Oliver Peabody* 9 . . . Exeter 1847
H.U. 1816; A.M.; Clergyman and Author. Springfield, Mass.
**Oliver William Bourne Peabody* 9 . . . Exeter 1848
H.U. 1816; A.M.; Editor and Clergyman. Burlington, Vt.
Aaron Peabody . . . . 20 . . . Bridgetown, Me.
Tallahassee, Fla.
George Washington Prescott . 20 . . . Salem, Mass.
*Benjamin Franklin Salter . . . 16 . . . Portsmouth 1858
Bowd. Coll. 1813; Merchant. New York, N.Y.
*William James Seaver . . . . 14 . . . Worcester, Mass. . . 1835
U.S. Consul. St. Croix.
*Theodore Sheafe . . . . 13 . . . Portsmouth 1840
Merchant. "
*Jonathan Silsby . . . . 20 . . . Acworth 1831
Dart. Coll. 1814; M.D.; Physician. Cazenovia, N.Y.
*Henry Stark . . . . 12 . . . Dunbarton.
Business. Washington, D.C.
*Richard Steele . . . . 11 . . . Durham 1870
Dart. Coll. 1815; A.M.; M.D.; Physician. Newburyport, Mass.
*William H. Tayloe . . . . . . 9 . . . Richmond, Va. . . . 1871
Planter. Mt. Airy, Richmond Co., Va.
*Jonas Underwood . . . . 19 . . . West Nottingham . . 1850
H.U. 1815; M.D.; Physician. Hingham, Mass.
William Willis . . . . 14 . . . Portland, Me.
H.U. 1813; A.M.; LL.D.; Lawyer. " "

35

1809.

*Crawford Allen . . . . 11 . . . Providence, R.I. . . 1872
B.U. 1815; A.M.; Manufacturer. " "
*Richard Bartlett . . . . 17 . . . Concord 1837
Dart. Coll. 1815; Lawyer. New York, N.Y.
Ebenezer Little Boyd . . . . . 11 . . . Exeter.
*Charles Bulfinch . . . . 15 . . . Boston, Mass. . . . 1862
" "
*Thomas Bulfinch . . . . 13 . . . Boston, Mass. . . . 1867
H.U. 1814; A.M.; Merchant and Author. " "
Stephen Crooker . . . . 23 . . . Halifax, N.S.
*John Amory Deblois . . . . . 11 . . . Boston, Mass. . . . 1855
H.U. 1816; A.M.; Business. Columbus, Ga.
*John Adams Dix . . . . 11 . . . Boscawen 1879
U.S. Sec. Treas.; Min. to France; Gov. N.Y.; New York, N.Y.
U.S. Senator; Author and Lawyer.
*Isaac Dodge . . . . 14 . . . Exeter 1832
Waterville, Me.
*Ephraim Fellowes . . . . . . 13 . . . Exeter 1849
Printer. "
*Nathaniel Folsom . . . . . . 17 . . . Portsmouth 1859
Shipmaster. Exeter.
*Josiah Gould . . . . 16 . . . Beverly, Mass. . . . 1836
Merchant. " "

*Joseph Chase Hilliard . . . . 21 . . . Kensington 1853
   Teacher.   "
*John Gorham Palfrey . . . . . 13 . . . Boston, Mass. . . . 1881
   H.U. 1815; A.M.; LL.D.; Prof. Sac. Lit. H.U.;   Cambridge, Mass.
   M.C.; Clergyman and Author.
*Benjamin Philbrick . . . . . . 15 . . . Exeter 1824
   Manufacturer.   Huntsville, Ala.
*George Pollard . . . . 12 . . . Littleton, Mass.
   Shipmaster.
Lucius Powers . . . . 19 . . . Shapleigh, Me.
William Pratt . . . . 14 . . . Charlestown, Mass.
*Jonathan Rollins . . . . 21 . . . Deerfield, Mass. . . 1840
   Teacher and Merchant.   Union, O.
*John Hale Sheafe . . . . 15 . . . Portsmouth 1840
   Merchant.   "
John H. Sherburne . . . . . . 15 . . . Portsmouth.
*Jared Sparks . . . . 20 . . . Willington, Conn. . 1866
   H.U. 1815; A.M.; LL.D.; Prof. Hist. H.U.;   Cambridge, Mass.
   Pres. H.U.; Clergyman and Author.
*George Simes . . . . 11 . . . Portsmouth 1825
   Shipmaster.   "
*Ebenezer Thompson . . . . . 12 . . . Durham 1826
   Farmer.   "
                                                      24

1810.

*George K. Apthorp . . . . . . 12 . . . 'Quincy, Mass.
                                             Surinam.
*Thomas Apthorp . . . . 13 . . . Boston, Mass.
*William Apthorp . . . . 10 . . . 'Boston, Mass.
                                             Surinam.
*Abraham Bazin, Jr. . . . . . . 12 . . . Boston, Mass. 1821
   Merchant.   "   "
William C. Bowers . . . . . . 14 . . . Middletown, Conn.
*William Bradford . . . . 13 . . . Wiscasset, Me. . . . 1858
   H.U. 1816; Author.
*Samuel Cartland . . . . 19 . . . Lee 1852
   Dart. Coll. 1816; A.M.; Lawyer; Prob. Judge.   Exeter.
William F. R. Chamberlain . . 14 . . . Exeter.
*Henry Cross . . . . 13 . . . Portland, Me.
*John Brazer Davis . . . . . . 11 . . . Boston, Mass. 1832
   H.U. 1815; A.M.; Lawyer.   "   "
*George Deering . . . . 12 . . . Portland, Me.
*James Ferdinand Deering . . . 12 . . . Portland, Me. 1830
   H.U. 1820; A.M.; Merchant.   "   "
*Elias Hasket Derby . . . . . . 14 . . . Salem, Mass. 1840
   Lawyer.   Medfield, Mass.
*John Abbot Douglass . . . . . 18 . . . Portland, Me. 1878
   Bowd. Coll. 1814; A.M.; Clergyman.   Waterford, Me.
*Thomas Huse Everett . . . . . 11 . . . Boston, Mass. 1839
   Accountant.   Lowell, Mass.
*Nicholas Gilman . . . . 10 . . . Exeter 1840
   Business.   Portland, Me.
*Samuel Kinsman Gilman . . . 14 . . . Exeter 1882
   Business.   Hallowell, Me.
*Stephen Leavitt Gordon . . . . 15 . . . Exeter 1843
   Music Teacher.   Portsmouth.

*Daniel Gilman Hatch . . . . . 12 . . . Exeter 1862
    H.U. 1817; A.M.; Merchant.   Covington, Ky.
John L. Hill. . . . . 12 . . . Georgetown, Me.
Mark L. Hill . . . . 11 . . . Georgetown, Me.
*Silas Holman . . . . 21 . . . Bolton, Mass. 1850
    M.D.
*Horace Hooker . . . . 16 . . . Windsor, Vt. 1864
    Yale Coll. 1815; A.M.; Clergyman.   Hartford, Conn.
Henry Hunnewell . . . . 14 . . . Portland, Me.
Samuel Hunt . . . . 15 . . . Charlestown, Mass.
*Josiah Stearns Hurd . . . . . 14 . . . Charlestown, Mass. . 1855
    M.D.; Physician.   "   "
William Hutchins . . . . 13 . . . Boston, Mass.
*George Goldthwaite Ingersoll . 13 . . . Keene 1863
    H.U. 1815; A.M.; D.D.; Clergyman.
Jeremiah Kews . . . . 20 . . . North Hampton.
*John Lamson . . . . 12 . . . Exeter.
John Walley Langdon . . . . 14 . . . Charlestown, Mass.
Joseph Osborne . . . . 21 . . . Salem, Mass.
Daniel Porter . . . . 12 . . . Conway, Mass.
Edward Pratt . . . . 13 . . . Charlestown, Mass.
Charles Preble . . . . 13 . . . Watertown, Mass.
Isaac H. Rand . . . . 13 . . . Boston, Mass.
Caleb Rand . . . . 11 . . . Boston, Mass.
*John Adams Richardson . . . 13 . . . Durham 1877
    Dart. Coll. 1819; Lawyer.   "
*Charles Robinson . . . . 13 . . . Exeter 1862
    H.U. 1818; A.M.; Clergyman.   Groton, Mass.
William Rollins . . . . 16 . . . Barrington.
Frederick Rowe . . . . 14 . . . Exeter.
    Butcher.   California.
Charles Russell . . . . 14 . . . Boston, Mass.
Thomas W. Shannon . . . . . 20 . . . Dover.
*William Smith. . . . . 10 . . . Exeter 1830
    H.U. 1817; A.M.; Lawyer.   "
David Taylor . . . . 25 . . . Plymouth.
Thomas Tyler . . . . 14 . . . Trinidad, W. I.
*James Underwood . . . . . . 20 . . . Nottingham 1842
    Agent.   Somerville, Mass.
*William Bicker Walter . . . . 14 . . . Boston, Mass. 1823
    Bowd. Coll. 1818; A.M.; Editor and Author.   "   "
*Henry Artemas Ward . . . . . 15 . . . Boston, Mass. 1870
    H.U. 1816; A.M.; M.D.; Physician.   "   "
Peter Wiggin . . . . 21 . . . Wakefield.
*William T. Wiggin . . . . . . 13 . . . Exeter 1862
Henry Willard . . . . 16 . . . Charlestown.

                                                    52

1811.

George Bancroft . . . . 11 . . . Worcester, Mass.
    H.U. 1817; A.M.; LL.D.; PH.D.; Sec. Navy; Washington, D.C.
    Min. to Eng.; Min. to Germany; Historian.
*Mark Barker . . . . 19 . . . Stratham 1868
    Farmer.   "

CATALOGUE. [1811.

Charles E. Bowers	12	Boston, Mass.	
Otis Bullard	25	Uxbridge, Mass.	
Isaac Butler	21	Pelham.	
William Channing	17	New London, Conn.	
Edwin Channing	16	New London, Conn.	
Samuel Clark	20	Limington, Me.	
*Jonathan Peter Cushing	18	Rochester	1835
Dart. Coll. 1817; A.M.; Prof. & Pres. Hamp. & Syd. Coll.		Raleigh, N.C.	
Loammi Davidson	21	Dunstable.	
Eppes Ellery	11	Exeter.	
*John Dean Gardner	11	Exeter	1869
Merchant.		Brooklyn, N.Y.	
John Gardner	14	Charlestown, Mass.	
*George Gilman	14	York, Me.	1825
M.D.; Physician.		" "	
*Samuel Taylor Gilman	10	Exeter	1835
H.U. 1819; Lawyer.		"	
*Thatcher Goddard	10	Boston, Mass.	1833
		New York, N.Y.	
Charles Hardy	14	Brighton, Mass.	
*Joseph Hatch	12	Kennebunk, Me.	1856
Shipmaster.		" "	
*Richard Hildreth	21	Sterling, Mass.	1857
*Abel Fletcher Hildreth	18	Sterling, Mass.	1864
H.U. 1818; A.M.; Teacher.		Derry.	
Elias Hull	12	Seabrook.	
George Jewett	15	Portland, Me.	
H.U. 1816.			
Reuben B. Lowell	25	Thomaston, Me.	
*Gideon Colcord Lyford	12	Exeter	1880
Merchant.		"	
*Samuel Tenny Moses	11	Exeter	1842
Printer.		"	
*George Odell	18	Stratham	1835
M.D.; Physician.		Greenland.	
Oliver William Osborne	12	Exeter.	
Business.		Boston, Mass.	
Alpheus Spring Packard	12	Wiscasset, Me.	
Bowd. Coll. 1816; A.M.; D.D.; Prof. Nat. & Revealed Religion, Bowd. Coll.		Brunswick, Me.	
Isaac Peasley	21	Boxford, Mass.	
*Joseph Philbrick	14	Exeter	1875
Potter.		Skowhegan, Me.	
*Joseph Ray	14	Beverly, Mass.	
Clergyman.		Georgia.	
Samuel Edmund Sewall	11	Boston, Mass.	
Lawyer.		" "	
*Lyndon Arnold Smith	16	Hopkinton	1865
Dart. Coll. 1817; A.M.; M.D.; Physician.		Newark, N.J.	
*James Smith	14	Exeter.	
*Daniel Winkley	19	Barrington	1883
Farmer.		Strafford.	
*Wilmot Wood	15	Wiscasset, Me.	1865
Bowd. Coll. 1816; A.M.; Lawyer.		" "	
Jonathan Woodbury	21	Barrington.	

1812.

*Abiel Abbot	11	Beverly, Mass.	1849
Business.		Boston, "	
*Charles E. Avery	18	Groton, Conn.	1854
Middlebury Coll. 1818.			
*George Barker	18	Stratham	1874
*Jacob Bartlett	16	Nottingham	1841
Farmer.		"	
Thomas Bickford	10	Boston, Mass.	
Cleophas Boyd	10	Exeter.	
Theophilus Boyd	12	Exeter.	
Abel Brown	22	South Hampton.	
*James E. Brooks	12	Exeter.	
Cushing Bryant	14	Nobleborough, Me.	
*John M. Channing	16	New London, Conn.	
*John M. Copp	17	Wakefield	1832
		New Orleans.	
Arthur G. Coffin	12	Gloucester, Mass.	
Francis A. Coffin	12	Beaufort, S.C.	
George Davis	12	Gloucester, Mass.	
*John Dorr	11	Boston, Mass.	1874
		" "	
*Edward Dorr	11	Boston, Mass.	1844
H.U. 1819; A.M.; Merchant.		" "	
*Ebenezer Ritchie Dorr	12	Boston, Mass.	1873
H.U. 1818; Lawyer.		" "	
*James Dudley	18	Raymond	1868
Business.		Malden, Mass.	
*Charles Octavius Emerson	13	York, Me.	1863
H.U. 1818; A.M.; Lawyer.		" "	
John Fifield	17	Stratham.	
Tilton French	18	East Kingston.	
George Gale	18	Kingston.	
Peter Gellineau	17	Trinidad, W. I.	
Sylvanus Gray	12	Boston, Mass.	
*Joseph Healey	14	Kensington	1829
Farmer.		"	
Joseph Hoit	16	Stratham.	
*Theodore Keating	14	Boston, Mass.	1829
H.U. 1821; A.M.; LL.B.; Lawyer.		" "	
*Andrew Thorndike Leach	14	Beverly, Mass.	1859
Shipmaster.		" "	
Samuel Mead	14	Amesbury.	
*David Lowell Nichols	18	Amesbury	1829
Dart. Coll. 1816; Clergyman.		Kingston.	
*Nathaniel Ward Osgood	14	Salem, Mass.	1863
Tanner.		" "	
*Gardner Paine	13	Worcester, Mass.	1854
Business.		" "	
*Edward Bass Peabody	10	Exeter	1830
*Daniel Hall Peirce	11	Portsmouth	1877
H.U. 1820; A.M.; M.D.		"	
*Enoch Perley	17	Boxford, Mass.	1814

*Richard Pickering . . . . 15 . . . Newington 1876		
H.U. 1819; Farmer.		"
*Ebenezer S. Piper . . . . 16 . . . Stratham 1835		
		Levant, Me.
William Rice . . . . 16 . . . Kittery, Me.		
John Rollins . . . . 20 . . . Andover.		
David Moore Russell . . . . . 16 . . . Plymouth.		
Fitz William Sargent . . . . . 12 . . . Gloucester, Mass.		
M.D.		Europe.
*Oliver Sheafe . . . . 13 . . . Portsmouth 1825		
H.U. 1817; A.M.; Merchant.		"
*Charles Smith . . . . 16 . . . Durham 1874		
Farmer.		Meredith.
Daniel R. Stanwood . . . . . . 10 . . . Gloucester, Mass.		
John Tilton . . . . 11 . . . Scarborough, Me.		
*Charles Walker . . . . 14 . . . Concord 1843		
H.U. 1818; Lawyer.		"
*Israel Whitney . . . . 14 . . . Beverly, Mass. . . . 1871		
Merchant.		" "
John P. Williams . . . . 15 . . . Nottingham.		
Teacher.		Spottsylvania Co., Pa.
		. 49

1813.

Stephen Ames . . . . 14 . . . Charlestown.		
Aaron Beach . . . . 18 . . . Whiting, Me.		
John Bowden . . . . 23 . . . Waterborough, Me.		
*John Kinsley Briggs . . . . . . 19 . . . Halifax, Mass. . . . 1843		
M.D.; Physician.		Dedham, Mass.
*Sidney Brooks . . . . 13 . . . Boston, Mass 1878		
H.U. 1819; A.M.; Merchant.		New York, N.Y.
*Peter Chardon Brooks . . . . . 14 . . . Boston, Mass 1880		
Merchant.		" "
Alpheus Spring Chandler . . . 17 . . . Elliot, Me.		
M.D.		
*Charles William Chauncy . . . 13 . . . Portsmouth 1864		
H.U. 1819; A.M.; M.D.		
Leader Dam . . . . 21 . . . Waterborough, Me.		
Charles Dana . . . . 15 . . . Charlestown, Mass.		
*John Elliot . . . . 12 . . . Portsmouth.		
		Kittery, Me.
*Robert Treat Paine Fiske . . . 14 . . . Worcester, Mass. . . 1866		
H.U. 1818; A.M.; M.D.; Physician.		Hingham, Mass.
*Charles Lane Folsom . . . . . 14 . . . Exeter 1829		
Dart. Coll. 1820; Teacher P.E.A.		"
George Williams Folsom . . . 10 . . . Exeter.		
*George Gardner . . . . 12 . . . Exeter 1857		
Merchant.		"
*John Gilchrist . . . . 21 . . . Goffstown.		
M.D.; Physician.		Port Hope, Canada.
*Joseph Gilman . . . . 21 . . . Marietta, O. 1823		
		Kentucky.
*Charles Gilman . . . . 19 . . . Meredith 1861		
Lawyer.		Baltimore, Md.
*Samuel Hammond . . . . . . 11 . . . Boston, Mass. . . . 1834		
Merchant.		" "

John Hedge	15	Wiscasset, Me.	1830
John Henry Hooper	10	Marblehead, Mass.	
Farmer.		Peoria, Ill.	
John Hurry	14	Wiscasset, Me.	
*Henry True Kelly	19	Hampstead	1840
Dart. Coll. 1819; A.M.; Clergyman.		Chatham, N.C.	
*William F. Lane	17	Stratham	1832
Business.		Hallowell, Me.	
Joseph Long	17	Amesbury, Mass.	
*John Lovering	19	Exeter	1837
Shoemaker.		"	
Enoch Martin	19	Brookfield.	
*Charles Paine	14	Williamstown, Vt.	1853
H.U. 1820; A.M.; Gov. Vermont.		Northfield, Vt.	
William B. Pearson	15	Gloucester, Mass.	
*Daniel Pickering	18	Greenland	1855
Business.		Wolfborough.	
David Riddle	15	Bedford.	
*Josiah Robinson	22	Exeter	1854
Farmer.		"	
*Trueworthy Robinson	19	Exeter	1833
Farmer.		"	
*Charles Robinson	20	Greenland	1862
Merchant.		Portsmouth.	
Edward B. Russell	14	Salem.	
*John Sevey	16	Wiscasset, Me.	1832
*Edward Bradstreet Sewall	11	Boston, Mass.	1830
Merchant.		New York, N.Y.	
*Gideon Lane Soule	17	Freeport, Me.	1879
Bowd. Coll. 1818; A.M.; LL.D.; Principal P.E.A.		Exeter.	
Francis Dana Stedman	12	Worcester, Mass.	
*John Sullivan	13	Exeter	1862
Lawyer; Attorney-General N.H.		"	
*Albert Thorndike	13	Beverly, Mass.	1858
Banker.		" "	
Noah Porter Wiggin	18	Stratham.	
Farmer.		"	
*James Wilson	16	Peterborough	1881
Middlebury Coll. 1820; M.C.; Lawyer.		Keene.	
*Benjamin Wilson	19	Brentwood.	
*Abner Wood	14	Newburyport, Mass.	1820
Supercargo.		Gottenburg, Sweden.	
*Benjamin Woodbury	20	New London, Conn.	1845
Dart. Coll. 1817; A.M.; Clergyman.		Plain, O.	

46

1814.

*Charles Benjamin Abbot	9	Exeter	1874
Farmer.		Glenburn, Me.	
Joseph Adams	17	Boston, Mass.	
George Bowen	11	Providence, R.I.	
Henry Briggs	16	Chatham, Mass.	
*Joseph Burley	21	Lee	1818
Teacher.		"	
Charles Chamberlain	12	Bridgetown, Me.	

*Frederic Augustus Cobb ... 12 ... Portland, Me. 1848
H.U. 1820; A.M.   Boston, Mass.
*Rufus Coffin .... 12 ... Epping.
*John Currier .... 13 ... Dover 1860
Merchant.   "
Thomas Currier .... 13 ... Dover.
                                  "
Carlton Dole .... 16 ... Alna, Me.
*Retier Parker Dow ...... 13 ... Exeter 1834
Business.   "
*Jeremiah Dow .... 11 ... Exeter 1836
Business.   "
*Andrew Leonard Emerson .. 12 ... York, Me. 1835
H.U. 1820; A.M.; LL.B.; Lawyer.   "   "
Moses J. Emery .... 14 ... Haverhill, Mass.
Farmer.   "   "
James Gerrish .... 22 ... Wenham, Mass.
Hollis Gerry .... 22 ... Sterling, Mass.
*Daniel Gilman .... 9 ... Exeter 1840
Merchant.   China.
Ezra Greene .... 19 ... Malden, Mass.
*Thomas W. Hale .... 17 ... Dover 1855
                     Lee.
*Charles Burdett Halsey .... 12 ... Providence, R.I. ... 1829
B.U. 1821; A.M.
*Samuel Hatch .... 11 ... Exeter 1873
H.U. 1821; A.M.; M.D.; Physician.   Hannibal, Mo.
John Hayden .... 13 ... Cambridgeport, Mass.
John Hodgdon .... 14 ... Dover.
Ivory Jefferds .... 15 ... Kennebunk, Me.
Payson Kendall .... 12 ... Weston, Mass.
William Frederic Lawrence .. 10 ... Exeter.
Merchant.   Epping.
*George Lee .... 17 ... Wiscasset, Me. ... ? 1825
James Lord .... 16 ... Effingham.
Levi Hilton Mead .... 16 ... Northwood.
Farmer.   "
John P. Mellen .... 15 ... Exeter.
*Samuel Morrill .... 14 ... Wells, Me. 1872
Bowd. Coll. 1820; A.M.; M.D.; Physician.   Boston, Mass.
Ebenezer H. Neil .... 16 ... Newmarket.
*Nathaniel Pearson ...... 16 ... Exeter 1841
Tanner.   Exeter.
*John Pedrick .... 10 ... Marblehead, Mass.
                                  "   "
*John Porter .... ,..... 22 ... Rye 1825
H.U. 1819; A.M.; Preacher.   Roxbury, Mass.
*John H. Ropes .... 15 ... Salem, Mass. 1820
                                  "   "
Henry R. Sadler .... 16 ... St. Mary's, Ga.
Charles Chauncy Sewall .... 12 ... Marblehead, Mass.
Clergyman (retired).   Medfield, Mass.
Burley Smart .... 22 ... Parsonsfield, Me.
M.D.; Physician.   Kennebunk, Me.
*Jonathan Smith .... 16 ... Peterborough 1840
H.U. 1819; A.M.; Lawyer.   Bath.
Henry Smith .... 11 ... Providence, R.I.

*Charles Stevens . . . . 15 . . . Beverly, Mass. . . . 1863
  Merchant.   "   "
James Tappan . . . . 11 . . . Gloucester, Mass.
John E. Trask . . . . 13 . . . Goffstown.
*Charles Walker . . . . 14 . . . Portsmouth 1856
  Miller.   Brooklyn, N.Y.
Caleb Wiggin . . . . 17 . . . Stratham.
  Farmer.   "
                                                        47

1815.

*John T. Apthorp . . . . 12 . . . Roxbury, Mass. . . . 1881
                                         Melrose, Mass.
*John P. Atkinson . . . . 14 . . . Dover 1825
                                         "
Benjamin Barker . . . . 16 . . . Rochester.
*Ward Chipman Brooks . . . . 11 . . . Boston, Mass. 1828
  H.U. 1822; A.M.; Merchant.   Baltimore, Md.
*Lawrence Brown . . . . 18 . . . Epping 1875
  Farmer.   Harristown, Ill.
*Welcome Arnold Burges . . . 13 . . . Providence, R.I. . . 1828
  B.U. 1820; Lawyer.   "   "
Galen C. Carter . . . . 20 . . . Bethel, Me.
  Middlebury Coll. 1819; A.M.
*Oliver W. Conner . . . . 14 . . . Exeter 1839
  Printer.   Boston, Mass.
*Abraham Drake Dearborn . . 13 . . . Exeter 1871
  M.D.
*John Samuel Hayes Durell . . 16 . . . Dover 1862
  Lawyer.   "
*Edward Henry Edes . . . . . 12 . . . Boston, Mass. 1845
  Clergyman.   "   "
*John Etheridge . . . . 13 . . . Charlestown, Mass.
                                         "   "
*William Jewett Farley . . . . 13 . . . Waldoborough, Me. . 1839
  Bowd. Coll. 1820; A.M.; Lawyer.   Thomaston, Me.
*Ebenezer Farley . . . . 11 . . . Boston, Mass. . . . 1850
  Merchant.   "   "
*Joseph Henry Farley . . . . . 10 . . . Boston, Mass. . . . 1860
  H.U. 1823; A.M.; Business.   "   "
*George Ffrost . . . . 14 . . . Durham 1879
  Merchant.   "
*David Wood Gorham . . . . . 15 . . . Canandaigua, N.Y. . 1873
  H.U. 1821; M.D.; Physician.   Exeter.
*Winthrop Gray . . . . 11 . . . Medford, Mass. . . . 1830
*Walter G. Greene . . . . 15 . . . Dover 1875
  Merchant.   Boston, Mass.
William R. Greene . . . . . . 15 . . . Providence, R.I.
William P. Hale . . . . 13 . . . Rochester.
Alpheus Hanscom . . . . 19 . . . Elliot, Me.
*Charles Harvey . . . . 14 . . . Northwood 1823
  Student.   "
George C. Johnston . . . . . . 14 . . . Hillsborough.
*Prescott Lawrence . . . . . . 20 . . . Epping 1834
  M.D.; Physician.   "
Jonas C. March . . . . 15 . . . Rochester.
Elias Megregory . . . . 26 . . . Newport, R.I.

George F. Mellen . . . . 11 . . . Exeter.
Nathan Merrill . . . . 17 . . . South Hampton.
Gilman Merrill . . . . 23 . . . Grafton.
*John Mooney . . . . 17 . . . Durham 1872
  Business.
Moses Merrill . . . . 12 . . . Wells, Me.
*Woodbury Langdon Orne . . . 17 . . . Wolfborough 1827
  Teacher.
*Frederic French Orne . . . . . 19 . . . Wolfborough 1822
Isaac H. Perkins . . . . 14 . . . Hanover.
Ebenezer Prescott . . . . 14 . . . Raymond.
  Farmer.   Monmouth, Me.
*Plumer Prescott . . . . 19 . . . Sanbornton 1850
  Business.   St. Louis.
Benjamin J. Randall . . . . . 19 . . . Hollis, Me.
Alexander Rice . . . . 15 . . . Kittery, Me.
Amos A. Richards . . . . . . 21 . . . Boston, Mass.
Edward Rowe . . . . 10 . . . Exeter.
  Tanner.   Skowhegan, Me.
*Edward Rundlett . . . . 10 . . . Portsmouth 1874
  H.U. 1825; M.D.; Physician.   "
*Charles Soule . . . . 20 . . . Freeport, Me. . . . 1869
  Bowd. Coll. 1821; A.M.; Clergyman.   Portland, Me.
*Charles Harrison Stedman . . 10 . . . Worcester, Mass. . . 1866
  M.D.
*David Robinson Straw . . . 20 . . . Newfield, Me. 1876
  B.U. 1822; Lawyer.   Guilford, Me.
*John Thompson . . . . 14 . . . Durham 1854
  H.U. 1822; A.M.; Farmer.   Moultonborough.
Israel Trask . . . . 18 . . . Goffstown.
Isaac Trask . . . . : 11 . . . Goffstown.
*Jonathan M. Tredick . . . . 12 . . . Portsmouth 1874
Enos Tuck . . . . 23 . . . Farmington, Me.
*Augustus Willard Walker . . 12 . . . Concord 1862
  Merchant.   Sebec, Me.
Benjamin Wheeler . . . . . . 13 . . . Boston, Mass.
*Bernard Whitman . . . . . . 19 . . . Bridgewater, Mass. . 1834
  Clergyman.   Waltham, Mass.
*William Augustus Whitwell . . 11 . . . Boston, Mass. . . . 1865
  H.U. 1824; A.M.; Clergyman.   Brookline, Mass.
*Frederick Henry Whitwell . . 9 . . . Boston, Mass. . . . 1816

55

1816.

*Nathaniel Sheafe Adams . . . 13 . . . Exeter 1849
  Printer.   "
Benjamin Allen . . . . 13 . . . Manchester, Mass.
George Briard . . . . 14 . . . Portsmouth.
Nathan Brown . . . . 23 . . . Stratham.
  Merchant.   New York, N.Y.
James F. Carter . . . . 18 . . . Bethel, Mo.
George Chase . . . . 12 . . . Boston, Mass.
John P. Coffin . . . . 11 . . . Boston, Mass.
Jonathan P. Darling . . . . . 14 . . . Henniker.

Timothy Darling . . . . 17 . . . Henniker 1871
H.U. 1822; Clergyman.   Bergen, N.Y.
*Daniel Dearborn . . . . 12 . . . Concord.
Lawyer.   Northwood.
*Samuel Dodge. . . . . 16 . . . Wenham, Mass. . . 1833
H.U. 1822; A.M.; M.D.; Physician.   "   "
William Dorr . . . . 13 . . . Boston, Mass.
*William Bradley Dorr . . . . . 13 . . . Boston, Mass. . . . 1875
H.U. 1821; A.M.   "   "
John Dow . . . . 17 . . . Salem.
*Alfred W. L. Elwyn . . . . . 12 . . . Portsmouth 1848
M.D.; Physician.   Philadelphia, Pa.
*Isaac Lord Folsom . . . . . 14 . . . Exeter 1851
Insurance Agent.   "
Ebenezer F. Gardner . . . . . 14 . . . Lynn, Mass.
John Taylor Gilman . . . . . 10 . . . Exeter.
Bowd. Coll. 1826; M.D.; Physician.   Portland, Me.
*William Dawes Hammond . . 10 . . . Boston, Mass. 1835
H.U. 1827; A.M.   West Indies.
*Robert Harris . . . . 14 . . . Portsmouth 1822
Midshipman, U.S. Navy.   "
*Richard Hildreth . . . . 9 . . . Exeter 1865
H.U. 1826; Editor and Author.   Boston, Mass.
*George Oliver Hilton . . . . 11 . . . Newmarket 1866
  "

Asa B. Hogins . . . . 24 . . . Piermont.
*Peter Holt . . . . 15 . . . Epping 1817
*Jeremiah Holt . . . . 13 . . . Epping 1816
Aaron Beede Hoyt . . . . . . 14 . . . Sandwich.
Dart. Coll. 1822; Farmer.   "
Amasa Jackson . . . . 11 . . . Middletown, Conn.
*Robert Jenkins . . . . 11 . . . Newburyport, Mass. 1822
Clerk.   "   "
*Theodore Kittredge . . . . . 14 . . . Epping 1879
M.D.; Physician.   Waltham, Mass.
*Phineas Miller Kollock . . . . 12 . . . Savannah, Ga. . . . 1872
H.U. 1823; M.D.; Physician.   "   "
*Calvin B. Magoun. . . . . . 18 . . . East Kingston . . . 1838
M.D.; Physician.   Woodville, Va.
*William Pitt Moses . . . . . 12 . . . Exeter 1863
Business.   "
*Horatio Gates Nelson . . . . 16 . . . Exeter 1831
Business.   Fayetville, N.C.
Oliver William Osborne . . . . 18 . . . Exeter.
Business.   Boston, Mass.
*Isaac Dow Parsons . . . . . . 17 . . . Rye 1850
Merchant.   Portsmouth.
Jonathan Phillips . . . . 16 . . . Lynn, Mass.
*John Porter . . . . 16 . . . Windham 1825
Charles Prescott. . . . . 15 . . . Newburyport, Mass.
Charles Richards . . . . 13 . . . Boston, Mass.
*Henry Perkins Salter . . . . . 14 . . . Portsmouth 1851
Merchant.   "
John Savage . . . . 14 . . . York, Me.
*Thomas Simpson . . . . 28 . . . Deerfield 1872
Clergyman.   Wisconsin.
Charles A. Swasey . . . . . . 16 . . . Exeter.

40   CATALOGUE.   [1816–17.

*Supply Clapp Thwing . . . . . 17 . . . Boston, Mass. 1877
  Merchant.   "   "
 Frederic Thomas . . . . 11 . . . Windsor, Vt.
*Nathaniel Gookin Upham . . 15 . . . Rochester 1869
  Dart. Coll. 1820; A.M.; LL.D.; Lawyer; Judge   Concord.
  Supr. Ct. N.H.
 Daniel Waldo . . . . 17 . . . Suffield, Conn.
*Jonathan Ward . . . . 18 . . . Alna, Me. 1826
  Dart. Coll. 1822; Clergyman.   Biddeford, Me.
 Wilson Ward . . . . 13 . . . Alna, Me.
 George M. Young . . . . . . 14 . . . Poughkeepsie, N.Y.
                                                              50

1817.

*Nathan Batchelder . . . . . . 16 . . . Epping 1834
  Business.   "
 Charles Barber . . . . 21 . . . Chelmsford, Mass.
*John McClintock Bartlett . . . 15 . . . Brattleborough, Vt. . 1849
  Bowd. Coll. 1823; Business.   Gibraltar.
 Christopher Bassett . . . . . . 13 . . . Newburyport, Mass.
  Manufacturer.   Salisbury.
 Andrew Watkins Bell . . . . . 14 . . . Portsmouth.
  Bookkeeper.   Brooklyn, N.Y.
 Gardiner Greene Chandler . . 11 . . . Boston, Mass.
  Artist.   Salem, Mass.
*Jonathan Chapman . . . . . . 10 . . . Boston, Mass. . . . 1848
  H.U. 1825; A.M.; Lawyer.   "   "
*Thomas Sheafe Coffin . . . . . 13 . . . Portsmouth 1879
  Shipmaster.   "
*Elijah Colburn . . . . 22 . . . Nottingham, West . 1881
  M.D.; Physician.   Nashua.
*Samuel Danforth . . . . 13 . . . Dorchester, Mass. . 1822
*Allen Washington Dodge . . . 13 . . . Newburyport, Mass. 1878
  H.U. 1826; Treasurer.   Wenham, Mass.
*Samuel Fox Dorr . . . . 12 . . . Boston, Mass. . . . 1844
  Merchant.   New York, N.Y.
*Thomas Wilson Dorr . . . . . 11 . . . Providence, R.I. . . 1854
  H.U. 1823; A.M.; Lawyer; Gov. R.I.   "   "
*William Dwight . . . . 12 . . . Springfield, Mass. . 1880
  Merchant.   Boston, Mass.
*Charles H. L. Elwyn . . . . . 10 . . . Portsmouth 1848
  H.U. 1826; A.M.; Lawyer.   New Orleans, La.
 Charles Andrews Farley . . . 12 . . . Boston, Mass.
  H.U. 1827; Clergyman (retired).   "   "
*Samuel Phillips Fisk . . . . . 16 . . . Claremont 1879
  Merchant.   "
*Daniel Gilman . . . . 12 . . . Exeter 1840
  Merchant.   China.
*George William Gordon . . . 15 . . . Exeter 1877
  Merchant; Consul Rio Janeiro.   Boston, Mass.
 William Hale . . . . 12 . . . Dover.
  Bowd. Coll. 1825; Merchant.   "
*Robert Louis Harris . . . . . 15 . . . Portsmouth 1828
  Mariner.   "
 William Hayward . . . . 12 . . . Boston, Mass.
*Josiah Stacy Hook . . . . . . 15 . . . Castine, Me. 1844
  Bowd. Coll. 1823; A.M.; M.D.; Physician. Adrian, Mich.

*John C. Jenkins 17	. . . Canandaigua, N.Y. .	1836
*Gilbert T. Jenkins 17	. . . Canandaigua, N.Y. .	1832
*John Kelly 21	. . . Plaistow	1877
Amh. Coll. 1825; A.M.; Lawyer.	Atkinson.	
*John Gale Merrill 20	. . . Nottingham.	
B.U. 1821; A.M.; M.D.		
*Samuel Moody 20	. . . York, Me.	1874
H.U. 1823.	Lisbon, Me.	
Abraham Moore 17	. . . Castine, Me.	
*Woodbridge Odlin 12	. . . Exeter.	
Wool Merchant	"	
*John Ham Williams Page . . . 14	. . . Gilmanton	1865
H.U. 1826; A.M.; Lawyer.	New Bedford, Mass.	
*William Frederic Rowland . . 10	. . . Exeter	1849
Yale Coll. 1826; Farmer.	"	
*George Robert Russell 17	. . . Providence, R.I. . .	1866
B.U. 1821; LL.D.; Lawyer.	" "	
*Francis Ormond Jonathan Smith 10	. . . Exeter	1876
Lawyer.	Portland, Me.	
Jonathan Ambrose Smith . . . 15	. . . Deerfield.	
M.D.; Physician.	Methuen, Mass.	
Russell Sturgis 12	. . . Boston, Mass.	
H.U. 1823; Banker.	London, Eng.	
*Henry Parkman Sturgis 10	. . . Boston, Mass.	1869
Merchant [Manila, Philippine Islands].	" "	
*Francis B. Todd 12	. . . Newburyport, Mass.	1841
Shipmaster.	" "	
Harris Turner 19	. . . Lyme.	
*Benjamin Greene Wainwright . 11	. . . Boston, Mass. . . .	1875
Merchant.	New York, N.Y.	
*Eliphalet K. Webster 15	. . . Hampton	1881
M.D.; Physician.	Boscawen.	
*Oliver C. Wyman 12	. . . Boston, Mass.	1877
Government Service.	" "	

1818.

William Boott 13	. . . Boston, Mass.	
*Henry Brooks 11	. . . Boston, Mass.	1833
*Dummer Rogers Chapman . . 10	. . . Boston, Mass.	1865
Broker.	" "	
*Horatio Gates Cilley 12	. . . Deerfield	1874
Dart. Coll. 1826; A.M.; Lawyer.	Lewiston, Me.	
*Hampden Cutts 16	. . . Portsmouth	1875
H.U. 1823; A.M.; Lawyer.	Hartland, Vt.	
*Samuel W. Dow 14	. . . Dover	1837
M.D.; Physician.	"	
William Ffrost 15	. . . Durham.	
Business.	"	
Lyman Gilman 15	. . . York, Me.	
*John Mark Gourgas 14	. . . Dorchester, Mass. . .	1862
H.U. 1824; A.M.; Lawyer.	Quincy, Mass.	
Samuel Greenleaf 13	. . . Salisbury.	
*Joseph Whipple Harris 14	. . . Portsmouth	1837
Lieut. U.S. Navy.	"	
*Herman Bremer Harris 17	. . . Portsmouth	1852
Merchant.	Masilon, O.	

*Edward Pratt Harris . . . . . 16 . . . Windham 1868
  Dart. Coll. 1826; A.M.; Lawyer. Avon, Mich.
*William Hatch . . . . 12 . . . Exeter 1876
  Bowd. Coll. 1824; A.M.; M.D.; Physician. Bloomington, Ill.
*William A. Hayden . . . . . . 13 . . . Cambridgeport, Mass. 1876
Hiram Hayes Hobbs . . . . . 17 . . . Berwick, Me.
  Bowd. Coll. 1823; Lawyer. South Berwick, Me.
Francis Carter Jenckes . . . . 15 . . . Providence, R.I.
  B.U. 1824. Havana.
Francis W. Jenkins . . . . . . 14 . . . New Haven, Conn.
George Lunt . . . . 15 . . . Newburyport, Mass.
  H.U. 1824; Editor and Author. Scituate, Mass.
*Alfred Mason . . . . 14 . . . Portsmouth 1828
  Bowd. Coll. 1825; M.D.; Physician. Boston, Mass.
*James J. Mason . . . . 12 . . . Portsmouth.
  Merchant. Boston, Mass.
Samuel McClintock . . . . . . 13 . . . Portsmouth.
*John McDonald . . . . 17 . . . Limerick, Me. 1867
  Bowd. Coll. 1823; A.M. Bangor, Me.
William P. Mellen . . . . . . 12 . . . Exeter.
*William Edward Payne . . 14 . . . Boston, Mass. 1838
  H.U. 1824; A.M. Paris, France.
Edward W. Payne . . . . . . 14 . . . Boston, Mass.
Henry Perkins . . . . 13 . . . Hanover.
*William Prentiss . . . . 15 . . . Medfield, Mass. . . . 1834
  H.U. 1825; A.M.; Teacher. Maryland.
*John Paul Robinson . . . . . 18 . . . Dover 1864
  H.U. 1823; A.M.; Lawyer. Lowell, Mass.
James Samuel Rowe . . . . 10 . . . Exeter.
  Bowd. Coll. 1826; Lawyer. Bangor, Me.
Rufus Rowe . . . . 20 . . . Exeter.
  Business. California.
*John Dennison Russ . . . . . 17 . . . Ipswich, Mass. . . . 1881
  Yale Coll. 1823; M.D.; Physician. Pompton, Conn.
*John Smith . . . . 21 . . . Peterborough 1822
  Business. "
*Jason Whitman . . . . 19 . . . Bridgewater, Mass. . . 1848
  H.U. 1825; A.M.; Clergyman. Lexington, Mass.
John Wilson . . . . 19 . . . Brentwood.

35

1819.

*William Bainbridge . . . . . . 12 . . . Boston, Mass. 1831
Francis R. Bigelow . . . . . . 13 . . . Medford, Mass.
*Samuel Burnham Buzell . . . 17 . . . Northwood 1852
  Farmer and Teacher. "
*George Washington Buzell . . 16 . . . Northwood 1830
  Farmer. "
*Solomon Clarke Buzell . . . 13 . . . Northwood 1882
  Treasurer P.E.A. Exeter.
*George Chapman . . . . . . 12 . . . Boston, Mass. 1834
  Clergyman. Framingham, Mass.
*Joseph Cloyes . . . . 15 . . . Charlestown, Mass.
  Teacher. Mobile, Ala.
*Augustus Gilman Deal . . . 18 . . . Exeter.
  Printer. "

*Charles C. P. Gale	20	Exeter	1838
Yale Coll. 1826; Teacher.		Derry.	
Joseph C. Gardner	12	Dorchester.	
*Charles Gilman	12	Bangor, Me.	1849
B.U. 1827; Lawyer.		Quincy, Ill.	
*Edward William Hook	12	Castine, Me.	1871
H.U. 1827; M.D.			
Joseph Sherbourne Jenckes	15	Providence, R.I.	
B.U. 1824; A.M.		Fairfax, Va.	
*Jerathmell Bowers Jenckes	12	Providence, R.I.	1848
B.U. 1825.			
*Samuel Junkins	19	York, Me.	1826
		Portland, Me.	
*Timothy Wiggin Little	14	Salisbury	1863
Business.		Manchester.	
*George Royal Makepeace	13	Cambridgeport, Mass.	1882
		Waltham, Mass.	
James Murdock	13	Havana, W.I.	
Shipmaster (retired).		Boston, Mass.	
*Charles Tracy Murdock	12	Havana, W.I.	1853
H.U. 1828; A.M.; LL.B.; Lawyer.		Cambridge, Mass.	
Thomas J. Parsons	15	Rye.	
Business.			
Oliver Porter	17	Waterford, Me.	
Business.			
*Benjamin Ridgeway	17	Philadelphia, Pa.	
John Langdon Sibley	14	Union, Me.	
H.U. 1825; A.M.; Clergyman; Librarian Emeritus H.U.; Author.		Cambridge, Mass.	
Josiah Smith	15	St. Augustine, Fla.	
Richard S. Stearns	16	Salem, Mass.	
*Samuel Henry Tudor	15	Hartford, Conn.	1844
William E. Wells	14	Hartford, Conn.	
*Charles Edward Whitwell	10	Boston, Mass.	1879
		" "	

28

1820.

Joshua Brackett	12	Greenland.	
*Stephen C. Brewster	16	Buxton, Me.	
*Alfred Chadwick	11	Exeter	1869
Business.		St. Louis, Mo.	
*Edward Groves Chamberlain	12	Exeter	1828
Business.		St. Jago de Cuba.	
*Joseph Longfellow Cilley	16	Nottingham	1868
Farmer.		Exeter.	
Allen Dorr	12	Providence, R.I.	
		Cumberland, R.I.	
*Jeremiah Dow	21	Kensington	1875
M.D.; Physician.		Hiram, Me.	
Alfred F. Dunham	14	New York, N.Y.	
*William Elliot	16	Marblehead, Mass.	1872
Dart. Coll. 1826; Lawyer.		Lewiston, Ill.	
*Joseph Farley	11	Ipswich, Mass.	1871
Francis Dennison Farley	11	Boston, Mass.	
Farmer.		Davenport, Iowa.	
*William Henry Gardner	13	Exeter	1873
Hotelkeeper.		Boston, Mass.	

*John Thomas Goddard . . . . 14 . . . Portsmouth 1837
  Capitalist.   "
*John Parker Hale . . . . . . 14 . . . Rochester 1874
  Bowd. Coll. 1827; LL.D.; Lawyer; M.C.; U.S. Dover.
  Sen.; Min. to Spain.
*Josiah Stover Little . . . . . . 19 . . . Newbury, Mass. . . 1862
  Bowd. Coll. 1825; A.M.; Lawyer.   Portland, Me.
*George W. Magoun . . . . . . 19 . . . East Kingston.
*George Mills . . . . 11 . . . Deerfield 1827
  Teacher.   Exeter.
 Josiah Preble Moody . . . . . 15 . . . York, Me.
  Bowd. Coll. 1827; Farmer.   Hampstead.
*Samuel Orr . . . . 17 . . . Bridgewater, Mass. . 1878
  M.D.; Physician.   E. Bridgewater, Mass.
 Oliver Peabody Pearse . . . . 12 . . . Portsmouth.
  Merchant.   Philadelphia, Pa.
*William Langdon Pickering . . 15 . . . Newington.
  Merchant.   New York, N.Y.
 Isaac Pitman . . . . 13 . . . Providence, R.I.
  Business (retired).   Somerville, Mass.
 Romulus Poole . . . . 15 . . . Gloucester, Mass.
 Augustus Luther Richardson . 15 . . . Boston, Mass.
  Merchant.   Cuba.
*Daniel H. Rundlett . . . . . . 12 . . . Exeter 1840
*Charles Gilman Safford . . . . 15 . . . Exeter 1847
  Dart. Coll. 1827; M.D.; Physician. Rutland, Mass.
*Francis George Shaw . . . . . 11 . . . Boston, Mass. . . . 1882
                                    Staten Island, N.Y.
*George Sheafe . . . . 13 . . . Portsmouth 1825
*John Fisher Sheafe . . . . . . 14 . . . Portsmouth 1882
  Capitalist.   New York, N.Y.
*John Frederic Skinner . . . . 13 . . . Charlestown, Mass.
  Merchant.   Concord, Mass.
 Charles A. Thompson . . . . . 12 . . . Baltimore, Md.
*John Rogers Thurston . . . . 11 . . . Exeter 1843
  H.U. 1829; A.M.; Lawyer.   Glenburn, Me.
*James Thurston . . . . 13 . . . Exeter 1872
  H.U. 1829; A.M.; Clergyman.   West Newton, Mass.
*Charles T. Ward . . . . 13 . . . Boston, Mass. . . . 1877
  Merchant.   "   "
 Jonas Whitman . . . . 15 . . . Barnstable, Mass.
 Charles Wirgman . . . . 10 . . . Baltimore, Md.
*Moses Emery Woodman . . 14 . . . Fryeburg, Me. . . . 1840
  Bowd. Coll. 1826; Lawyer.   Brunswick, Me.
                                                          37

1821.

*George Frederic Amory . . . . 12 . . . Dorchester, Mass. . 1850
  Farmer.   Iowa.
 Samuel W. Archer . . . . . . 15 . . . Philadelphia, Pa.
*William K. Atkinson . . . . . 14 . . . Dover 1837
                                      "
*Henry Vose Baxter . . . . . . 15 . . . Quincy, Mass. . . . 1867
                                    New Orleans, La.
*Samuel Stillman Boyd . . . . 14 . . . Portland, Me. 1867
  Bowd. Coll. 1826; Lawyer; Jud. Supr. Ct. Miss. Natchez, Miss.
 Washington Brown . . . . . . 13 . . . Portsmouth.

CATALOGUE.

*Charles Parker Coffin . . . . . 12 . . . Beaufort, S.C. . . . 1868
  H.U. 1828; M.D.; Physician.   Pontatoch, Mich.
John Templeman Coolidge . . 11 . . . Boston, Mass.
  Pres. Columbian Bank.   " "
Thomas Tingy Craven . . . . 13 . . . Portsmouth.
  Rear Admiral, U.S.N.   Kittery, Me.
*Alfred W. Craven . . . . 11 . . . Portsmouth 1879
  Civil Engineer.   New York, N.Y.
*Blowers Danforth . . . . 13 . . . Dorchester, Mass. . . 1852
Henry Dow . . . . 16 . . . Dover.
  Farmer.   "
Frederic Henry Dow . . . . . 13 . . . Roxbury, Mass.
*St. John Durell . . . . 15 . . . Dover 1826
  Cadet, West Point.   "
*Charles John Fox Durell . . . 14 . . . Dover 1840
        "
*Thomas Dwight . . . . 13 . . . Springfield, Mass. . . 1876
  H.U. 1827.   Boston, Mass.
*Francis Dwight . . . . 13 . . . Springfield, Mass. . . 1845
  H.U. 1827; Sec. Board of Education.   New York, N.Y.
Alpheus Felch . . . . 16 . . . Limerick, Me.
  Bowd. Coll. 1827; LL.D.; U.S. Sen. 1847–53;   Ann Arbor, Mich.
  Judge Supr. Ct. Mich. 1842–45; Gov. Mich.
  1845–47; Prof. Law, Univ. Mich.
*Charles Edwin Gilman . . . . 13 . . . Exeter 1840
  Mariner.
*John A. Harris . . . . 16 . . . Dorchester, Mass. . . 1882
  Teacher.   South Boston, Mass.
*James Winthrop Harris . . . . 15 . . . Dorchester, Mass. . . 1881
  Secretary.   Cambridge, Mass.
*George Haskell . . . . 22 . . . Waterford, Me. . . . 1876
  Dart. Coll. 1827; M.D.
*Samuel Foster Haven . . . . . 15 . . . Dedham, Mass. . . . 1881
  Amh. Coll. 1826; A.M.; LL.D.; Lawyer.   Worcester, Mass.
John Hodgdon . . . . 20 . . . Weare.
  Bowd. Coll. 1827; Lawyer.   Dubuque, Iowa.
Joshua Holt . . . . 16 . . . Exeter.
*Richard Kimball . . . . 22 . . . Dover 1881
  Lawyer.   "
Joseph W. Munson . . . . . . 14 . . . Chelmsford, Mass.
*George Paine . . . . 14 . . . Williamstown, Vt. . 1836
  Dart. Coll. 1827; Lawyer.   Masilon, O.
*Ephraim Peabody . . . . 14 . . . Wilton 1855
  Bowd. Coll. 1827; D.D.; Clergyman.   Boston, Mass.
Frederic Robinson . . . . . . 22 . . . Exeter.
John J. Sanborn . . . . 24 . . . Epsom.
*James E. Sheafe . . . . 11 . . . Portsmouth 1830
        "

Alfred R. Shute . . . . 10 . . . Exeter.
Forrest Shepherd . . . . 21 . . . Boscawen.
  Dart. Coll. 1827; Geologist.   Potosi, Mo.
William Smith . . . . 21 . . . Cavendish, Vt.
  Farmer.   Proctorsville, Vt.
*Charles Waldron . . . . 15 . . . Dover 1868
  Merchant.   "
*William N. Weston . . . . . . 12 . . . Eastport, Me.
  Lawyer.   " "

1822.

*John Stevens Abbot . . . . . 15 . . . Temple, Me. 1881
   Bowd. Coll. 1827; A.M.; Lawyer.   Thomaston, Me.
Theodore Thomas Abbot . . . 23 . . . Greenland.
   Farmer.   Lunenburg, Mass.
*Lewis G. Barnes. . . . . 14 . . . Portsmouth 1843
   Merchant.   New York, N.Y.
*William Bartol . . . . 15 . . . Portland, Me. 1840
   Merchant.   New York, N.Y.
*Robert Anthony Baxter . . . . 13 . . . Quincy, Mass.
      Providence, R.I.
Thomas Bellows . . . . 14 . . . Walpole.
   Farmer.   "
*William P. Blodgett. . . . . . 13 . . . Providence, R.I. . . 1873
   Business.   "   "
William Thurston Boutwell . . 19 . . . Lynborough.
   Dart. Coll. 1828; Clergyman.
*Charles Dexter Cleveland . . . 19 . . . Charlestown, Mass. . 1869
   Dart. Coll. 1827; A.M.; LL.D.; Teacher.   Philadelphia, Pa.
William Crosby . . . . 15 . . . Dover.
*Alpheus Crosby . . . . 11 . . . Gilmanton 1874
   Dart. Coll. 1827; A.M.; Prof. Lat. and Greek   Hanover.
   Dart. Coll.; Author.
Samuel F. Dearborn . . . . . 12 . . . Exeter.
William A. Doak . . . . 15 . . . Bath, Me.
Valorous Drew . . . . 19 . . . Newfield, Me.
*John Hubbard Eaton . . . . . 16 . . . Boxford, Mass. . . . 1862
   H.U. 1827; A.M.; Clergyman.
Abel Fletcher . . . . 20 . . . Kennebunk, Me.
*Joseph Buckminster Gardner . 10 . . . Exeter 1882
   Business Manager.   Boston, Mass.
*Joseph Taylor Gilman . . . . 10 . . . Exeter 1862
   Merchant [Canton, China].   "
*Albert Gallatin Greene . . . . 13 . . . Bath, Me. 1830
   Bowd. Coll. 1828.   "   "
*Alfred Greenleaf . . . . 18 . . . W. Newbury, Mass. 1872
   Teacher.   "   "
*George Henry Hartwell . . . . 13 . . . Littleton, Mass. . . 1848
   Business.   Cincinnati, O.
Johnson Hatch . . . . 12 . . . Exeter.
   Apothecary.   Jacksonville, Ill.
Horace L. Hazelton . . . . . . 14 . . . Sanbornton.
   Lawyer.   Boston, Mass.
Cyrus Holmes . . . . 21 . . . Halifax, Mass.
Jacob K. Kettell . . . . 19 . . . Limerick, Me.
Jeremiah Kimball . . . . 25 . . . Canterbury.
   Business.   Concord.
Gilman Kimball . . . . 17 . . . New Chester.
   A.M.; M.D.; Prof. Surg. Med. Coll. Vt. and   Lowell, Mass.
   Berks. Med. School; Physician.
*Isaac Knight . . . . 25 . . . Waterford, Me. . . . 1850
   Bowd. Coll. 1829; Clergyman.   Fisherville, N.H.
*William Marrett . . . . 18 . . . Standish, Me. 1859
   M.D.
Jeremiah Willey Marsh . . . . 10 . . . Exeter.
   Preacher.   Virginia.

*Stephen Minor	15	Natchez, Miss.	1830
Cotton Planter.		Vidalia, La.	
*Charles Grandison Parsons	15	Rye	1844
Dart. Coll. 1829; A.M.; M.D.; Physician.		Shongaloo, Miss.	
*James Handyside Perkins	12	Boston, Mass.	1849
Clergyman and Author.		Cincinnati, O.	
*David Pillsbury	20	Candia	1862
Dart. Coll. 1827; Lawyer.		Concord.	
Roman L. Putnam	24	Houlton, Me.	
*George Martin Richmond	14	Providence, R.I.	1866
Business.		" "	
Benjamin M. Saul	14	New Orleans, La.	
*George Yeaton Sawyer	16	Wakefield	1882
Bowd. Coll. 1826; A.M.; Lawyer; Judge Supr. Ct. N.H.		Nashua.	
Luther Dearborn Sawyer	19	Wakefield.	
Bowd. Coll. 1828; Lawyer.		"	
John Sawyer	13	Exeter.	
*Hamilton Smith	17	Durham	1875
Dart. Coll. 1829; Lawyer.		Washington, D.C.	
Moses Soule	18	Freeport, Me.	
Bowd. Coll. 1829; A.M.; Teacher.		Lyons, Iowa.	
*Samuel F. Stevens	11	Exeter	1854
Business.		New York, N.Y.	
*James Sullivan	11	Exeter	1878
Dart. Coll. 1829; Lawyer.		Michigan.	
*John Henry Warland	15	Cambridge, Mass.	1872
H.U. 1827; Editor.		Lowell, Mass.	
*David Wells	18	Deerfield	1876
M.D.; Physician.		Lowell, Mass.	
Lemuel Smith Williams	13	New Bedford, Mass.	
Luther T. Wilson	20	Fairhaven, Mass.	
*Robert Wilson	10	Keene	1870
Amh. Coll. 1832.		"	

49

1823.

*Ezra Abbot	17	Wilton	1876
Bowd. Coll. 1830; Teacher.		Owatonna, Minn.	
Obed E. Adams	21	Medfield, Mass.	
*Horace Bartol	12	Freeport, Me.	1881
Gov't Service.		Washington, D.C.	
*Joseph March Chadwick	10	Exeter	1836
Business.		St. Louis, Mo.	
Lovell Childs	22	Newton, Mass.	
William Conner	14	Exeter.	
Farmer.		"	
Ralph Cutter	13	Portsmouth.	
Merchant.		Brooklyn, N.Y.	
*Oliver C. Demerritt	21	Madbury	1873
Carbuilder.		Lawrence, Mass.	
*Francis Fiske Dorr	12	Boston, Mass.	1870
Merchant.		New York, N.Y.	
George Oliver Harris	13	Charlestown, Mass.	
Bookkeeper (Boston).		Salem, Mass.	
*Charles Hatch	11	Exeter	1825

*Thomas Albert Haven. . . . . 12 . . . Portsmouth 1853
  Merchant.   Philadelphia, Pa.
Thomas T. Helen . . . . 14 . . . Washington, D.C.
*Howard Millet Henderson. . . 20 . . . Dover 1841
  Teacher.   Frankfort, Ky.
*John Hubbard. . . . . 13 . . . Berwick, Me. 1848
  H.U. 1829; A.M.; Lawyer.   South Berwick, Me.
*Charles Currier Ingalls . . . . 15 . . . Durham 1877
  Dart. Coll. 1829; M.D.; Physician.   Andover, Mass.
John Ingalls . . . . 18 . . . Durham.
                                         Andover, Mass.
*Haven Ladd. . . . . 14 . . . Portsmouth 1829
  Dart. Coll. 1829; Teacher.   Philadelphia, Pa.
Henry Ladd . . . . 13 . . . Portsmouth.
  Merchant.   "
*Lewis Flanders Laine . . . . . 17 . . . Loudon.
  Clergyman.   Canistro, N.Y.
*Alexander Hamilton Lawrence 11 . . . Exeter 1857
  Dart. Coll. 1833; LL.B.; Lawyer.   Washington, D.C.
*William Bell Marsh . . . . . . 11 . . . Exeter 1846
  Editor.   Brooklyn, N.Y.
*Alexander McCulloch . . . . . 17 . . . Kennebunk, Me.
Nahum Morrill . . . . 14 . . . Wells, Me.
Joseph Murdoch. . . . . 12 . . . Havana, W.I.
  Insurance Broker.   Boston, Mass.
*James Cook Richmond . . . . 15 . . . Providence, R.I. . . 1866
  H.U. 1828; A.M.; Clergyman; Philanthropist; Poughkeepsie, N.Y.
  Author.
*Thomas Andrews Richmond. . 11 . . . Providence, R.I. . . 1859
  Lawyer.   New York, N.Y.
Charles Russell . . . . 22 . . . Northborough, Mass.
John L. Sherriff. . . . . 15 . . . Exeter.
*Joseph Dennie Tyler . . . . . 19 . . . Brattleborough, Vt. . 1852
  Yale Coll. 1829; A.M.; Teacher.   Staunton, Va.
*John Adams Vinton . . . . . . 22 . . . Boston, Mass. 1877
  Dart. Coll. 1828; A.M.; Clergyman.   "   "
Charles March Weeks. . . . . 14 . . . Greenland.
  M.D.; Physician.   Crawford, Ga.

32

1824.

*Charles Abbot. . . . . 15 . . . Wilton 1878
  Dart. Coll. 1833; Merchant.   Newark, N.J.
William Ebenezer Abbot . . . . 14 . . . Beverly, Mass.
  Bowd. Coll. 1830; Clergyman (retired). Dorchester, Mass.
*Charles Tilden Appleton . . . 15 . . . Baltimore, Md. . . . 1859
  Merchant.   Boston, Mass.
William Channing Appleton. . 11 . . . Baltimore. Md.
  H.U. 1832; LL.B.; Lawyer.   Boston, Mass.
Charles H. Badger . . . . . . 14 . . . Pepperell, Mass.
Elbridge Bradbury . . . . . . 19 . . . Framingham, Mass.
  Amh. Coll. 1831; A.M.; Clergyman.   New Boston, Mass.
William S. Caldwell. . . . . . 13 . . . Newburyport, Mass.
                                         Ipswich, Mass.
William B. Crown. . . . . . . 21 . . . East Kingston.
*David Stearns Devens . . . . . 14 . . . Charlestown, Mass. . 1858
  M.D.; Clergyman; Physician.   Lake Village.

[1824-25.]   CATALOGUE.   49

Samuel Moody Emery . . . . . 20 . . . West Newbury, Mass.
H.U. 1830; A.M.; Clergyman (retired).   "   "
Nathaniel Smith Folsom . . . 17 . . . Portsmouth.
Dart. Coll. D.D.; Prof. West. Res. Coll. 1833–36;   Wellesley Hills, Mass.
Prof. Meadville Sem. 1849–61; Clergyman
(retired).
*William Emerson Foster . . . 15 . . . Boston, Mass. . . . 1842
H.U. 1829; A.M.; M.D.; Physician.   "   "
*Barzillai Frost . . . . 20 . . . Effingham 1858
H.U. 1830; Clergyman.   Concord, Mass.
Samuel C. Gilman . . . . 24 . . . Buffalo, N.Y.
Albert G. Gridley . . . . 13 . . . Exeter.
Henry Rundlett Hall . . . . . 12 . . . Exeter.
Gov't Service.   Washington, D.C.
Charles Harris . . . . 14 . . . Providence, R.I.
Charles Henry Holmes . . . 14 . . . Alfred, Me.
B.U. 1829.   Topsfield, Mass.
Samuel Jaques . . . . 13 . . . Charlestown, Mass.
Real Estate Broker.   Boston, Mass.
*Minor Kenner . . . . 16 . . . New Orleans, La. . . 1863
Increase Sumner Kimball . . . 22 . . . Dover.
Lawyer.   Sanford, Me.
*George D. Lamson . . . . . . 12 . . . Beverly, Mass. . . . 1841
Mariner.   "   "
*William W. Orne . . . . 13 . . . Springfield, Mass. . 1852
Business.   "   "
Augustus John Rowe . . . . . 12 . . . Exeter.
   "
*Thomas Sparhawk . . . . . . 17 . . . Concord 1874
Dart. Coll. 1828; M.D.; Physician.   "
William H. Sullivan . . . . . . 10 . . . Exeter.
Business.   St. Joseph, Minn.
James Madison Tappan . . . . 13 . . . East Kingston.
Farmer.   "   "
*Abraham Rand Thompson . . 14 . . . Charlestown, Mass. . 1830
Student.
Richard T. Tink . . . . 12 . . . Manchester, Mass.
John Waldron . . . . 19 . . . Farmington.
**Henry Augustus Walker* . . . 14 . . . Charlestown, Mass. . 1838
H.U. 1830; Clergyman.   "   "
Edward White . . . . 13 . . . Haverhill, Mass.
Charles William Woodman . . 14 . . . Rochester.
Dart. Coll. 1829; Lawyer.   Dover.

33

1825.

Abiel Abbot . . . . 16 . . . Wilton.
Bowd. Coll. 1831; Teacher.   Owatonna, Minn.
Charles Aikin . . . . 23 . . . Bedford.
A.M.; Lawyer; Notary Public.   Wright's, Cal.
*William Austin . . . . 13 . . . Charlestown, Mass. . 1835
H.U. 1831; A.M.; Teacher.   Brookline, Mass.
*Otis Baker . . . . 21 . . . Templeton, Mass. . . 1834
Yale Coll. 1831.   "   "
*James Benjamin . . . . 14 . . . Dunstable 1853
H.U. 1830; Lawyer.   Boston, Mass.
Timothy Boutelle . . . . 14 . . . Waterville, Me.
Lawyer.

*Horatio Brooks . . . . 16 . . . Boston, Mass. 1843
   Shipmaster.   "   "
Robert J. Brown . . . . 13 . . . Boston, Mass.
*Henry Phillips Chamberlain . . 13 . . . Exeter 1867
   Merchant.   St. Iago de Cuba.
*Robert Adams Coker . . . . . 18 . . . West Newbury, Mass. 1833
   H.U. 1831; Teacher.   "   "   "
*Ebenezer Ellingwood Cox . . . 11 . . . Beverly, Mass. . . . 1837
   Mariner.   "   "
Samuel Fay . . . . 19 . . . Framingham, Mass.
James P. Fogg . . . . 13 . . . Exeter.
George Albert Frost . . . . . 12 . . . Sanford, Me.
   Merchant.   Springvale, Me.
*John W. Graves . . . . 15 . . . Deerfield 1872
   M.D.; Physician.   Lowell, Mass.
*Charles Howe Greenleaf . . . 19 . . . West Newbury, Mass. 1838
   Dart. Coll. 1832; Teacher.   Brooklyn, N.Y.
George Harris . . . . 13 . . . Boston, Mass.
Charles Harris . . . . 12 . . . Boston, Mass.
   Dentist.   Brooklyn, N.Y.
Jonathan William Hartwell . . 14 . . . Littleton, Mass.
                                               Xenia, O.
Nathaniel Hills . . . . 13 . . . Haverhill, Mass.
Robert G. Hobbs . . . . 14 . . . Weston, Mass.
Nathaniel H. Hubbard . . . 12 . . . Berwick, Me.
   Lawyer.   Winterport, Me.
*Samuel Richards Hutchinson . 13 . . . Alstead 1869
   Miner.   Nevada.
Jeremiah Knight . . . . . . 18 . . . Providence, R.I.
Thomas H. Liddle . . . . . . 14 . . . New Orleans, La.
*Nathaniel Lord . . . . 17 . . . Kennebunk, Me. . . ? 1850
                                               California.
*Ezekiel Marsh . . . . 16 . . . Danvers, Mass. . . . 1844
   Bowd. Coll. 1831; Clergyman.   Ellington, Conn.
Theodore H. McCaleb . . . 15 . . . Port Gibson, Miss.
   Judge U.S. Dist. Ct.   Louisiana.
John Hopkins Morison . . . . 19 . . . Peterborough.
   H.U. 1831; A.M.; D.D.; Clergyman and Author.   Boston, Mass.
Nathan Watson Monroe . . . . 19 . . . Cambridge, Mass.
   H.U. 1830; A.M.; Clergyman.   Greenfield, Mass.
*William Saxon Morton . . . 16 . . . Milton, Mass. 1871
   H.U. 1831; A.M.; Lawyer.
*James Pearson . . . . 14 . . . Waterville, Me. . . . 1868
   Merchant.   Chicago, Ill.
Robert Smith . . . . 12 . . . Exeter.
George Washington Towle . . 15 . . . Epping.
   Clerk.   Newcastle.
*Henry Waldron . . . . 18 . . . Portsmouth 1876
   Bowd. Coll. 1830; Lawyer.   New York, N.Y.
*Nathaniel Wells . . . . 20 . . . Salisbury 1864
   Yale Coll. 1829; M.D.; Physician.   Mississippi.
*Nathaniel Wells . . . . 20 . . . Deerfield 1878
   Lawyer.   Great Falls.

1826.

*William P. Abbot . . . . 14 . . . Dunstable 1880
  Merchant [Boston, Mass.].   Keene.
Benjamin Dana Baxter . . . . 14 . . . Quincy, Mass.
                                        California.
Arthur Burley . . . . 14 . . . Exeter.
  Merchant.   Chicago, Ill.
John Langdon Carlton . . . . 15 . . . Bath.
  Dart. Coll. 1831; Lawyer.   "
*Sullivan Caverno . . . . 19 . . . Strafford 1881
  Dart. Coll. 1831; A.M.; Lawyer.   Lockport, N.Y.
Phineas Conner . . . . 12 . . . Newbury, Mass.
Thomas Conner . . . . 14 . . . Exeter.
  Merchant.   "
*George Caspar Crowninshield . 15 . . . Salem, Mass. 1857
                                         Brookline, Mass.
*James Augustus Dorr . . . . . 13 . . . Boston, Mass. 1869
  H.U. 1832; Lawyer.   New York, N.Y.
*William Henry Duncan . . . . 18 . . . Candia 1883
  Dart. Coll. 1830; A.M.; Lawyer.   Hanover.
Edward Henry Durell . . . . . 15 . . . Dover.
  H.U. 1831; Lawyer; Judge U.S. Dist. Ct.   Louisiana.
*Josiah Henry Folsom . . . . . 18 . . . Exeter 1870
  Farmer.   "
*Moses French Hoit . . . . . . 13 . . . Exeter 1867
  Dart. Coll. 1835; A.M.; Lawyer.   Nevada, Cal.
Calvin Hubbard . . . . 18 . . . Shapleigh, Me.
*George W. Hutchins . . . . . 17 . . . Bath 1839
  Lawyer.   "
*William Parry Jones . . . . . 14 . . . Portsmouth 1872
  Merchant.   "
*John Kimball . . . . 17 . . . Kensington 1868
  Merchant.   Salisbury, Mass.
John McDuffie Knight . . . 14 . . . Rochester.
Abiel Abbot Livermore . . . . 15 . . . Wilton.
  H.U.-1833; A.M.; Clergyman; Pres. Meadville   Meadville, Pa.
  Theol. Sem.; Author.
*Franklin McDuffie . . . . . . 17 . . . Rochester 1832
  Lieut. U.S. Army.
Samuel H. Merrill . . . . . . 21 . . . Buxton, Me.
*John Murdoch . . . . 13 . . . Havana, W.I. 1871
  Merchant.   Boston, Mass.
*William Murdoch . . . . 11 . . . Havana, W.I. . . . 1882
  Planter.   "   "
George Henry Nichols . . . . 11 . . . Portland, Me.
  H.U. 1833; M.D.; Physician.   Boston, Mass.
*Merrill Ordway . . . . 22 . . . West Newbury, Mass. 1830
Hamilton Elliot Perkins . . . . 19 . . . Hopkinton.
  Lawyer.   Concord.
→Huntington Porter . . . . . . 13 . . . Rye 1836
  H.U. 1833.
Thomas Stackpole . . . . . . 19 . . . Rochester.
John B. Stacy . . . . 13 . . . Gloucester, Mass.
*Henry Stearns . . . . 14 . . . Medford, Mass. . . . 1859
Winslow Marston Watson . . 13 . . . Plymouth, Mass.
  H.U. 1833; Journalist.   Washington, D.C.

Morrill Wyman . . . . 14 . . . Charlestown, Mass.
  H.U. 1833; A.M.; M.D.; Adj. Prof. Theory and   Cambridge, Mass.
  Prac. H.U. 1853-56; Physician.
*Jeffries Wyman . . . . 12 . . . Charlestown, Mass. . 1874
  H.U. 1833; A.M.; M.D.; Prof. Anatomy, H.U.;   Cambridge, Mass.
  Author.

33

1827.

*Ezra Abbot . . . . 17 . . . Andover, Mass. . . . 1872
  M.D.; Physician.   Canton, Mass.
Josiah Abbot . . . . 16 . . . Framingham, Mass.
  Yale Coll. 1835; A.M.; M.D.; Physician.   Winchendon, Mass.
*Ebenezer Adams . . . . 13 . . . Hanover 1837
  Dart. Coll. 1831; A.M.; Teacher.   "
*Levi S. Bartlett . . . . 15 . . . Kingston 1865
  M.D.; Physician.   "
*Joseph L. Beckett . . . . 13 . . . Exeter 1882
  Printer (Boston, Mass.).   Brentwood.
Seth Bemis . . . . 13 . . . Watertown, Mass.
  Manufacturer.   "   "
*Alexander Ramsey Bradley . . 17 . . . Hollis, Me. 1862
  H.U. 1831; Lawyer.   Fryeburg, Me.
Daniel Bray . . . . 13 . . . Salem, Mass.
George E. Brodhead . . . . . 13 . . . Newmarket.
  Business.   New York, N.Y.
John S. Brown . . . . 20 . . . New Ipswich.
  Editor.   Kansas.
*Edmund Chadwick . . . . . . 11 . . . Exeter 1879
  Business [St. Louis].   "
Jacob Chapman . . . . 17 . . . Tamworth.
  Dart. Coll. 1835; A.M.; Clergyman.   Exeter.
John Copp . . . . 18 . . . Wakefield.
  Bowd. Coll. 1832; A.M.; Teacher.   "
*John Morrill Currier . . . . . 18 . . . Amesbury, Mass. . . 1844
  Yale Coll. 1833; M.D.; Physician.   Woodville, Miss.
*Gilman Dane . . . . 22 . . . Greenfield, Mass. . . 1839
  Union Coll. 1833; Agent.   "   "
George Washington Dearborn . 12 . . . Exeter.
  Business.   "
John Adams Dearborn . . . . 12 . . . Exeter.
  Business.   Oakland, Cal.
John Homer Dix . . . . 14 . . . Boston, Mass.
  H.U. 1833; M.D.; Oculist.   "   "
Joseph W. Ellis . . . . 15 . . . Exeter.
John N. Evans . . . . 17 . . . Louisiana.
*Edward Gray Fales . . . . . . 15 . . . Boston, Mass. 1842
  Bowd. Coll. 1832; LL.B.; Lawyer.   Baltimore, Md.
Moses Hall Fitts . . . . 19 . . . Candia.
  Dart. Coll. 1831; A.M.; Lawyer.   San Francisco, Cal.
*Henry French . . . . 13 . . . Kingston 1840
  Dart. Coll. 1836; Instructor P.E.A.   Exeter.
*Christopher Gore Greene . . . 18 . . . Saco, Me. 1853
Timothy Gridley . . . . 13 . . . Exeter.
James Hall . . . . 23 . . . Cambridge, Mass.
*Joseph Harrington . . . . . . 14 . . . Roxbury, Mass. . . . 1852
  H.U. 1833; A.M.; Clergyman.

John Walker Hartwell . . . . 14 . . . Littleton, Mass.
Insurance Agent.   Cincinnati, O.
*Silas Holman Hill . . . . 19 . . . Portsmouth 1860
Dart. Coll. 1832; A.M.; Lawyer.   Washington, D.C.
*Charles Davis Jackson . . . . 17 . . . Salem, Mass. 1871
Dart. Coll. 1833; D.D.; Clergyman.   Westchester, N.Y.
*Robert Tucker Kerr . . . . . . 16 . . . New Orleans, La.
Thomas C. Lane . . . . 17 . . . Hollis, Me.
Frederic A. Locke . . . . . . 17 . . . Boston, Mass.
*Benjamin F. Magoun . . . . . 20 . . . East Kingston. . . . 1829
  "   "
Richard S. Maloney . . . . . . 16 . . . Northfield.
*Henry Brown Osgood . . . . . 15 . . . Fryeburg, Me. . . . 1843
Bowd. Coll. 1832; Lawyer.   Portland, Me.
*William Harrison Parsons. . . 14 . . . Rye 1867
Shipmaster.
Benjamin Perkins . . . . 19 . . . Exeter.
Farmer.   "
John Lewis Ringe . . . . 23 . . . Alton.
William G. Smith . . . . 20 . . . England.
Henry Gookin Storer . . . . . 13 . . . Scarborough, Me.
Bowd. Coll. 1832; A.M.; Clergyman.   "   "
*George Sturgis . . . . 10 . . . Boston, Mass. 1857
Merchant.   Manila, Philippine Islands.
*Henry Tuck . . . . 29 . . . Kensington 1845
M.D.
Nathaniel Saville Tucker . . . 13 . . . Newton, Mass.
H.U. 1833; A.M.; M.D.; Physician.   Illinois.
David D. Wedgwood . . . . . 15 . . . Exeter.
*Theodore Wells . . . . 20 . . . Deerfield 1862
M.D.; Physician.   Scarborough, Me.
John B. Wentworth . . . . . . 14 . . . Exeter.
Business.   Lynn, Mass.
Oramel White . . . . 20 . . . Randolph, Mass.
*Asa Woodbury . . . . 16 . . . Beverly, Mass. . . . 1844
Jeweller.   New York, N.Y.
Jere. Hall Woodman . . . . . 15 . . . Rochester.
Farmer.   Ashtabula, O.

50

1828.

*Rufus Abbot . . . . 20 . . . Wilton 1873
Yale Coll. 1833; M.D.; Physician.   Pleasant Hills, Mo.
*George Jacob Abbot . . . . . 15 . . . Windham 1879
H.U. 1835; A.M.; U.S. Consul, Sheffield, Eng.;   Meadville, Pa.
Prof. Latin, Meadville Theol. Sem.
Charles Vose Bemis . . . . . . 12 . . . Watertown, Mass.
H.U. 1835; M.D.; Physician.   Medford, Mass.
Lyman Blake . . . . 18 . . . Chichester.
John J. Bradley . . . .
Union Coll. 1835.
*Cyrus Parker Bradley . . . . 10 . . . Concord 1838
Dart. Coll. 1837.   "
Thomas S. Bradley . . . . . . 17 . . . Fryeburg, Me.
Payton Bradshaw . . . . 19 . . . Prince Edward's Island,Va.
Isaac Austin Brooks . . . . . 14 . . . Charlestown.
  Cambridge.

George Chandler . . . . 18 . . . Fryeburg, Me.
Rufus W. Clark . . . . 14 . . . Newbury, Mass.
  Clergyman.   Albany, N.Y.
Elias M. Clark . . . . 16 . . . Winthrop, Me.
*Horatio Coffin . . . . 16 . . . Portsmouth 1857
  Capitalist.   "
*Phineas Sanborn Conner . . . 15 . . . Newbury, Mass. . . 1854
  Dart. Coll. 1835; M.D.; Physician.   Cincinnati, O.
Edwin Coolidge . . . . 16 . . . Boston, Mass.
Samuel Dodge . . . . 13 . . . Portsmouth.
Henry Joseph Gardner . . . . 10 . . . Dorchester.
  Gov. Mass. 1855-7; Business.   Chicago, Ill.
James M. Goodwin . . . . . . 21 . . . Saco, Me.
Elisha Goodwin . . . . 18 . . . Saco, Me.
Samuel T. Gove . . . . 15 . . . St. John, N.B.
  M.D.; Physician.   St. Andrew, C.B.
*Albert F. Hanson . . . . 14 . . . Dover 1858
  Merchant.   Philadelphia, Pa.
Henry Francis Harrington . . 14 . . . Roxbury, Mass.
  H.U. 1834; Clergyman.   New Bedford, Mass.
James Lawrence Hartwell . . . 13 . . . Littleton, Mass.
  Contractor.   New York, N.Y.
*Hugh Horatio Henry . . . . . 13 . . . Rockingham, Vt. . . 1869
  Dart. Coll. 1833.   Chester.
John L. Jewell . . . . 14 . . . Stratham.
  Business.   "
Alexander Hamilton Ladd . . 13 . . . Portsmouth.
  Merchant.   "
*Nathaniel Knowles Lombard . 20 . . . Boston, Mass. 1876
  Merchant.   Smyrna.
*James Henry Mitchell . . . . . 15 . . . Bridgewater, Mass. . 1872
  Merchant (Boston, Mass.).   East Bridgewater, Mass.
*Christopher Morton . . . . . . 14 . . . Portland, Me.
Nicholas E. Paine . . . . 20 . . . Newmarket.
*Lucius Parker . . . . 20 . . . Southborough, Mass. 1868
  H.U. 1834; Clergyman.   Laramie, Neb.
Grenville Parker . . . . 15 . . . Chelmsford, Mass.
  Lawyer.   Lowell, Mass.
Daniel Parker . . . . 22 . . . Billerica, Mass.
*Charles Henry Peirce . . . . . 14 . . . Cambridge, Mass. . . 1855
  H.U. 1833; A.M.; M.D.; Physician.   "   "
Sherburne Blake Piper . . . . 20 . . . Northwood.
  Dart. Coll. 1832; A.M.; Lawyer.   Lewiston, N.Y.
*Charles Edwin Stratton . . . . 15 . . . Watertown, Mass. . 1871
  Merchant.   Boston, Mass.
Albert G. Thornton . . . . . . 16 . . . Saco, Me.
*Charles Turner Torrey . . . . 14 . . . Chelsea, Mass. . . . 1846
  Yale Coll. 1833; A.M.; Clergyman.   Baltimore, Md.
True Tucker . . . . 17 . . . Meredith Bridge.
*Noah Worcester . . . . 15 . . . Gloucester, Mass. . . 1847
                                                              40

1829.

James Bean . . . . 19 . . . Warner.
Francis Bowen . . . . 17 . . . Boston, Mass.
  H.U. 1833; A.M.; LL.D.; Prof. Nat. and Moral   Cambridge, Mass.
  Phil. and Civ. Polit. H.U.; Author.

*Joseph Boyden . . . . 17 . . . Tamworth 1842
Teacher.   Alabama.
Benjamin Franklin Butler . . . 11 . . . Deerfield.
C.U. 1838; A.M.; LL.D.; M.C. 1867-75;   Lowell, Mass.
Gov. Mass. 1883.
Edmund Chadwick . . . . . . 17 . . . Middleton.
Teacher.   Starkey, N.Y.
Moses T. Chapin . . . . 15 . . . Barrington, R.I.
*Heber Chase . . . . 21 . . . Hopkinton 1850
M.D.; Physician.   Philadelphia, Pa.
Alfred Conner . . . . 14 . . . Exeter.
Carpenter.   "
Horatio Sprague Cook . . . . 12 . . . Dorchester, Mass.
Herman Elves Davidson . . . 14 . . . Charlestown, Mass.
H.U. 1836; A.M.; M.D.; Physician.   Boston, Mass.
John Taylor Gilman Davies . . 13 . . . Portland, Me.
M.D.; Physician.   "   "
*George Clinton Durell . . . . . 14 . . . Dover 1838
*Edward Fox . . . . 14 . . . Portland, Me. 1881
H.U. 1834; LL.B.; Judge U.S. Dist. Ct.; Lawyer. "   "
William F. Gordon . . . . . . 18 . . . Exeter.
Business.   Lawrence, Mass.
Joshua P. Haven . . . . 11 . . . Philadelphia, Pa.
James B. Kelly . . . . 22 . . . Hopkinton.
Farmer.   "
Charles Mason . . . . 17 . . . Dublin.
H.U. 1834; A.M.; LL.B.; Lawyer.   Fitchburg, Mass.
Leonard W. Merrill . . . . . . 15 . . . Portland, Me.
*William Oxnard Moseley . . . 14 . . . Newburyport, Mass.
H.U. 1836; Clergyman.   "   "
John Taylor Gilman Nichols . 12 . . . Portland, Me.
H.U. 1836; Clergyman.   Saco, Me.
Hezekiah O'Calloghan . . . 14 . . . St. Jago de Cuba.
John Parsons . . . . 13 . . . Rye.
*Benjamin Hurd Rhoades . . . 17 . . . Boston, Mass. 1880
B.U. 1833; A.M.; Librarian.   Newport, R.I.
Benjamin F. Russell . . . . . 14 . . . Newburyport, Mass.
*Charles Woodman Scates . . . 13 . . . Middleton 1873
H.U. 1838; Lawyer.   Williamsport, Va.
William F. Tarbell . . . . . . 16 . . . Cambridge, Mass.
John L. W. Tilton . . . . . . 17 . . . Exeter.
Royal Tyler . . . . 17 . . . Brattleborough, Vt.
H.U. 1834; A.M.; Lawyer; Probate Judge.   "   "
Worcester Willey . . . . 21 . . . Campton.
Will. Coll. 1835; A.M.; Clergyman.
*William Wiswall . . . . 14 . . . Exeter.
Timothy Roberts Young . . . . 18 . . . Dover.
Bowd. Coll. 1835; M.C.; Lawyer.   Marshall, Ill.

31

1830.

Harris Abbot . . . . 17 . . . Wilton.
Farmer.   "
*John Quincy Adams . . . . . 14 . . . Quincy, Mass. . . . 1853
Lieut. U.S. Navy.
*George W. Beale . . . . 14 . . . Quincy, Mass. . . . 1870
                                          Burlington, Iowa.

*John Abner Briggs . . . . . . 14 . . . Newburyport, Mass. 1845
H.U. 1835; A.M.; M.D.; Physician. " "
Abijah Brigham . . . . 18 . . . Sudbury, Mass.
Farmer. South Acton, Mass.
*Horace Butler . . . . 16 . . . Deerfield 1861
Dart. Coll. 1836; Lawyer; Prob. Judge. Libertyville, Ill.
Josiah Butler . . . . 14 . . . Deerfield.
Broker. New York, N.Y.
Edward Buxton . . . . 26 . . . New Boston.
*David Joseph Clark . . . . . . 17 . . . Stratham 1866
Dart. Coll. 1836; Lawyer. Manchester.
*Robert Augustine Cross . . . 14 . . . Exeter 1861
Printer. Boston, Mass.
*Thomas Cutts . . . . 19 . . . Biddeford, Me. . . . 1870
Nathaniel Gardiner Gilman . . 11 . . . Exeter.
Farmer. "
*David Green Goodall . . . . 16 . . . Bath 1882
Business. Beloit, Wis.
*James Harrison Gray . . . . . 11 . . . Boston, Mass. 1853
M.D.; Physician. Springfield, Mass.
*Augustus C. L. Hartwell . . . 14 . . . Littleton, Mass. . . . 1865
Business. New Orleans, La.
*_Ephraim Nelson Hidden_ . . . . 19 . . . Tamworth 1880
Dart. Coll. 1836; Clergyman. Norfolk, Mass.
*Samuel Tenney Hildreth . . . 13 . . . Gloucester, Mass. . . 1839
H.U. 1837.
Francis Parkman Hurd . . . . 10 . . . Exeter.
H.U. 1839; M.D.; Farmer. Wakefield, Mass.
*Horace Green Hutchins . . . 18 . . . Bath 1877
Dart. Coll. 1835; A.M.; Lawyer. Boston, Mass.
Ephraim A. Hyde . . . . 16 . . . Freeport, Me.
Austin Daniel Kilham . . . . . 12 . . . Beverly, Mass.
Merchant (retired). " "
John Savillian Ladd . . . . . . 20 . . . Epping.
Dart. Coll. 1835; A.M.; Lawyer. Cambridge, Mass.
*Fitz Henry Lawrence . . . . . 13 . . . Exeter.
Mariner. "
Thomas Atkins Livermore . . 17 . . . Milford.
Dentist.
Nathaniel Lovering . . . . . . 11 . . . Exeter.
Farmer. Newton.
John Gilman Lovering . . . 13 . . . Exeter.
Business. Epping.
Jarvis McDuffie . . . . 20 . . . Rochester.
Yale Coll. 1836; Farmer. Exeter.
William Henry McCrillis . . . 16 . . . Somersworth.
Lawyer. Bangor, Me.
*_John H. Murdough_ . . . . . . 19 . . . Wakefield 1869
Clergyman. Gorham, Me.
Theodore Bland Moses . . . . 13 . . . Exeter.
Surveyor. West Roxbury, Mass.
*John Fitz Henry Muzzey . . . 13 . . . Portland, Me. 1846
H.U. 1835.
James William Odlin . . . . . 10 . . . Exeter.
"

*George W. Pendexter . . . . . 15 . . . Dover.
Shipmaster. Galveston, Texas.
*Nathaniel Gorham Phillips . . 14 . . . Andover, Mass. . . . 1882
John T. G. Pike . . . . 16 . . . Hampton Falls.

*Joseph Hicks Richards .... 14 ... Nottingham 1835
M.D.; Physician.   Portland, Me.
John Riley .... 15 ... Dover.
Shipmaster.   New York, N.Y.
Abraham Hazen Robinson .. 17 ... Concord.
Yale Coll. 1835; A.M.; M.D.; Physician.   "
*Benning W. Sanborn ..... 17 ... Deerfield 1874
Business.   Concord.
John Smith .... 23 ... Brentwood.
Charles William Storer .... 13 ... Newburyport, Mass.
Lawyer.   Boston, Mass.
*Joseph Dudley Thyng ..... 15 ... Exeter 1881
Merchant.   "
*Benjamin A. Thompson .... 17 ... Deerfield 1837
Teacher.   Concord.
Ebenezer Trask .... 20 ... Gloucester, Mass.
Erastus S. Tuttle .... 13 ... Newmarket.
Francis William Upham .... 13 ... Rochester.
Bowd. Coll. 1837; LL.D.; Prof. Phil., Rutgers Coll.   Brunswick, N.J.
Author.
George Brown Webster .... 16 ... East Kingston.
Farmer.   " "
Jacob S. Wentworth ..... 13 ... Exeter.
Tolman Willey .... 21 ... Campton.
Lawyer.   Boston, Mass.
Hollis Willey .... 22 ... Epping.
Carlos Willey .... 14 ... Hanover.
John F. Winkley .... 15 ... Amesbury, Mass.
Theodore Chase Woodman .. 15 ... Rochester.
Dart. Coll. 1835; Lawyer.   Belfast, Me.

53

1831.

William Allen .... 15 ... Bridgewater, Mass.
H.U. 1837; A.M.; Government Service.   Boston, Mass.
*Henry David Austin ..... 13 ... Charlestown, Mass. .. 1879
H.U. 1839; LL.B.; Lawyer.   Wakefield, Mass.
William Charles Balch .... 12 ... Newburyport, Mass.
R.R. Clerk.   Boston, Mass.
Joshua Berry .... 25 ... Portsmouth.
Nicholas Arthur Clarke ... 17 ... Exeter.
H.U. 1838; A.M.; Insurance Agent.   Salem, Mass.
*John M. Dow .... 16 ... Dover 1871
Broker.   New York, N.Y.
Ezekiel Gilman .... 14 ... Deerfield.
H.U. 1839.   New York, N.Y.
John Gilman .... 12 ... Deerfield.
Printer.
*Seth Hayes .... 21 ... Farmington 1832
    "
J. M. Henderson .... Dover.
Aaron Hobart .... 13 ... East Bridgewater, Mass.
Corporation Treasurer (Boston, Mass.).   " " "
Nathaniel Holmes .... 17 ... Peterborough.
H.U. 1837; A.M.; Lawyer and Author; Prof. of   St. Louis, Mo.
Law, H.U. 1868-72; Judge Supr. Ct. Mo.

Frederic Jones . . . . 17 . . . Dublin.
H.U. 1835; A.M.; M.D.; Physician.   New Ipswich.
*Edward M. E. Keating . . . 14 . . . York, Me. 1837
Bowd. Coll. 1835; Lawyer.   Alton, Ill.
*Henry Lorenzo Low . . . . . . 14 . . . Concord 1852
Dart. Coll. 1836; A.M.; Prof. Ancient Lang., Geneva, N.Y.
Hobart Coll.
*George Minot . . . . 14 . . . Haverhill, Mass. . . . 1858
H.U. 1836; LL.B.; Lawyer.   Malden, Mass.
*Horace Morison . . . . 21 . . . Peterborough 1870
H.U. 1837; A.M.; Prof. Math., Univ. Maryland.   Baltimore, Md.
James Colman Moses . . . . . 13 . . . Exeter.
Nathaniel Noyes . . . . 18 . . . West Newbury, Mass.
Business.   Haverhill, Mass.
Edwin A. C. Page . . . . 14 . . . Exeter.
Daniel P. Pike . . . . 16 . . . Kensington.
Clergyman.   Newburyport, Mass.
William B. Porter . . . . 11 . . . Newburyport, Mass.
Preacher.   Illinois.
William Pitt Preble . . . . . . 12 . . . Portland, Me.
Bowd. Coll. 1840; Lawyer.   "   "
*George William Rice . . . . . 14 . . . Portsmouth 1881
H.U. 1836; A.M.; Bank Cashier.   Boston, Mass.
*Nathaniel Gilman Rogers . . . 13 . . . Exeter 1847
C.U. 1838; Teacher.
*John Francis Rogers . . . . . 11 . . . Exeter 1870
Business.   Lowell, Mass.
*William Sherman Rowland . . 13 . . . Windsor, Conn. . . . 1856
Yale Coll. 1836; Lawyer.   New York, N.Y.
James M. Saunders . . . . . . 15 . . . Portsmouth.
*William Henry Shackford . . . 16 . . . Portsmouth 1842
H.U. 1835; A.M.; Prof. Math. P.E.A.   Exeter.
Charles Chauncy Shackford . . 15 . . . Portsmouth.
H.U. 1835; A.M.; Clergyman; Prof. Rhet. and Ithaca, N.Y.
Lit., Cornell Univ.
*James Foster Shores . . . . . 17 . . . Portsmouth 1877
Bank Cashier.   "
Isaac Smith Shute . . . . 13 . . . Exeter.
Merchant.   "
*Henry Augustus Shute . . . 10 . . . Exeter 1841
Dart. Coll. 1840.   "
*David Scott Sloan . . . . 16 . . . Haverhill 1841
Dart. Coll. 1836; A.M.; Teacher.   Geneva, N.Y.
John M. Story . . . . 12 . . . Newburyport, Mass.
Merchant.   New York, N.Y.
Jere. Webster Tuck . . . . . . 19 . . . Kensington.
Amh. Coll. 1840; Clergyman.   Middletown, Conn.
Samuel Parsons Tuck . . . . . 19 . . . Kensington.
Farmer.   "
Daniel A. Veasey . . . . 14 . . . Exeter.
Business.   Indiana.
Ashton S. H. White . . . . . 11 . . . Portsmouth.
*George Henry Wills . . . . . . 11 . . . Newburyport, Mass. 1860
Business.   "   "
Henry L. Wiswall . . . . 13 . . . Exeter.
Government Clerk.   Washington, D.C.

41

1832.

Ebenezer Allen . . . . 21 . . . Townsend, Mass.
*Daniel Wells Alvord . . . . . 15 . . . Greenfield, Mass. . . 1871
   Union Coll. 1838; A.M.; Lawyer.   Virginia.
Joseph W. Batchelder. . . . . 22 . . . Loudon.
*Coffin March Chadwick . . . . 13 . . . Exeter 1865
   Steamer Captain.   San Francisco, Cal.
John Chadwick . . . . 10 . . . Exeter.
   Shipmaster; Business Agent (Boston, Mass.).   "
William H. Chandler . . . . . 17 . . . Providence, R. I.
*Jacob Morrill Currier . . . . . 18 . . . Dover 1847
   Pensacola.
Edward Henry Davies . . . . 14 . . . Portland, Me.
   Bowd. Coll. 1838; LL.B.; Lawyer.   "
*Charles G. Dow . . . . 15 . . . Dover 1837
   Clerk.   "
James M. Elliot . . . . 12 . . . Chester.
   Farmer.
Josiah Fogg . . . . 17 . . . Exeter.
   Farmer.   Deerfield.
*Albert Gassett . . . . 14 . . . Boston, Mass. 1838
John Gardiner Gilman . . . . 11 . . . Exeter.
   Farmer.   "
Edward St. L. Haven . . . . . 12 . . . Philadelphia, Pa.
*Charles Jarvis . . . . 11 . . . Weathersfield, Vt. . . 1862
   Univ. Vt. 1839; LL.B.
Edward R. Johnston . . . . . 21 . . . Hillsborough.
Samuel Livermore . . . . 15 . . . Plymouth.
John Langdon Lovering . . . 12 . . . Exeter.
   Florist.   "
William H. Low . . . . 13 . . . Dover.
   Merchant.   Chicago, Ill.
*Asa Mitchell . . . . 14 . . . Bridgewater, Mass. . 1876
William Perry Moulton . . . . 11 . . . Exeter.
   Insurance Agent.   "
Edward S. Osgood . . . . . . 14 . . . Denmark, Me.
*Samuel H. Pendexter . . . . . 14 . . . Dover 1880
   Banker.   New York, N.Y.
Matthew Pike . . . . 19 . . . Hampton Falls.
   Farmer.   "   "
John Fox Potter . . . . 16 . . . Augusta, Me.
   M.C. 1858–61; Lawyer.   East Troy, Wis
*George Augustus Richmond . . 15 . . . Providence, R.I. . . . 1868
   Havana.
*Edward Sullivan . . . . 12 . . . Exeter 1843
Andrew W. Thompson . . . . 12 . . . Durham.
   R. R. Employ.   Portland, Me.
*Albert Gallatin Upham . . . . 13 . . . Rochester 1847
   Bowd. Coll. 1840; A.M.; M.D.; Physician.   Boston, Mass.
*John Wright Warren . . . . . 21 . . . Lincoln, Mass. . . . 1869
   M.D.; Physician.   Boston, Mass.
Francis Brown Webster . . . . 16 . . . Salisbury.
   Dart. Coll. 1841; Manufacturer.   Boston, Mass.
Bernard Bemus Whittemore . . 15 . . . Peterborough.
   H.U. 1839; Lawyer and Journalist.   Nashua.

*George A. Wood . . . . 15 . . . Newburyport, Mass. 1883
Business.   Philadelphia, Pa.
Lewis Young . . . . 16 . . . Exeter.
                                                                  34

1833.

*Thornton Fleming Brodhead . 12 . . . Newmarket 1862
LL.B.; Lawyer.   Detroit, Mich.
William Clough . . . . 14 . . . Exeter.
*John Parker Conner . . . . . 14 . . . Exeter 1848
Dart. Coll. 1840; A.M.; M.D.; Physician.   Astoria, N.Y.
James Davis . . . . 14 . . . Amesbury, Mass.
Dart. Coll. 1841; Teacher.   "   "
George Nehemiah Eastman . . 13 . . . Farmington.
Dart. Coll. 1839; A.M.; Lawyer.   "
Bagley Favor . . . . 21 . . . New Chester.
Nathaniel Gordon . . . . 12 . . . Exeter.
Dart. Coll. 1841; LL.B.; Capitalist.   "
Oliver Lethbridge Gridley . . . 15 . . . Great Falls.
Merchant (retired).   Fayville, Mass.
*Edward Wheelock Hatch . . . 15 . . . Exeter.
Francis Brown Hayes . . . . . 13 . . . South Berwick, Me.
H.U. 1839; A.M.; Lawyer.   Boston, Mass.
William Pickering Hill . . . . 13 . . . Concord.
Dart. Coll. 1839; A.M.; Editor.   "
Richard Lovering . . . . 14 . . . Exeter.
Business.   Lynn, Mass.
Charles H. Mitchell . . . . . . 14 . . . Portland, Me.
Business.   San Francisco, Cal.
Frederic Morrill . . . . 18 . . . Brentwood.
Lawyer.   Baltimore, Md.
William Gilman Perry . . . . . 10 . . . Exeter.
Dart. Coll. 1842; M.D.; Physician.   "
*Edward Warren Putnam . . . 13 . . . Portsmouth 1863
Dart. Coll. 1840; A.M.; Clergyman.   North Whitefield, Me.
Edward Shaw . . . . 14 . . . Portland, Me.
                                       Boston, Mass.
Charles Emery Soule . . . . . 10 . . . Exeter.
Bowd. Coll. 1842; A.M.; Assistant Surrogate;   New York, N.Y.
Lawyer.
William Cutter Tenney . . . 16 . . . Newmarket.
H.U. 1838; Clergyman.   Kansas City, Mo.
Munroe G. I. Tukesbury . . . 14 . . . Amesbury, Mass.
*Charles Tompson . . . . 12 . . . South Berwick, Me. . 1875
Printer.
Richard S. Varnum . . . . . . 16 . . . Haverhill, Mass.
*James Smith Walker . . . . . 12 . . . Peterborough 1840
Lewis Warrington . . . . 14 . . . Norfolk, Va.
Paymaster, U.S. Navy.
Edmund Burke Whitman . . . 20 . . . East Bridgewater, Mass.
H.U. 1838; A.M.   Cambridge, Mass.
                                                                  25

1834.

*Nathaniel Bradley Baker . . . 15 . . . Concord 1876
H.U. 1839; Gov. N.H.; Lawyer.   Des Moines, Ia.
David A. Barker . . . . 12 . . . Rochester.
Amos R. Binney . . . . 15 . . . Boston, Mass.

John Brooks	15 ...	Boston, Mass.
James Watson Brown	21 ...	Framingham, Mass.
M.D.; Physician (retired).		Framingham Centre, Mass.
Charles Burley	14 ...	Exeter.
Florist.		"
Augustus Burley	15 ...	Exeter.
Business.		Chicago, Ill.
Bradbury Poor Cilley	10 ...	Nottingham.
Dart. Coll. 1843; Lawyer.		Manchester.
Thomas Clements	20 ...	Dover.
Thomas Bartlett Doe	24 ...	Somersworth.
Farmer.		Danville, Va.
*George O. J. Durell	24 ...	Lee 1853
M.D.; Physician.		Goshen, N.Y.
Charles Dwinell	16 ...	Bangor, Me.
James E. Farnum	17 ...	Boston, Mass.
*George Dennis Fowle	12 ...	Alexandria, D.C. ... 1867
Business.		" "
*William Graves	16 ...	Brentwood.
*William Henderson	20 ...	Dover 1839
Farmer.		"
*George Hobart	14 ...	E. Bridgewater, Mass. 1843
Merchant.		New Orleans, La.
Samuel Emerson Howard ...	14 ...	Newburyport, Mass.
Merchant.		Brooklyn, N.Y.
Aaron M. Hubbard	21 ...	Acton, Me.
Joseph Hurd Ladd	14 ...	Portsmouth.
Merchant.		New York, N.Y.
*Joseph Lewis Leach......	19 ...	Concord.
Merchant.		Boston, Mass.
*Horatio Merrill	17 ...	Brownfield, Me.... 1878
Dart. Coll. 1840; Clergyman.		
Nathaniel Holmes Morison ..	18 ...	Peterborough.
H.U. 1839; A.M.; LL.D.; Teacher.		Baltimore, Md.
John Leese Moses	12 ...	Exeter.
C.U. 1841; A.M.; Treasurer.		Knoxville, Tenn.
*David M. Noyes	14 ...	Newburyport, Mass. 1839
George Gilman Odiorne	11 ...	Exeter.
M.D.; Preacher.		Jefferson City, Ia.
Joseph Osgood.	18 ...	Kensington.
Clergyman.		Cohasset, Mass.
Francis Edward Parker	12 ...	Portsmouth.
H.U. 1841; LL.B.; Lawyer.		Boston, Mass.
Nathaniel G. Robinson	14 ...	Brentwood.
Farmer.		"
*William Ballard Smith	14 ...	Durham 1866
Dart. Coll. 1840; Lawyer; Judge Circ. Ct.		Louisville, Ky.
John Babson Lane Soule ...	18 ...	Freeport, Me.
Bowd. Coll. 1840; Clergyman.		Highland Park, Ill.
*Walter Harris Tenney	14 ...	Concord 1844
Dart. Coll. 1839; Lawyer.		Dunbarton.
*George Timothy Upham ...	14 ...	Portsmouth 1857
Merchant.		San Francisco, Cal.
*Edward Webster	13 ...	Boston, Mass. ... 1848
Dart. Coll. 1841; Civil Engineer.		" "
Henry Cummings Whitman ..	17 ...	Billerica.
Lawyer.		Cincinnati, O.
John M. Williams	16 ...	Dover.
Clerk.		Boston, Mass.

1835.

Ezra Abbot . . . . 16 . . . Jackson, Me.
  Bowd. Coll. 1840; A.M.; LL.D.; Prof. New   Cambridge, Mass.
  Test. Crit. H.U.; Author.
William Benjamin Bacon . . . 12 . . . Boston, Mass.
  H.U. 1841; A.M.; Merchant.   "   "
George Murillo Bartol . . . . . 14 . . . Portland, Me.
  B.U. 1842; Clergyman.   Lancaster, Mass.
Charles T. Bradley . . . . . . 17 . . . Haverhill, Mass.
  Merchant.   Milwaukee, Wis.
Enoch Payson Bullard . . . . 15 . . . Concord.
  Merchant.   New York, N.Y.
*Gardner Elliot . . . . 22 . . . Exeter 1876
  Business.   New York, N.Y.
*Nicholas Emery . . . . 13 . . . Portland, Me. 1840
Benjamin F. Fish . . . . 17 . . . Thornton.
  Business.   Detroit, Mich.
Robert Ilsley Frothingham . . 13 . . . Newburyport, Mass.
  Business.   New York, N.Y.
*Augustus K. Gardner . . . . . 14 . . . Roxbury, Mass. . . 1876
  M.D.; Physician.   New York, N.Y.
Daniel Swan Gilchrist . . . . 13 . . . Charlestown.
  Lawyer.   Boston, Mass.
Charles Jervis Gilman . . . 11 . . . Exeter.
  M.C. 1858-9; Farmer.   Brunswick, Me.
James W. Greene . . . . 23 . . . Smithfield, R.I.
Rufus H. Hilliard . . . . 20 . . . Kensington.
  Farmer.   "
*Edward Frothingham Howard. 13 . . . Newburyport.
  Business.   "
*Nathaniel Dean Hubbard . . . 14 . . . Charlestown 1865
  H.U. 1840; Broker.   Boston, Mass.
William Augustus Kimball . . 22 . . . Shapleigh, Me.
  Lawyer.   Rochester.
Timothy J. Murray . . . . . . 15 . . . Newmarket.
  Business.   "
*Frederic O. Pendexter . . . . 16 . . . Dover 1872
  Merchant.   New York, N.Y.
Elvin J. Pike . . . . 13 . . . Hampton Falls.
Fitz John Porter . . . . 14 . . . Alexandria, D.C.
  West Point, 1845; Gen. U.S.A.   Morristown, N.Y.
*Charles Henry Porter . . . . 18 . . . Portland, Me. 1841
  Yale Coll. 1839; Theol. Student.   "   "
Barrett Edwards Potter . . . . 16 . . . Augusta, Me.
  Bowd. Coll. 1841; Banker.   "   "
Daniel Fox Potter . . . . . . 16 . . . Augusta, Me.
  Bowd. Coll. 1841; Clergyman.   Brunswick, Me.
Edward Reed . . . . 14 . . . Yarmouth, Me.
  Dart. Coll. 1841; Business.   Boston, Mass.
*James Smith . . . . 19 . . . Peterborough 1846
  Yale Coll. 1840; LL.B.; Lawyer.   New Orleans, La.
Nicholas Emery Soule . . . . . 10 . . . Exeter.
  H.U. 1845; A.M.; M.D.; Teacher [Cincinnati].   "
Samuel Storer . . . . 15 . . . Portsmouth.
  Lawyer.   San Diego, Cal.
Jonas M. Tebbets . . . . 16 . . . Rochester.

[1835-36.] CATALOGUE. 63

*Nathaniel Tracy . . . . 13 . . . Newburyport, Mass. 1843
  Student.   "   "
William Orne White . . . . . . 14 . . . Salem, Mass.
  H.U. 1840; A.M.; Clergyman.   Brookline, Mass.
*Joseph Addison White . . . . 18 . . . Peterborough 1843
  H.U. 1840; Teacher.   Middletown, Pa.
Joseph Phinney Whittemore . 14 . . . Peterborough.
  Lawyer.   Detroit, Mich.
*Augustus Whitman . . . . . . 14 . . . Abington, Mass. . . . 1880
                                                   Worcester, Mass.
George Dudley Wildes . . . . . 17 . . . Newburyport, Mass.
  Clergyman (Riverdale).   New York, N.Y.
William Gray Wise . . . . . . 14 . . . Portsmouth.
  Manufacturer.   Auburn, N.Y.

                                                                                   36

1836.

*Amos Tappan Akerman . . . . 15 . . . Portsmouth 1880
  Dart. Coll. 1842; U.S. Att. Gen. 1870-72; Law-   Cartersville, Ga.
  yer.
Stephen Rowe Bellows . . . . 14 . . . Walpole.
  Lawyer.   "
James Blodgett . . . . 24 . . . Westford, Mass. . . . 1845
  H.U. 1841; Clergyman.
Joseph D. L. Davis . . . . . . 14 . . . New York, N.Y.
David Fogg Drew . . . . 16 . . . Milton, Mass.
  Dart. Coll. 1842; A.M.; M.D.; Physician.   Lynn, Mass.
*Walter Moody Elliot . . . . . 12 . . . Exeter 1873
  Business.   San Francisco, Cal.
*John Abbot Emery . . . . . . 17 . . . Springfield 1842
*Marcus Fox . . . . 16 . . . Fitchburg, Mass.
*Philemon Brown Francis . . . 22 . . . Lunenburg, Mass. . 1841
                                                   Quincy, Ill.
Benjamin F. Gilman . . . . . 22 . . . Boston, Mass.
  M.D.
Moses F. Greene . . . . 23 . . . Smithfield, R.I.
Eldridge Gurney . . . . 18 . . . Abington, Mass.
  Business.   St. Joseph, Mo.
Wells Healey . . . . 16 . . . Hampton Falls.
  Farmer.   "   "
Howland Holmes . . . . 21 . . . East Bridgewater, Mass.
  H.U. 1843; A.M.; M.D.; Physician.   Lexington, Mass.
*Richard Hubbard . . . . 13 . . . Charlestown 1882
  Broker.   • Boston, Mass.
Aaron Dean Hubbard . . . . . 10 . . . Charlestown.
  Broker.   Boston, Mass.
*William Jarvis . . . . 12 . . . Weathersfield, Vt. . 1842
Leonard Fitz Edw. Jarvis . . 17 . . . Surry, Me.
  Bowd. Coll. 1840 ; A.M.; Lawyer.   Columbia, Cal.
John Prentiss Proctor Kelly . 16 . . . Exeter.
  Merchant.   "
Samuel Kimball . . . . 20 . . . Shapleigh, Me.
  Teacher.   Cane Spring Depot, Ky.
Samuel Connor Lawrence . . 13 . . . Exeter.
  Capitalist.   "
James W. Locke . . . . 21 . . . Roxbury, Mass.

*Samuel B. Locke . . . . 20 . . . W. Cambridge, Mass. 1838
Albert W. Lovering . . . . . 11 . . . Exeter.
   Bookseller.   New York, N.Y.
Samuel Adams Morison . . . . 18 . . . Peterborough.
   Business.   Oaklands, Cal.
*James Morison . . . . 18 . . . Peterborough 1882
   H.U. 1844; A.M.; M.D.; Physician.   Quincy, Mass.
Nathan Andrew Moulton . . . 12 . . . Hampton Falls.
   Business.   Newburyport, Mass.
*John Chandler Nourse . . . . 14 . . . Hallowell, Me. . . . 1844
   H.U. 1840.
*William Nudd . . . . 18 . . . Kensington 1863
   Farmer.   Exeter.
George Osgood . . . . 18 . . . Kensington.
   Farmer.   "
William Plumer . . . . 12 . . . Epping.
   H.U. 1845; LL.B.; Business.   Lexington, Mass.
*Henry Sargent . . . . 14 . . . Leicester, Mass. . . 1858
   Yale Coll. 1841; A.M.; M.D.; Physician.   Worcester, Mass.
Samuel Smith . . . . 11 . . . Mississippi.
   Planter.   "
Richard Wenman Swan . . . . 19 . . . West Cambridge, Mass.
   H.U. 1842; A.M.; Prof. Lang. and Lit.; Iowa Coll.   Grinnell, Iowa.
George Walker . . . . 12 . . . Peterborough.
   Dart. Coll.1842; A.M.; LL.B.; U.S. Consul Gen.   Paris, France.
John S. Ware . . . . 13 . . . Hampton Falls.
*Horatio Woodman . . . . . . 15 . . . Buxton, Me. 1879
   LL.B; Lawyer.   Boston, Mass.

37

1837.

Samuel Augustus Badger . . . 15 . . . Kittery, Me.
   Yale Coll. 1844; Business.   Boston, Mass.
*John Bradford Ball . . . . . . 16 . . . Portsmouth 1844
   Clerk.   Boston, Mass.
Jeremy Belknap Barker . . . 20 . . . Wakefield.
   Lawyer.   White Plain Co., Nevada.
William Barker . . . . 23 . . . Ellsworth, Me.
   Wheelwright.   River Falls, Wis.
John B. Beale . . . . 18 . . . Scituate, Mass.
Charles Henry Bell . . . . . . 13 . . . Chester.
   Dart. Coll. 1844; LL.D.; Lawyer; U.S. Sen. 1879;   Exeter.
   Gov. N.H. 1881-2.
Abel Herbert Bellows . . . . . 14 . . . Walpole.
   H.U. 1842; A.M.; L.L.B.   Boston, Mass.
Adino Nye Brackett . * . . . . 15 . . . Lancaster.
   Dart. Coll. 1844; M.D.; Physician.   Negrofoot, Va.
*Joseph Hildreth Bradley . . . 15 . . . Haverhill, Mass. . . 1882
   Dart. Coll. 1844; Lawyer.   Boston, Mass.
*George Henry Bullard . . . . 13 . . . Concord.
Daniel Chaplin . . . . 16 . . . Cambridgeport, Mass.
   M.D.
George Faber Clark . . . . . . 20 . . . Dublin.
   Clergyman.   Mendon, Mass.
William Henry Cobbs . . . . . 14 . . . Exeter.
   R.R. Clerk.   North Springfield, Mo.
*George Washington Copp . . 17 . . . Wakefield 1864
   Bowd. Coll. 1842.

Stephen W. Drew . . . . 19 . . . Milton.
*Joel S. Furber . . . . 14 . . . Exeter.
*Andrew Bowers Gale . . . . . 12 . . . Salem, Mass.
Business. New York, N.Y.
William Henry Gorham . . . . 10 . . . Exeter.
M.D. "
*Charles Hammond . . . . . . 13 . . . Boston, Mass.
*William Samuel Hatch . . . . 14 . . . Diniwiddie Co., Va. . 1868
Merchant. Georgetown, Ky.
Henry Y. Hayes. . . . . 18 . . . Durham.
Business. Dover.
*Charles Edwin Kimball . . . . 15 . . . Kensington 1850
Clerk. "
John William Kingman . . . . 16 . . . Madbury.
H.U. 1843; Lawyer; Judge Supreme Court. Wyoming Territory.
Benjamin H. Merrill . . . . . 14 . . . Alna, Me.
George Osborne Odlin . . . . 14 . . . Exeter.
Farmer. Morison, Ill.
John Quincy Adams Perkins . 12 . . . Exeter.
Business. North Bend, Ind.
Oliver James Rand . . . . . . 17 . . . Exeter.
Treasurer. Boston, Mass.
*Alfred Rodman . . . . 16 . . . New Bedford, Mass. 1853
John Eastman Sanborn . . . . 13 . . . Exeter.
M.D.; Physician. Rockport, Me.
Augustus Lord Soule . . . . . 10 . . . Exeter.
H.U. 1846; Lawyer; Judge Supreme Court Boston, Mass.
Mass. 1879-81.
Ebenezer Carlton Sprague . . 14 . . . Buffalo, N.Y.
H.U. 1843; Lawyer. " "
Samuel Stevens Thyng . . . . 16 . . . Exeter.
Merchant. "
*Ebenezer Franklin Tucke . . . 15 . . . Kensington 1857
Dart. Coll. 1843; Lawyer. Exeter.
*John M. C. Veazey . . . . . . 14 . . . Exeter 1880
Lawyer. Indiana.
John C. Wadleigh . . . . . . 21 . . . Meredith.
*Seth Webb . . . . 14 . . . Scituate, Mass. . . . 1862
H.U. 1843; Lawyer.

36

1838.

Henry H. Barstow . . . . . . 14 . . . Kingston.
Sherburne Pierce Blake . . . . 12 . . . Raymond.
Business. "
Ozias Goodwin Chapman . . . 18 . . . Boston, Mass.
Business. Canada.
*John Coe . . . . 16 . . . Durham 1879
Business. Cambridge, Mass.
*Charles D. Dudley . . . . . . 15 . . . Roxbury, Mass. . . . 1843
*Caleb Ellis Farley . . . . . . 20 . . . Hampton Falls . . . 1852
Dart. Coll. 1843; Teacher. Seguin, Tex.
William Perry Fogg. . . . . . 12 . . . Exeter.
Merchant; Author. New York, N.Y.
William Nathaniel Folsom . . 11 . . . Exeter.
Shipmaster.

Ezra White Gale . . . . 14 . . . Kingston.
Dart. Coll. 1843; A.M.; Insurance Agent. St. John, N.B.
*William Henry Gilman . . . 12 . . . Exeter 1860
Yale Coll. 1847; Lawyer. "
Samuel Hutchins Goodall . . . 15 . . . Bath.
Dart. Coll. 1844; Lawyer. Boston, Mass.
Charles Henry Gould . . . . . 13 . . . Exeter.
Business. New York, N.Y.
Benjamin Emerson Hall . . . 18 . . . Exeter.
Charles Hosea Hildreth . . . . 12 . . . Gloucester, Mass.
M.D.; Physician. " "
Joseph Chase Hilliard . . . . . 17 . . . Kensington.
Insurance Agent. Boston, Mass.
Samuel Allison Holmes . . . . 15 . . . Peterborough.
Lawyer. St. Louis, Mo.
Abram Jacquith . . . . 22 . . . Greenfield.
Franklin Lane . . . . 15 . . . Exeter.
M.D.; Physician. Baltimore, Md.
Daniel Flagg Melcher . . . . . 14 . . . Exeter.
Business. Springfield, Mass.
Abner Little Merrill . . . . . 12 . . . Exeter.
H.U. 1846; M.D.; Merchant. Boston, Mass.
Samuel Blake Osgood . . . . . 12 . . . Epping.
*George C. Peavey . . . . . . 22 . . . Strafford 1876
Lawyer. "
*Nathaniel Gilman Perry . . . 11 . . . Exeter 1855
H.U. 1846. "
*Richard Saltonstall . . . . . . 14 . . . Salem, Mass 1875
Real Estate Broker. Brooklyn, N.Y.
*Charles H. Sanborn . . . . . . 23 . . . Falmouth, Me.
John Edward Shackford . . . 13 . . . Portsmouth.
George Smith Shute . . . . . 11 . . . Exeter.
Govt. Clerk (Boston, Mass.). "
Amos Towle . . . . 15 . . . Exeter.
Teacher. Mobile, Ala.
*Joseph Hurd Walker . . . . . 15 . . . Charlestown, Mass. . 1858
H.U. 1843; Civil Engineer. Boston, Mass.
Joseph Burbeen Walker . . . 16 . . . Concord.
Yale Coll. 1844. "
*Augustus Henry Weeks . . . . 14 . . . Exeter 1879
Merchant. "
James Wilson . . . . 19 . . . Rochester.
*Augustus Wiswall . . . . . . 15 . . . Exeter 1880
Business. Newton, Mass.
*Jasper Hazen York . . . . . . 22 . . . Rochester 1874
M.D.; Physician. Dover.
William Young . . . . 21 . . . Scituate, Mass.
Journalist.

35

1839.

Francis Peabody Abbot . . . . 12 . . . Glenburn, Me.
Dentist. Berlin, Prussia.
George Edward Balch . . . . 16 . . . Newburyport, Mass.
Expert Accountant. New York, N.Y.
*Daniel Webster Barber . . . . 16 . . . Epping 1881
Clergyman.

Charles Henry Branscomb . . 17 . . . Newmarket.
Dart. Coll. 1845; Business.   Manchester, Eng.
*Charles Harod Brown . . . . . 13 . . . Haverhill, Mass.
Hotel Keeper.   " "
*James Jackson Cruft . . . . . 12 . . . Boston, Mass 1849
H.U. 1846.   " "
John L. Davis . . . . 14 . . . Kittery, Me.
Benjamin Rice Davison . . . . 14 . . . Boston, Mass.
George Faulkner . . . . 20 . . . Billerica, Mass.
H.U. 1844; M.D.; Physician.   Jamaica Plain, Mass.
*Robert Farris Fisk . . . . . . 19 . . . Cambridge, Mass. . 1863
Yale Coll. 1844; A.M.; LL.B.; Business.   " "
Samuel Augustus Fisk . . . . 17 . . . Cambridge, Mass.
Yale Coll. 1844; A.M.; M.D.; Physician.   Northampton, Mass.
James Cooly Fletcher . . . . . 16 . . . Indianapolis, Ind.
B.U. 1846; Clergyman; Author.   Naples, Italy.
George Silsbee Hale . . . . . 13 . . . Keene.
H.U. 1844; LL.B.; Lawyer.   Boston, Mass.
Moses Wingate Hayes . . . . 15 . . . Madbury.
Lawyer.   Providence, R. I.
*Jonathan Homer Lane . . . . 19 . . . Hornby, N.Y. 1880
Yale Coll. 1846; A.M.; Coast Survey Official.   Washington, D.C.
Abram Bracket Lord . . . . . 21 . . . Ossipee.
Rolla Oscar Page . . . . 18 . . . Canton, N.Y.
H.U. 1845; Clergyman; A.M.; Prof. Math.   Brooklyn, N.Y.
Hobart Coll. 1850-51.
Horace Parker . . . . 22 . . . Kittery, Me.
Bowd. Coll. 1845; Teacher.   Eliot, Me.
John Jacob Pickering . . . . . 16 . . . Portsmouth.
Bank Cashier.   "
William Lawrence Plumer . . 14 . . . Epping.
Farmer.   "
Joseph Plummer . . . . 19 . . . Milton.
Farmer.   "
*Jonathan Russell . . . . 14 . . . Milton, Mass. 1875
H.U. 1846; A.M.; Merchant.   Manila, Phil. Islands.
*Charles Henry Boylston Snow . 17 . . . Fitchburg, Mass. . . 1875
H.U. 1844; LL.B.; Lawyer.   " "
Samuel Stanton . . . . 18 . . . Barnstead.
*Robert Swain . . . . 16 . . . New Bedford, Mass. 1843
Edward Prentiss Tucke . . . . 14 . . . Kensington.
H.U. 1846; Teacher.   Williamsburg, S.C.
George William Tuxbury . . . 16 . . . Salisbury, Mass.
Dart. Coll. 1845; Lawyer.   Boston, Mass.
John Stoughton Watson . . . 13 . . . Cambridge, Mass.
William Webster . . . . 15 . . . Kingston.
Dart. Coll. 1844; A.M.; Teacher.   Port Chester, N.Y.
*Albert Gallatin Weeks . . . . 19 . . . Gilford 1853
Dart. Coll. 1844; M.D.; Physician.   Barnstead.
*George Henry Williams . . . . 14 . . . Roxbury, Mass.
Levi Thayer Woodman . . . . 22 . . . Candia.

32

1840.

*George W. Badger . . . . . . 14 . . . Kittery, Me. 1847
Shipmaster.   " "
Leonidas Balch . . . . 16 . . . Newburyport, Mass.
Clerk.   " "

Ezra Barker . . . . 20 . . . Ellsworth, Me.
  Farmer.   La Grange, Me.
George Albert Blake . . . . . 12 . . . Raymond.
  Will. Coll. 1849; M.D.; Physician.   Walpole.
John Smith Cavender . . . . . 16 . . . St. Louis, Mo.
  Business.   "   "
*Hiram Chase . . . . 20 . . . Chester 1845
  Union Coll. 1844.   "
John Quincy Adams Clark . . 15 . . . Sanbornton.
  Fruit Grower.   California.
Joseph Manning Cleaveland . 16 . . . Exeter.
  Coll. N.J. 1846; M.D.; Supt. Insane Asylum.   Poughkeepsie, N.Y.
*George Nehemiah Cleaveland . 14 . . . Exeter 1877
  Yale Coll. 1847; M.D.; Physician.   New York, N.Y.
Henry Martin Crane . . . . . 11 . . . Exeter.
*Frederic Farley . . . . 16 . . . Newcastle, Me. . . . 1841
James Wilson Green . . . . . 21 . . . Chester.
Seth Walker Hartwell . . . . . 16 . . . Littleton, Mass.
  Civil Engineer.   Washington, D.C.
*John Adams Hastings . . . 16 . . . Brighton, Mass. . . 1851
  H.U. 1846; Teacher.   Erie, Pa.
Charles Newell Healey . . . 14 . . . Hampton Falls.
  Farmer.   Stratham.
*John Locke . . . . 17 . . . W. Cambridge, Mass. 1862
*Charles Lowe . . . . 11 . . . Exeter 1874
  H.U. 1847; A.M.; Clergyman; Sec. Unit. Assoc.   Somerville, Mass.
Henry Rowland Merrill . . . 12 . . . Exeter.
  Merchant.   Boston, Mass.
Charles William Orne . . . . . 13 . . . Boston, Mass.
*George Howard Pearson . . 16 . . . Boston, Mass. . . . 1870
  Business.   Lowell, Mass.
William Camp Porter . . . . . 18 . . . Fredericksburg, Va.
Eliphalet Porter Robinson . . 15 . . . Brentwood.
Jacob Rogers . . . . 11 . . . Exeter.
  Business.   Lowell, Mass.
William Rogers . . . . 13 . . . New Orleans, La.
James Henry Rundlett . . . . 18 . . . Exeter.
  Business.   Groveland, Mass.
George William Shackford . . 18 . . . Barrington.
Charles Gilman Smith . . . . . 12 . . . Exeter.
  H.U. 1847; A.M.; M.D.; Physician.   Chicago, Ill.
*Jonathan Coolidge Stone . . . 13 . . . Newburyport, Mass. 1868
  H.U. 1848; M.D.; Physician.   New York, N.Y.
James Camp Tappan . . . . . 15 . . . Vicksburg, Miss.
  Yale Coll. 1845; Lawyer.   Helena, Ark.
Joseph Warren Towle . . . . . 15 . . . Epping.
  H.U. 1851; Lawyer.   Exeter.
Nathaniel Warren . . . . 23 . . . Brookfield.
*Charles Henry West . . . . . . 12 . . . Charlestown 1865
  Business.   "
Henry Trowbridge Wiswall . . 20 . . . Exeter.
  Yale Coll. 1847; A.M.; Lawyer.   Washington, D.C.

1841.

George Bicknell Ager . . . . . 15 . . . East Bridgewater, Mass.
Accountant; City Treasury. Boston, Mass.
Ebenezer Bacon . . . . 11 . . . Boston, Mass.
Merchant. " "
*Jeremiah Olney Carr . . . . . 17 . . . Providence, R.I. . . 1856
B.U. 1848; Lawyer. " "
*Samuel Fulton Clark . . . . . 23 . . . Peterborough 1861
Clergyman. Ware, Mass.
Charles Edward Clark . . . . . 15 . . . Exeter.
Business. Boston, Mass.
Henry William Cleaveland . . 13 . . . Exeter.
Architect. San Francisco, Cal.
George Washington Collamore 23 . . . Boston, Mass.
Frederic Augustus Copp . . . 18 . . . Wakefield.
Yale Coll. 1847; A.M.
Isaac Ilsley Cummings . . . . 15 . . . Portland, Me.
H.U. 1846; A.M.; M.D. " "
Henry Damon . . . . 16 . . . West Cambridge, Mass.
Business. Boston, Mass.
William Abbot Everett . . . . 13 . . . Beverly, Mass.
H.U. 1849; A.M.; LL.B. Cambridge, Mass.
*Francis Augustus Faulkner . . 16 . . . Keene 1879
H.U. 1846; Lawyer.
William Cranch Bond Fifield . 12 . . . Weymouth, Mass.
M.D.; Physician. Boston, Mass.
Abraham Hilliard Flanders . . 13 . . . Exeter.
Union Coll. 1848; M.D.; Physician. Slatersville, R.I.
*Ira Freeman Folsom . . . . . 20 . . . Gilford 1859
Dart. Coll. 1848; Lawyer. "
Josiah James Folsom . . . . . 14 . . . Exeter.
Farmer. "
Jonathan Folsom French . . . 19 . . . Danville.
Charles Stephen Gale . . . . . 16 . . . Meredith.
Daniel Francis Grant . . . . . 17 . . . Exeter.
*Samuel Hale . . . . 16 . . . Portsmouth 1853
·Agriculturist. Rollinsford.
Angier March Hobbs . . . . . 14 . . . Exeter.
*John Samuel Hoitt . . . . . . 15 . . . Exeter 1852
Sacramento, Cal.
*Henry Whitcomb Holman . . . 16 . . . Bolton, Mass. 1853
H.U. 1848; Lawyer. New Orleans, La.
Peter Thacher Hunt . . . . . . 20 . . . Ashburnham, Mass.
Dart. Coll. 1847.
*Charles Kimball . . . . 11 . . . Exeter.
John Kittredge . . . . 16 . . . Andover, Mass.
M.D.; Physician. Taunton, Mass.
William H. Lackey . . . . . . 23 . . . Marblehead, Mass.
Collector. " "
*Howard Malcolm Moses . . . . 10 . . . Exeter 1857
Paper Manufacturer. Newmarket.
*Samuel Dodge Moses . . . . . 14 . . . Exeter 1872
M.D.; Physician. Knoxville, Tenn.
Thomas Kitson Perkins . . . . 14 . . . Exeter.
Business. Newmarket.
*Joseph Richards . . . . 22 . . . Braintree, Mass. . . . 1879
Quincy, Mass.

Robert Lambert Robinson . . . 14 . . . Roxbury, Mass.
*Albert Smith Scott . . . . . . 17 . . . Peterborough 1877
   Lawyer.   "
William Henry Slocum . . . . 23 . . . Boston, Mass.
   Merchant.   "   "
Elijah Brigham Stoddard . . . 15 . . . Upton, Mass.
   B.U. 1847; A.M.; Lawyer.   Worcester, Mass.
*George Dalton Thomes . . . . 22 . . . Ossipee 1845
*Charles Hall Thyng . . . . . . 17 . . . Exeter 1881
   Tailor.   Boston, Mass.
George Henry Torr . . . . . . 16 . . . Rochester.
George White . . . . 19 . . . Quincy, Mass.
   Yale Coll. 1848; LL.B.; Lawyer; Probate Judge   Dedham, Mass.
   (Boston, Mass.).
Ephraim White . . . . 21 . . . Rochester.
*Rufus Anderson Whitman . . 21 . . . New Gloucester, Me.
   Teacher.
Bernard Crosby Whitman . . . 13 . . . Waltham, Mass.
   H.U. 1846; Lawyer; Judge Supr. Ct., Nevada,   Virginia City, Nevada.
   1869-75; Ch. J. 1872-74.
Samuel Wood Winter . . . . . 16 . . . Ossipee.

                                                     43

1842.

George W. Babcock . . . . . 23 . . . Boston, Mass.
   Dermatologist.   "   "
Nathaniel Parsons Brown . . . 19 . . . Stratham.
Edwin Augustus Buck . . . . . 17 . . . Bucksport, Me.
   Yale Coll. 1849; Clergyman.
Charles Putnam Carter . . . . 15 . . . Wakefield.
   Business.   Franklin, Mass.
*Paul Ansel Chadbourne . . . . 18 . . . Somersworth 1883
   Will. Coll. 1848; A.M.; LL.D.; M.D.; Pres.   Williamstown, Mass.
   Will. Coll.; Pres. Agric. Coll., Mass.; Author.
James Luther Chamberlain . . 16 . . . Alexandria, D.C.
   Merchant.   Baltimore, Md.
*Nathaniel Williams Cilley . . . 16 . . . Nottingham 1855
   Mechanic.   "
John Henry Robertjat Crosby . 14 . . . Alexandria, D.C.
Francis Curtis . . . . 15 . . . Newton, Mass.
   Paper Manufacturer.   Clarendon Hills, Mass.
John Locke Doggett . . . . . 17 . . . Jacksonville, Fla.
*Levi Farwell . . . . 14 . . . Fitchburg, Mass. . . 1851
Watson Freeman . . . . 12 . . . Boston, Mass.
   Business.   "   "
Ebenezer Folsom . . . . 13 . . . Exeter.
   Business.   "
John Bradbury Frothingham . 14 . . . Exeter.
   Business.   St. Louis, Mo.
Robert Henry Fuller . . . . . 16 . . . Cambridge, Mass.
   Surrogate Clerk.   New York, N.Y.
*George Lowell Gardner . . . . 11 . . . Exeter 1845
John Herbert . . . . 19 . . . Salisbury, Mass.
*Gardner James Hoitt . . . . . 12 . . . Exeter 1856
Israel Small Hopkinson . . . 20 . . . Limington, Me.
*John Augustine Hurd . . . . . 17 . . . Charlestown, Mass. . 1845

William Frederic Lane	24 . . .	Exeter.
Bank Cashier.		Pa.
Mark Smith Palmer	17 . . .	New Bedford, Mass.
Silas Franklin Peirce	16 . . .	Frankfort. Me.
Real Estate Agent.		Boston, Mass.
John Scott Pickett	18 . . .	Triana, Ala.
M.D.; Physician.		Danville, Ala.
*Francis Edward Prevaux . . .	20 . . .	Amesbury, Mass. . . . 1860
B.U. 1846; A.M.; Clergyman.		
Henry Saltonstall	14 . . .	Salem, Mass.
H.U. 1848; A.M.; Corporation Treasurer.		Boston, Mass.
Luther Eastman Shepard . . .	21 . . .	Raymond.
Dart. Coll. 1851; A.M.; Lawyer.		Lowell, Mass.
Walter Durgin Smith	18 . . .	Newmarket.
James Caleb Smith	18 . . .	Culpepper, Va.
Rodney Metcalf Stimson . . .	19 . . .	Milford.
Marietta Coll. 1847; Treas. Marietta Coll.		Marietta, O.
Nathan Batchelder Tilton . . .	22 . . .	East Kingston.
Farmer.		" "
John Fogg Towle	20 . . .	Lee.
Farmer.		Exeter.
*Elijah Munroe Tubbs	19 . . .	Hancock 1878
John Whitman	17 . . .	Calais, Me.
*Charles Wellington Wilder . .	14 . . .	Leominster, Mass. . 1871
M.D.; Physician.		Fitchburg, Mass.
*Frederic William Williams . .	13 . . .	Exeter.
Jeweller.		Boston, Mass.
*William Frederic Williams . .	12 . . .	Exeter 1846
Mariner.		"
Augustus Atkinson Woodbury	14 . . .	Exeter.

38

1843.

Henry Quincy Adams	16 . . .	West Cambridge, Mass.
		Sacramento, Cal.
*Adams Ayer	20 . . .	Haverhill, Mass. . . . 1882
H.U. 1848; Clergyman.		Montreal, Canada.
Horace Clinton Bacon	19 . . .	West Cambridge, Mass.
Lawyer.		Lawrence, Mass.
Josiah Bartlett	13 . . .	Stratham.
Dart. Coll. 1851; Treasurer.		New York, N.Y.
*James Francis Brown	23 . . .	Quincy, Mass. . . . 1853
Clergyman.		West Cambridge, Mass.
John Wesley Clement	17 . . .	Exeter.
Business.		"
*George Washington Cogswell .	13 . . .	Peterborough 1854
H.U. 1849; Law Student.		Le Roy, N.Y.
Thomas Kittredge Cummins .	14 . . .	Springfield, Mass.
Merchant.		Boston, Mass.
Henry Curtis	18 . . .	Newton, Mass.
James Bolivar Dunlap	18 . . .	Indianapolis, Ind.
Lebeus Bayley Fifield	17 . . .	Yarmouth, N.S.
Amh. Coll. 1853; A.M.; Clergyman.		Kearney Junc., Neb.
John Parker Gale	17 . . .	South Hampton.
John Williams Getchell	11 . . .	Exeter.
Business.		"

Gardiner Gilman . . . . 14 . . . Exeter.		
Farmer.	"	
Charles Henry Goodwin . . . . 14 . . . Exeter.		
Business.	Stoneham, Mass.	
Francis James Gould . . . . . 15 . . . Charlestown, Mass.		
H.U. 1850; M.D.; Physician.	Jacksonville, Fla.	
*Chester Harding . . . . 16 . . . Springfield, Mass. . 1875		
H.U. 1847; Lawyer.	St. Louis, Mo.	
Horace Harding . . . . 15 . . . Springfield, Mass.		
H.U. 1848; State Engineer.	Tuscaloosa, Ala.	
John Lovell Hatch . . . . . . 22 . . . Boston, Mass.		
Cornelius Henry Herman . . . 14 . . . Norfolk, Va.		
Daniel Clark Hill . . . . 19 . . . Farmington.		
*Thomas Sanford Jamieson . . 15 . . . Alexandria, D.C. . . 1862		
Engine Builder.	"	"
John Henry Kimball . . . . . 15 . . . Exeter.		
Farmer.	"	
Samuel Plumer Ladd . . . . . 14 . . . Epping.		
Farmer.	"	
*Charles William Little . . . . 13 . . . Cambridge, Mass. . . 1872		
H.U. 1850; A.M.	Brattleborough, Vt.	
John Alexander Munroe . . . 22 . . . Bradford, Mass.		
William Osgood . . . . 20 . . . Kensington.		
H.U. 1850; A.M.; M.D.; Physician.	Boston, Mass.	
*George Henry Peirce . . . . . 14 . . . Dover 1873		
Contractor.	"	
*Woodbridge Odlin Perkins . . 12 . . . Exeter. 1883		
Painter.	"	
John Taylor Perry . . . . . . 11 . . . Exeter.		
H.U.1852; A.M.; Editor & Author [Cincinnati, O.]	"	
George Washington Plumer . . 15 . . . Epping.		
Farmer.	"	
Jonathan Robinson . . . . . . 23 . . . Brentwood.		
Nathaniel Isaac Sawyer . . . . 10 . . . Cincinnati, O.		
*Samuel Abbot Smith . . . . 14 . . . Peterborough 1865		
H.U. 1849; A.M.; Clergyman.	West Cambridge, Mass.	
Samuel Taylor . . . . 22 . . . Brentwood.		
John Heartbury Thyng . . . . 24 . . . Brentwood.		
Farmer.	"	
*Joseph Trumbull . . . . 17 . . . Worcester, Mass. . . 1880		
Broker.	New York, N.Y.	
*Elbridge Gerry Wellington . . 16 . . . Lexington, Mass. . . 1849		
Charles Sidney Whitehouse . . 16 . . . Rochester.		
Gov't Service.	Boston, Mass.	
John Samuel Whiting . . . . . 14 . . . Charlestown, Mass.		
H.U. 1850; M.D.; Physician.	"	"
George Henry Wiggin . . . . 13 . . . Exeter.		
Business.	St. Louis, Mo.	
Joseph C. A. Wingate . . . . 12 . . . Stratham.		
Bowd. Coll. 1851; A.M.; U.S. Consul.	Shanghai, China.	
George Washington Young . . 17 . . . Strafford.		
	Lowell, Mass.	

43

1844.

Curtis Coe Bean	16	Gilmanton.	
Miner.		Prescott, Arizona.	
Robert C. M. Bowles	15	Roxbury, Mass.	
Business.		London, Eng.	
Robert Waterston Chase	14	South Berwick, Me.	
Merchant.		Baltimore, Md.	
Samuel Greely Clarke	17	Pittsfield.	
H.U. 1851; Lawyer.		St. James, L.I.	
*George Spencer Cobbs	15	Exeter	1864
Willis Strong Colton	15	Lockport, N.Y.	
Yale Coll. 1850; A.M.; Clergyman.		Warren, Conn.	
Charles Doe	14	Somersworth.	
Dart. Coll. 1849; LL.D.; Lawyer; Ch. Just. Supr. Ct., N.H.		Rollinsford.	
Charles Franklin Dunbar	14	Abington, Mass.	
H.U. 1851; Editor; Prof. Polit. Econ. H.U.		Cambridge, Mass.	
Benjamin Franklin Folsom	19	Stratham.	
Business.		Philadelphia, Pa.	
William Whittlesey Frost	18	Pierpont, O.	
*Nathaniel Gorham, jr.	14	Canandaigua, N.Y.	1853
Business.		Detroit, Mich.	
William Bartleman Gregory	15	Alexandria, D.C.	
M.D.; Physician.		" "	
James Harding	14	Springfield, Mass.	
R.R. Commissioner.		Jefferson City, Mo.	
George Walker Hartwell	10	Cincinnati, O.	
H.U. 1853; Business.		" "	
Joseph Alfred Harwood	17	Littleton, Mass.	
Manufacturer.		Boston, Mass.	
Augustus Lord Hayes	17	South Berwick, Me.	
H.U. 1849.		" "	
Alexander Henderson	12	Portland, Me.	
*James Walker Kendall	19	Leominster, Mass.	1847
Caleb Lamson	26	Hamilton, Mass.	
James White Mackintosh	25	Cambridge, Mass.	
David Webster Merrill	14	Exeter.	
Farmer.		"	
John Moore	19	Somersworth.	
John Noble	15	Somersworth.	
H.U. 1850; LL.B.; Clerk Supr. Ct.		Boston, Mass.	
Joseph Wentworth Peirce	14	Greenland.	
Clergyman.		Portsmouth.	
Joshua Rindge Peirce	12	Greenland.	
H.U. 1851; A.M.; Clergyman.		Dorchester, Mass.	
George Francis Richardson	14	Tyngsborough, Mass.	
H.U. 1850; A.M.; LL.B.; Lawyer.		Lowell, Mass.	
*Charles Archibald Robertson	18	Beverly, Mass.	1880
H.U. 1850; A.M.; M.D.; Oculist.		Albany, N.Y.	
*William Sheafe	14	Portsmouth	1882
Merchant.		Boston, Mass.	
*William Henry Sinclair	16	Stratham	1847
*Nicholas J. Staats	15	Buffalo, N.Y.	1853
Business.		" "	
Horatio Stebbins	23	Wilbraham, Mass.	
H.U. 1848; A.M.; D.D.; Clergyman.		San Francisco, Cal.	

Franklin Tuxbury . . . . 14 . . . Amesbury 1879
  Clergyman.   Watertown, Conn.
Ebenezer Gowell Wallace . . . 21 . . . Berwick, Me.
  Business.   Rochester.
Edwin Wallace . . . . 21 . . . Berwick, Me.
  Business.   Rochester.
Augustus Woodbury . . . . . . 18 . . . Beverly, Mass.
  A.M.; Clergyman.   Providence, R.I.

35

1845.

Everett Colby Banfield . . . . 16 . . . Boston, Mass.
  H.U. 1850; Lawyer.   Wolfborough.
George Frederic Benson . . . 11 . . . Bradford, Mass.
*George William Burleigh . . . 14 . . . Somersworth. 1878
  Dart. Coll. 1851; LL.B.; Lawyer.   Great Falls.
George Washington Clark . . 13 . . . Exeter.
  Business.   Boston, Mass.
Charles Gilman Conner . . . . 12 . . . Exeter.
  H.U. 1854; Lawyer; Clerk of Courts.   "
Daniel Hoit Durgin . . . . . . 19 . . . Tuftonborough.
*Jacob Edwin Elliot . . . . . . 12 . . . Exeter 1853
                                                   "
Charles Franklin Folsom . . . 12 . . . Exeter.
  Saloon Keeper.   "
*Walter Gassett . . . . 16 . . . Boston, Mass. . . . 1846
William Pickering Healey. . . 14 . . . Hampton Falls.
Joseph Hobart . . . . 13 . . . Abington, Mass.
  Farmer.   Nordhoff, Ventura Co., Cal.
Christopher Columbus Langdell 18 . . . New Boston.
  H.U. 1851; A.M.; LL.D.; Dane Prof. Law, H.U.   Cambridge, Mass.
John Edward Lockwood. . . . 16 . . . Alexandria, D.C.
*James Peirce . . . . 19 . . . Dorchester, Mass. . 1853
                   "   "
Thomas Ryan . . . . 18 . . . Amesbury, Mass.
Elijah Merrill Shaw . . . . . . 18 . . . Kensington.
  Manufacturer.   Lewiston, Me.
Nathaniel Appleton Shute . . 12 . . . Exeter.
William True Sleeper . . . . . 23 . . . Smyrna, Me.
  Univ. Vt. 1850; A.M.; Clergyman.   Worcester, Mass.
*Howard Sleeper . . . . 13 . . . Roxbury, Mass. . . 1859
  Journalist.
George Washington Smith . . 20 . . . Stratham.
  Business.   Manchester.
*George Samuel Sullivan . . . 12 . . . Exeter 1869
  Lawyer.   Boston, Mass.
Richard Henry Sylvester . . . 16 . . . Charlestown.
  Editor.   St. Louis, Mo.
Theodore Tebbets . . . . 14 . . . Rochester 1863
  H.U. 1851; A.M.; Clergyman.   Medford, Mass.
Reuben Tower . . . . 16 . . . Waterville, N.Y.
                   "   "
*Patrick Henry Townsend . . . 21 . . . Salisbury 1864
  Bowd. Coll. 1850; Lawyer.   Washington, D.C.
Norris James Wiggin . . . . . 15 . . . Exeter.
  Business.   Memphis, Tenn.

26

1846.

Oscar Dunreath Abbot	22	Manchester.	
M.D.; Physician.		"	
William Fessenden Allen	14	Bangor, Me.	
Collector Gen. of Customs.		Honolulu, S.I.	
Hendrick Dearborn Batchelder	18	North Hampton.	
Lawyer		Haverstraw, N.Y.	
Lester Clark	15	Hartford, Conn.	
		" "	
John Wingate Clark	14	Stratham.	
Gov't Clerk.		Washington, D.C.	
Albe Cady Clarke	20	Sanbornton.	
Lawyer.		Boston, Mass.	
Thomas Currier	14	Dover.	
Farmer.		"	
*John Currier	15	Dover	1875
Lawyer.		Sioux City, Iowa.	
Josiah Hamilton Dearborn	16	Effingham.	
Lawyer.		Silver Lake, Kansas.	
*Wilder Dwight	13	Springfield, Mass.	1862
H.U. 1853; LL.B.; Lawyer.		Boston, Mass.	
*Robert Warren Folsom	11	Gordon, Ga.	1864
M.D.; Physician.		" "	
James Daniel Hewitt	13	Boston, Mass.	
Trinity Coll. 1854; M.D.			
William Wirt Hewitt	11	Boston, Mass.	
Robert Jamieson	13	Alexandria, D.C.	
Insurance Agent.		Danville, Va.	
John Henry Jenkins	22	New York, N.Y.	
*Charles H. Kingman	19	Durham	1868
Farmer.		Madbury.	
William Henry Lemon	19	West Cambridge, Mass.	
Alexander Chadbourne Low	13	Dover.	
Merchant.		Memphis, Tenn.	
James Fowler Lyman	15	Northampton, Mass.	
H.U. 1850; Lawyer.		New York, N.Y.	
John Godfrey Neil	16	Columbus, O.	
		St. Louis, Mich.	
Charles Horatio Nye	14	New Bedford, Mass.	
William Henry Page	19	Rochester.	
M.D.; Physician.		Los Vegas, New Mexico.	
Kingman Fogg Page	14	Rochester.	
Bowd. Coll. 1853; A.M.; Real Estate Agent.		New York, N.Y.	
*John Safford Parsons	18	Amesbury, Mass.	1862
Yale Coll. 1852; A.M.; Teacher.		So. Byfield, Mass.	
*Ivers Carter Phillips	15	Fitchburg, Mass.	1877
Business.			
Alexander William Purdy	18	Washington, D.C.	
George Orlando Smith	20	Bradford, Mass.	
George Washington Smith	14	Gloucester, Mass.	
Moody Adoniram Stevens	19	Bradford.	
Joseph Augustus Stickney	17	Somersworth.	
Bank Cashier.		"	
Russell Sturgis	15	Boston, Mass.	
Merchant (retired).		Brookline, Mass.	

Edward Wade . . . . 16 . . . Watervliet, N.Y.
Lawyer. Albany, N.Y.
Henry Chadwick Whittemore . 17 . . . West Cambridge, Mass.
Clerk. Arlington, Mass.
*Horatio H. F. Whittemore . . 16 . . . W. Cambridge, Mass. 1872
H.U. 1852; M.D. Marblehead, Mass.
34

1847.

*Day Fayette Ayer . . . . . . 22 . . . Haverhill, Mass. . . 1856
William Babson . . . . 13 . . . Gloucester, Mass.
Bank Cashier. " "
Ezra Bartlett . . . . 15 . . . Stratham.
Clerk. Boston, Mass.
David T. Chamberlain . . . . 23 . . . Weathersfield, Vt.
*Nathan Clifford . . . . 15 . . . Newfield, Me 1854
*John Marshall Cobbs . . . . . 11 . . . Exeter.
Mariner. "
Edward Charles Cole . . . . . 19 . . . Rochester.
*Edward Joseph Conner . . . . 12 . . . Exeter 1868
West Point, 1857; Lieut. U.S. Army. "
John Langdon Dearborn . . . 12 . . . Exeter.
H.U. 1857. Dorchester, Mass.
William Edward Dorsheimer . 15 . . . Buffalo, N.Y.
Lawyer. New York, N.Y.
Edward Forrest Eaton . . . . 16 . . . Newmarket.
H.U. 1851.
Joseph Low Elkins . . . . . . 12 . . . Newmarket.
Dart. Coll. 1856; M.D.; Physician. "
John Bryant Emerson . . . . 16 . . . Chelmsford, Mass.
Billings Farnsworth . . . . . . 18 . . . Buffalo, N.Y.
James Buonaparte Farrington . 16 . . . Rochester.
Bowd. Coll. 1854; A.M.; Lawyer. San Jose, Cal.
*William Frederic Faulkner . . 16 . . . Keene 1874
Business. Sioux City, Iowa.
John Henry French . . . . . . 18 . . . Pittsfield.
B.U. 1855; LL.B.; Lawyer. Eastport, Me.
*Charles William Gale . . . . . 12 . . . Exeter 1865
Business. "
*Nicholas Gilman . . . . 13 . . . Exeter 1854
H.U. 1854. "
George Gordon . . . . 13 . . . Boston, Mass.
Business. " "
Joseph Gilman Gordon . . . . 12 . . . Exeter.
Business. San Francisco, Cal.
Charles Wells Gray . . . . . . 15 . . . Exeter.
Business. Boston, Mass.
Orin McCrillis Head . . . . . 12 . . . Exeter.
Business. Pittsburg, Pa.
Amos Houlton . . . . 19 . . . Houlton, Me.
James Monroe Johnson . . . . 19 . . . Pittsfield.
Elias Davis Knight . . . . . . 14 . . . Gloucester, Mass.
James Lovell Loring . . . . . 14 . . . Boston, Mass.
*Stephen Eldridge Merrihew . . 15 . . . New Bedford, Mass. . 1868
William Curtis Mills . . . . . 21 . . . Boston, Mass.
Clergyman. Creston, Iowa.

Oliver White Peabody .... 13 ... Springfield, Mass.
Banker. Boston, Mass.
William Bourne Peabody ... 13 ... Springfield, Mass.
Boston, Mass.
*Samuel Perham .... 17 ... Chelmsford, Mass. . 1873
M.D.; Physician. Exeter.
*Henry Perry .... 15 ... Keene 1848
Student. "
John Rice Reynolds ..... 13 ... Honolulu, S.I.
Charles Clifford Smith .... 18 ... Bradford.
Washington Solomon ..... 14 ... Gordon, Ga.
George B. N. Tower ..... 13 ... Boston, Mass.
*Hamilton Ela Towle ..... 14 ... Lee 1881
Civil Engineer.
*Edward Walden .... 15 ... Buffalo, N.Y. 1854
Yale Coll. 1853. " "
William Henry Walker .... 22 ... West Cambridge, Mass.
Clergyman.
William Robert Ware ..... 14 ... Milton, Mass.
H.U. 1852; S.B.; Architect; Prof. Arch. Inst. New York,.N.Y.
Tech. 1867–81; Prof. Arch. Sch. Mines,
Columb. Coll.
Marquis D. Warren ...... 20 ... Wardsborough, Vt.
Sylvester Waterhouse ..... 16 ... Barrington.
H.U. 1853; LL.B.; Prof. Greek, Wash. U. St. Louis, Mo.
John Buffington Webster ... 12 ... New Market.
Henry Bellows Wells ..... 13 ... Exeter.
Business. Boston, Mass.
*Ephraim Weston .... 23 ... Hancock 1861
Farmer; Teacher. "
Henry King Wetherbee .... 15 ... New Market.
James Henry Wheeler .... 15 ... Dover.
M.D.; Physician. "

48

1848.

John Henry Alley .... 15 ... Lynn, Mass.
Treasurer Electric Light Co. " "
John Perry Allison ...... 16 ... Peterborough.
H.U. 1854; Lawyer. Sioux City, Iowa.
Richard Aylett Barrett .... 15 ... St. Louis, Mo.
William Henry Bass ..... 16 ... Boston, Mass.
*John Gorham Bond ..... 14 ... Boston, Mass. ... 1854
George Boynton .... 17 ... Peterborough.
Stephen Higginson Brooks .. 14 ... Exeter.
Theodore Edson Colburn ... 14 ... Boston, Mass.
H.U. 1854; Architect. " "
Oliver Sawyer Cressy ..... 13 ... Hamilton, Mass.
Charles Bartlett Crockett ... 14 ... Boston, Mass.
Business. Medford, Mass.
William Pitt Drew .... 18 ... Augusta, Me.
Russell Perkins Eaton .... 18 ... Augusta, Me.
Advertising Agent. Boston, Mass.
Amasa Fogg .... 20 ... Parsonsfield, Me.
John Edward Gardner .... 12 ... Exeter.
H.U. 1856; Merchant. "

Walter Scott Gove . . . . . . 16 . . . New Orleans, La.
*David Leavitt Hobbs . . . . . 16 . . . North Hampton . . . 1854
   Farmer.   "   "
Robert Porter Kimball . . . . 14 . . . Exeter.
*Henry Lord Page King . . . . 17 . . . St. Simon's Island, Ga. 1862
   Yale Coll. 1852; LL.B.
*Jonathan Marston Lamprey . . 17 . . . Hampton 1848
George Palfrey . . . . 18 . . . New Orleans, La.
   Yale Coll. 1853; Engineer U.S. Army.
William Wirt Pendergast . . . 14 . . . Durham.
Edward James Purdy . . . . . 13 . . . Exeter.
   Trinity Coll. 1857; A.M.; Clergyman.   Winona, Minn.
Lucius Junius Reed . . . . . . 14 . . . Boston, Mass.
Alphonso Allison Rice . . . 17 . . . Framingham, Mass.
   Civil Engineer.   Farmington, Van Buren Co., Ia.
*James Sullivan Roby . . . . . 12 . . . Exeter 1870
   Clerk.
Robert Russell . . . . 14 . . . Biddeford, Me.
George William Sawyer . . . . 18 . . . Wakefield.
James Nowell Smart . . . . . 14 . . . So. Newmarket.
Uriah Smith . . . . 16 . . . Wilton.
James Horace Stevens . . . 19 . . . Lawrence, Mass.
   Lawyer.   Boston, Mass.
*Frederic Wheeler . . . . . . 16 . . . Framingham, Mass. 1857
   H.U. 1854; LL.B.; Lawyer.

                                      31

1849.

John William Abbot . . . . . 15 . . . Westford, Mass.
   Manufacturer. (Graniteville, Mass.)   "   "
Frederic Lothrop Ames . . . . 14 . . . North Easton, Mass.
   H.U. 1854; Capitalist and Manufacturer.   Boston, Mass.
Joseph Addison Carter . . . . 13 . . . Bridgewater, Vt.
*Jonathan Chapman . . . . . . 13 . . . Boston, Mass. . . . 1882
   H.U. 1856; A.M.; Business.   Cincinnati, O.
Elias Hutchins Cheney . . . . 17 . . . Holderness.
   Editor.   Lebanon.
William Henry Coelho . . . . 12 . . . Montevideo, S.A.
*Thomas Palfrey Cole . . . . . 15 . . . Hallowell, Me. . . . ? 1867
George Luna Davenport . . . 15 . . . Exeter.
*Payson Perrin Ellis . . . . . . 16 . . . Boston, Mass. . . . 1863
   H.U. 1855; Merchant.   East Indies.
Cornelius Fiske . . . . 19 . . . Lincoln, Mass.
   H.U. 1853; Lawyer.   New York, N.Y.
*Thomas Groom . . . . 13 . . . Boston, Mass. . . . 1855
George Wells Healey . . . . . 14 . . . Lynn, Mass.
   H.U. 1856; Business.
William Elwyn Jewell . . . 14 . . . Stratham.
   Dart. Coll. 1856; Lawyer.   Boston, Mass.
George Henry Johnson . . . . 17 . . . Charlestown, Mass.
                                        Greenpoint, N.Y.
Frederic Burditt Kilner . . . . 21 . . . Barre, Mass.
Lewis Carr Lawton . . . . . . 17 . . . Providence, R.I.
William Smith Leonard . . . . 17 . . . Dublin.
   Dart. Coll. 1856; M.D.; Physician.   Hinsdale.

George Putnam Moore . . . . 23 . . . Manchester.
Wilbur Fiske Newhall . . . . 16 . . . Lynn, Mass.
Sec. Insurance Co.   Saugus, Mass.
Jeremiah Smith . . . . 12 . . . Lee.
H.U. 1856; A.M.; Lawyer; Judge Supreme   Dover.
Court, N.H. 1867-74.
George Stickney . . . . 21 . . . Georgetown, Mass.
Benjamin Saxon Story . . . . 16 . . . New Orleans, La.
David Henry Taylor . . . . . 15 . . . Lynn, Mass.
John Samuel Titcomb . . . . . 15 . . . Somersworth.
Titus Salter Tredick . . . . . 14 . . . Portsmouth.
H.U. 1854; A.M.   "
Warren Van Buren Tuxbury . 13 . . . Amesbury, Mass.
Merchant.   New London, Conn.
Joseph Rowe Webster . . . . 15 . . . Milton, Mass.
H.U. 1854; M.D.; Physician.   "   "

27

1850.

Robert Edward Babson . . . . 12 . . . Gloucester, Mass.
H.U. 1856; Teacher Eng. High School.   Boston, Mass.
Willard Flagg Bliss . . . . . . 20 . . . St. Louis, Mo.
H.U. 1855; Teacher.   "   "
Edward Jackson Brown . . . . 17 . . . Fitchburg, Mass.
H.U. 1855; Business.   St. Louis, Mo.
Langley Boardman Brown . . 15 . . . Kensington.
Farmer.   "
*James Sterrett Cenas . . . . . 13 . . . New Orleans, La. . . . 1853
*Sylvester W. Chadbourne . . . 23 . . . Kennebunk, Me. . . . 1863
Teacher.   Freehold, N.J.
Benjamin Graves Chambers . . 13 . . . St. Louis, Mo.
Gardiner Hubbard Clarke . . . 18 . . . Brookline, Mass.
Albert Dickerman . . . . 19 . . . Stoughton, Mass.
LL.B.; Lawyer.   Boston, Mass.
Daniel Appleton Dwight . . . 14 . . . Brookline, Mass.
Business.   Boston, Mass.
*Howard Dwight . . . . 13 . . . Brookline, Mass. . . . 1862
H.U. 1857; A.M.; Business.   Memphis, Tenn.
Raymond Egerton . . . . 14 . . . New Orleans, La.
H.U. 1856; Lawyer.   New York, N.Y.
Edward Thornton Fisher . . . 13 . . . Oswego, N.Y.
H.U. 1856; A.M.; Teacher.   Brooklyn, N.Y.
George Washington Gale . . . 13 . . . Exeter.
*John Gardner Gibson . . . . . 14 . . . Boston, Mass. . . . 1856
Charles Hammond Gibson . . 13 . . . Boston, Mass.
Merchant.   "   "
Michael Cavan Martinez . . . 19 . . . St. Thomas, W.I.
James Perley Page . . . . . . 12 . . . Exeter.
Broker.   New York, N.Y.
Daniel Hussey Page . . . . . . 16 . . . Rochester.
Farmer.   Lindsburg, Kansas.
Daniel Dearborn Parsons . . . 17 . . . Rye.
Mariner.
Willard Quincy Phillips . . . . 16 . . . Cambridge, Mass.
H.U. 1855; A.M.; LL.B.
Benjamin Franklin Prescott . . 17 . . . Epping.
Dart. Coll. 1856; Gov. N.H. 1877-8; Farmer.   "

Charles Otis Roddin	15	Lynn, Mass.
*Edward Grenville Russell	16	Groton, Mass. ... 1880
H.U. 1855; A.M.; Clergyman; Business.		Cambridge, Mass.
Allen Schenck	20	Manhassett, N.Y.
Business.		New York, N.Y.
Nathaniel Stone Simpkins	16	Yarmouthport, Mass.
Dart. Coll. 1856; Merchant.		New York, N.Y.
George Washington Spofford	18	Peterborough.
Business.		Chicago, Ill.
Charles Edward Stetson	15	Braintree, Mass.
H.U. 1854; A.M.; Teacher.		" "
George Harrison Stevens	19	Deerfield.
Farmer.		"
*Edward Seth Tisdale	14	Ellsworth, Me. ... 1861
Samuel Brooks Wyman	18	Newburyport, Mass.
H.U. 1856; A.M.; Lawyer.		Lowell, Mass.

1851.

Roger Newton Allen	14	Greenfield, Mass.
Capitalist.		Boston, Mass.
Stephen Barker	22	Boxford. Mass.
Clergyman.		Northampton, Mass.
George Frederic Barker	15	Rochester.
Merchant.		Chicago, Ill.
Joshua William Beede	18	Poplin.
Dart. Coll. 1858; M.D.; Physician.		Auburn, Me.
*Daniel Reynolds Carter	16	Wakefield 1865
Dart. Coll. 1857; Teacher.		"
*Ward Chadwick	20	West Boxford, Mass. 1862
Lawyer.		
Bradbury Longfellow Cilley	12	Exeter.
H.U. 1858; A.M.; Prof. Anc. Lang. P.E.A.		"
John Theodore Clarke	17	Pittsfield.
Dart. Coll. 1858; A.M.; Supt. Pub. Schools.		Chicopee, Mass.
William Travis Clarke	22	Boston, Mass.
Clergyman.		Harlem, N.Y.
*Samuel Rowland Crocker	14	Boston, Mass..... 1878
Bowd. Coll. 1855; Editor.		" "
Thomas Augustus Cushing	16	Somersworth.
Dart. Coll. 1857; Clerk.		Washington, D.C.
Presley Judson Edwards	19	St. Louis, Mo.
Artemas Clinton Field	24	Lempster.
Clergyman.		Hinesburg, Vt.
Francis Freeman Fogg	17	Cambridgeport, Mass.
John Henry Gale	17	Gloucester, Mass.
Selah Bancroft Howard	21	Winchester, Mass.
*Henry Oxnard Hooper	16	Boston, Mass.
Horace Jewett	17	South Berwick, Me.
Maj. U.S. Army.		
Chauncey Hastings Kidder	14	Exeter.
Joseph Dana Littlefield	23	Randolph, Mass.
M.D.; Physician.		Youngstown, O.
Benjamin Smith Lyman	15	Northampton.
H.U. 1855; Mining Engineer.		Philadelphia, Pa.
*Horace Houlton Meloon	13	Exeter 1867
Gov't Service.		New Orleans, La.

Edward Bagley Merrill . . . . 16 . . . New Bedford, Mass.
Bowd. Coll. 1857; A.M.; Lawyer.   New York, N.Y.
Washington Hill Merritt . . . 23 . . . Warren, Mass.
H.U. 1856; A.M.; Teacher.   Boston, Mass.
*Edward Palfrey . . . . 15 . . . New Orleans, La. . . 1862
Planter.   St. Mary's, La.
*John Dexter Porter . . . . . . 14 . . . New Salem, Mass. . 1867
Farmer.   Pennington's Pt., Ill.
Franklin Benjamin Sanborn . 19. . . . Hampton Falls.
H.U. 1855; Journalist and Author.   Concord, Mass.
Henry Francis Snow . . . . . 19 . . . Effingham.
Clergyman.   Cornish, Me.
Robert Kermit Stewart . . . . 12 . . . New York, N.Y.
*Charles A. Coffin Thompson . 16 . . . Durham 1868
Farmer.   "
Peter Sanborn Thompson . . . 12 . . . Exeter.
  Brentwood.
William Hale Thompson . . . 13 . . . Durham.
Business.   Chicago, Ill.
*Newell Tibbets . . . . 23 . . . Stewartstown 1859
Antioch Coll. 1857.   "
Samuel Hidden Wentworth . . 16 . . . Concord.
H.U. 1858; A.M.; LL.B.; Lawyer.   Boston, Mass.
*Wilbur Winchester . . . . . . 17 . . . Charlestown, Mass. . 1863
Machinist.   "   "
*George Lafayette Wise . . . . 15 . . . Portland, Me.   . . . 1854
Edward Woods . . . . 15 . . . Bath.
Dart. Coll. 1856; Lawyer.   Albany, N.Y.

37

1852.

James Burditt Barnes . . . . . 16 . . . Dover.
Lawyer.   "
William Augustus Boyd . . 11 . . . New York, N.Y.
John Kelly Cilley . . . . 12 . . . Exeter.
Merchant.   New York, N.Y.
Francellus Gordon Dalton . . 11 . . . Exeter.
Wendell Davis . . . . 16 . . . Greenfield, Mass.
Dart. Coll. 1857.   New Bedford, Mass.
John Edwin Dodge . . . . . . 15 . . . Exeter.
Clerk.   Boston, Mass.
John Foster . . . . 19 . . . Dublin.
Dart. Coll. 1858; Teacher.   Faribault, Minn.
Francis Ormond French . . . . 14 . . . Washington, D.C.
H.U. 1857; LL.B.; Banker.   New York, N.Y.
*James Paulus French . . . . . 12 . . . Exeter 1867
Amh. Coll. 1859; A.M.
William Delesdenier Fuller . . 15 . . . Calais, Me.
  Washington, D.C.
George Gorham . . . . 15 . . . Canandaigua, N.Y.
H.U. 1857; Lawyer.   Buffalo, N.Y.
Edward Dromgool Grant . . . 16 . . . Norfolk, Va.
Yale Coll. 1858; Business.   New York, N.Y.
Charles Hutchins Hapgood . . 16 . . . Petersham, Mass.
B.U. 1857; Business.   Chicago, Ill.
William Franklin Hathaway . 16 . . . New Bedford, Mass.
Dart. Coll. 1858; Business.   "   "

Alfred Houston Haven . . . . 16 . . . Portsmouth.
   H.U. 1858; M.D.; Physician.   "
Edward Livingston Hill . . . 19 . . . Portsmouth.
   Lawyer.   Peabody, Mass.
Isaac Wallingford Hobbs . . . 14 . . . Effingham.
   Dart. Coll. 1859; Farmer.   Pembroke.
Lewis French Hobbs . . . . . 16 . . . North Hampton.
   Teacher.   West Medford, Mass.
William F. B. Jackson . . . . 16 . . . Boston, Mass.
   Clergyman.   Providence, R.I.
Joseph Edward Janvrin . . . . 13 . . . Exeter.
   M.D.; Physician.   New York, N.Y.
Richard Montgomery Johnson 16 . . . Dover.
   Salesman.   Boston, Mass.
*John A. La Forest Julian . . . 15 . . . Exeter 1856
   Clerk.   Chicago, Ill.
*John Avery Parker Lothrop. . 15 . . . New Bedford, Mass.
Charles King Luzenburg . . . 15 . . . New Orleans, La.
   Coll. N.J. 1857; A.M.; Judge Dist. Ct.   "   "
Jesse Page Marshall . . . . . 23 . . . Kingston.
   Farmer.   "
Henry Mathes . . . . 12 . . . Portsmouth.
   H.U. 1862.   "
*George Mathes . . . . 16 . . . Portsmouth 1868
   Shipmaster.   "
Malcolm McIntire . . . . 17 . . . Parsonsfield, Me.
   Bowd. Coll. 1857; Lawyer.   Owensborough, Ky.
*John Boardman Morse . . . . 17 . . . Dover 1868
   Clerk.   Chelsea, Mass.
William Moulton . . . . 19 . . . Ossipee.
*Edwin Augustus Nye . . . . Milo, Me. 1879
Charles Pomeroy Otis . . . . . 12 . . . Rye.
   Yale Coll. 1861; A.M.; Ph.D.; Prof. Mod. Lang.   Boston, Mass.
   Inst. Tech.
John McClary Perkins. . . . . 18 . . . Somersworth.
   Lawyer.   Washington, D.C.
Robert Cutts Pierce . . . . . . 12 . . . Greenland.
   Banker.   Portsmouth.
*Treat Wentworth Potter . . . 16 . . . Manchester 1879
   Business.   "
*Joseph Warren Rowe . . . . . 17 . . . Kensington.
      Illinois.
Edmund Rowland . . . . . . 17 . . . Springfield, Mass.
   Clergyman.   Cincinnati, O.
John Warren Sanborn . . . . 18 . . . East Kingston.
   Farmer.   Kingston.
*Richard Willard Sears . . . . 16 . . . Boston, Mass. . . . 1880
   Business.   "   "
Walter Devereux Sewall . . . 17 . . . Watertown, N.Y.
   Bookkeeper.   "   "
William Gardner Shackford . . 12 . . . Portsmouth.
   Shipmaster.   South Orange, N.J.
John Elbridge Sinclair . . . . 14 . . . Exeter.
   Prof. Scientific School, Dart. Coll. 1866–69;   Worcester, Mass.
   Teacher, Free Inst.
Henry James Stevens . . . . . 15 . . . North Andover, Mass.
   H.U. 1857; Lawyer.   Boston, Mass.
*Horace Nathaniel Stevens . . . 14 . . . N. Andover, Mass. . . 1876
   Manufacturer.   "   "

Benjamin Franklin Swasey . . 15 . . . Exeter.
Business. "
John Pearse Treadwell . . . . 13 . . . Portsmouth.
H.U. 1858; LL.B.; Lawyer. Boston, Mass.
*John Tredick . . . . 14 . . . Wakefield 1881
Dart. Coll. 1860; M.D.; Physician. Perrymansville, Md.
Wheelock Graves Veazey . . . 17 . . . Exeter.
Dart. Coll. 1859; LL.B.; Lawyer; Judge Sup'r Rutland, Vt.
Ct., Vt.
George Albert Wentworth . . 16 . . . Wakefield.
H.U. 1858; A.M.; Prof. Math. P. E. A.; Author. Exeter.
Jesse Alexander Wilkins . . . 21 . . . Middleton, Mass.
Farmer. Woodstock, Conn.
Solomon Walker Young . . . 16 . . . Barnstead.
M.D.; Physician. Pittsfield.

51

1853.

Benjamin Barnes . . . . 14 . . . Dover.
Insurance Agent. Portland, Me.
Isaac Increase Blaisdell . . . . 21 . . . Jay, Me.
Dwight Boyden . . . . 15 . . . Boston, Mass.
Frederic Boyden . . . . 14 . . . Boston, Mass.
*Augustus Warren Chapman . 15 . . . St. Joseph, Mich. . . 1864
Univ. Mich. 1859.
*Jacob Abbot Cram . . . . . . 17 . . . Hampton Falls . . . 1872
H.U. 1859; Lawyer. Chicago, Ill.
*James Aiken Crockett . . . . 16 . . . Boston, Mass. . . . 1878
Business. " "
James Clarke Davis . . . . . . 15 . . . Greenfield, Mass.
H.U. 1858; Lawyer. Boston, Mass.
James Samuel Dearborn . . . 13 . . . Exeter.
Printer. Boston, Mass.
Richard Draper Douglass . . . 17 . . . Plattsburg, N.Y.
William Bradbury Drew . . . 16 . . . Nahant, Mass.
Charles William Eaton . . . . 19 . . . Boston, Mass.
Samuel Johnson Edgerly . . . 22 . . . Pittsfield.
Dart. Coll. 1859; Farmer. Seneca, Kan.
Simeon Bartlett Folsom . . . . 16 . . . Dover.
Commercial Traveller. "
Walter Gale . . . . 19 . . . Northborough, Mass.
LL.B.; Lawyer. " "
Edward John Handiboe . . . 17 . . . Boston, Mass.
James Alexander Hartness . . 20 . . . Cleveland, O.
Dart. Coll. 1859; Broker. " "
*Edward Autis Hayes . . . . . 17 . . . Canandaigua, N.Y. . . 1863
Charles Ela Hill . . . . 14 . . . Newmarket.
Charles Adams Horne . . . . 16 . . . Somersworth.
H.U. 1860; Teacher. Albany, N.Y.
George Naylor Julian . . . . . 12 . . . Exeter.
Business. San Francisco, Cal.
*Henry Martyn Keith . . . . . 23 . . . Warren Mass. . . . 1881
Teacher. Chicago, Ill.
James Morrill Larrabee . . . . 19 . . . Wales, Me.
Farmer. Gardiner, Me.
Henry Knight Leaver . . . . . 14 . . . Concord.
Gov't Service. Washington, D.C.

Nathaniel Low, jr. . . . . 15 . . . Dover.
    New Hampton.
Virgil Homer McDaniel . . . . 17 . . . Barrington.
*Benjamin Batchelder McNeal . 16 . . . Exeter 1874
Hiram Augustus Merrill . . . 15 . . . Watertown, N.Y.
  Lawyer.   "   "
James Henry Mulholland . . . 18 . . . Eastport, Me.
  Lawyer.   Presque Isle, Me.
Horatio Cheever Newhall . . . 16 . . . Galena, Ill.
  Lawyer.   San Francisco, Cal.
George W. C. Noble . . . . . 16 . . . Somersworth.
  H.U. 1858; A.M.; Teacher.   Boston, Mass.
*Amos Masters Paul . . . . . . 14 . . . So. Newmarket. . . 1858
Edwin Ruthven Perkins . . . . 20 . . . Tamworth.
  Dart. Coll. 1857; Cashier.   Cleveland, O.
Marcus Morton Poole . . . . . 17 . . . New York, N.Y.
Lawrence Vernon Poole . . . 14 . . . New York, N.Y.
*Henry Augustus Richardson . 17 . . . Cambridge, Mass. . 1863
  H.U. 1858; M.D.; Surg. U.S. Navy.
Daniel Webster Sanborn . . . 17 . . . East Kingston.
  Dart. Coll. 1860; A.M.; Teacher.   Philadelphia, Pa.
Charles Haven Sawyer . . . . 12 . . . Wakefield.
William Scrimgeour . . . . . . 16 . . . Brooklyn, N.Y.
Jonathan Addison Severance . 19 . . . Kingston.
Joseph Alden Shaw . . . . . . 17 . . . Sudbury, Mass.
  H.U. 1858; A.M.; Teacher.   Worcester, Mass.
Edward Rowland Sill . . . . . 12 . . . Cuyahoga, O.
  Yale Coll. 1861; Prof. Eng. Lang. and Lit.   Oakland, Cal.
  Univ. Cal.
*James Wesley Stephenson . . 18 . . . Cambridge, Mass. . 1867
  H.U. 1859; LL.B.; Lawyer.   San Francisco, Cal.
Warren Carlton Stevens . . . 15 . . . North Andover, Mass.
  Salesman.   Boston, Mass.
Edward Swett Tappan . . . . 15 . . . Somerville, Tenn.
John Harvey Treat . . . . . . 14 . . . Pittsfield.
  H.U. 1862; A.M.; Business.   Lawrence, Mass.
James Oberlin Treat . . . . . 12 . . . Pittsfield.
    Melrose, Mass.

    47

1854.

George Edward Henry Abbot . 16 . . . Westford, Mass.
  H.U. 1860; A.M.; Teacher.   Groton, Mass.
Elijah Harrison Austin . . . . 15 . . . Madbury.
    Brooklyn, N.Y.
George Washington Barber . . 19 . . . Epping.
  Clergyman.   Maine.
William Butler Blake . . . . . 16 . . . Raymond.
  Business.   Marshall, Mich.
*Henry French Brown . . . . . 14 . . . North Hampton . . . 1863
  Law Student.
Philo Chase . . . . 23 . . . Munroe, Me.
  Lawyer.   New York, N.Y.
*William Webster Claflin . . . 20 . . . Leominster, Mass. . 1864
  M.D.; Physician.   Hudson, Mass.
*Ellery Channing Clarke . . . . 18 . . . Westford, Mass.
  Business.   Manchester.

Stephen Wells Clarke . . . . . 16 . . . Pittsfield.
Dart. Coll. 1862; A.M.; Business. Manchester.
*Edmund Henry Cushing . . . 16 . . . Charlestown 1869
H.U. 1859; Paymaster U. S. Navy.
Samuel Page Dame . . . . . . 13 . . . Brentwood.
Bowd. Coll. 1862; A.M.; Druggist. Sharon, Pa.
*George William Dewhurst . . 15 . . . Exeter 1866
Business. Savannah, Ga.
*Henry Weld Farrar . . . . . . 13 . . . Bangor, Me. 1881
H.U. 1861; Editor. Chicago, Ill.
Daniel Brainard Fitts . . . . . 17 . . . Epping.
 Providence, R. I.
Frederic Augustus Fuller . . . 14 . . . Bangor, Me.
James Gilchrist . . . . 16 . . . Charlestown.
Broker. Boston, Mass.
Charles Snelling Gill . . . . . 13 . . . Exeter.
Merchant. Boston, Mass.
Charles Glidden Haines . . . . 14 . . . Biddeford, Me.
Bowd. Coll. 1861. " "
*Frederic Hallett . . . . 18 . . . Yarmouth, Mass. . . 1861
Lawyer.
James Lang Harriman . . . . 20 . . . Dalton.
M.D.; Physician. Hudson, Mass.
Jedediah Kilborn Haywood . . 19 . . . Concord.
Ira Gustavus Hoitt . . . . . . 21 . . . Lee.
Dart. Coll. 1860; A.M.; Broker. San Francisco, Cal.
Jesse Harrison Houghton . . . 23 . . . Boston, Mass.
*John Simeon Chase Kelly . . . 16 . . . Atkinson 1861
Albert Etheridge Kennard . . 17 . . . South Newmarket.
William Arthur Kilbourn . . . 16 . . . Groton, Mass.
H.U. 1858; A.M.; Farmer. Lancaster, Mass.
*Simeon Swett Leavitt . . . . 12 . . . Exeter.
Business. Boston, Mass.
Washington Marsh . . . . . . 14 . . . Nottingham.
Charles Edward Perkins . . . 15 . . . Pittsfield.
Farmer. Madbury.
Warren Warner Porter . . . . 16 . . . New Salem, Mass.
Teacher. Bridgeport, Conn.
*William James Quinn . . . . . 12 . . . Newmarket 1882
Lawyer. Lawrence, Mass.
Edward Mussey Rand . . . . 15 . . . Portland, Me.
Bowd. Coll. 1859; A.M.; Lawyer. " "
Wilson Ward Robinson . . . . 15 . . . Brentwood.
Frederic Atherton Ross . . . . 20 . . . Terre Haute, Ind.
Real Estate Broker. " " "
*Francis Wallingford Sabine . . 16 . . . Bangor, Me. 1864
Bowd. Coll. 1859; A.M.
Winborne Adams Shaw . . . . 17 . . . Kensington.
Clergyman. Cincinnati, O.
John Darrah Smith . . . . . . 15 . . . Brentwood.
*Francis Bartlett Smith . . . 16 . . . Portland, Me. . . . 1879
Business. " "
Alfred Stebbins . . . . 18 . . . Vernon, Vt.
Amh. Coll. 1860; Farmer. San Buenaventura, Cal.
Calvin Stebbins . . . . 18 . . . So. Wilbraham, Mass.
Amh. Coll. 1862; Clergyman. Detroit, Mich.
Arthur Judson Swain . . . . . 18 . . . Leominster, Mass.
Teacher. Port Austin, Mich.

*Charles Lewis Swan . . . . . . 14 . . . So. Easton, Mass. . 1865
H.U. 1859; LL.B.
Warren Lincoln Swett . . . . 13 . . . Lawrence, Mass.
John Laning Taylor . . . . . . 15 . . . Owego, N.Y.
*Pearson Cogswell Tebbets . . 15 . . . Madbury 1867
Charles Collins Thatcher . . . 20 . . . Stockholm, N.Y.
Broker. St. Louis, Mo.
Jacob Hall Thompson . . . . 16 . . . Portsmouth.
Bowd. Coll. 1860; A.M.; Journalist. New York, N.Y.
Minot Tirrell . . . . 19 . . . Roxbury, Mass.
John Sheldon Treat . . . . . . 16 . . . Portsmouth.
Marble Worker. "
Edward Tuck . . . . 11 . . . Exeter.
Dart. Coll. 1862; Banker. New York, N.Y.
Alonzo Claudius Whitridge . . 14 . . . Charleston, S.C.
Business. New York, N.Y.
*Augustus Wiswall Wiggin . . 13 . . . Wakefield 1875
Dart. Coll. 1862; M.D.; Surg. U.S. Army.
John Winslow . . . . 18 . . . Lynn, Mass.
H.U. 1859; A.M.; M.D.; Physician. Ithaca, N.Y.
Charles Jones Wyeth . . . . . 18 . . . Galena, Ill.
George Sylvester York . . . 19 . . . Exeter.

55

1855.

Luther Cheney Abbot . . . . . 24 . . . New Salem, Mass.
Lawyer. Richmond, Ind.
George Ayer . . . . 25 . . . Haverhill, Mass.
Business. " "
Marcellus Bailey . . . . 15 . . . Washington, D.C.
Lawyer. " "
*Thomas Kelly Bolton . . . . . 15 . . . Cleveland, O. 1879
H.U. 1861; Lawyer. " "
*Alfred Brewster . . . . 18 . . . Tamworth 1879
Farmer. "
Perley Blodgett Bryant . . . . 18 . . . Barrington.
Buel Clinton Carter . . . . . . 15 . . . Ossipee.
Yale Coll. 1862; Lawyer. Dover.
*Simon Leavitt Chapman . . . 19 . . . North Hampton . . . 1880
Farmer. Minnesota.
*Howard Malcolm Chase . . . . 15 . . . Stratham 1863
Dart. Coll. 1862. "
Daniel Gilman Conner . . . . 13 . . . Exeter.
Business. New York, N.Y.
William Ellery Copeland . . 16 . . . Roxbury, Mass.
H.U. 1860; A.M.; Clergyman. Omaha, Neb.
Samuel Quarles Dearborn . . . 19 . . . Effingham.
Dart. Coll. 1860; Lawyer. Effingham Falls.
Frederic M. Dearborn . . . . 13 . . . Newton, Mass.
M.D.
Sherburne Blake Eaton . . . . 15 . . . Lawrence, Mass.
Yale Coll. 1862; Lawyer. New York, N.Y.
William Conner Ellis . . . . . 16 . . . Thibodeaux, La.
*Samuel Fessenden . . . . . . 14 . . . Portland, Me. 1862
Bowd. Coll. 1861. "
George Fuller Gill . . . . . . 12 . . . Exeter.
Dart. Coll. 1862; M.D.; Physician. St. Louis, Mo.

William Henry Grant	21 . . .	Ossipee.
M.D.; Physician.		Ossipee Center.
*Gasper Spurzheim Grant . . .	18 . . .	Ossipee 1865
Dart. Coll. 1861; M.D.		"
Charles Walter Greene	13 . . .	Newmarket.
George Sears Greene	17 . . .	Bristol, R.I.
George Washington Harrison .	16 . . .	Westfield, Mass.
		Worthington, Mass.
William Hawes	20 . . .	Boston, Mass.
Mayo Williamson Hazeltine . .	14 . . .	Belfast, Me.
H.U. 1862; A.M.; Editor and Author; Lawyer.		Elizabeth, N. J.
Gilman Clark Hickok	16 . . .	Boston, Mass.
George Frank Hobbs	13 . . .	Wakefield.
Abijah Hollis	18 . . .	Milton, Mass.
LL.B.; Contractor.		Concord.
George William Hoover	14 . . .	Washington, D.C.
Joseph Albert Locke	15 . . .	Lawrence, Mass.
Jerome Fenelon Manning . . .	16 . . .	Lowell, Mass.
Lawyer.		Boston, Mass.
John Buzzell Mathews	16 . . .	Wakefield.
Edward Paschal McKinney . .	17 . . .	Binghampton, N.Y.
Yale Coll. 1861; Merchant.		" "
Henry McLaughlin	15 . . .	Bangor, Me.
Joseph William Merrill	12 . . .	Exeter.
Business.		"
Daniel Gage Neal	17 . . .	South Newmarket.
Albert Lane Norris	16 . . .	Epping.
M.D.; Physician.		Cambridge, Mass.
*Rufus Greenleaf Norris	16 . . .	Epping 1873
Farmer.		"
*John Sawyer Page	15 . . .	North Berwick, Me. . 1876
		Boston, Mass.
Hersey Goodwin Palfrey . . .	16 . . .	Belfast, Me.
H.U. 1860; Civil Engineer.		St. Louis, Mo.
Retire Hathorn Parker	15 . . .	Exeter.
Merchant.		Boston, Mass.
Arthur Livermore Payne . . .	20 . . .	Center Harbor.
Henry Edward Prescott	14 . . .	Chicago, Ill.
Samuel Dalton Quarles	22 . . .	Ossipee.
Lawyer.		"
Daniel Webster Ranlet	12 . . .	Exeter.
Business.		Boston, Mass.
George Rice	17 . . .	Framingham, Mass.
Yale Coll. 1860; A.M.; M.D.; Physician.		So. Framingham, Mass.
*Samuel Comings Richardson .	25 . . .	Cornish, Me. 1859
Teacher.		Petaluna, Cal.
*George William Robinson . . .	15 . . .	Exeter 1864
Rufus Price Rose	18 . . .	Stephentown, N.Y.
Charles Edwin Rundlett . . .	13 . . .	Exeter.
Machinist.		Providence, R.I.
*Charles Christie Salter	15 . . .	Portsmouth 1870
H.U. 1861; Clergyman.		
*Hiram Moore Sanborn	22 . . .	Tamworth 1879
Teacher.		New York, N.Y.
Noah Sanborn	16 . . .	Tamworth.
M.D.; Physician.		New Jersey.
Charles Edward Smith	12 . . .	Durham.

Alvah Augustus Smith . . . . 23 . . . Candia.
Broker. Boston, Mass.
George Webster Stevens . . . 18 . . . Nottingham.
Charles Christopher Stuart . . 18 . . . Mobile, Ala.
Merchant. " "
John Sullivan . . . . 15 . . . Exeter.
Apothecary. Boston, Mass.
*Jeremiah Hall W. Tebbets . . 14 . . . Nashua 1880
Business. Lynn, Mass.
*Charles Edwin Thurrell . . . . 16 . . . North Berwick, Me. 1857
*George Carter Thurston . . . 17 . . . Ossipee 1883
Supt. Street R. R. Boston, Mass.
*Orestes Topliff . . . . 19 . . . Freedom 1864
Lawyer. "

61

1856.

George Everett Adams . . . . 16 . . . Chicago, Ill.
H.U. 1860; LL.B.; Lawyer. " "
John Allyn . . . . 13 . . . Belfast, Me.
Business. Boston, Mass.
*Timothy Kneeland Ames . . . 18 . . . Peterborough 1862
Lawyer. "
George Washington Atherton . 18 . . . Danvers, Mass.
Yale Coll. 1863; A.M.; Prof. Hist., Polit. Econ., State College, Pa.
Rutgers Coll.; Pres. State Coll., Pa.
William Nelson Batchelder . . 18 . . . Holliston, Mass.
Amh. Coll. 1863; Merchant. La Crosse, Wis.
Benjamin Franklin Boyden . . 14 . . . Tamworth.
Cyrus Osgood Brown . . . . . 21 . . . Kensington.
Farmer. Chichester.
William Ripley Brown . . . . 16 . . . Ashby, Mass.
Charles Henry Brown . . . . . 18 . . . Candia.
Insurance Agent. Boston, Mass.
William Ela Buck . . . . 18 . . . Hampstead.
Supt. Pub. Schools. Manchester.
James Henry Buckner . . . . . 19 . . . Covington, Ky.
M.D.; Physician. Cincinnati, O.
*James Dearborn Butler . . . . 13 . . . Nottingham 1877
H.U. 1864; A.M.; Lawyer. Portsmouth.
Albert Clarke Buzell . . . . . 11 . . . Exeter.
H.U. 1865; A.M.; LL.B.; Lawyer. "
Joseph Henry Byne . . . . . . 16 . . . Stafford Point, Tex.
Business. San Antonio, Tex.
*John Treadwell Cole . . . . . 14 . . . Exeter 1871
H.U. 1860; M.D.; Physician. Newburyport, Mass.
George Thomas Conner . . . . 13 . . . Exeter.
Business. Boston, Mass.
Horace Stuart Cummings . . . 15 . . . Hillsborough.
Dart. Coll. 1862; Lawyer. Washington, D.C.
Edmund Joseph Curley . . . . 20 . . . West Newbury, Mass.
Distiller. Lexington, Ky.
Charles Seth Cushman . . . . 19 . . . Jamesville, Wis.
John Daland . . . . 18 . . . Salem, Mass.
Insurance Agent. Boston, Mass.
Elleus Gardner Dalton . . . . 11 . . . Exeter.
Nathaniel Russell Davis . . . 14 . . . Greenfield, Mass.
Stock Raising. Cheyenne, Wy. Territory.

Timothy Spaulding Dodge . . 27 . . . Boston, Mass.
*Horace Drew . . . . 19 . . . Barrington 1864
Clerk. Boston, Mass.
Charles Droun . . . . 31 . . . Troy, N.Y.
Frederic Henry Elder . . . . . 16 . . . Rochester, N.Y.
Orlando Marcellus Fernald . . 15 . . . East Kingston.
H.U. 1864; A.M.; Prof. Greek, Will. Coll. Williamstown, Mass.
Charles Winthrop Fifield . . . 13 . . . So. Newmarket.
Yale Coll. 1864; Clergyman. Champion, N.Y.
Charles Henry Folsom . . . . 14 . . . Exeter.
William Merchant R. French . 12 . . . Exeter.
H.U. 1864; Landscape Engineer. Chicago, Ill.
Jesse Franklin Frisbee . . . . 18 . . . Rochester.
M.D.; Physician. Newton, Mass.
Paul Chadbourne Garvin . . . 21 . . . Acton, Me.
M.D.; Physician. Frankfort, Kan.
John Gordon . . . . 13 . . . Exeter.
Piano Tuner. Chelsea, Mass.
Henry Francis Gould . . . . . 14 . . . Kennebunkport, Me.
Weigher. Boston, Mass.
Frank Warren Hackett . . . . 15 . . . Portsmouth.
H.U. 1861; A.M.; Lawyer. Washington, D.C.
William Henry Hadselle . . . 16 . . . Hancock, Mass.
Farmer. " "
*Samuel Cushman Haven. . . . 13 . . . Portsmouth 1863
H.U. 1862.
William Brownell Heath . . . 20 . . . Lunenburg, Mass.
Clergyman. Fall River, Mass.
*Leander Massilon Hoitt . . . . 20 . . . Lee 1859
Richard Hopkins Jackson . . 16 . . . Clarksville, Tex.
John McKenzie Jackson . . 14 . . . Clarksville, Tex.
Josiah Weare Kingsbury . . . 17 . . . Tamworth.
Dart. Coll. 1862; Clergyman. Exeter.
Abraham Gordon Ladd . . . . 19 . . . Deerfield.
Business. Raymond.
Roscius Henry Leach . . . . . 15 . . . Somersworth.
Newton Littlefield . . . . 16 . . . Haverhill, Mass.
Clerk. " "
Timothy Morison Longley . . 18 . . . Peterborough.
Royalston, Mass.
Francis Alexander Marden . . 16 . . . Windham.
H.U. 1863; A.M.; Lawyer. New York, N.Y.
Elias Hutchins Marston . . . . 13 . . . North Hampton.
Teacher. Boston, Mass.
James Rundlett May . . . . . 14 . . . Portsmouth.
H.U. 1861; A.M.; M.D.; Surg. U.S. Navy. "
Collin Swain McKenzie . . . . 17 . . . Cleveland, O.
Printer. " "
*John Folsom Moses . . . . . . 14 . . . Knoxville, Tenn. . . 1857
James Franklin Powers . . . . 19 . . . Boston, Mass.
Nathaniel Appleton Prentiss . 16 . . . West Cambridge, Mass.
H.U. 1862; A.M.; Lawyer. New York, N.Y.
Granville Bradstreet Putnam . 21 . . . Danvers, Mass.
Amh. Coll. 1861; Teacher Franklin School. Boston, Mass.
*Edward Jackson Reynolds . . 18 . . . Honolulu, S.I. . . . 1865
Civil Engineer. " "
Charles Asa Smith . . . . . . 17 . . . Somersworth.
Boston, Mass.

Lucius Smith	21	Bristol, Wis.
Edward Gray Stetson	15	So. Scituate, Mass.
H.U. 1863; A.M.; LL.B.; Lawyer.		San Francisco, Cal.
Norman Story	15	Plaquemine, La.
*Edwin Alonzo Sturtevant	14	Rochester 1858
Stephen Thomas Swift	13	Lexington, Ky.
Business.		" "
Algernon Sydney Symmes	19	Ryegate, Vt.
George Grosvenor Tarbell	15	Lincoln, Mass.
H.U. 1862; M.D.; Physician.		Boston, Mass.
Edward Payson Ten Broeck	17	Portland, Me.
Amos Towle	18	Freedom.
Teamster.		Boston, Mass.
Jabez Nelson Trask	23	Westbrook, Me.
H.U. 1862; Clergyman.		New Salem, Mass.
Joseph Badger Upham	15	Portsmouth.
Bowd. Coll. 1861; A.M.; Engineer U.S. Navy.		
Daniel Barber Veazey	14	Brentwood.
Teacher and Agent.		Hematite, Mo.
George Albert Wadleigh	16	Somersworth.
U.S. Navy.		
Joseph Dennis Wadsworth	16	Barre, Mass.
Druggist.		" "
Daniel French Wells	16	Brooklyn, N.Y.
M.D.; Journalist.		Exeter.
William Henry Wescott	16	Boston, Mass.
M.D.; Physician.		" "
Alexander Wilson Wheeler	15	Cleveland, O.
M.D.; Physician.		" "
Russell Homer White	16	Belfast, Me.
Business.		Leadville, Col.
*Heber Milton White	12	Belfast, Me.
Joseph Fernald Wiggin	18	Exeter.
Lawyer; Prob. Judge (Exeter). 1871–76.		Boston, Mass.
George Washington Wiggin	20	North Hampton.
Insurance Agent.		Exeter.
Joseph Henry Willard	13	Chicago, Ill.
William Ayer Wood	15	Somersworth.

1857.

*Forrester Andrew	16	Salem, Mass.
Edward Larke Appleton	17	Bangor, Me.
James Edward Bates	15	Somersworth.
H.U. 1864; Lawyer.		Boston, Mass.
James Dana Bell	17	Exeter.
LL.B; Lawyer and Farmer.		Hawthorne, Fla.
Charles Upham Bell	14	Exeter.
Bowd. Coll. 1863; A.M.; Lawyer.		Lawrence, Mass.
Clarke Blaisdell	16	Marblehead, Mass.
Cotton Printer.		Manchester.
Marshall William Blake	15	New York, N.Y.
Merchant.		" "
Charles Edward Blake	12	Condersport, Pa.
Yale Coll. 1865; M.D.; Physician.		" "
*Charles Malcolm Boyd	18	West Newbury, Mass. 1864

Solomon Hoyt Brackett . . . . 18 . . . Framingham, Mass.
H.U. 1862; A.M.; Teacher.   St. Johnsbury, Vt.
Francis Erving Bradford . . . 13 . . . Raymond.
*Addison Reese Brown . . . . 13 . . . Kensington 1880
Farmer.   "
*William Jason Cain . . . . . . 17 . . . Rutland, Vt. 1877
Freight Supt.   Sedalia, Mo.
Charles Monroe Carleton . . . 17 . . . Waterford, Me.
M.D.; Physician.   Norwich, Conn.
Charles Abbot Cheney . . . . 13 . . . Stratham.
Joseph Longfellow Cilley . . . 14 . . . Exeter.
H.U. 1864; Merchant.   New York, N.Y.
William Augustine Cram . . . 19 . . . Hampton Falls.
Clergyman.   " "
David Franklin Davis . . . . . 24 . . . Nottingham.
Dart. Coll. 1862; Hotel Keeper.   Waco, Texas.
Clarkson Dearborn . . . . . . 16 . . . Seabrook.
Merchant.   Amesbury, Mass.
Addison Leonard Demerritt . . 22 . . . Nottingham.
Farmer.   "
Charles Follen Folsom . . . . 15 . . . Meadville, Pa.
H.U. 1862; A.M.; M.D.; Physician.   Boston, Mass.
Robert Plummer Foss . . . . . 22 . . . Strafford.
Lawyer.   Harlem, Iowa.
Jonathan John French . . . . 12 . . . Philadelphia, Pa.
Samuel Harvey Gleason . . . 17 . . . Barnet, Vt.
Lawyer.   Sedalia, Mo.
Mercer Goodrich . . . . 14 . . . Portsmouth.
Business.   "
Richard Lewis Gove . . . . . 16 . . . Seabrook.
  Newburyport, Mass.
John Phipps Munroe Green . . 17 . . . Kensington.
Shoe Dealer.   Haverhill, Mass.
Charles Ezra Green . . . . . . 15 . . . Cambridge, Mass.
H.U. 1862; Prof. Civil Engineering, Univ. Mich.   Ann Arbor, Mich.
John Dean Hall . . . . 14 . . . Eddyville, Iowa.
H.U. 1863; M.D.; A.M.; U.S. Army.
James William Hanson . . . . 19 . . . Lee.
  Arizona.
Daniel Thomas V. Huntoon . 14 . . . Marblehead, Mass.
  Canton, Mass.
*James Mills Kingsbury . . . . 22 . . . Tamworth 1863
*Harlan Page Kingsbury . . . . 16 . . . Tamworth 1864
Otis Lyscom Leonard . . . . . 14 . . . East Marshfield, Mass.
H.U. 1866; Clergyman.   " " "
James Lovejoy Libby . . . . . 12 . . . New York, N.Y.
Business.   " "
Rufus Pratt Lincoln . . . . . 16 . . . Amherst, Mass.
Amh. Coll. 1862; M.D.; Physician.   New York, N.Y.
Joshua Elbridge G. Lyford . . 16 . . . Brentwood.
*Albert George Manson . . . . 20 . . . Limington, Me. . . . 1878
Bowd. Coll. 1862; A.M.; Teacher.   Cleveland, O.
*James Knowles Medbery . . . 18 . . . Portsmouth 1873
Editor and Author.   New York, N.Y.
Payson Merrill . . . . 15 . . . Stratham.
Yale Coll. 1865; LL.B.; Lawyer.   New York, N.Y.
George Shattuck Morison . . . 14 . . . Milton. Mass.
H.U. 1863; A.M.; LL.B.; Civil Engineer.   New York, N.Y.

*William Henry Morrill . . . . 15 . . . Exeter 1862
   Teacher.   "
Wareham Morse . . . . 14 . . . New Haven, Conn.
*William Francis Munroe . . . 17 . . . Bradford, Mass . . . 1875
   M.D.; Physician.   Boston, Mass.
*James Woodbury Norris . . . 17 . . . Nottingham 1882
   Merchant.   Rice, Tex.
Francis Cushing Nye . . . . . 17 . . . New Bedford, Mass.
   H.U. 1862; Lawyer.   New York, N.Y.
*William Albert Odell . . . . . 16 . . . Durham 1867
   H.U. 1864; A.M.
John McCleary Parker . . . . 20 . . . Fitzwilliam.
   Business.   "
John William Parsons . . . . 16 . . . Rye.
   M.D.; Physician.   Portsmouth.
Edward Augustus Penniman . 15 . . . Boston, Mass.
Edward Cranch Perkins . . . 13 . . . Cincinnati, O.
   H.U. 1866; A.M.; Lawyer.   Boston, Mass.
Benjamin Judson Perkins . . . 19 . . . Exeter.
   Farmer.   "
Ezra Pray . . . . 25 . . . Rochester.
   M.D.; Physician.   "
Garland Roberts . . . . 17 . . . Stratham.
   Farmer.   "
William Rotch Robeson . . . . 14 . . . New Bedford, Mass.
   H.U. 1864; A.M.; LL.B.; Lawyer.   -   Boston, Mass.
George Frank Rollins . . . . . 13 . . . Exeter.
   Mason.   "
Frederic Moseley Sackett . . . 17 . . . Providence, R.I.
   B.U. 1861; Manufacturer.   "   "
Charles Adams Sackett . . . . 14 . . . Providence, R.I.
   Lawyer.   New York, N.Y.
Ira Otis Sawyer . . . . 19 . . . Haverhill, Mass.
   Shoe Manufacturer.   "   "
Nathaniel Curtis Scoville . . . 21 . . . Pitcairn, N.Y.
   H.U. 1864; LL.B.; Lawyer.   Lee, Summit Co., Kan.
Joseph Herbert Senter . . . . 14 . . . Portsmouth.
   H.U. 1861; Clergyman.   Portland, Me.
*Frederic William Smith . . . 20 . . . Manchester, Mass. . 1869
   Capt. Cavalry U.S. Army.   Texas.
Albert Stetson . . . . 23 . . . Kingston, Mass.
   H.U. 1861; A.M.; Teacher.   Normal, Ill.
Chester Colton Stevens . . . . 22 . . . Brentwood.
Charles Brigham Stoddard . . 15 . . . Plymouth, Mass.
   H.U. 1862; Merchant.   "   "
Stephen Millet Thompson . . . 19 . . . Lee.
   Real Estate Agent.   Providence, R.I.
John Wool Wheeler . . . . . . 14 . . . Cleveland, O.
   M.D.; Physician.   "   "
James Willey . . . . 18 . . . Exeter.
   Painter.   Haverhill, Mass.

1858.

*Augustus Barker . . . . 16 . . . Albany, N.Y. 1863
William Elbridge Boardman . . 14 . . . Boston, Mass.
   H.U. 1865; M.D.; Physician.   "   "

CATALOGUE.

Samuel Henry Bradley . . . . 15 . . . Olean, N.Y.
Business. " "
Charles Albert Bunker . . . . 18 . . . Barnstead.
Dart. Coll. 1864; A.M.; Supt. Public Schools. Peacham, Vt.
Elbridge Tyler Burley . . . . . 16 . . . Newmarket.
Lawyer. Lawrence, Mass.
Henry Sanborn Cate . . . . 16 . . . Greenland.
Business. Millerstown, Pa.
Harrison Cole . . . . 17 . . . Southbridge, Mass.
Optician. Columbus, O.
*Henry Clinton Corey . . . . . 21 . . . Chaplin, Conn. . . . 1864
New York, N.Y.
Elmer Lawrence Corthell . . . 17 . . . South Abington, Mass.
B.U. 1867; Civil Engineer. New York, N.Y.
Frederic Balch Deane . . . . . 17 . . . Uxbridge, Mass.
Lawyer. Marlborough, Mass.
Brainerd Dearborn . . . . . . 16 . . . North Hampton.
M.D.; Physician. Portsmouth.
Warren Everett Eaton . . . . 19 . . . North Reading, Mass.
Master Harlow School. Boston, Mass.
George Prentiss Edgerly . . . 17 . . . Farmington.
*John Marshall Eldridge, jr. . . 19 . . . Hampton, Conn. . . 1865
Journalist. Jersey City, N.J.
James Henry Elliot . . . . . . 15 . . . Keene.
H.U. 1864; A.M.; Lawyer. New York, N.Y.
*Benjamin Brown French . . . 13 . . . Washington, D.C. . 1881
Civil Engineer. South America.
William Gerrish . . . . 16 . . . Chelsea, Mass.
Real Estate Agent. " "
LeRoy Sunderland Gove . . . 20 . . . Milford.
H.U. 1864; Lawyer. New York, N.Y.
John Orne Green . . . . 17 . . . Lowell, Mass.
H.U. 1863; A.M.; M.D.; Aurist. Boston, Mass.
Henry Gremmels . . . . 20 . . . Gottingen, Germany.
Farmer. Hampton.
Moses Uriah Hall . . . . 23 . . . Exeter.
Mason. "
John Samuel Hayes . . . . . . 17 . . . Durham.
Teacher. Somerville, Mass.
Laban Mark Hill . . . . 19 . . . Barrington.
George Irving Hoitt . . . . . 15 . . . Durham.
Business. Boston, Mass.
Edward Robbins Howe . . . . 15 . . . Detroit, Mich.
H.U. 1864; A.M.; Engineer. Boston, Mass.
George William Kittredge . . 16 . . . Dover.
M.D.
*William Newell Locke . . . . 16 . . . Lee 1865
Henry Lunt . . . . 16 . . . Quincy, Mass.
H.U. 1863; A.M.; Lawyer. Boston, Mass.
Charles Brown Marsh . . . . . 17 . . . Waltham, Mass.
Clerk. Tewksbury, Mass.
William Henry Marsh . . . . . 15 . . . Waltham, Mass.
George Henry Morse . . . . . 21 . . . Walpole, Mass.
Farmer. " "
Samuel Badger Neal . . . . . 16 . . . Kittery, Me.
H.U. 1864; A.M.; Clerk. Boston, Mass.
Edward Gookin Parker . . . . 17 . . . Kittery, Me.
Benjamin Sewall Pike . . . . 16 . . . Newburyport, Mass.
Govt. Service. Washington, D.C.

Henry Webster Powers . . . . 20 . . . South Abington, Mass.
Clerk. New York, N.Y.
Gustavus Percival Pratt . . . 17 . . . Cohasset, Mass.
M.D.; Physician. " "
William Scollay Prentiss . . . 19 . . . Baltimore, Md.
Hosea Mason Quinby . . . . . 18 . . . Pittsfield.
B.U. 1865; M.D.
Edwin Sanborn Reed . . . . . 21 . . . Uxbridge, Mass.
*Daniel Smyth Sayles . . . . . 24 . . . Burrillville, R.I. . . . 1871
John Benton Shaw . . . . . . 16 . . . Olean, N.Y..
Telegraph Supt. Jamestown, N.Y.
Marshall Solomon Snow . . . 16 . . . East Dennis, Mass.
H.U. 1865; A.M.; Prof. Polit. Lit. and Hist., St. Louis, Mo.
Wash. Univ.
Edward Lewis Sturtevant . . . 16 . . . Winthrop, Me.
Bowd. Coll. 1863; A.M.; M.D.; Physician. South Framingham, Mass.
John Robinson Swinerton . . . 17 . . . Milton.
Hotel Keeper. Long Branch, N.J.
Daniel Locke Tubbs . . . . . 25 . . . Olean, N.Y.
Ransom Tiphiania Tubbs . . . 18 . . . Olean, N.Y.
Charles Henry Warren . . . . 14 . . . New York, N.Y.
Business. Providence, R.I.
*Thomas Jefferson Washburn . 19 . . . Bridgewater, Mass. . 1866
Alonzo Bond Wentworth . . . 18 . . . Somersworth.
LL.B.; Lawyer. Boston, Mass.
Allen Baston Wheeler . . . . . 32 . . . Exeter.
Mechanic. Blackberry Station, Ill.

50

1859.

*Edward Stanley Abbot . . . . 17 . . . Beverly, Mass. . . . 1863
George Henry Adams . . . . . 17 . . . Middleton, Mass.
Charles Alphonso Ames . . . 20 . . . Peterborough.
Merchant. Denver, Col.
Daniel Baker . . . . 17 . . . Milton, Me.
John Augustus Balestier . . . 17 . . . New York, N.Y.
Lawyer. " "
Francis Barnes . . . . 18 . . . Portland, Me.
*Alfred William Barnes . . . . 20 . . . Owosso, Mich. . . . 1866
Teacher. Muskingum, O.
Sidney Kenedy Beckwith . . . 17 . . . Chelsea, Mich.
William Parmenter Bennett . . 22 . . . Groton, Mass.
Will. Coll. 1862; Clergyman. Ames, Iowa.
Egbert Byron Bingham . . . 21 . . . Scotland, Conn.
Yale Coll. 1863; Clergyman. Rockville, Conn.
Albert Blair . . . . 18 . . . Barry, Ill.
H.U. 1863; Lawyer. Macon, Mo.
*William Francis Brigham . . . 20 . . . Feltonville, Mass. . 1865
Annapolis, Md.
Augustus Scott Campbell . . . 16 . . . Galena, Ill.
Lawyer. Chicago, Ill.
Henry Converse Carter . . . . 18 . . . Flushing, N.Y.
John White Chadwick . . . . . 18 . . . Marblehead, Mass.
Clergyman. Brooklyn, N.Y.
Henry Clusky . . . . 19 . . . St. Louis, Mo.
Lawyer. San Francisco, Cal.

Henry Newton Comey . . . . 19 . . . . Holliston, Mass.
Lucien Alfred Cox . . . . . . 19 . . . Marlborough, Mass.
Druggist.   Providence, R.I.
James Love Crittenden . . . . 17 . . . San Francisco, Cal.
George Selden Cullum . . . . 16 . . . Meadville, Pa.
Supt. Gas and Water Co's.   "   "
Prentiss Cummings . . . . . . 18 . . . Sumner, Me.
H.U. 1864; LL.B.; Lawyer.   Boston, Mass.
Jeremiah Curtin . . . . 23 . . . Greenfield, Wis.
H.U. 1863.
Benjamin Price Davis . . . . . 15 . . . Brooklyn, N.Y.
Merchant.   New York, N.Y.
*George Washington Davis . . 17 . . . Canton, Mo. 1873
Cyrus William Dearborn . . . 14 . . . Amesbury, Mass.
Moses Ayer Drew . . . . 15 . . . Alfred, Me.
Lawyer.   "   "
Edward Smith Eveleth . . . 17 . . . Essex, Mass.
M.D.; Physician.   Gloucester, Mass.
George Seward Ffrost . . . 14 . . . Durham.
H.U. 1865; A.M.; Lawyer.   Dover.
*William Abijah Flagg . . . . . 20 . . . Bloomington, Ill. . . . 1877
M.D.; Physician.   Veria, Ill.
Cleaveland Foote . . . . 17 . . . Springfield, Mass.
Business.   New York, N.Y.
Charles Fuller . . . . 16 . . . Lincoln, Me.
Bowd. Coll. 1865; A.M.; M.D.; Physician. "   "
Charles Allen Gilman . . . . . 15 . . . Effingham.
*William Lawrence Gordon . . 19 . . . Exeter 1864
                                       Andersonville, Ga.
Francis Gorman . . . . 18 . . . Springfield, Mass.
H.U. 1864; A.M.; Teacher.   Cambridge, Mass.
John Fordyce Gould . . . . . 18 . . . Wilton, Me.
Samuel Lampson Gould . . . 19 . . . Albany, Me.
M.D.
Henry Clay Gowdey . . . . . 15 . . . Eutaw, Ala.
Teacher.   Paris, Tex.
William Holder Gray . . . . . 18 . . . Walpole, Mass.
Manufacturer.   Boston, Mass.
Preston Gurney . . . . 16 . . . South Abington, Mass.
B.U. 1866; Clergyman.   Central Falls, R.I.
Elijah Brown Hazen . . . . . 18 . . . Deerfield.
*Lewis Reyburne Hempstead . 17 . . . Galena, Ill. 1872
Lawyer.   "   "
George Anthony Hill . . . . . 17 . . . Sherburne, Mass.
H.U. 1865; A.M.; Asst. Prof. Math. H.U. Cambridge, Mass.
Charles Edmund James . . . . 15 . . . Exeter.
Clerk U.S. Navy.   Portsmouth.
Nathaniel March Jewett . . . 17 . . . Bangor, Me.
Merchant.   Boston, Mass.
George Clayton Latham . . . . 17 . . . Springfield, Ill.
Merchant.   "   "
Edward Newbold Lawrence . . 17 . . . Flushing, N.Y.
Heywood Lee . . . . 18 . . . Lenox, Mass.
Business.   Philadelphia, Pa.
*Douglas Lee . . . . 14 . . . Lenox, Mass. 1864
Robert Todd Lincoln . . . . . 16 . . . Springfield, Ill.
H.U. 1864; U.S. Sec. War; Lawyer.   Chicago, Ill.
Henry Burnham Mead . . . . 18 . . . Hingham, Mass.
Yale Coll. 1866; A.M.; Clergyman.   Stonington, Conn.

*Richard Jones Meconkey ... 17 ... West Chester, Pa. . 1878
*Charles Sewall Merrick .... 18 ... Walpole, Mass. ... 1866
　Chemist; S.B.
James Christie Moore ..... 20 ... Topsfield, Me.
　Business.　　　　　　　　　　　　　　East Cambridge, Mass.
John Cousins Mordough ... 15 ... Hamilton, Mass.
Ralph Keniston Nichols .... 16 ... Portsmouth.
　Agent Water Co.　　　　　　　　　　Lower Lake, Lake Co., Cal.
Joseph Franklin Noone .... 18 ... Peterborough.
　Miller.　　　　　　　　　　　　　　　　"
Josiah Alonzo Osgood. .... 17 ... Chelsea, Mass.
　Mechanical Engineer.　　　　　　　　Boston, Mass.
Boyd Cummings Packer .... 16 ... Harrisburg, Pa.
　　　　　　　　　　　　　　　　　　　Lock Haven, Pa.
John Davis Parker ...... 18 ... Salem, Mass.
　Business.　　　　　　　　　　　　　　Boston, Mass.
Edward Everett Parker .... 17 ... Brookline.
　Dart. Coll. 1860; Lawyer; Prob. Judge.　Nashua.
William Peters .... 17 ... Ogdensburg, N.Y.
　Lawyer.　　　　　　　　　　　　　　　New York, N.Y.
*John Thomas Pope ...... 17 ... Halifax, Mass. ... 1874
　B.U. 1865; LL.B.; Lawyer.　　　　　Jersey City, N.J.
Seth Gurney Reed. ...... 19 ... Baltimore, Md.
John Monat Rice .... 27 ... Northborough, Mass.
　Prof. Math. Naval Acad.　　　　　　Annapolis, Md.
George H. M. Rowe ..... 18 ... Salmon Falls.
　Dart. Coll. 1864; A.M.; M.D.; Physician.　Boston, Mass.
George Briggs Russell .... 15 ... Plymouth, Mass.
　Major U.S. Army.
James Milton Sawin. ..... 17 ... Brookline.
　Teacher.　　　　　　　　　　　　　　　Providence, R.I.
Henry Chapin Sawin ..... 16 ... Brookline.
　Teacher.　　　　　　　　　　　　　　　Newton, Mass.
Andrew Homer Scott ..... 18 ... Dover, Ark.
　M.D.; Physician.　　　　　　　　　　Little Rock, Ark.
Charles Jinks Simons ..... 16 ... Prome Birmah.
*Job Randall Smith ...... 16 ... Manchester 1863
　Student, Bost. Univ.
Frank Russell Stoddard. ... 15 ... Plymouth, Mass.
　H.U. 1866; A.M.; City Cashier.　　　Boston, Mass.
James Breckenridge Sumner . 16 ... Dalton.
　M.D.; Physician.　　　　　　　　　　Bloomington, Neb.
George Milmore Taylor .... 14 ... Baltimore, Md.
George Weeks Thompson ... 22 ... Barrington.
John Brown Thompson .... 18 ... Oldtown, Me.
Frederic Henry Thompson .. 15 ... New Salem, Mass.
　M.D.; Physician.　　　　　　　　　　Fitchburg, Mass.
Charles Walter Tower .... 17 ... Randolph, Mass.
　M.D.; Physician.　　　　　　　　　　Marshfield, Oregon.
Henry Herbert Townsend ... 17 ... Milton.
Jay Tuttle .... 17 ... Nottingham.
　M.D.; Physician.　　　　　　　　　　Portland, Oregon.
*William Henry Twilight .... 21 ... Exeter.
Alphonzo White. .... 16 ... Chelsea, Mass.
Charles Edward Wiggin ... 16 ... Durham.
　Shoe Manufacturer.　　　　　　　　　Haverhill, Mass.
Charles Sidney Wilder .... 18 ... Holliston, Mass.
　Business.　　　　　　　　　　　　　　　"　　　　"

Joseph Henry Wilder . . . . . . 16 . . . Holliston, Mass.
Henry Thomas Wing . . . . . 17 . . . Sandwich, Mass.
  H.U. 1864; A.M.; LL.B.; Lawyer.   New York, N.Y.
James Lawrence Young . . . . 14 . . . Lawrence, Mass.
                                                                                 87

1860.

Morison Alexander . . . . . . 19 . . . Derry.
Edward Lowell Anderson . . . 17 . . . Cincinnati, O.
                                        "   "
Charles Alvan Beach . . . . . 16 . . . Springfield, Mass.
Frank Arthur Brackett . . . . 18 . . . Framingham, Mass.
  Teacher.   Bristol, Conn.
Albert Lawrence Brown . . . 13 . . . Exeter.
  LL.B.; Broker.   Boston, Mass.
*William Gerrish Brown . . . . 19 . . . Manchester 1866
                                                "
*Clarence Colman Buck . . . . 22 . . . Gorham, Me. 1871
Francis Marion Caldwell . . . 23 . . . Golden Ridge, Me.
  Farmer.   Sherman, Me.
Leonard Hathaway Caldwell . 21 . . . Golden Ridge, Me.
                                                Jacksonville, Fla.
Maro Johnson Chamberlain . . 18 . . . Dublin.
  Miner.   Frisco, Utah.
William Edwin Chamberlain . 19 . . . Sacramento, Cal.
Albro Elmore Chase . . . . . 16 . . . Paris Hill, Me.
  H.U. 1865; Editor; Prin. High Sch.   Portland, Me.
Clement Cleveland . . . . . . 16 . . . Cambridge, Mass.
  H.U. 1867; A.M.; M.D.; Physician.   New York, N.Y.
John Franklin Clifford . . . . 15 . . . Portland, Me.
Ira Lathrop Davies . . . . . . 15 . . . Oldtown, Me.
George Henry Davis . . . . . 18 . . . Portland, Me.
*George Washington Davis . . 14 . . . Exeter 1881
  Printer.
William Coffin Davis . . . . . 13 . . . Gloucester, Mass.
*Frank Fiske Dinsmoor . . . . 15 . . . Keene 1870
  H.U. 1867.
Pierre Cheaseman Dubois . . . 15 . . . Fishkill Landing, N.Y.
  Supt. of Mines.   San Francisco, Cal.
Thomas Chandler Edwards . . 17 . . . Keene.
  Business.   Chicago, Ill.
Manning Emery . . . . 15 . . . Portsmouth.
  Business.   Boston, Mass.
Willard Francis Esty . . . . . 20 . . . Canton, Mass.
  Lawyer.   Boston, Mass.
David Webber Farquar . . . . 16 . . . Holliston, Mass.
  Business.   Boston, Mass.
George Albert Fisher . . . . . 20 . . . Dorchester, Mass.
  H.U. 1865; LL.B.; Lawyer.   Boston, Mass.
George Augustus Flagg . . . . 15 . . . Holliston, Mass.
  H.U. 1866; A.M.; LL.B.; Manufacturer. Millbury, Mass.
James Greely Flanders . . . . 15 . . . Milwaukee, Wis.
  Yale Coll. 1867; LL.B.; Lawyer.   "   "
Robert Hall French . . . . . . 17 . . . Bedford.
Orville Knight Gerrish . . . . 19 . . . Sumner, Me.
  Lawyer.   Portland, Me.

Charles Llewellyn Gibbs . . . 17 . . . Framingham, Mass.
Le Roy Freeze Griffin . . . . . 15 . . . Epsom.
B.U. 1866; A.M.; Prof. Lake Forest Coll.   Illinois.
Leverett Duncan Gunter . . . 21 . . . Queensbury, N.B.
M.D.; Physician.   Chelsea, Mass.
Meldon Leroy Hanscom . . . . 17 . . . Portsmouth.
H.U. 1867; Merchant.   Parkersburg, Oregon.
Charles Hayes . . . . 20 . . . Berwick, Me.
M.D.; Physician.   Providence, R.I.
*Orville Pomeroy Higgins . . . 17 . . . Flint, Mich. 1861
*Otis Hinkley . . . . 23 . . . New Harmony, Ind.
William Carey Howard . . . . 19 . . . South Easton, Mass.
James Otis Hoyt . . . . 17 . . . Haverhill, Mass.
H.U. 1865; A.M.; LL.B.; Lawyer.   New York, N.Y.
Sanford Benton Hubbard . . . 19 . . . Shelburne.
Govt. Service.   Cambridge, Mass.
John Webster Johnson . . . . 18 . . . Southborough, Mass.
Frank William Jones . . . . . 14 . . . Portsmouth.
Capitalist.   Boston, Mass.
Ludlow Ap Jones . . . . 16 . . . Cincinnati, O.
H.U. 1865; A.M.; Lawyer.   " "
William Harding King . . . 14 . . . Springfield, Mass.
Merchant.   " "
William Jones Ladd . . . . . . 16 . . . Portsmouth.
Mining Engineer.   Milton, Mass.
George Hobart Latham . . . . 13 . . . East Bridgewater, Mass.
Business.   Memphis, Tenn.
Anson Hapgood Lawrence . . 17 . . . Barre, Mass.
Lawyer.   Chicago, Ill.
*John Edwards Leonard . . . 14 . . . Fairville, Pa. 1878
H.U. 1867; A.M.; M.C.; Lawyer; Ch. Just.   Louisiana.
Supr. Ct.
*Arthur Jones Loud . . . . 14 . . . Plymouth, Mass. . . . 1872
H.U. 1867; A.M.
*Henry Clay McCreary . . . 18 . . . Sacramento, Cal. . . . 1869
Yale Coll. 1865; Lawyer.   " "
Franklin Miller . . . . 18 . . . Sacramento, Cal.
Cashier.   " "
John Ames Mitchell . . . . . . 15 . . . East Bridgewater, Mass.
Editor.   New York, N.Y.
Charles Coburn Morgan . . . 17 . . . Dracut, Mass.
Clinton Morrill . . . . 15 . . . Bangor, Me.
George Lyman Morse . . . . . 13 . . . Boston, Mass.
Business.   " "
George William Neal . . . . 16 . . . Kittery, Me.
H.U. 1865; A.M.; Teacher.   Boston, Mass.
*David Leighton Ordway . . . 16 . . . Haverhill, Mass. . . . 1869
H.U. 1865; A.M.; LL.B.
Calvin Page . . . . 15 . . . North Hampton.
Lawyer.   Portsmouth.
*Henry Harrison Pearson . . . 20 . . . Lincoln, Ill. 1864
Leonard Hobart Pillsbury . . 24 . . . Derry.
Merchant.   "
Almon Porter . . . . 13 . . . Haverhill, Mass.
Samuel Plumer Prescott . . . 15 . . . Haverhill, Mass.
Dart. Coll. 1867; Lawyer.   Princeton, Ill.
George Newton Proctor . . . 18 . . . Fitchburg, Mass.
Merchant.   " "

Henry Foster Ranney	19	Brattleborough, Vt.
Samuel Augustus Russell	17	New York, N.Y.
Clifford Saville	19	Lexington, Mass.
Merchant.		" "
Edwin Pliny Seaver	22	Northborough, Mass.
H.U. 1864; A.M.; Supt. Public Schools.		Boston, Mass.
Andrew Coolidge Stone	20	Marlborough, Mass.
Lawyer.		Lawrence, Mass.
William Prescott Stoddard	14	Plymouth, Mass.
H.U. 1866; Corporation Treasurer.		" "
Ezra Knight Sweetser	27	Cumberland, Me.
		" "
Samuel Swett	14	Exeter.
Miner.		Georgetown, Cal.
*James Monroe Tappan	19	East Kingston ... 1862
John Horace Taylor	15	Chelsea, Mass.
Sheep Ranching.		Larned, Kan.
Godfrey Siegen Thaler	19	Stillwater, Minn.
LL.B.		
Alonzo Towle	16	Freedom.
M.D.; Physician.		"
Charles Jackson Train	15	Framingham, Mass.
*Thomas Logan Tullock	15	Portsmouth 1870
Paymaster U.S. Navy.		"
Augustus Van Wyck	14	Pendleton, S.C.
Lawyer.		New York, N.Y.
Frank Thomas Vinal	15	North Andover, Mass.
M.D.; Physician.		Scituate, Mass.
*Henry Ware	14	Cambridgeport, Mass. 1862
Charles Edwin Webster	19	Portland, Me.
Bowd. Coll. 1866; A.M.; M.D.; Physician.		" "
Charles Eben Wentworth	15	Portsmouth.
Publisher.		Cambridge, Mass.
Rufus Lawrence Wilder	15	Leominster, Mass.
M.D.; Physician.		New York, N.Y.
Joseph Woodward Wilder	13	Leominster, Mass.
		" "
Gorham Deane Williams	18	Deerfield, Mass.
H.U. 1865; Lawyer.		Greenfield, Mass.
George Washington Wilson	16	Upper Marlborough, Md.
Merchant.		" " "

85

1861.

Richard Franklin Alley	16	Newmarket.
Frank Benjamin Arnold	17	New York, N.Y.
H.U. 1866; Merchant.		" "
George William Ayers	15	Stratham.
Farmer.		"
Josiah Bartlett Batchelder	18	Exeter.
Clerk.		Boston, Mass.
William Henry Bennett	17	Hampton, Conn.
Yale Coll. 1866; LL.B.; Lawyer.		Stirling, Ill.
*Charles Wilbert Bickford	18	Rochester 1875
Wilmon Whiledin Blackmar	20	Boston, Mass.
Lawyer.		" "

Henry Thatcher Boutwell . . . 17 . . . Nashua.
H.U. 1866; M.D.; Physician. Manchester.
Benjamin Franklin Brickett . . 15 . . . Haverhill, Mass.
Dart. Coll. 1867; Lawyer. " "
*Joseph Emmons Briggs . . . . 20 . . . Dighton, Mass. . . . 1867
H.U. 1866.
Francis Wayland Butler . . . 19 . . . Bennington.
James William Carlisle . . . . 17 . . . Exeter.
Business. "
*Frank Augustus Carpenter . . 17 . . . Foxborough, Mass. . 1867
H.U. 1866.
*Josiah Andrews Chandler . . . 15 . . . Portsmouth 1877
Engineer. Belmont, Mass.
George Washington Cobb . . . 17 . . . Dighton, Mass.
Samuel Adams Coburn . . . . 17 . . . Portsmouth.
Clerk. Boston, Mass.
Nathan Cutler . . . . 16 . . . Augusta, Me.
Lawyer. New York, N.Y.
Elbridge Gerry Cutler . . . . . 14 . . . Augusta, Me.
H.U. 1868; M.D.; Physician. Boston, Mass.
William Franklin Davis . . . 21 . . . Lowell, Mass.
H.U. 1867; Clergyman. Chelsea, Mass.
William Henry Dodge . . . . . 14 . . . Hampton Falls.
Lawyer. Dover.
*Lewis Francis Dupee . . . . . 22 . . . No. Wrentham, Mass. 1871
Teacher.
John Edwin Earley . . . . . . 19 . . . Walpole, Mass.
Civil Engineer. El Paso, Tex.
*George Frederic Emery . . . . 16 . . . Portland, Me. . . . 1873
H.U. 1866; A.M.; Merchant. San Francisco, Cal.
Charles Gershom Fall . . . . . 15 . . . Malden, Mass.
H.U. 1868; A.M.; Lawyer and Author. Boston, Mass.
Joseph Allen Fay . . . . 17 . . . Milford, Mass.
M.D.; Physician. "
Charles Coolidge Flagg . . . . 14 . . . Exeter.
Clerk. San Francisco, Cal.
*John Howard Folsom . . . . . 13 . . . Exeter 1872
Clerk. Boston, Mass.
William Henry Fuller . . . . . 13 . . . Cambridge, Mass.
Carlton Clark Fyler . . . . . . 24 . . . West Killingly, Conn.
Charles Sibley Gage . . . . . . 17 . . . Concord.
H.U. 1867; Lawyer. New York, N.Y.
Justin Edwards Gale . . . . . 18 . . . Rockport, Mass.
H.U. 1866; A.M.; Teacher. Cambridge, Mass.
Edward Francis Gale . . . . . 15 . . . Exeter.
Business. Chicago, Ill.
Clifford Belcher Gill . . . . . . 16 . . . Exeter.
Farmer. Junction City, Kan.
Thomas Herbert Gray . . . . . 16 . . . Walpole, Mass.
H.U. 1867; Merchant. Boston, Mass.
George Wheelock Grover . . . 16 . . . Concord.
M.D.
William Penn Hammond . . . 17 . . . Plympton, Mass.
Amh. Coll. 1869; M.D.; Physician. Boston, Mass.
William Allen Hayes . . . . . 18 . . . Washington, D.C.
H.U. 1866; A.M.; LL.B.; Lawyer. Boston, Mass.
George Franklin Hubbard . . . 16 . . . Winterport, Me.
M.D.

Arthur Hunnewell . . . . 15 . . . Boston, Mass.
H.U. 1868; Business.
Samuel Champion Hunt . . . . 19 . . . Franklin, Mass.
Frederic Guion Ireland . . . . 15 . . . New York, N.Y.
H.U. 1868; LL.B.; Teacher and Author.
Alfred Brayton Irons . . . . . 19 . . . Providence, R.I.
Thomas Loomis Knapp . . . . 18 . . . Ogdensburg, N.Y.
Rens. Polytechnic Inst. 1866; Civil Engineer; Santa Barbara, Cal.
Fruit Ranching.
William Fowle Ladd . . . . . 15 . . . Portsmouth.
Merchant. Galveston, Tex.
Charles Edward Lane . . . . . 18 . . . Exeter.
Clerk.
William Latimer . . . . 16 . . . Boston, Mass.
Edward Hemstead Latham . . 18 . . . Columbus, O.
Irving Leland . . . . 16 . . . Holliston, Mass.
Business. Boston, Mass.
James Pickering Lewis . . . . 19 . . . New Hampton.
M.D.; Clerk P.O. Dept. Washington, D.C.
*Charles Selden Mead . . . . . 17 . . . Hingham, Mass. . .'. 1864
Lewis Cass Melcher . . . . . . 16 . . . Exeter.
Business. Boston, Mass.
Edwin Forrest Melcher . . . . 16 . . . Exeter.
Business. Boston, Mass.
George Stephen Minot . . . . 16 . . . Reading, Mass.
Business. Boston, Mass.
James Frederic Morse . . . . 20 . . . Hartford, Conn.
Robert Mendom Otis . . . . . 16 . . . Kittery, Me.
H.U. 1866; M.D.; Physician. Boston, Mass.
Thomas Manning Page . . . . 19 . . . St. Louis, Mo.
Bookkeeper. " " "
Elbridge John Pattee . . . . . 20 . . . Port Fairfield, Me.
Charles Harrison Pennypacker 16 . . . West Chester, Pa.
Lawyer. Philadelphia, Pa.
Charles Elliot Philbrook . . . . 19 . . . Shelburne.
Charles Theodore Roberts . . . 18 . . . Shirley, Mass.
Lewis Calvin Sanders . . . . . 14 . . . Durham.
Lawyer. Dover.
James Emery Corckin Sawyer . 18 . . . Searsport, Me.
*Walter Henry Seaver . . . . . 20 . . . Northborough, Mass. 1867
Student, H.U.
Josiah Lafayette Seward . . . 16 . . . East Sullivan.
H.U. 1868; A.M.; S.T.B.; Clergyman. Lowell, Mass.
Swithin Chandler Shortlidge . . 20 . . . Fairville, Pa.
H.U. 1866; A.M.; Teacher. Media, Pa.
George Edward Smith . . . . . 19 . . . Worcester, Mass.
Broker. Boston, Mass.
John Winthrop Spooner . . . . 15 . . . Dorchester, Mass.
H.U. 1867; A.M.; M.D.; Physician. Hingham, Mass.
George Stackpole . . . . 19 . . . Gorham, Me.
John Ward Taylor . . . . . . 21 . . . Hebron, Me.
H.U. 1866; Merchant. San Francisco, Cal.
Daniel Gordon Thompson . . . 18 . . . Durham.
Teacher. Milton, Mass.
James Mason Towle . . . . . 18 . . . Somerville, Mass.
Byron Howard Waterman . . . 18 . . . Providence, R.I.
Leonard Wheeler . . . . 15 . . . Lincoln, Mass.
H.U. 1866; M.D.; Physician. Worcester.

Joseph Warren Whittier . . . 18 . . . Exeter.
Henry Willey . . . . 14 . . . Goffstown.
Merchant. Santa Cruz, Cal.
Frank Wright . . . . 16 . . . Auburn, N.Y.
H.U. 1866; A.M.; Business. " "

76

1862.

Frederic Morse Adams . . . . 21 . . . Dublin.
Law Reporter. New York, N.Y.
Willis Laws Ames. . . . . . . 16 . . . Peterborough.
Editor. Golden Dale, Wash. Ter.
Albert Holmes Ammidown . . 16 . . . Southbridge, Mass.
H.U. 1868; A.M.; Lawyer. New York, N.Y.
Charles Henry Arnold . . . . 14 . . . New York, N.Y.
Business. " " "
Thomas Ira Atwood. . . . . . 14 . . . Hudson, N.Y.
Josiah Calef Bartlett . . . . . 16 . . . Exeter.
H.U. 1869; A.M.; Teacher. Taunton, Mass.
Franklin Bartlett . . . . 16 . . . New Bedford, Mass.
H.U. 1869; A.M.; Ph.D.; LL.B.; Lawyer. New York, N.Y.
*George Leonard Barton . . . 16 . . . Gill, Mass. 1879
H.U. 1867; A.M.; Lawyer. Greenfield, Mass.
Edward Sawyer Batchelder . . 16 . . . Exeter.
Salesman. Boston, Mass.
Jeremiah Sinclair Bean . . . . 21 . . . Rochester.
Samuel Folsom Beede. . . . . 22 . . . Sandwich.
Teacher; Supt. Public Schools. Northfield, Minn.
Christopher Columbus Blake . 23 . . . Dahlonega, Iowa.
Nathaniel Briggs Borden . . . 18 . . . Fall River, Mass.
Corporation Treasurer. " " "
Charles Lee Follen Bridge . . 13 . . . Hampton Falls.
Business. Boston, Mass.
Luke Smith Brooks . . . . . . 15 . . . Stow, Mass.
Farmer. Maynard, Mass.
John Tilton Busiel . . . . . . 14 . . . Laconia. .
H.U. 1868; Manufacturer. "
*Rollo Marble Cole. . . . . . . 15 . . . Paris, Me. 1868
Bowd. Coll. 1867.
Herbert Jonathan Cooke . . . 16 . . . Hadley, Mass.
Lawyer.
John Sherwin Crosby . . . . . 20 . . . Unity, Me.
Lawyer. St. Joseph, Mo.
*Charles Jewett Demeritt . . . 18 . . . Durham 1881
Business. Kansas City, Mo.
Edwin Demeritt. . . . . 16 . . . Durham.
Dart. Coll. 1869; Teacher. Boston, Mass.
*Moses Beede Dillingham . . . 21 . . . W. Falmouth, Mass. 1863
Samuel Dinsmoor . . . . 15 . . . Keene.
Business. "
*William Henry Dolby . . . . . 24 . . . Saco, Me. 1868
Teacher. Lowell, Mass.
Horace Paul Downs . . . . . . 22 . . . Tamworth.
M.D.; Physician. Washington Territory.
Charles Henry Dunlap . . . . 17 . . . Andover, Me.
Insurance Agent. Lewiston, Me.

Amos Sheldon Edwards . . . . 19 . . . Fayetteville, N.Y.
M.D.; Physician. Syracuse, N.Y.
Charles Bowdoin Fillebrown . . 19 . . . Winthrop, Me.
Business. Boston, Mass.
Arthur Irving Fiske . . . . . . 14 . . . Holliston, Mass.
H.U. 1869; A.M.; Teacher. Boston, Mass.
Taylor Barnum Fletcher . . . . 15 . . . Exeter.
Tufts Coll. 1869; Dentist. Portage, Wis.
*William Henry French . . . . 14 . . . Laconia 1878
H.U. 1869; M.D.; Physician. California.
Charles Baker Godfrey . . . . 17 . . . Milford, Mass.
Business. " "
Sydney Kendall Gold . . . . . 14 . . . Washington, D.C.
H.U. 1869; A.M.; Business. Faribault, Minn.
Henry Hosford Hale . . . . . 15 . . . Haverhill, Mass.
Manufacturer. Bradford, Mass.
William Weaver Heaton . . . 17 . . . Salem, O.
Broker. New York, N.Y.
William Hartwell Hildreth . . 19 . . . New Ipswich.
M.D.; Physician. Newton, Mass.
William Henry Hoag . . . . . 22 . . . Albany, N.Y.
M.D.
Izaak Taylor Hoague . . . . . 17 . . . Deerfield
H.U. 1867; LL.B.; Lawyer. Boston, Mass.
George Albert Holt . . . . . . 18 . . . Hampton, Conn.
Edgar Huidekoper . . . . . . 17 . . . Meadville, Pa.
H.U. 1868; A.M.; Stock Farmer. " "
Hiram Jewell . . . . 21 . . . Brentwood.
Carriage Manufacturer. Amesbury, Mass.
Daniel Parry Lippincott . . . . 17 . . . Morristown, N.J.
Teacher. Cairo, Ill.
John Pickering Lyman . . . . 15 . . . Portsmouth.
H.U. 1868; A.M.; Business. Boston, Mass.
Herschel Main . . . . 17 . . . Washington, D.C.
Engineer, U.S. Navy.
Charles Marseilles . . . . 16 . . . Philadelphia, Pa.
Editor. Kingston, N.Y.
Allison Zaman Mason . . . . . 22 . . . Dublin.
Business. Boston, Mass.
Elisha Burr Maynard . . . . . 19 . . . Springfield, Mass.
Dart. Coll. 1867; Lawyer. " "
Henry Putnam Merrill . . . . 20 . . . Andover, Me.
M.D.; Physician. Portland, Me.
Henry Mitchell . . . . 17 . . . Norwich, N.Y.
Robert Swain Morison . . . . 15 . . . Milton, Mass.
H.U. 1869; A.M.; S.T.B.; Clergyman. Peterborough.
John Henry Morse . . . . . . 16 . . . Methuen, Mass.
Manufacturer. " "
Francis Appleton Morse . . . 19 . . . Dublin.
Teacher. West Roxbury, Mass.
*George Parker Nelson . . . . . 13 . . . Peekskill, N.Y. 1882
Factory Supt. New York, N.Y.
William Morton Ogden . . . . 21 . . . Boston, Mass.
M.D.; Physician. " "
Edward Osgood Otis . . . . . 13 . . . Rye.
H.U. 1871; M.D.; Physician. Boston, Mass.
Walter Page . . . . 15 . . . Watertown, Mass.
Business. Boston, Mass.
Thomas Clarkson Parrish . . . 15 . . . Philadelphia, Pa.
Miner. Colorado.

Joab Peaslee . . . . 19 . . . Plaistow.
Business. Haverhill, Mass.
*Willets Peaslee . . . . 18 . . . Plaistow 1873
Lawyer. Cincinnati, O.
Albert Field Pike . . . . 16 . . . Boston, Mass.
Jerome Bonaparte Poole . . . 17 . . . East Abington, Mass.
H.U. 1867; Teacher. Boston, Mass.
Joseph Wheeler Reed . . . . . 18 . . . Acton, Mass.
H.U. 1867; LL.B. Maynard, Mass.
William Whitlock Richards . . 16 . . . New York, N.Y.
H.U. 1868; A.M.; Business. " "
Nathaniel Morton Safford . . . 14 . . . Dorchester, Mass.
H.U. 1869; A.M.; LL.B.; Lawyer. Boston, Mass.
Albert Ivory Sands . . . . . . 16 . . . Cambridge, Mass.
James Scammon . . . . 18 . . . Stratham.
B.U. 1868; LL.B.; Lawyer. Kansas City, Mo.
Charles Franklin Smith . . . . 17 . . . Exeter.
John Lefavour Stanley . . . 20 . . . Beverly, Mass.
Dart. Coll. 1869; A.M.; Teacher. Concord.
James Rindge Stanwood . . . 15 . . . Portsmouth.
Merchant. Boston, Mass.
Charles Onslow Stearns . . . . 16 . . . Concord.
H.U. 1867; Civil Engineer. Boston, Mass.
Morton Burr Stelle . . . . . . 14 . . . Washington, D.C.
Calvin Amory Stevens . . . 17 . . . Groton, Mass.
Business. New York, N.Y.
Solomon Thayer Streeter . . . 20 . . . Vernon, Vt.
Amh. Coll. 1867; LL.B.; Lawyer. New York, N.Y.
Charles Howard Thyng . . . . 15 . . . Exeter.
R.R. Clerk (New York, N.Y.). Roselle, N.J.
George Thomas Tilden . . . . 17 . . . Boston, Mass.
Architect. " "
George Clark Travis . . . . . 16 . . . Holliston, Mass.
H.U. 1869; A.M.; Lawyer. " "
*William Abram Van Buren . . 15 . . . New York, N.Y. . . . 1863
Frank Alvord Warfield . . . . 15 . . . Holliston, Mass.
Clergyman. Brockton, Mass.
Thomas Fenner Wentworth . . 16 . . . Greenland.
Yale Coll. 1868; Lawyer. New York, N.Y.
Arthur Nathaniel Whiting . . 17 . . . Watertown, Mass.
Business. Haydenville, Mass.
*Henry Medill Whitman . . . . 17 . . . Cincinnati, O. 1869
H.U. 1868.
Channing Wood Whitman . . 16 . . . Cincinnati, O.
H.U. 1868; A.M.; U.S. Consul. Huddersfield, Eng.
Samuel Beede Wiggin . . . . . 24 . . . Sandwich.
Dentist. "
George Winslow Wiggin . . . 21 . . . Sandwich.
Lawyer. Franklin, Mass.
Charles Issacher Wiggin . . . 15 . . . Durham.
Clerk. Boston, Mass.
Charles Dearborn Wiggin . . . 21 . . . Meredith.
B.U. 1868; A.M.; M.D.; Physician. Providence, R.I.
Joseph Colburn Wilson . . . . 17 . . . Orono, Me.
Bowd. Coll. 1867; Lawyer. " "
William Seal Windle . . . . . 16 . . . Fairville, Pa.
H.U. 1869; A.M.; Lawyer. West Chester, Pa.
Edward Leander Wood . . . . 16 . . . Fitchburg, Mass.
H.U. 1867; A.M.; Treasurer. Lewiston, Me.

George Albert Wood . . . . . 17 . . . Brentwood.
Musician.   "
                                              90

1863.

William Pomeroy Alexander . 15 . . . Springfield, Mass.
H.U. 1870; Govt. Service.   "   "
Charles De Lancey Alton . . . 18 . . . Summit, N.J.
Henry Green Atwater . . . . . 13 . . . Peekskill, N.Y.
H.U. 1869; LL.B.; Lawyer.   New York, N.Y.
Fordyce Dwight Barker . . . . 15 . . . New York, N.Y.
Broker.   "   "
Washington Becker . . . . . . 16 . . . South Worcester, Mass.
Joseph Hartwell Bridge . . . . 16 . . . Augusta, Me.
S.B.; Mining Engineer.   Leadville, Col.
*Samuel Emmons Brown . . . 16 . . . Exeter 1877
H.U. 1870; Clergyman.
Charles Rufus Brown . . . . . 14 . . . Exeter.
H.U. 1877; Master U.S. Navy; Clergyman.   Franklin Falls.
Edward Chelonday Bullard . . 19 . . . Schuylerville, N.Y.
Paper Manufacturer.   "   "
James Hardy Burgess . . . . . 18 . . . Oldtown, Me.
Lawyer.   "   "
Frederic Wilcox Chapin . . . . 13 . . . Springfield, Mass.
H.U. 1870; M.D.; Physician.   "   "
*Leander Chapin . . . . 19 . . . Milford, Mass. . . . 1865
James Rundlett Cheney . . . . 16 . . . Stratham.
Washington Choate . . . . . . 17 . . . Essex, Mass.
Amh. Coll. 1870; Teacher.   Brooklyn, N.Y.
Arthur Dearborn Clarke . . . . 16 . . . Franklin.
Lumber Merchant.   Jefferson, Tex.
William Bullard Cutler . . . . 16 . . . Holliston, Mass.
M.D.; Physician.   Boston, Mass.
*Frank Demeritt . . . . 15 . . . Durham 1874
Dart. Coll. 1870; Business.   Boston, Mass.
St. Clair Denny . . . . 17 . . . Pittsburg, Pa.
John Francis Dwight . . . . . 19 . . . North Wrentham, Mass.
H.U. 1870; Teacher.   Boston, Mass.
Theodore Holbrook Emerson . 15 . . . Orland, Me.
Philemon Eveleth . . . . 18 . . . Essex, Mass.
Sewall Allen Faunce . . . . . 22 . . . Kingston.
William Nelson Ferris . . . . 14 . . . Peekskill, N.Y.
Omar Alphonso Flint . . . . . 19 . . . Acton, Mass.
William Rice Foster . . . . . 17 . . . Stafford Springs, Conn.
George Ephraim Foskett . . . 16 . . . Louisville, Ky.
Samuel Ham Garvin . . . . . 21 . . . Acton, Mass.
Joseph Farwell Gordon . . . . 20 . . . Tyngsborough, Mass.
Lyman Frank Gooch . . . . . 15 . . . Exeter.
Business.   Boston, Mass.
Friend Humphrey Gregory . . 17 . . . Beverly, Mass.
Charles Goodwin Hale . . . . 15 . . . Hanover
William Gardner Hale . . . . 14 . . . Peterborough.
H.U. 1870; Prof. Latin, Cornell Univ.   Ithaca, N.Y.
John Haley . . . . 15 . . . Newmarket.
Business.   "

Joseph William Hall . . . . . 20 . . . Dennis, Mass.
　Merchant.　　　　　　　　　　　Boston, Mass.
Frederic Robert Halsey . . . . 16 . . . New York, N.Y.
　H.U. 1868; A.M.; LL.B.; Lawyer.　　"　　"
Frank Elisha Hatch . . . . . . 19 . . . Hillsborough.
George Hill . . . . 20 . . . North Hoosick, N.Y.
　H.U. 1869; A.M.; Lawyer.　　　　New York, N.Y.
John Edwin Hill . . . . 15 . . . Stoneham, Mass.
　H.U. 1870; Merchant.　　　　　　Boston, Mass.
John Hillis . . . . 17 . . . Maynard, Mass.
　H.U. 1868; A.M.; Lawyer (Boston, Mass.).　"　"
Joseph Henry Holway . . . . 21 . . . Sandwich, Mass.
Henry Newell Hoxie . . . . . 22 . . . East Sandwich, Mass.
　Prin. Friends School.　　　　　　Germantown, Pa.
William Edwin Hoyt . . . . . 18 . . . Portsmouth.
　Civil Engineer.　　　　　　　　Rochester, N.Y.
Joseph Alexander D. Hughes . 16 . . . Nashua.
Arthur Clarke Huidekoper . . 15 . . . Meadville, Pa.
　LL.B.; Treas. Glass Co.　　　　　"　　"
*Joseph Hayden Jewell . . . . 16 . . . Brentwood 1872
　B.U. 1871; Med. Student, H.U.
George Henry Lawrence . . . 15 . . . Milwaukee, Wis.
　Yale Coll. 1869; A.M.; Lawyer.　　"　　"
Joshua Holmes Leach . . . . . 15 . . . Nashua.
　M.D.; Physician.　　　　　　　Keene.
Leverett Lyndon Leggett . . . 18 . . . Zanesville, O.
　Lawyer.　　　　　　　　　　　Cleveland, O.
Edwin Benson Lent . . . . . . 14 . . . Peekskill, N.Y.
　Clerk, Pub. Works.　　　　　　New York, N.Y.
George Langdon Lothrop . . . 17 . . . Lexington, Mass.
　Merchant.　　　　　　　　　　Boston, Mass.
George Washington Mann . . 18 . . . Hanover.
Lo Palmer Moore . . . . 25 . . . Manchester.
Charles Adams Morrill . . . . 20 . . . Haverhill, Mass.
　H.U. 1868; A.M.; Teacher, St. Paul.　Concord.
William Walter Nason . . . . . 15 . . . Exeter.
　Clergyman.　　　　　　　　　New Scotland, N.Y.
William Martin Newton . . . . 18 . . . Rochester, N.Y.
Frederic George Noonan . . . 15 . . . Milwaukee, Wis.
　Business.　　　　　　　　　　Kansas City, Mo.
Charles Cushing Odlin . . . . 15 . . . Exeter.
　M.D.; Physician.　　　　　　　Melrose, Mass.
Samuel Longstreth Parrish . . 14 . . . Philadelphia, Pa.
　H.U. 1870; Lawyer.　　　　　　New York, N.Y.
David Walton Perkins . . . . 16 . . . Milwaukee, Wis.
　Music Teacher.　　　　　　　Chicago, Ill.
James Handyside Perkins . . . 15 . . . Cincinnati, O.
　H.U. 1870; LL.B.; Lawyer.　　　"　　"
Robert J. W. Phinney . . . . 16 . . . Barnstable, Mass.
　Business.　　　　　　　　　　Boston, Mass.
Bard Berge Plummer . . . . . 17 . . . Milton.
　Farmer.　　　　　　　　　　　"
David Gurney Pratt . . . . . . 14 . . . Brighton, Mass.
　Business.　　　　　　　　　　Boston, Mass.
Francis Rawle . . . . 17 . . . Williamsport, Pa.
　H.U. 1869; LL.B.; Lawyer.　　　Philadelphia, Pa.
Robert Hallowell Richards . . 19 . . . Boston, Mass.
　Prof. Mining Engineering, Inst. Tech.　"　"

Henry Bullard Richardson . . 18 . . . Medway, Mass.
Amh. Coll. 1869; A.M.; Prof. German, Amh.   Amherst, Mass.
Andrew Howland Russell . . . 16 . . . Plymouth, Mass.
Lieut. U.S. Army.
Edward Russell . . . . 18 . . . New York, N.Y.
*Joseph Leavitt Sanborn . . . . 19 . . . Hampton Falls . . . 1873
H.U. 1867; A.M.
Hezekiah Scammon . . . . . . 20 . . . Stratham.
Business.   Exeter.
Joseph Lyman Silsbee . . . . 14 . . . Northampton, Mass.
H.U. 1869; Architect.   Syracuse, N.Y.
William Cowper Simmons . . . 21 . . . North Wrentham, Mass.
H.U. 1868; Prof. Greek, Univ. Vermont.   Burlington, Vt.
Thomas Hart Smith . . . . . . 17 . . . Philadelphia, Pa.
M.D.; Physician.   "   "
Elliot Smith . . . . 16 . . . New York, N.Y.
Lawyer.   "   "
Sanford Sydney Smith . . . . 14 . . . New York, N.Y.
H.U. 1870; LL.B.; Lawyer.   "   "
Charles Henry Smith . . . . . 14 . . . Newmarket.
Yale Coll. 1869; Lawyer.   "
William Eliot Sparks . . . . . 15 . . . Cambridge, Mass.
H.U. 1869; A.M.   Taunton, Mass.
Winthrop Flint Stevens . . . . 15 . . . Stoneham, Mass.
Dart. Coll. 1869; M.D.; Physician.   "   "
Thomas Strahan . . . . 17 . . . West Cambridge, Mass.
Business. (Boston, Mass.)   Chelsea, Mass.
Theodore Sutro . . . . 18 . . . Baltimore, Md.
H.U. 1871; Lawyer.   New York, N.Y.
Charles Frederic Swett . . . . 18 . . . Portland, Me.
Stephen Swift Taft . . . . . . 14 . . . Upton, Mass.
H.U. 1870; Lawyer.   Palmer, Mass.
Frederic Thompson . . . . . . 17 . . . Conway.
John Todhunter . . . . 16 . . . Philadelphia, Pa.
H.U. 1868; LL.B.; Lawyer.   New York, N.Y.
Everett Albert Towne . . . . . 17 . . . Southbridge, Mass.
*Elijah Van Sickel Townsend . 13 . . . Philadelphia, Pa.
Willis Tuxbury . . . . 13 . . . Exeter.
Business.   Boston, Mass.
*George Albert Warren . . . . 14 . . . Exeter 1879
                                                     Denver, Col.
William James Waters . . . . 21 . . . New Bedford, Mass.
Berlin White . . . . 17 . . . South Easton, Mass.
Arthur Dunlap Whitehouse . . 16 . . . Rochester.
Eli Whitney . . . . 16 . . . New Haven, Conn.
Yale Coll. 1869; A.M.
William Scollay Whitwell . . . 17 . . . Jamaica Plain, Mass.
H.U. 1869; A.M.; M.D.; Physician.   San Francisco, Cal.
James Cornelius Wilson . . . . 15 . . . Philadelphia, Pa.
M.D.; Physician.   "   "
Douglas Dousman Wolcott . . 19 . . . Milwaukee, Wis.
Yale Coll. 1868.
Frank Woodman . . . . 16 . . . Mineral Point, Wis.
H.U. 1869; A.M.; Manufacturer.   Charleston, West Va.

1864.

Edwin Augustus Alger .... 17 ... Lowell, Mass.
LL.B.; Lawyer.   Boston, Mass.
*Francis Atwood .... 18 ... Franklin, Mass. ... 1882
H.U. 1869; A.M.; M.D.; Physician.   St. Paul, Minn.
James Knox Averill ..... 17 ... Sand Lake, N.Y.
LL.B.
Edward Rinaldo Bacon .... 17 ... Le Roy, N.Y.
Lawyer.   New York, N.Y.
George Ashton Badger .... 15 ... Boston, Mass.
Bookkeeper.   "   "
Albert Clifford Barney .... 16 ... Dayton, O.
B.U. 1869.   "   "
Leslie Peese Barnum ..... 18 ... Adrian, Mich.
James Roberts Beede ..... 20 ... Center Sandwich.
John Clemons Benton ..... 14 ... Covington, Ky.
Lawyer.   "   "
Leander Augustus Bevin ... 19 ... East Hampton, Conn.
*William Rice Boardman ... 16 ... Portsmouth 1880
Lawyer.   "
*John Kittredge Brown ..... 21 ... Saxonville, Mass.
H.U. 1869; A.M.; Missionary.   Syria.
George Cole Brown ...... 16 ... Rehoboth, Mass.
M.D.; Physician.   "   "
Walter Henderson Bryant ... 17 ... Pittsburg, Pa.
Edward Fisher Chapin .... 18 ... Boston, Mass.
Merchant.   Chicago, Ill.
Henry Lincoln Clapp ..... 25 ... Taunton, Mass.
H.U. 1870; Teacher.   Boston, Mass.
*Galen Alonzo Clark ...... 18 ... Stow, Mass 1873
H.U. 1871.   California.
Francis Edmeston Cooke ... 17 ... St. Louis, Mo.
Teacher.   "   "
Lowell Mason Cummings ... 17 ... Farmersville, N.Y.
Lawyer.   Springville, N.Y.
Ellwood Harvey Darlington .. 19 ... West Chester, Pa.
Carpenter.   "   "
*Frank Dupont Davis ..... 16 ... Cambridge, Mass. . 1879
Broker.   Boston, Mass.
Joseph Henry Dearborn .... 15 ... Deerfield.
Business.   Boston, Mass.
Henry James Dutton ..... 18 ... Ellsworth, Me.
Yale Coll. 1869; Lawyer.
Henry Warren Eldredge ... 19 ... Kensington.
Amh. Coll. 1871; Clergyman.   Turners Falls, Mass.
Benjamin Marvin Fernald ... 17 ... Exeter.
H.U. 1870; LL.B.; Lawyer.   Boston, Mass.
Channing Folsom .... 16 ... Newmarket.
Supt. Public Schools.   Dover.
*Thomas Brown Frost ..... 19 ... North Hampton ... 1867
Farmer.   "   "
*Charles Brown Godfrey .... 16 ... Epping 1873
Business.   "
Francis Irving Gray ..... 17 ... Barnstable, Mass.
Journalist.   Boston, Mass.

Henry Greenough	16	Cambridge, Mass.
Merchant.		Philippine Island.
Lewis Benedict Hall	16	Albany, N.Y.
H.U. 1869; A.M.; Lawyer.		" "
Hiram Putnam Harriman	18	Groveland, Mass.
Rufus Everett Hilliard	21	Kensington.
Shoe Dealer.		Lynn, Mass.
William Barker Hills	14	Plaistow.
H.U. 1871; M.D.; Instructor Med. School, H.U.		Boston, Mass.
Charles Emerson Hoar	14	Concord, Mass.
H.U. 1870; Farmer.		Newbury Park, Col.
John Osborn Hobbs	16	Delevan, Wis.
Edward Francis Hodges	13	New York, N.Y.
H.U. 1871; M.D.; Physician.		Indianapolis, Ind.
Henry Prichard Holden	15	Cincinnati, O.
Lawyer.		" "
Artemas Henry Holmes	15	New York, N.Y.
H.U. 1870; Lawyer.		" "
John Hubbard	15	Exeter.
Lieut. U.S. Navy.		
James Lemuel Humphrey	14	Springfield, Mass.
Merchant.		
Charles Greene Jackson	17	San Francisco, Cal.
Charles Warren Johnson	16	Swatow, China.
Edward Lyon	17	Williamsport, Pa.
Gardiner Felch McCandless	17	Pittsburg, Pa.
William Spencer McLelland	17	Huntsville, Ala.
Royal Whitman Merrill	14	Andover, Mass.
H.U. 1869; A.M.; Journalist.		Philadelphia, Pa.
John Cooper Montgomery	17	Danville, Pa.
LL.B.		
Ernest Nathaniel Morison	15	Baltimore, Md.
H.U. 1870; Insurance Agent.		" "
Charles William Moseley	16	Newburyport, Mass.
Broker.		Boston, Mass.
Charles Howard Moses	16	Knoxville, Tenn.
Edward Hallam Movius	16	Buffalo, N.Y.
Lawyer.		" "
James Jefferson Myers	21	Frewsburg, N.Y.
Thomas Nesmith	16	Lowell, Mass.
H.U. 1871; Business.		" "
William Fisher Packer	16	Williamsport, Pa.
Charles Lane Palmer	15	Cambridge, Mass.
H.U. 1871; Farmer.		Hawley, Minn.
Asa Lovejoy Peabody	24	Virden, Ill.
*John Odenham Pearce	17	Maysville, Ky. 1878
		" "
Charles Pearce	16	Maysville, Ky.
Merchant.		Cincinnati, O.
Lewis Edward Pearce	15	Maysville, Ky.
Merchant.		" "
Herbert Henry Davis Pierce	15	Cambridge, Mass.
Robert Franklin Pennell	14	Freeport, Me.
H.U. 1871; Prof. Latin, P.E.A. 1875–82; Author.		Exeter.
Thomas Matthew Porter	17	Covington, Ky.
Merchant.		Cincinnati, O.
John Mason Williams Pratt	16	Taunton, Mass.
H.U. 1869; A.M.; S.T.B.; Clergyman.		Pembroke, Mass.

Horace Sylvester Shapleigh	. . 20 . . .	Lebanon, Me.
Nathaniel Stevens Smith	. . . 17 . . .	Kingston, N.Y.
H.U. 1869; Lawyer.		New York, N.Y.
George Phillips Spooner	. . . 15 . . .	Dorchester, Mass.
Business.		Detroit, Mich.
Frank Nash Stuart	. . . . . . 17 . . .	Springfield, Ill.
Postal Clerk.		Omaha, Neb.
Emanuel Sullavon	. . . . . . 19 . . .	New Bedford, Mass.
Lawyer.		" "
Frank Henry Towle	. . . . . . 15 . . .	Exeter.
James Fisher Tweedy	. . . . . 15 . . .	Milwaukee, Wis.
Univ. Mich. 1870; Business.		New York, N.Y.
John Butler Tytus	. . . . . . 15 . . .	Middletown, O.
Paper Manufacturer.		" "
Charles Mitchell Underwood	. 15 . . .	Adrian, Mich.
Daniel Barker Veazey	. . . . . 22 . . .	Brentwood.
Teacher and Agent.		Hematite, Mo.
William Rotch Ware	. . . . . 15 . . .	Baltimore, Md.
H.U. 1871; Architect and Editor.		Boston, Mass.
Arthur Harrison Weston	. . . 21 . . .	Skowhegan, Me.
Mandell Webster Weston	. . . 18 . . .	Skowhegan, Me.
Judson Boardman Wilds	. . . 17 . . .	New York, N.Y.
H.U. 1871; Lawyer.		" "
Walter Thaxter Winsor	. . . . 16 . . .	Brookline, Mass.
H.U. 1870; Business.		Boston, Mass.
Dillwyn Wistar	. . . . 19 . . .	Philadelphia, Pa.
Conveyancer.		" "

80

1865.

Wallace Conduit Barker	. . . 17 . . .	Michigan City, Ind.
*Frank James Bean	. . . . . . 13 . . .	Deerfield.
Business.		Boston, Mass.
Horace Berry	. . . . 19 . . .	Newington.
M.D.; Physician.		Boston, Mass.
Henry Otis Billings	. . . . . . 18 . . .	Newton, Mass.
Charles Roberts Brickett	. . . 14 . . .	Haverhill, Mass.
H.U. 1872; Lawyer.		" "
Edward Burritt Brown	. . . . 17 . . .	Seaford, Del.
Horace Brown	. . . . 14 . . .	West Newbury, Mass.
H.U. 1872; LL.B; Lawyer.		Salem, Mass.
William Nelson Callender	. . . 22 . . .	Albany, N.Y.
Frank Linus Childs	. . . . . . 15 . . .	Worcester, Mass.
B.U. 1870; A.M.; LL.B.; Lawyer.		" "
George Enoch Cilley	. . . . . 14 . . .	Exeter.
Business.		Boston, Mass.
*Benjamin Franklin Clark	. . . 13 . . .	Stratham 1873
Student, Dart. Coll.		
Walter Clifford	. . . . 16 . . .	New Bedford, Mass.
H.U. 1871; LL.B.; Lawyer.		" " "
Charles Ross Clifton	. . . . . 22 . . .	McCleary, Pa.
LL.B.; Clerk War Dept.		Washington, D.C.
Virgil Roscoe Connor	. . . . . 18 . . .	Fairfield, Me.
H.U. 1871; Business.		" "
Edwin Dillingham Crowell	. . 14 . . .	East Dennis, Mass.
Dorrance Babcock Currier	. . . 19 . . .	Hanover.
Real Estate Agent.		"

*George Wallace Damon	16	No. Marshfield, Mass. 1868
Edwin Calvin Eastman	16	Exeter.
Apothecary.		South Berwick, Me.
Winfield Scott Edgerly	19	Farmington.
Lieut. U.S. Army.		
Walter Ela	16	Washington, D.C.
H.U. 1871; M.D.; Physician.		Cambridge, Mass.
Richard Ela	14	Washington, D.C.
H.U. 1871; LL.B.; Business.		Cambridge, Mass.
William Henry Elliot	15	Keene.
H.U. 1872; LL.B.; Lawyer.		"
Lewis Jonathan Elliot	15	Exeter.
Dentist.		
Joseph Albert Fairbrother	19	St. Albans, Me.
Gilman Clark Fisher	24	Brookline.
C.U. 1869; Supt. Public Schools.		Weymouth, Mass.
Edgar Adams Fletcher	16	Exeter.
Teacher.		Grand Rapids, Mich.
Herbert Folsom	14	Newmarket.
Farmer.		Kansas.
John Brown Gerrish	16	New Bedford, Mass.
H.U. 1871; Business.		New York, N.Y.
Moses Brooks Gould	15	Cincinnati, O.
Gustavus Goward	18	Newton, Mass.
H.U. 1869; A.M.; Consular Service.		
David Calvin Hedden	17	New Orleans, La.
Merchant.		" " "
Louis Prevaux Hervey	17	Exeter.
Business.		Boston, Mass.
*Joseph Gibson Hoyt	14	Hanover 1871
Dart. Coll. 1870; Clerk.		
Frank Whittemore Hunt	16	Nashua.
William Marshall Janes	17	Paris, Tenn.
Yale Coll. 1871; Lawyer.		" "
Edward Adolphus Joachimson	17	Birmingham, Conn.
William Neil King	16	Columbus, O.
H.U. 1871; Bank Cashier.		Cincinnati, O.
John Lord King	15	Springfield, Mass.
H.U. 1871; Lawyer.		Syracuse, N.Y.
*Elijah Howard Lewis	19	Brooklyn, N.Y. 1875
H.U. 1871.		
David Loring	15	Concord, Mass.
Civil Engineer.		Portland, Oregon.
Francis Ogden Lyman	19	Hilo, Hawaiian Islands.
H.U. 1871; LL.B.; Lawyer.		Chicago, Ill.
Tilly Lynde	15	Milwaukee, Wis.
Real Estate Agent.		" "
John Drake Marston	13	Rye.
Farmer.		"
James McCobb	16	Portland, Me.
Business.		" "
*Herbert James McDonald	20	Boston, Mass. 1876
William McGregor	21	Boston, Mass.
George Ashbury McLaughlin	14	Newmarket.
Clergyman.		Haverhill, Mass.
Gordon Mitchell	23	Plainville, Conn. 1878
Union Coll. 1869; Clergyman.		Morrisiana, N.Y.
*Alfred Johnson Monroe	16	Belfast, Me. 1875
Bowd. Coll. 1871; Law Student.		" "

112　　　　　　　　　CATALOGUE.　　　　　　　　　[1865.

Robert Brown Morison . . . . 14 . . . Baltimore, Md.
M.D.; Physician.　　　　　　　　　　　　　"　　　　"
Charles Freeman Nye . . . . . 15 . . . Champlain, N.Y.
H.U. 1870; Lawyer.　　　　　　　　　　　"　　　　"
Edward Luther Parks . . . . . 15 . . . Boston, Mass.
M.D.; Physician.　　　　　　　　　　　　 "　　　　"
Willard Silsbee Peele . . . . . 17. . . . Salem, Mass.
　　　　　　　　　　　　　　　　　　　　Boston, Mass.
John Howard Phelps . . . . . 14 . . . Boston, Mass.
*Vincent Enyart Phipps . . . . 16 . . . Cincinnati, O. 1869
George Arthur Poor. . . . . . 22 . . . Andover, Me.
Farmer.　　　　　　　　　　　　　　　　Oxford, Me.
George Adin Pushee . . . . . 14 . . . Exeter.
Tailor.　　　　　　　　　　　　　　　　Boston, Mass.
Dwight Rice Putnam . . . . . 17 . . . Newtonville, Mass.
John Edwin Reid . . . . 20 . . . Greenfield, Ill.
John Hamilton Rice . . . . . . 16 . . . Boston, Mass.
Business.　　　　　　　　　　　　　　　"　　　　"
Sylvester Warren Rice . . . . 22 . . . Roseburg, Oregon.
H.U. 1871; Lawyer.　　　　　　　　　　Portland, Oregon.
*Homer Richardson . . . . . . 19 . . . Dover 1870
Charles Edwin Richmond . . . 15 . . . Exeter.
*George Willabee Rogers . . . 15 . . . Salem, Mass. 1881
　　　　　　　　　　　　　　　　　　　　"　　　　"
Morgan Rotch . . . . 17 . . . New Bedford, Mass.
H.U. 1871; Business.　　　　　　　　　　"　　　"　　　"
Walter Rednal Ruddock . . . 15 . . . West Newbury, Mass.
Business.　　　　　　　　　　　　　　　Boston, Mass.
John Owen Stearns . . . . . . 15 . . . Elizabeth, N.J.
Daniel Avery Stevens . . . . . 15 . . . Exeter.
Ralph Stone . . . . 16 . . . Norridgewock, Me.
H.U. 1872; Lawyer.　　　　　　　　　　Buffalo, N.Y.
Josiah Eugene Stone . . . . . 18 . . . Saxonville, Mass.
George Seabury Sumner . . . 15 . . . Boston, Mass.
Business.　　　　　　　　　　　　　　　"　　　　"
Henry Walton Swift . . . . . 15 . . . New Bedford, Mass.
H.U. 1871; LL.B.; Lawyer.　　　　　　　Boston, Mass.
William Thornton . . . . 16 . . . New Bedford, Mass.
Salesman.　　　　　　　　　　　　　　 Brooklyn, N.Y.
Charlemagne Tower . . . . . . 17 . . . Pottsville, Pa.
H.U. 1872; Lawyer.　　　　　　　　　　Philadelphia, Pa.
Eugene Treadwell . . . . 14 . . . New York, N.Y.
H.U. 1872; LL.B.; Lawyer.　　　　　　　 "　　　　"
Samuel Epes Turner . . . . . 18 . . . Baltimore, Md.
H.U. 1869; A.M.; LL.B.　　　　　　　　　"　　　　"
George Albert Tuxbury . . . . 15 . . . Amesbury, Mass.
Business.　　　　　　　　　　　　　　　Haverhill, Mass.
Lucian Augustus Wait . . . . 19 . . . Highgate, Vt.
H.U. 1870; Assist. Prof. Math. Corn. Univ.　Ithaca, N.Y.
William Brigham Walker . . . 16 . . . Springfield, Mass.
Business.　　　　　　　　　　　　　　　"　　　　"
Raymond Lee Ward . . . . . 17 . . . New York, N.Y.
Business.　　　　　　　　　　　　　　　"　　　　"
Eli Washburn . . . . 17 . . . Middleborough, Mass.
Eliott Butler Whiting . . . . . 15 . . . New York, N.Y.
Treasurer.　　　　　　　　　　　　　　　"　　　　"
*Francis Eugene Whitney . . . 15 . . . Stow, Mass. 1873
H.U. 1872.

Richard Clark Wilby . . . . . 15 . . ·. Cincinnati, O.
Lawyer. " "
Ellwood Wilson . . . . 16 . . . Philadelphia, Pa.
Lawyer. " "
Arno Samuel Wilson . . . . . 17 . . . Kittery, Me.
Farmer. " "
Leon Baldwin Wolfe . . . . . 17 . . . Lewisburg, Pa.
Manufacturer. " "
Charles Fuller Woodard. . . . 17 . . . Bangor, Me.
H.U. 1870; LL.B.; Teacher. " "
Augustus Gustavus Wooster . 25 . . . Hancock, Me.

                                                                                 89

1866.

Herbert Baxter Adams . . . . 16 . . . Amherst, Mass.
Amh. Coll. 1872; A.M.; Ph.D.; Fellow in Hist.,   Baltimore, Md.
Johns Hopkins Univ.
Joseph Longworth Anderson . 15 . . . Cincinnati, O.
M.D.; Physician. " "
John Avery . . . . 21 . . . Brandon, Vt.
M.D.; Physician. Wallingford, Vt.
John Coleman Avery . . . . . 18. . . . Cincinnati, O.
H.U. 1872.
Charles Edwin Batchelder. . . 17 . . . North Hampton.
H.U. 1873; Lawyer. Portsmouth.
George Schuyler Bates . . . . 15 . . . New York, N.Y.
H.U. 1872; LL.B.; Journalist. Boston, Mass.
William Appleton Bell . . . . 15 . . . Boston, Mass.
H.U. 1873; M.D.; Physician. Somerville, Mass.
Woodbury Blair. . . . . 15 . . . Washington, D.C.
H.U. 1874; Lawyer. " "
Nathaniel Horace Blodgett . . 16 . . . Kensington.
Clerk. Boston, Mass.
Osborn Francis Brashear . . . 15 . . . Cincinnati, O.
Accountant. Minneapolis, Minn.
*George Henry Bragdon . . . . 14 . . . Exeter 1875
Henry Judson Brickett . . . . 16 . . . Haverhill, Mass.
M.D.; Physician. Columbus, Neb.
Frank Obadiah Briggs . . . . 15 . . . Hillsborough.
West Point, U.S.A.
William Russell Burleigh . . . 15 . . . Great Falls.
Lawyer. " "
Alonzo Chapman . . . . 17 . . . Plaistow.
Salesman. Chicago, Ill.
Charles Henry Cushman . . . 18 . . . Portland, Me.
George Boyce Darley . . . . . 16 . . . Fishkill, N.Y.
Thomas Manley Dillingham . . 15 . . . Waterville, Me.
M.D.; Physician. Boston, Mass.
Elbridge Miner Eaton . . . . . 20 . . . Haverhill, Mass.
M.D.; Physician. Chattanooga, Tenn.
Charles Newton Fessenden . . 20 . . . Fitchburg, Mass.
H.U. 1872; Teacher. Chicago, Ill.
Roswell Martin Field . . . . . ·15 . . . St. Louis, Mo.
Journalist. Kansas City, Mo.
Frederic Nason Footman . . . 17 . . . Great Falls.
Architect. Boston, Mass.

Solon Tenney French . . . . . 14 . . . St. Louis, Mo.
   Amh. Coll. 1872; A.M.; Teacher.   Chicago, Ill.
Walter Russell Gardner . . . . 16 . . . Nantucket, Mass.
   B.U. 1871; Clergyman.   Boston, Mass.
William Thomas Gilbert . . . 16 . . . New Bedford, Mass.
   Reporter.   Boston, Mass.
Daniel Gilman . . . . 15 . . . Exeter.
                                                   Chicago, Ill.
John Greenfield . . . . 17 . . . Rochester.
   Auctioneer.   "
Elisha Gunn . . . . 15 . . . Springfield, Mass.
   H.U. 1873; Lawyer.   New York, N.Y.
Ogden Haight . . . . 16 . . . New York, N.Y.
                                                       "   "
John Oxenbridge Heald . . . . 16 . . . Orange, N.Y.
   Yale Coll. 1873; Lawyer.   New York, N.Y.
Henry Clay Higginbotham . . 16 . . . Leavenworth, Kan.
   Lawyer.   Leadville, Col.
Walter Clinton Hill . . . . . . 15 . . . Stoneham, Mass.
   H.U. 1873; Teacher.   "   .   "
Samuel Hoyt . . . . 15 . . . Salisbury.
   Gov't Service (Boston, Mass.).   Newburyport, Mass.
Lucius Lee Hubbard . . . . . 17 . . . Cincinnati, O.
   H.U. 1872; Lawyer (Boston, Mass.).   Cambridge, Mass.
Charles Dustin Hunking . . . 16 . . . Haverhill, Mass.
   H.U. 1871; M.D.; Physician.   "   "
Oliver Alvaro Hutchinson . . . 20 . . . Milford.
   Lawyer.   Farmington, Whitman Co., W.T.
Daniel Baxter Hyde . . . . . . 17 . . . Winchendon, Mass.
   Carpenter.   Fitchburg, Mass.
George Irving Jones . . . . . 18 . . . Templeton, Mass.
   H.U. 1871; Business.   St. Louis, Mo.
Camillus George Kidder . . . . 16 . . . Baltimore, Md.
   H.U. 1872; LL.B.; Lawyer.   New York, N.Y.
Francis Boott Loring . . . . . 16 . . . Boston, Mass.
   M.D.; Physician.   Washington, D.C.
Henry Livermore Manning . . 14 . . . Baltimore, Md.
Samuel Lord Morison . . . . . 14 . . . Boston, Mass.
   H.U. 1873; Business.   New York, N.Y.
Andrew Morse Moulton . . . . 19 . . . Hampstead.
   Farmer.   "
Rufus William Nason . . . . . 18 . . . Great Falls.
   H.U. 1873; Lawyer.   "   "
Joseph Wiswell Palmer . . . . 18 . . . Fitchburg, Mass.
   H.U. 1872; Dentist.   "   "
Joseph Bruce Palmer . . . . . 14 . . . Nantucket, Mass.
                                                Mission San Jose, Cal.
*Frank Monroe Parsons . . . 17 . . . Jacksonville, Ill. . . . 1877
   Yale Coll. 1871.
Henry Rockey Pendery . . . . 17 . . . Leavenworth, Kan.
   H.U. 1873; Lawyer.   Leadville, Col.
Richard Peters . . . . 15 . . . Philadelphia, Pa.
Newton Williams Reid . . . . 18 . . . Jacksonville, Ill.
   Business.   "   "
John Franklin Richardson . . 18 . . . Fitchburg, Mass.
   H.U. 1872; Govt. Service.   Boston, Mass.
Eugene Kincaid Sackett . . . 20 . . . Attlebury, N.Y.
Charles William Sanborn . . . 17 . . . Wakefield.
   Dart. Coll. 1872; Lawyer.   Wolfborough Junction.

John Wentworth Sanborn . . . 18 . . . South Newmarket.
Clergyman. Batavia, N.Y.
Frank Haller Sawyer . . . . . 16 . . . Biddeford, Me.
Reporter. San Francisco, Cal.
Charles Harvey Shepley . . . . 18 . . . Fitchburg, Mass.
Business. Boston, Mass.
Charles Arthur Sinclair . . . . 17 . . . Bethlehem.
Business. Boston, Mass.
William Columbus Smith . . . 15 . . . Exeter.
Farmer. North Sandwich.
Andrew Gustavus Smith . . . 17 . . . Providence, R.I.
R.R. Superintendent. Brandywine, Md.
James Decker Spencer . . . . 17 . . . Watertown, N.Y.
M.D.; Physician. " "
Henry Pease Starbuck . . . . 15 . . . Nantucket, Mass.
H.U. 1871; LL.B.; Lawyer. New York, N.Y.
Charles Nathaniel Thomas . . 18 . . . Hartford, Vt.
Book Agent. Cambridge, Mass.
Frank Edgar Thompson . . . . 17 . . . Dover.
Teacher. Newport, R.I.
Jeremy Wingate Titcomb . . . 17 . . . Farmington.
Business. Sacramento, Cal.
Everett Totman . . . . 16 . . . Fairfield, Me.
Dart. Coll. 1872; Business. " "
Joseph Weatherhead Warren . 17 . . . Springfield, Mass.
H.U. 1871; M.D.; Assist. in Physiol. H.U. Boston, Mass.
Thomas Barnes Warren . . . . 15 . . . Springfield, Mass.
H.U. 1873; Lawyer. " "
John Blake White . . . . 15 . . . New York, N.Y.
M.D.; Physician. " " "
Moses Perkins White . . . . . 16 . . . South Hampton.
H.U. 1872; LL.B.; Lawyer. Boston, Mass.
Clarence Mortimer White . . . 18 . . . Coldwater, Mich.
Teacher. Sandwich Islands.
George Dudley Wildes . . . . 17 . . . Ipswich, Mass.
H.U. 1873; Merchant. Boston, Mass.

71

1867.

Abiel Jacob Abbot . . . . . . 17 . . . Westford, Mass.
Manufacturer (Graniteville, Mass.). " "
Charles William S. Adams . . 16 . . . Chelmsford, Mass.
Lowell Douglas Allen . . . . . 17 . . . Cambridge, Mass.
H.U. 1873; Business. Manchester.
Thomas William Baldwin . . . 17 . . . Bangor, Me.
H.U. 1873; Civil Engineer. " "
Henry Hudson Barrett . . . . 16 . . . Malden, Mass.
H.U. 1874; Lawyer. Boston, Mass.
Frank Eastham Burley . . . . 16 . . . Exeter.
Business. Chicago, Ill.
George Hyland Campbell . . . 16 . . . Nashua.
Business. Boston, Mass.
Ezra Bailey Chase . . . . . . 19 . . . Exeter.
Marietta Coll. 1873; Clergyman. West Bloomfield, O.
James Harvey Chichester . . . 28 . . . New York, N.Y.
" "
*Arthur Clifford . . . . 15 . . . New Bedford, Mass. 1881
H.U. 1874; M.D.; Physician. " " "

Frank Seymour Coit . . . . . 16 . . . Buffalo, N.Y.
Business.   " "
John Edward Connor . . . . . 15 . . . Newmarket.
Louis Atwood Cook . . . . . . 19 . . . North Blackstone, Mass.
Lawyer.
Ammi Cutter . . . . 15 . . . Buffalo, N.Y.
H.U. 1872; Lawyer.   " "
*Thomas Albert Davis . . . . . 17 . . . Leavenworth, Kan. . 1870
Frank Martin Davis . . . . . . 20 . . . Leavenworth, Kan.
M.D.; Surgeon, U.S. Army.
John Wheelock Elliot . . . . . 14 . . . Keene.
H.U. 1874; M.D.; Physician.   Boston, Mass.
Addison Ely . . . . 14 . . . Elizabeth, N.J.
George Emerson . . . . 19 . . . South Reading, Mass.
Frank Walker Fiske . . . . . . 16 . . . Concord.
Business.   Kansas City, Mo.
John Dana Folsom . . . . . . 25 . . . Raymond.
Clergyman.   Centre Sandwich.
William Plumer Fowler . . . 16 . . . Concord.
Dart. Coll. 1872; Lawyer.   Boston, Mass.
Richard Augustine Gambrill . 17 . . . Baltimore, Md.
H.U. 1872; LL.B.; Lawyer.   New York, N.Y.
Charles Alexander Gambrill . 16 . . . Baltimore, Md.
Business.   " "
Arthur Lewis Goodrich . . . . 15 . . . Stratham.
H.U. 1874; Teacher, High School.   Salem, Mass.
Luther Waterman Griffin . . . 17 . . . Haverhill, Mass.
Business.   Boston, Mass.
John Kimball Hall . . . . . . 21 . . . Nashua.
George Henry Hardy . . . . . 17 . . . Brookline.
Wes. Univ. 1874; A.M.; Clergyman.   Gilford Village.
George Porter Hardy . . . . . 17 . . . Biddeford, Me.
Bookkeeper.   " "
Roscoe Edwin Hewitt . . . . . 27 . . . Santa Clara, Cal.
Joseph Crowell Holmes . . . . 15 . . . Marshfield, Mass.
Bank Clerk.   Boston, Mass.
George Rockwell Kent . . . . 14 . . . New York, N.Y.
Thomas Worthington King . . 16 . . . Columbus, O.
Journalist.   " "
Francis Wilson Lee . . . . . . 15 . . . Boston, Mass.
Business.   " "
George Frank Merrill . . . . . 18 . . . Bangor, Me.
M.D.; Physician.   Cambridge, Mass.
*Eugene Usher Mitchell . . . . 15 . . . Newfield, Me. . . . 1881
H.U. 1874; Teacher.   Portland, Me.
Charles Francis Cook Moor . 14 . . . Waterville, Me.
Theodore William Moses . . . 16 . . . Exeter.
H.U. 1874; M.D.
Edward Beverly Nelson . . . . 16 . . . Poughkeepsie, N.Y.
H.U. 1873; Prin. Inst. for Deaf Mutes.   Rome, N.Y.
Francis Albert Newell . . . . 20 . . . Salem, Mass.
William French Pierce . . . . 16 . . . Cambridge, Mass.
Jesse Byam Phelps . . . . . . 19 . . . New Haven, Vt.
Samuel Rawson Prentiss . . . 18 . . . Bangor, Me.
Business.   Oakland, Cal.
Joseph Vila Prichard . . . . . 16 . . . Boston, Mass.
H.U. 1873; Journalist.   Tompkinsville, N.Y.
Alphonso Bartlett Ramsdell . . 19 . . . South Hanson, Mass.

Charles Cotton Robinson . . . 18 . . . Groton, Mass.
Business.   Boston, Mass.
Edgar William Robinson . . . 21 . . . Cambridge, Mass.
Robert William Sawyer . . . . 17 . . . Wakefield, Mass.
H.U. 1874.   Bangor, Me.
Edwin Frank Sawyer . . . . . 21 . . . Templeton, Mass.
James Patterson Scott . . . . 18 . . . Philadelphia, Pa.
H.U. 1871; Business.   "   "
Charles Otis Scott . . . . . . 15 . . . Cleveland, O.
Business.   "   "
Amos William Seavey . . . . . 18 . . . Greenland.
Wes. Univ. 1874; A.M.; Clergyman.   Princeton, Mass.
Thomas Ely Secor . . . . . . 19 . . . New York, N.Y.
H.U. 1875; Lawyer.   "   "
George Langdon Shorey . . . 17 . . . Lynn, Mass.
H.U. 1873; Lawyer.   "   "
Jeremiah Smith . . . . 15 . . . Peterborough.
Lawyer.   San Francisco, Cal.
Henry St. John Smith . . . . 15 . . . Portland, Me.
H.U. 1872; LL.B.; Lawyer.
William Harris Stearns . . . . 17 . . . Malden, Mass.
Henry Baldwin Stone . . . . . 15 . . . New Bedford, Mass.
H.U. 1873; Supt. C.B. & Q.R.R.   Chicago, Ill.
Frederic Swift . . . . 14 . . . New Bedford, Mass.
H.U. 1874; Business.   "   "
Josiah Richmond Talbot . . . 17 . . . Bristol, R.I.
Charles Francis Tarbell . . . . 14 . . . Lincoln, Mass.
H.U. 1873; Cotton Broker.   Providence, R.I.
Rolla Alonzo Tyler . . . . . . 21 . . . Greenfield, Mass.
Agent.   Exeter.
Charles Rumford Walker . . . 15 . . . Concord.
Yale Coll. 1874; M.D.   "
Hiram Willson . . . . 15 . . . Cambridge, Mass.
Ernest Windsor . . . . 15 . . . Brookline, Mass.
Business.   Boston, Mass.
Frank Herbert Wright . . . . 17 . . . Portland, Me.
Yale Coll. 1873; Business.   Denver, Col.

66

1868.

Walter Baker . . . . 19 . . . Dorchester, Mass.
H.U. 1874; Clergyman.   New York, N.Y.
Henry Baldwin . . . . 18 . . . Canterbury, Conn.
Yale Coll. 1874; Farmer.   South Canterbury, Conn.
*Cecil Barnes . . . . 16 . . . Portland, Me. 1880
H.U. 1872; Teacher.   Chicago, Ill.
George Bates . . . . 16 . . . Boston, Mass.
Gorham Beals . . . . 16 . . . Canandaigua, N.Y.
August Belmont . . . . 15 . . . New York, N.Y.
Business.   "   "
Ellery Jarvis Bennett . . . . . 17 . . . Dover.
Shoe Manufacturer.   "
Charles Gilman Brown . . . . 19 . . . Hampton.
Business.   Lynn, Mass.
George Washington Brown . . 20 . . . East Salisbury, Mass.
Teacher.   Newburyport, Mass.

Frederic William Carleton . . 16 . . . New York, N.Y.
Henry Arnott Chisholm . . . . 16 . . . Cleveland, O.
H.U. 1874; Supt. Chisholm Works. " "
Daniel Gano Chittenden . . . 16 . . . Mont Clair, N.J.
Editor. New York, N.Y.
Charles Baldwin Chittenden . . 13 . . . Mont Clair, N.J.
Salesman. New York, N.Y.
Chester Ward Clark . . . . . . 17 . . . Glover, Vt.
Lawyer (Boston, Mass.). Wilmington, Mass.
Melville Lubeck Cobb . . . . . 15 . . . Dighton, Mass.
Everett Thyng Collins . . . . 13 . . . Exeter.
Musician. Lawrence, Mass.
*Oliver Goldsmith Corwin . . . 17 . . . Suckasunny, N.J. . . 1872
Student, Yale Coll.
Charles Greeley Cunningham . 16 . . . Milton, Mass.
Mining Engineer. Laporte, Cal.
Charles Jackson Cushing . . . 18 . . . Barnston, P.Q.
Charles Francis Dean . . . . . 17 . . . New York, N.Y.
William Whitwell Dewhurst . 18 . . . Exeter.
Lawyer. St. Augustine, Fla.
Francis Child Faulkner . . . . 15 . . . Keene.
H.U. 1874; Lawyer. "
Frank Winslow Fiske . . . . . 19 . . . Peterborough.
Frank William French . . . . 16 . . . South Newmarket.
Frank Camden Geer . . . . . 16 . . . Minersville, Pa.
George Whitefield Goodsoe . . 18 . . . Kittery, Me.
Moses Sanborn Gordon . . . . 13 . . . Exeter.
Yale Coll. 1875. Calistoga, Cal.
William McCrillis Griswold . . 14 . . . Bangor, Me.
H.U. 1875; Assist. Librarian, Cong. Library. Washington, D.C.
Charles Morrison Hickey . . . 15 . . . Exeter.
Bookkeeper. Boston, Mass.
George La Fayette Hobbs . . 17 . . . Dover.
*Isaac Henry Hobbs . . . . . . 19 . . . South Berwick, Me. . 1870
Edward Hammond Hoyt . . . 18 . . . Haverhill, Mass.
Business. " "
Oliver Templeton Johnson . . 16 . . . New York, N.Y.
James Keenan . . . . 20 . . . Dover.
Sheldon Leavitt Kent . . . . . 15 . . . Brooklyn, N.Y.
Robert Kerr . . . . 22 . . . Killingly, Conn.
Charles Francis Lighthipe . . 15 . . . Orange, N.J.
H.U. 1875; Lawyer. " "
James Duane Lowell . . . . . 15 . . . Duanesburg, N.Y.
Engineer, Bur. & Mo. R.R.
Charles Adams Merrill . . . . 19 . . . Andover, Me.
Teacher. Machias, Me.
*William George Morison . . . 15 . . . Baltimore, Md. . . . 1869
James Nagle . . . . 19 . . . Stow, Mass.
Walter Spaulding Norcross . . 14 . . . Wakefield, Mass.
Carmi Alfred Norton . . . . . 18 . . . Greenland.
Harold Parker . . . . 14 . . . Lancaster, Mass.
Civil Engineer. " "
Charles Edgar Parkinson . . . 21 . . . Oakland, Cal.
William Peirce . . . . 19 . . . Lynn, Mass.
Arthur Wellesley Plimpton . . 18 . . . Boston, Mass.
Merchant. " "

Sylvester Primer . . . . 25 . . . Le Roy, N.Y.
  H.U. 1874; Prof. Mod. Lang., Coll. of Charleston.   Charleston, S.C.
John Rufus Ranney . . . . . . 16 . . . Cleveland, O.
  Lawyer.   " "
George Albert Sargent . . . . 17 . . . Haverhill, Mass.
  Business.   " "
Milton Adelbert Shumway . . . 20 . . . Killingly, Conn.
  Lawyer.   Danielsonville, Conn.
John Franklin Simmons . . . . 17 . . . West Scituate, Mass.
  H.U. 1873; Lawyer.   Abington, Mass.
Edwin Francis Small . . . . . 15 . . . Biddeford, Me.
  Trin. Coll. 1874; A.M.; Clergyman.   ' " "
Howard Augustus Smith . . . 17 . . . New York, N.Y.
  Lawyer.   " "
Benjamin Cunningham Snyder 17 . . . Pottsville, Pa.
*Edward Evans Spring . . . . . 17 . . . Portland, Me. . . . 1870
  Business.   So. America.
Richard Sprague Stearns . . . 15 . . . Malden, Mass.
Cyrus Abbot Stone . . . . . . 20 . . . Dorchester, Mass.
  Will. Coll. 1872.
Charles Wellington Stone . . . 14 . . . Templeton, Mass.
  H.U. 1874; Teacher.   Boston, Mass.
Eugene Edmond Strang . . . . 16 . . . New York, N.Y.
  Merchant.   Cleveland, O.
Henry Adgate Strong . . . . . 22 . . . Colchester, Conn.
  Yale Coll. 1873; LL.B.; Lawyer.   Cohoes, N.Y.
John Bazleel Stuart . . . . . . 16 . . . Steubenville, O.
Nelson Taylor, jr. . . . . 14 . . . New York, N.Y.
  H.U. 1875; Lawyer.   South Norwalk, Conn.
Henry Grant Thompson . . . . 15 . . . New York, N.Y.
William Elliott Thompson . . . 22 . . . Bristol, R.I.
  B.U. 1873; A.M.; Teacher.   Lima, N.Y.
Lucian Sanford Tilton . . . . 16 . . . Exeter.
  Bookseller.   Williamsport, Pa.
Charles Edward Travers . . . 16 . . . San Francisco, Cal.
Deshler Welsh . . . . 14 . . . Buffalo, N.Y.
  Journalist.   New York, N.Y.
Hugh Lawrence White . . . . 16 . . . Williamsport, Pa.
  Business.   " "
*John Bellinger White . . . . . 16 . . . New York, N.Y. . . . 1883
  Petroleum Broker.   " "
William Henry Whiting . . . . 16 . . . Upton, Mass.
Daniel Bechtel Young . . . . . 15 . . . Reading, Pa.
  Lawyer.   Chicago, Ill.

                                        72

1869.

Lucius Edwin Ammidown . . . 17 . . . Southbridge, Mass.
Charles John Bell . . . . 14 . . . Boston, Mass.
  Chemist, State College, Pa.   State College, Pa.
Samuel Fairbank Blodgett . . 19 . . . Jacksonville, Ill.
William Lee Bond . . . . 18 . . . Hawaii, S.I.
Albert Davis Bosson . . . . . 15 . . . Chelsea, Mass.
  B.U. 1875; A.M.; Lawyer.   Boston, Mass.
William Edmund Boynton . . . 16 . . . Winchester, Mass.
  Business.   Boston, Mass.

William Mason Bradley .... 15 ... Bucksport, Me.
H.U. 1876; LL.B.; Business.   Boston, Mass.
Erastus Brainerd .... 14 ... Middletown, Conn.
H.U. 1874; Journalist.   Philadelphia, Pa.
George Edwin Brewer ..... 19 ... Southborough, Mass.
Insurance Agent.   Woonsocket, R.I.
George Herbert Bridgman ... 16 ... Keene.
Dart. Coll. 1876; M.D.; Physician.   Boston, Mass.
Henry Glover Brown ..... 19 ... Fishkill, N.Y.
Henry Morgan Burdett ... 16 ... New York, N.Y.
H.U. 1874; Business.   " " "
John Ammi Butler ...... 17 ... Milwaukee, Wis.
Lawyer.   " "
Frank Clement .... 15 ... Haverhill, Mass.
Business.   " "
Frank Cochran Cockey .... 16 ... Baltimore, Md.
*Wayman Crow, jr.. ...... 16 ... St. Louis, Mo. 1878
Walter Salisbury Cutler .... 15 ... Albany, N.Y.
Richard Wellington Davidge . 16 ... Amherst, Mass.
Frederic Fobes Doggett .... 14 ... Pembroke, Mass.
H.U. 1877.
Nathan Haskell Dole ..... 16 ... Norridgewock, Conn.
H.U. 1874; Teacher and Journalist.   Philadelphia, Pa.
Frank Edwards .... 17 ... Southbridge, Mass.
William Gurnee Felter ..... 27 ... New Brunswick, N.J.
Andrew Fiske .... 15 ... Boston, Mass.
H.U. 1875; LL.B.; Lawyer (Boston, Mass.).   Weston, Mass.
Lewellyn Eugene Fiske .... 16 ... Peterborough.
Nathan'l Langdon Frothingham 13 ... Boston, Mass.
H.U. 1875; Lawyer.   " "
Henry Gardner .... 17 ... Sparta, Ill.
Elbridge Gerry, jr. ...... 16 ... Portland, Me.
Addison Gilmore .... 15 ... Cambridge, Mass.
Ulysses Simpson Grant .... 16 ... Washington, D.C.
H.U. 1874; LL.B.; Lawyer.   New York, N.Y.
John Arbuthnot Green .... 16 ... Syracuse, N.Y.
Travelling Agent.   Chicago, Ill.
*Henry Heatly Green ..... 15 ... Syracuse, N.Y. 1872
George Richard Green .... 14 ... Fishkill, N.Y.
Charles Knapp Hale ...... 17 ... New Orleans, La.
Clerk.   " " "
Arthur Dudley Hale ...... 17 ... Medford, Mass.
Chauncey Hammett ...... 21 ... Killingly, Conn.
William Wesley Hapgood ... 17 ... Boston, Mass.
John Tasker Harvey ..... 17 ... Pittsfield.
*John Monroe Haynes ..... 19 ... Dover 1878
Civil Engineer.
Edward Williamson Hill ... 21 ... Cambridgeport, Vt.
Albert Hoa .... 26 ... New Orleans, La.
John Charles Holman ..... 15 ... Cambridge, Mass.
H.U. 1876; Business.   Boston, Mass.
Robert Bloomer Holmes .... 15 ... New York, N.Y.
Broker.   " " "
James Murray Howe ..... 15 ... Cambridge, Mass.
Real Estate Agent.   Boston, Mass.
Henry McGuire Hunt ..... 19 ... Gilford.

Lawrence Roscoe Jerome	15	New York, N.Y.
Broker.		" " "
*Alfred Henry Jones	17	Williamsville, Vt. . . . 1873
Edward Lorenzo Lillibridge	20	Brookline, Conn.
Herbert Walter Marshall	16	Kingston.
Carriagemaker.		"
George Frederic McMillan	17	Wayland, Mass.
James Métivier	16	Boston, Mass.
H.U. 1877; Teacher.		Cambridge, Mass.
Josiah Byram Millett	16	Bridgewater, Mass.
H.U. 1877.		
Martin Moore	17	Ipswich, Mass.
Business.		Lynn, Mass.
William Lambert Morse	20	Marlborough, Mass.
H.U. 1874; Business.		" "
Frederic McCraven Nichols	17	Galveston, Tex.
State Assessor.		" "
George Langdon Ordway	16	Washington, D.C.
Lawyer; Territorial Auditor.		Pierre, Da.
Walter Joseph Otis	16	Chicago, Ill.
M.D.; Physician.		Boston, Mass.
Henry Parsons	18	Great Barrington, Mass.
John Sidney Patton	21	Hillsborough, Ill.
H.U. 1874; LL.B.; Lawyer.		Boston, Mass.
Nelson William Perry	16	Cincinnati, O.
Mining Engineer.		" "
•Charles Ashton Place	16	East Walpole, Mass.
M.D.		
Lewis Henry Plimpton	16	Walpole, Mass.
H.U. 1875; M.D.		Boston, Mass.
Frank Hinkley Pope	15	Sandwich, Mass.
Reporter (Boston, Mass.).		Leominster, Mass.
Edward Fay Rice	17	Northborough, Mass.
*Homer Richardson	23	Dover 1870
Alfred Loring Rust	18	Portsmouth.
Teacher.		Seneca, Johnson Co., Kan.
Alfred Francis Sears	16	Newark, N.J.
Lawyer.		Portland, Oregon.
Benjamin Charles Starr	21	Cleveland, O.
H.U. 1877; Lawyer.		" "
*Edward Stetson	15	Bangor, Me. 1879
H.U. 1876; Lawyer.		" "
William Edward Sutliff	19	Salisbury, Mass.
Elijah Jeffreys Snitcher	20	Salem, N.J.
Carter Tevis	17	San Francisco, Cal.
Henry Knox Thatcher	15	Bangor, Me.
Frederic Winthrop Thayer	15	Belmont, Mass.
William Sewell Tibbets	15	Great Falls.
Business.		" "
Benjamin Currier Travis	19	Holliston, Mass.
Business.		" "
Louis Kossuth Travis	17	Holliston, Mass.
Lawyer.		Westborough, Mass.
Benjamin Stevens Van Wyck	14	Pendleton, S.C.
Manufacturer.		Denver, Col.
Horace Cheney Wait	17	Highgate, Vt.
Teacher.		Jersey City, N.J.

James Howard Welles . . . . . 16 . . . Glastonbury, Conn.
  Paper Manufacturer.   Barre, Mass.
Jacob Bradford Whittemore . . 17 . . . Hillsborough Bridge.
John Wiggins . . . . 15 . . . St. Louis, Mo.
  M.D.; Physician.   "   "   "
Frank Holland Wilcox . . . . 15 . . . Springfield, Mass.
                                                . 82

1870.

*George Blake Adams . . . . 20 . . . Medbury, Mass. . . . 1881
  Amh. Coll. 1875; Clergyman.   Northborough, Mass.
Frank Vandyke Andrews . . . 17 . . . Cincinnati, O.
  Lawyer.   "   "
Clifford Andrews . . . . 15 . . . Cincinnati, O.
  Clerk.   "   "
Arthur Anthony . . . . 17 . . . Fall River, Mass.
  City Auditor.   "   "   "
James Blackburn Attrill . . . 17 . . . Baltimore, Md.
Edward David Baldwin . . . . 21 . . . Le Roy, N.Y.
  H.U. 1875; Editor.   Meriden, Conn.
Richard Stearns Barrett . . . 16 . . . Malden, Mass.
  Business.   "   "
Horace Irving Bartlett . . . . 14 . . . Amesbury, Mass.
  Amh. Coll. 1876; Lawyer.   Salisbury, Mass.
William Edward Bates . . . . 23 . . . Colchester, Vt.
George William Bennett . . . 19 . . . Hampton, Conn.
  Farmer.   "   "
Robert Burns Blodgett . . . . 15 . . . Charlestown, Mass.
Charles Albert Blymer . . . . 16 . . . Lewistown, Pa.
  Business.   "   "
*George Gilbert Blymer . . . . 16 . . . Lewistown, Pa. . . . 1882
  Business.   "   "
Edward Franklin Bradford . . 18 . . . Cincinnati, O.
                                        "   "

Robert Stow Bradley . . . . . 15 . . . Boston, Mass.
  H.U. 1876; Business.   "   "
Frank Brainerd . . . . 15 . . . Portland, Conn.
  Business.   "   "
Charles Briggs . . . . 19 . . . Rochester, N.Y.
John Briggs . . . . 19 . . . Rochester, N.Y.
Henry Sigourney Butler . . . 15 . . . Madison, Wis.
  H.U. 1877; LL.B.; Lawyer.
George Folger Canfield . . . 15 . . . New York, N.Y.
  H.U. 1875; Lawyer.   "   "
William Daniels Carpenter . . 18 . . . Foxborough, Mass.
Martin Luther Cate . . . . . . 15 . . . Exeter.
  H.U. 1877; Business.   Fitchburg, Mass.
Edward Hilton Cilley . . . . . 15 . . . Exeter.
  Farmer.   "
Moses Henry Cilley . . . . . . 20 . . . South Newmarket.
Arthur Josiah Clough . . . . . 14 . . . Exeter.
  Teacher.   Nantucket, Mass.
Walter Stow Collins . . . . . . 16 . . . Cleveland, O.
  H.U. 1876; Lawyer.   "   "
Charles Ward Copeland . . . 18 . . . Fall River, Mass.
  M.D.; Physician.   "   "

*Andrew Roger Culver . . . . . 16 . . . Brooklyn, N.Y. . . . 1871
Joseph Warren Dart . . . . . 17 . . . New London, Conn.
M.D.; Physician.   "   "
William Davis . . . . 16 . . . Plymouth, Mass.
H.U. 1876; M.D.; Physician.   Syracuse, N.Y.
Orrando Perry Dexter . . . . . 15 . . . New York, N.Y.
A.M.; Oxford, Eng.; Lawyer.   "   "
Amory Eliot . . . . 14 . . . Chicopee, Mass.
H.U. 1877; Lawyer.   Boston, Mass.
Levi Asa Farwell . . . . Fitchburg, Mass.
Stock Raising.   Denver, Col.
*William Russell Foster . . . . 15 . . . Portsmouth 1883
H.U. 1875; Lawyer.   "
Franklin Pierce Foulkes . . . 17 . . . Toledo, O.
H.U. 1875; LL.B.; Lawyer.   "   "
Thomas Trueman Gaff . . . . 16 . . . Cincinnati, O.
Business.   "   "
James Wade Gaff . . . . Cincinnati, O.
H.U. 1875; Lawyer.   "   "
George Walton Green . . . . . 16 . . . New York, N.Y.
H.U. 1876; Lawyer.   "   "
Herbert Green . . . . 17 . . . Brooklyn, N.Y.
H.U. 1876; LL.B.; Lawyer.   New York, N.Y.
Albert Brewer Guptill . . . . . 16 . . . Lubec, Me.
Lawyer.   Fargo, D.T.
Allen Joseph Hackett . . . . . 16 . . . Belmont.
Journalist.   "
James Ben-Ali Haggin . . . . 17 . . . San Francisco, Cal.
Henry Steeley Hale . . . . . . 18 . . . Bellefonte, Pa.
Merchant.   "   "
Philip Hale . . . . Northampton, Mass.
Yale Coll. 1876; Lawyer.   Albany, N.Y.
Thomas Handley . . . . 24 . . . New York, N.Y.
William Frank Hapgood . . . 16 . . . Worcester, Mass.
Lawyer.   New York, N.Y.
Emor Herbert Harding . . . . 16 . . . Boston, Mass.
H.U. 1876; A.M.; LL.B.; Merchant.   "   "
Azariah Boody Harris . . . . . 17 . . . Springfield, Mass.
H.U. 1876; R.R. Supt.   "   "
Walker Hartwell . . . . 16 . . . Cincinnati, O.
H.U. 1875; LL.B.; Lawyer.   "   "
Herbert Joseph Harwood . . . 16 . . . Littleton, Mass.
H.U. 1877; Business.   Boston, Mass.
Edmund Trowbridge Hastings 19 . . . Medford, Mass.
H.U. 1876; Business.   Boston, Mass.
George Burnap Hobart . . . . 16 . . . East Bridgewater, Mass.
H.U. 1875; Lawyer.   Kingston, Mass.
Willis Farrar Hobbs . . . . . 16 . . . North Hampton.
Manufacturer.   Bridgeport, Conn.
Henry Martin Hooper . . . . . 19 . . . Griggstown, N.J.
Student.   "   "
Arthur Burley Hosmer . . . . 16 . . . Chicago, Ill.
M.D.; Physician.   "   "
William Henry Hotchkiss . . . 19 . . . Ansonia, Conn.
Yale Coll. 1875; Business.   Buffalo, N.Y.
Louis Gilman Hoyt . . . . . . 14 . . . Exeter.
Lawyer.   Kingston.
John Trull Jacobs . . . . 15 . . . Concord, Mass.

William Channing Kellogg . . 20 . . . Tilton.
Middletown Coll. 1875; Lawyer. Yarmouth, Mass.
Edward Wyatt Kimball . . . . 17 . . . Concord.
Artist. Chicago, Ill.
Joseph Emerson Knight. . . . 19 . . . North Hatfield, Mass.
Business. Haverhill, Mass.
Charles Fuller Leslie . . . . . 22 . . . Patten, Me.
M.D.
Walter Emerson Lufkin . . . . 15 . . . Galveston, Tex.
Business. " "
George Lyon, jr. . . . . 21 . . . St. Joseph, Mo.
Theological Student. Cambridge, Mass.
James Cameron Mackenzie . . 18 . . . Wilkesbarre, Pa.
Lafayette Coll.; Ph.D.; Teacher. Lawrenceville, N.J.
Edward Baxter Marsh . . . . 16 . . . Greenfield, Mass.
Amh. Coll. 1876; Assist. Librarian, Amh. Coll. Amherst, Mass.
Daniel Cady McMartin . . . 17 . . . Johnston, N.Y.
H.U. 1876; Lawyer. Des Moines, Ia.
Rodney Augustus Mercur . . . 18 . . . Towanda, Pa.
Lawyer. " "
John Davis Mercur . . . . . . 17 . . . Towanda, Pa.
M.D.; Physician. Philadelphia, Pa.
Richard Montague . . . . 17 . . . Westborough, Mass.
H.U. 1875; Clergyman. Providence, R.I:
William Radcliffe Morris . . . 14 . . . Derry.
H.U. 1877; Govt. Service. Omaha, Neb.
Arthur St. John Newbury . . 16 . . . Cleveland, O.
H.U. 1876; Lawyer. " "
George Osgood . . . . 17 . . . Cohasset, Mass.
Farmer. Kensington.
John Percyville Parker . . . . 21 . . . Ripley, O.
Robert Logan Patton . . . . . 21 . . . Morgantown, N.C.
Amh. Coll. 1876; Teacher. " "
Anson Walcott Peet. . . . . . 22 . . . Shelburn, Vt.
Farmer. Huntington, Vt.
Palo Alto Peirce . . . . 17 . . . Assonet, Mass.
" "

George Arthur Plimpton . . 15 . . . Walpole, Mass.
Amh. Coll. 1876; Publisher. New York, N.Y.
Jonathan Washbourn Pratt . . 16 . . . Bridgewater, Mass.
Thomas Freeman Quimby . . 15 . . . Biddeford, Me.
M.D.; Physician. Minneapolis, Minn.
William Dougherty Rusk . . . 21 . . . St. Joseph, Mo.
Lawyer. " "
George Hobbs Sanborn . . . . 16 . . . Rochester.
George Hoit Sanborn . . . . . 16 . . . Dover.
Druggist. Chicago, Ill.
*John Williamson Scott . . . . 15 . . . Cleveland, O. 1872
William Shepard Seamans . . 15 . . . Exeter.
H.U. 1877; M.D.; Physician. New York, N.Y.
David Theodore Seligman . . . 14 . . . New York, N.Y.
H.U. 1876; LL.B.; Lawyer. " "
Herbert Shaw . . . . 16 . . . Boston, Mass.
Arthur Wilson Silsby . . . . . 17 . . . Concord.
Lawyer. "
Thomas Morrison Sloane . . . 16 . . . Sandusky, O.
H.U. 1877; Lawyer. " "
William Hale Stevens . . . . . 18 . . . Camden, Me.

Maynard French Styles .... 16 ... Tunbridge, Vt.
H.U. 1877; Lawyer.   Gunnison City, Col.
Edwin Davis Stoddard .... 14 ... Worcester, Mass.
Insurance Business.   "   "
George Mead Storrs ..... 14 ... Chicago, Ill.
Robert Newton Stubbs .... 14 ... Lisbon.
Bookkeeper.   St. Louis, Mo.
William Low Swett ...... 15 ... Exeter.
Stock Raising.
William Nye Swift ...... 16 ... New Bedford, Mass.
H.U. 1877; M.D.; Physician.   "   "
Alonzo Lily Thompson .... 15 ... Baltimore, Md.
Frederic Manning Tucker ... 15 ... New York, N.Y.
Wm. Van Alstyne Van Duzer . 16 ... New York, N.Y.
Business.
William Edward Verplanck .. 14 ... Fishkill, N.Y.
Lawyer (New York, N.Y.).   Rye, N.Y.
George Plumb Waldorf .... 20 ... Lima, O.
Postmaster.   "   "
James Smith Walker ..... 15 ... Springfield, Mass.
Business.   Paris, France.
*Frank Wilson Winchester ... 16 ... Whitewater, Wis... 1881
Mad. Univ.; Manufacturer.   "   "
Frederic Perkins Wiswall ... 15 ... Washington, D.C.
Francis Joseph Woodman ... 19 ... Great Falls.
Journalist.   "   "

105

1871.

John Hopkins Allen ...... 16 ... Old Saybrook, Conn.
Clerk.   New York, N.Y.
William Hall Allen ...... 13 ... Old Saybrook, Conn.
H.U. 1878; Business.   New York, N.Y.
Charles Gordon Bacon .... 14 ... New London, Conn.
Clerk.   "   "   "
Alfred Young Barker ..... 24 ... Lowell, Mass.
William Morse Barnard .... 15 ... Franklin.
Dart. Coll. 1876; Lawyer.   "
William Clinton Bates ..... 17 ... Hingham, Mass.
Supt. Public Schools.   "   "
John James Berry .... 14 ... Exeter.
Lafayette Gilman Blair .... 23 ... Kansas City, Mo.
H.U. 1878; Lawyer.   Cambridge, Mass.
George Washington Blodgett . 15 ... Seneca Falls, N.Y.
M.D.; Prof. Phys., Homœopathic Med. Coll.   New York, N.Y.
Charles Chester Bolton .... 16 ... Cleveland, O.
Business.   "   "
Frank Bowler .... 20 ... Nashua.
Amh. Coll. 1876; Clergyman.   Florence, Mass.
Charles Froome Bragg .... 17 ... Cincinnati, O.
Henry Hobart Brown ..... 17 ... Chester, Pa.
H.U. 1876; Teacher.   Philadelphia, Pa.
Arthur Henry Brown ..... 18 ... East Princeton, Mass.
H.U. 1878.
Edward Stark Burleigh .... 14 ... Great Falls.
Dart. Coll. 1878; Planter.   Florida.

Charles Henry Chapman ... 23 ... Boston, Mass.
Frank Arthur Colby ...... 19 ... Lancaster.
  M.D.; Physician.   "
George Watson Cole ...... 20 ... Waterville, Conn.
Percival Courtney Colley ... 15 ... Boston, Mass.
Quincy Adams Cranch .... 16 ... West Brighton, N.Y.
Frank Culbertson .... 14 ... Cincinnati, O.
  Will. Coll. 1877; Stock Raising.   San Angela, Tex.
George Miller Cumming ... 16 ... Pottsville, Pa.
  H.U. 1876; Lawyer.   "   "*
Henry Gold Danforth ..... 17 ... Rochester, N.Y.
  H.U. 1877; Lawyer.
William Church Davenport .. 17 ... Taunton, Mass.
  Business.   "   "
Lincoln Lear Eyre ...... 14 ... Philadelphia, Pa.
  Lawyer.   "   "
Frank O'Farrell .... 16 ... Lafayette, Ind.
David Dunlap Gilman ..... 17 ... Brunswick, Me.
  Bookkeeper.   "   "
Ralph Waldo Grover ..... 14 ... Earlville, Ill.
  Shoe Manufacturer.   Chicago, Ill.
Revere Charles Gunning ... 19 ... New York, N.Y.
Henry Hale .... 18 ... Elizabethtown, N.J.
  Lawyer.   "   "
Joseph Churchill Hale ..... 16 ... Elizabethtown, N.J.
   "   "

Roderick Floyd Hale ..... 17 ... Grantville, Mass.
Edward Cunningham Hall .. 18 ... Kingston, Mass.
  H.U. 1876; Govt. Service.   Newburg, N.Y.
*Roe Hasbrouck .... Newburg, N.Y. 1879
  H.U. 1876.
Robert Paul Hastings ..... 16 ... San Francisco, Cal.
  H.U. 1877; Lawyer.   "   "   "
Henry Hankins .... 17 ... Dayton, O.
  Bookkeeper.   "   "
Truman Heminway ...... 16 ... New York, N.Y.
  H.U. 1877; Banker.   "   "
Charles Francis Hodges .... 18 ... Worcester, Mass.
  Stock Raising.   San Antonio, Tex.
Frank Holyoke .... 16 ... South Natick, Mass.
  M.D.; Physician.   Holyoke, Mass.
Rush Shippen Huidekoper .. 17 ... Meadville, Pa.
  M.D.; Veterinary Surg.   Philadelphia, Pa.
Friend Humphrey .... 15 ... Albany, N.Y.
  Merchant.   New York, N.Y.
Oscar Richard Hundley .... 16 ... Huntsville, Ala.
  Vanderbilt Univ. 1877; Lawyer.   "   "
David Kilbourn Jackman ... 15 ... Bath.
Edward Arthur Jones ..... 16 ... Boston, Mass.
Charles Samuel Kelsey .... 18 ... Le Roy, N.Y.
  Business.   "   "   "
Herbert Seymour Kelsey ... 16 ... Le Roy, N.Y.
  Bank Teller.   "   "   "
Frederic Cleveland Kent ... 13 ... Brooklyn, N.Y.
  Business.   New York, N.Y.
Herbert Dix Kingsbury .... 16 ... Grantville, Mass.
  H.U. 1875; Clerk.   Boston, Mass.
William Fargo Kip ...... 16 ... Buffalo, N.Y.
  H.U. 1876; LL.B.; Lawyer.   ".   "

Thomas Macauley . . . . 25 . . . Belleville, N.J.
H.U. 1877; A.M.   Newark, N.J.
Daniel Martin . . . . 19 . . . Williamstown, Vt.
Supt. Pub. Schools.   Pullman, Ill.
William Mason, jr. . . . . . . 15 . . . Taunton, Mass.
H.U. 1876; Business.   "
Henry Goodwin McKaye . . . 15 . . . Cambridge, Mass.
Julian Augustus Mead . . . . 15 . . . West Acton, Mass.
H.U. 1878; M.D.   •
Martin Henry Mead . . . . . . 24 . . . Stamford, N.Y.
James Watts Mercur . . . . . 14 . . . Towanda, Pa.
H.U. 1878; Lawyer.   Philadelphia, Pa.
Joseph Davis Milne . . . . . . 15 . . . Fall River, Mass.
B.U. 1877; Business.
Frank Hatch Morgan . . . . . 18 . . . Le Roy, N.Y.
H.U. 1876; Journalist.   "   "   "
*William Sterne Morse . . . . . 15 . . . Boston, Mass. . . . 1875
Alonzo Seaman Morse . . . . 18 . . . Dover Plains, N.Y.
Business.   Syracuse, N.Y.
Herbert Henry Moses . . . . . 15 . . . Exeter.
Business.   Boston, Mass.
John Hoffman Murray . . . . . 19 . . . Goshen, N.Y.
Merchant.   Kansas City, Mo.
James Earnest Nesmith . . . . 15 . . . Lowell, Mass.
Henry Gilman Nichols . . . . 17 . . . Saco, Me.
H.U. 1877; Lawyer.   Boston, Mass.
George Hyatt Nye . . . . . . 16 . . . Auburn, N.Y.
Carpet Manufacturer.   "
John Bartow Olmsted . . . . . 17 . . . Le Roy, N.Y.
H.U. 1876; Lawyer.   "   "
Henry Sharwood Otis . . . . . 16 . . . Exeter.
Assist. House Surg., Hartford Hospital.   Hartford, Conn.
Walter Andrews Phipps . . . 17 . . . Hopkinton, Mass.
M.D.
James Edward Plimpton . . . 14 . . . Walpole, Mass.
Business.   Liverpool, Eng.
Edward Osgood Richards . . . 14 . . . New York, N.Y.
Amh. Coll. 1878; Secretary.   "   "
William Duncan Robertson . . 18 . . . Stanstead, P.Q.
M.D.
*James Dixon Roman . . . . . 17 . . . Hagerstown, Md. . . . 1875
John Ponder Saulsbury . . . . 18 . . . Georgetown, Del.
Lawyer.   Dover, Del.
*Digby Gordon Seymour . . . . 16 . . . Fall River, Mass.
Franklin Brett Sherman . . . 15 . . . East Abington, Mass.
Business.   Boston, Mass.
William Washburn Sleeper . . 16 . . . Sherman Mills, Me.
Amh. Coll. 1878; Missionary.   Samokove, Bulgaria.
Franklin Augustus Smith . . . 15 . . . New London, Conn.
Clerk.   "   "
Augustus Daniel Smith . . . . 20 . . . Aurora, Ill.
Clergyman.   Marshfield, Mass.
Vinton Stillings . . . . 18 . . . Leavenworth, Kan.
Lawyer.   "   "
Charles Pratt Strong . . . . . 16 . . . East Bridgewater, Mass.
H.U. 1876; M.D.   Boston, Mass.
Albert Slocomb Terry . . . . . 17 . . . Ansonia, Conn.
Bookkeeper.   "   "

Isaiah Thomas . . . . 15 . . . Boston, Mass.
Farmer.   Goffstown.
Henry Burton Thompson . . . 17 . . . Hillsborough, O.
Charles Henry Vinton . . . . 16 . . . Boston, Mass.
H.U. 1878.   "   "
*Donald Reed Watson . . . . . 16 . . . Windsor Hill, Conn. 1875
*Charles Warren Weeks . . . . 16 . . . Lake Village 1879
Barge Christopher Weidman . 16 . . . Lebanon, Pa.
William Lang Wheeler . . . . 16 . . . New York, N.Y.
Lawyer.   "   "
John William Whidden . . . . 15 . . . Lancaster.
M.D.; Physician.   Saco, Me.
Edgar Adams Wilson . . . . . 17 . . . Meriden, Conn.
M.D.; Physician.   Rockville, Conn.
John Flack Winslow . . . . . 16 . . . Cincinnati, O.
H.U. 1876; Lawyer.   "   "
Charles Henry Wiswell . . . . 19 . . . Little Falls, N.Y.
H.U. 1877; Teacher.   Boston, Mass.
George Edward Woodberry . . 16 . . . Beverly, Mass.
H.U. 1877; Journalist; Author.   "   "
                                                92

1872.

Harlan Page Amen . . . . . . 19 . . . Portsmouth, O.
H.U. 1879; Teacher.   Poughkeepsie, N.Y.
Benjamin Francis Bailey . . . 17 . . . Columbia, S.C.
Teacher.   Union, S.C.
William Amos Bancroft . . . . 19 . . . Groton, Mass.
H.U. 1878; Lawyer.   Cambridge, Mass.
Richard Banfield . . . . 16 . . . Washington, D.C.
Edmond Lincoln Baylies . . . 14 . . . Taunton, Mass.
H.U. 1879; Lawyer.   "   "
*John Anderson Blodgett . . . 17 . . . Kensington 1880
M.D.; Physician.   Detroit, Mich.
Henry Albert Brown . . . . . 17 . . . Peabody, Mass.
M.D.; Physician.   Reading, Mass.
John Augustus Brown . . . . 15 . . . Exeter.
H.U. 1880; Teacher.   "
Edgar Stickney Buffum . . . . 16 . . . Great Falls.
Yale Coll. 1877; Manufacturer.   "   "
Melville Bull . . . . 17 . . . Newport, R.I.
H.U. 1877; Farmer.   "   "
John Micajah Burleigh . . . . 17 . . . South Berwick, Me.
Will. Coll.; Lawyer.   Lafayette, Ind.
George Henry Burrill . . . . . 15 . . . Gloversville, N.Y.
H.U. 1879; Theological Student, Union Sem. New York, N.Y.
Harry Butler . . . . 14 . . . Portland, Me.
H.U. 1879; Bank Clerk.   "   "
George Minot Butler . . . . . 16 . . . Philadelphia, Pa.
H.U. 1881; Miner.   Bonanza, Col.
George Byron Chapman . . . 22 . . . Dover Plains, N.Y.
M.D.; Physician.   Amenia, N.Y.
*Edward Francis Chase . . . . 14 . . . New York, N.Y. . . . 1880
Law Student.   "   "
John Edwin Chesley . . . . . 18 . . . Amesbury, Mass.
Agent.   "   "
Alva Hector Cluck . . . . . . 14 . . . Niagara Falls, N.Y.

Frederic Fletcher Cole . . . . 17 . . . Rochester, Minn.
Edward Colony . . . . 19 . . . Keene.
Business. "
Samuel Wells Cummings . . . 16 . . . Boston, Mass.
Rome, Italy.
Henri Duquesnet Dillaye . . . 18 . . . Syracuse, N.Y.
Lawyer. " "
*George Lyman Dolloff . . . . 14 . . . Exeter 1882
H.U. 1879; Teacher. "
Herbert Hamilton Drake . . . 16 . . . Newport, R.I.
H.U. 1877; Banker. New York, N.Y.
William Riddle Duncklee . . . 15 . . . New York, N.Y.
Business. Fredonia, N.Y.
Frank De Maurice Dunn . . . 18 . . . Northbridge, Mass.
H.U. 1879; Teacher. " "
Frederic Augustus Faulkner . 17 . . . Keene.
Manufacturer. "
John Winthrop Fiske . . . . . 15 . . . Bath, Me.
Amh. Coll. 1876; Lawyer. New York, N.Y.
*Otis Ward Garland . . . . . . 15 . . . Gloucester, Mass. . . 1877
Student, Bowd. Coll.
Edward Hale . . . . 14 . . . Northampton, Mass.
H.U. 1879; Secretary. Cambridge, Mass.
John Butterworth Harding . . 21 . . . Philadelphia, Pa.
H.U. 1878; Clergyman. Bryn Maur, Pa.
Robert Orr Harris . . . . . . 17 . . . Boston, Mass.
H.U. 1877; Lawyer. East Bridgewater, Mass.
Melvin George Hartzell . . . . 17 . . . St. Joseph, Mo.
Clerk. Sabetha, Kan.
Charles Bell Hibbard . . . . . 16 . . . Laconia.
Dart. Coll. 1876; Lawyer. Boston, Mass.
Jerome Hilbourn . . . . 18 . . . Chelsea, Mass.
Merchant (Boston, Mass.). " "
William Burr Hill . . . . 14 . . . New Rochelle, N.Y.
Student, Yale Coll.
Hector Morrison Hitchings . . 16 . . . New York, N.Y.
Lawyer. " " "
Oscar William Hodgdon . . . 17 . . . Kensington.
Medical Student.
George Arthur Holbrook . . . . 15 . . . Portsmouth.
Bowd. Coll. 1877; A.M.; Clergyman. Bellevue, O.
*Isaac Tatem Hopper . . . . . 16 . . . Philadelphia, Pa.
William De Creet Howard . . 16 . . . Chicago, Ill.
H.U. 1879; Business. " "
Edward Wells Huntington . . 16 . . . Lowell, Mass.
Business. " "
William De Witt Hyde . . . . 13 . . . Southbridge, Mass.
H.U. 1879; Clergyman.
Alexander Fridge Jamieson . . 15 . . . Alexandria, D.C.
Johns Hopk. Univ. 1879; Teacher. Trenton, N.J.
Benjamin Newhall Johnson . . 16 . . . Saugus, Mass.
Lawyer (Boston, Mass.). Lynn, Mass.
Herbert Stanton Jordan . . . . 14 . . . Exeter.
M.D.; Physician. Brownfield, Me.
Aaron Hobart Latham . . . . 17 . . . East Bridgewater, Mass.
H.U. 1877; Lawyer. Boston, Mass.
Charles Samuel Mack . . . . . 15 . . . St. Louis, Mo.
H.U. 1879.
Joseph Griffiths Masten . . .'. 19 . . . Buffalo. N.Y.
Student in Architecture. " "

Frederic Tidd Merrill . . . . . 15 . . . Haverhill.
Frank Warren Miller . . . . . 15 . . . Albany, N.Y.
Lawyer.   New York, N.Y.
Charles Emmett Miller . . . . 19 . . . St. Joseph, Mo.
Teacher.   "   "   "
*William Edwin Moore . . . . . 16 . . . Helena, Ark. 1883
Bookkeeper.   "   "
*Hickey Hunt Morgan . . . . . 14 . . . New Orleans, La. . . 1880
John James Nairn. . . . . . . 15 . . . Washington, D.C.
Mikkel Nielson . . . . 22 . . . Lindbergmark, Denmark.
R.R. Business.   Boston, Mass.
Edwin Jay Nelson . . . . . . 17 . . . Little Falls, N.Y.
Business.   "   "   "
William Taylor Newton . . . 22 . . . Boston, Mass.
Corporation Cashier.   "   "
Abner Merrill Osgood . . . . . 20 . . . Raymond.
Boston Univ.; A.M.; S.T.B.; Teacher.   Provincetown, Mass.
Harrison Perry Page . . . . . 15 . . . Watertown, Mass.
Jacob Cansler Patton . . . . . 19 . . . Morganstown, N.C.
H.U. 1877.   Cambridge, Mass.
George Rose Peck. . . . . . . 19 . . . Auburn, N.Y.
Editor.   "   "
Guy Carlton Phinney . . . . . 20 . . . Wilmot, N.S.
Real Estate Agent.   Seattle, Washington Ter.
Earl Bill Putnam . . . . 16 . . . Waterville, N.Y.
H.U. 1879; Lawyer.   Rochester, N.Y.
George Randolph . . . . 16 . . . Norwalk, O.
Auditor.   St. Louis, Mo.
Frank Thomas Ransom . . . . 21 . . . St. Joseph, Mo.
*Edward Prescott Reed . . . . 17 . . . Stow, Mass. 1882
H.U. 1878.
Gilman Parker Robinson . . . 16 . . . Providence, R.I.
Stock Raising.   Colorado.
Herbert Judson Robinson . . . 13 . . . Brentwood.
U.S. Navy.
Warren Merton Robinson . . . 15 . . . Taunton, Mass.
H.U. 1878; Bookkeeper.   Lynn, Mass.
Bronson Rumsey . . . . 19 . . . Buffalo, N.Y.
Business.   "   "
Frank Thomas Rusk . . . . . 19 . . . St. Joseph, Mo.
H.U. 1877; Principal High School.   "   "   "
George Wilcox Salter . . . . . 15 . . . New York, N.Y.
Henry Augustus Shute . . . . 15 . . . Exeter.
H.U. 1879; Lawyer; Judge Police Court.   "
James Theophilus Simpson . . 16 . . . Exeter.
Forrest Starr Smith . . . . . . 15 . . . Durham.
Farmer.   "
Willard Everett Smith . . . . 16 . . . Schenectady, N.Y.
H.U. 1879; Medical Student, H.U.
Gerardus Smith . . . . 14 . . . Schenectady, N.Y.
Lawyer.   "   "
Edward Eppes Sparhawk . . . 19 . . . Boston, Mass.
Teacher.   "   "
*Albert Eri Spaulding . . . . . 19 . . . Milford 1875
Teacher.   Princeville, Ill.
James Page Stimson . . . . . 14 . . . Wiscasset, Me.
Lawyer.   Leavenworth, Kan.
Gerrit Smith Sykes . . . . . . 20 . . . Mercer, Pa.
H.U. 1877; Teacher.   Cincinnati, O.

*George Phillips Tappan . . . . 14 . . . Helena, Ark. 1877
  Bookkeeper.   "   "
Frederic Winslow Taylor . . . 16 . . . Philadelphia, Pa.
  Mechanical Engineer.   Germantown, Pa.
William Reuben Taylor . . . . 20 . . . Jefferson, N.Y.
  H.U. 1877; Lawyer.   "   "
Hubert Engelbert Teschemacher 16 . . . San Francisco, Cal.
  H.U. 1878; Stock Raising.   Cheyenne, Wyoming Ter.
Roswell Payson Thompson . . 19 . . . Exeter.
  Business.   "
Edward Kimball Trickey . . . 16 . . . Belmont. Mass.
  R.R. Contractor.   Indian Cove, P.Q.
James Arthur Tufts . . . . . . 16 . . . Alstead.
  H.U. 1878; Instructor, P.E.A.   Exeter.
Charles Tuttle . . . . 18 . . . Oakland, Cal.
Joseph Warren Ware . . . . . 22 . . . Sherburne, Mass.
  R.R. Contractor.   Memphis, Tenn.
Edward Graeff West . . . . . 17 . . . Exeter.
  H.U. 1877; M.D.; Physician.   Boston, Mass.
John Charles Wheeler . . . . . 13 . . . New York, N.Y.
    "   "   "
Joseph White . . . . 18 . . . Winchendon, Mass.
  H.U. 1877; Teacher.   Cincinnati, O.
John Howard Willard . . . . . 17 . . . Boston, Mass.
  Farmer.   Lexington, Mass.
Henry Austin Wood . . . . . 16 . . . West Upton, Mass.
  H.U. 1878; M.D.; Physician.   Boston, Mass.
James Anderson Wright . . . 15 . . . Philadelphia, Pa.
  H.U. 1879; Business.   "   "

                                                                                                    96

1873.

Joseph Tarbell Adams . . . . . 17 . . . Cherryfield, Me.
  Salesman.   Portland, Me.
Charles William Allen . . . . 18 . . . Flemington, N.J.
  M.D.; Physician.   New York, N.Y.
Thomas Ray Ashbrook . . . . 19 . . . St. Joseph, Mo.
  Clerk.   "   "
Edward Richardson Bacon . . 16 . . . Chicago, Ill.
  H.U. 1878; Merchant.   "   "
Charles William Bacon . . . . 17 . . . Natick, Mass.
  H.U. 1879; Lawyer.   Boston, Mass.
Frank Woods Baker . . . . . 17 . . . Boston, Mass.
  H.U. 1881.
Frederic Ogden de Billier . . . 16 . . . Yonkers, N.Y.
  H.U. 1878; Stock Raising.   Cheyenne, Wyoming Ter.
John Boit . . . . 15 . . . Boston, Mass.
  Student in Architecture.   New York, N.Y.
Benjamin Davis Bond . . . . . 20 . . . Hawaii Kohala, S.I.
Nicholas Penniman Bond . . . 18 . . . Baltimore, Md.
  Lawyer.   "   "
Hugh Lenox Bond . . . . . . 14 . . . Baltimore, Md.
  H.U. 1880; Lawyer.   "   "
Graham Bennett Bristol . . . . 20 . . . Brooklyn, N.Y.
Edward Brooks . . . . 16 . . . Boston, Mass.
  Broker's Clerk.   "   "
Henry Brooks . . . . 16 . . . Boston, Mass.
  Student in Arboriculture.   "   "

Harry Austin Buffum . . . . . 15 . . . Great Falls.
Yale Coll. 1880; Manufacturer. Milton.
Walter Allen Burleigh . . . . 17 . . . South Berwick, Me.
Manufacturer. " " "
*Francis Micajah Burleigh . . . 16 . . . Great Falls 1876
Charles Ernest Byington . . . 17 . . . Exeter.
Bank Clerk. "
John Daniel Canerdy . . . . . 18 . . . Waterbury, Vt.
Austin Kilham Chadwick . . . 15 . . . Exeter.
Bank Clerk. Lowell, Mass.
George Locke Cheney . . . . 16 . . . Essex, Conn.
H.U. 1878; Lawyer. New York, N.Y.
*William George Cochrane . . . 14 . . . Malden, Mass.
*Franklin Dyer . . . . 17 . . . Gloucester, Mass. . . . 1875
Student, Bowd. Coll.
Daniel Henry Felch . . . . . . 16 . . . Ayer, Mass.
Bowd. Coll. 1878; Teacher. Cheney, Wash. Ter.
William Proctor Ferguson . . 20 . . . Shapleigh, Me.
Bowd. Coll. 1880; Teacher. " "
Frank Morrill Fogg . . . . . . 18 . . . Deerfield.
Journalist. Auburn, Me.
William Howard Folsom . . . 15 . . . Exeter.
H.U. 1881; Clerk. Boston, Mass.
*Gideon Sheldon Fuller . . . . 17 . . . North Ferrisburg, Vt. 1883
Univ. Vt. 1879; Lawyer. Denver, Col.
Zebina Allston Gleason . . . . 18 . . . Westborough, Mass.
H.U. 1878; Surveyor. San Angelo, Tex.
Nathaniel Gordon, jr. . . . . . 14 . . . Exeter.
Yale Coll. 1880; Bank Clerk. New York, N.Y.
*Arthur Gorham . . . . 15 . . . Exeter 1873
Thomas Bryan Gunning . . . 14 . . . New York, N.Y.
Dentist. " "
George Howell Halberstadt . . 17 . . . Pottsville, Pa.
M.D.; Physician. " "
John Cooley Halstead . . . . . 15 . . . Harrison, N.Y.
Edward Holland Hastings . . 16 . . . Walpole.
Treasurer Bijou Theatre. Boston, Mass.
Henry Clinton Hay . . . . . . 20 . . . Portland, Me.
H.U. 1878; Theological Student. Boston, Mass.
Charles Peter Hemenway . . . 16 . . . Machias, Me.
 Portland, Me.
George Howard Henderson . . 16 . . . Dover.
Bookkeeper. "
George Andrew Henderson . . 17 . . . New York, N.Y.
William Bancroft Hill . . . . . 16 . . . Temple.
H.U. 1879; Lawyer. Baltimore, Md.
William Preston Hill . . . . . 15 . . . St. Louis, Mo.
Henry Hitchings . . . . 13 . . . Gravesend, L.I.
Yale Coll. 1881; Law Student. New York, N.Y.
Charles Austin Hobbs . . . . 16 . . . Exeter.
H.U. 1880; Teacher, St. Marks. Southborough, Mass.
Walter Allston Holman . . . 15 . . . Cambridge, Mass.
Business. Boston, Mass.
Frederic Eleazer Horne . . . . 17 . . . Dover.
Commercial Traveller. Boston, Mass.
Rufus King Howell, jr. . . . . 14 . . . New Orleans, La.
H.U. 1880; Planter. Bayou Sara, La.
James King Hoyt . . . . 14 . . . New York, N.Y.

Rufus Peabody Hubbard . . . 17 . . . Wells, Me.
M.D.; Physician. Boston, Mass.
Samuel Hutchings . . . . . . 21 . . . Louisville, Ky.
Ernest Henry Jackson . . . . 15 . . . New York, N.Y.
Coll. N.J. 1880; Lawyer. " "
William Henry Judson . . . . 19 . . . Mendon, Mass.
M.D.; Physician. Wauregan, Conn.
Curtis Asahel Kibling . . . . . 15 . . . South Strafford, Vt.
Dart. Coll. 1880; Teacher. Elk Point, D.T.
John Cone Kimball . . . . . . 16 . . . Brookfield, Mass.
Student in Archæology. Boston, Mass.
Henry Wilson King . . . . . . 16 . . . North Brookfield, Mass.
Lawyer. Worcester, Mass.
Frank Learned . . . . 19 . . . Pittsfield, Mass.
Manufacturer. " "
William Pollock Learned . . . 16 . . . Pittsfield, Mass.
H.U. 1880.
James Lewis Manker . . . . . 22 . . . Shenandoah, Page Co., Ia.
William Halleck McCord . . . 18 . . . St. Joseph. Mo.
Merchant. Omaha, Neb.
Francis McLennan . . . . . . 16 . . . Montreal, P.Q.
H.U. 1879; Law Student. " "
Ogden Mills . . . . 16 . . . San Francisco, Cal.
H.U. 1878; Business. New York, N.Y.
Edwin Wilson Morse . . . . . 18 . . . Natick, Mass.
H.U. 1878; Journalist. New York, N.Y.
Samuel Newell Nelson . . . . 17 . . . Milford, Mass.
H.U. 1878; M.D.; Physician. Cambridge, Mass.
Charles Stuart Nisbet . . . . . 17 . . . Avon, Livingston Co.,N.Y.
Lawyer. Amsterdam, N.Y.
*Frederic Bennett Oakes . . . . 17 . . . South Berwick, Me. . 1877
M.D.
John O'Connor . . . . 20 . . . Indianapolis, Ind.
Lawyer. Huron, D.T.
Walter Henry Parker . . . . . 17 . . . Exeter.
Business. St. Louis, Mo.
Charles Booth Peck . . . . . . 16 . . . Bridgeport, Conn.
Chester Mead Perry . . . . . . 18 . . . East Abington, Mass.
Lawyer. Boston, Mass.
John Quincy Adams Pettingill 17 . . . East Salisbury, Mass.
Lawyer.
John Quincy Pike . . . . 18 . . . Epping.
Business. "
Arthur Salem Plimpton . . . . 15 . . . Stockbridge, Mass.
Clerk. Brooklyn, N.Y.
Barrett Potter . . . . 16 . . . Topsham, Me.
Bowd. Coll. 1878; Law Student. Brunswick, Me.
William Carroll Price . . . . . 15 . . . St. Clair, Pa.
Eddington, Pa.
Henry King Richardson . . . . 16 . . . Boston, Mass.
Edwards Roberts . . . . 18 . . . Boston, Mass.
R.R. Business. Denver, Col.
John Whipple Robinson . . . 19 . . . Concord.
Journalist. Biddeford, Me.
Henry Ellis Ruggles . . . . . . 15 . . . Upton, Mass.
Charles Frederic Sampson . . . 18 . . . North Brookfield, Mass.
Merchant. Worcester, Mass.
Stewart Shillito . . . . 16 . . . Cincinnati, O.
Business. " "

Joseph Theophilus Stevens . . 16 . . . West Epping.
Business. Epping.
William Wallace Stickney . . . 20 . . . Tyson Furnace, Vt.
Lawyer. Ludlow, Vt.
Ambrose Talbot . . . . 13 . . . Everett, Mass.
H.U. 1881; Medical Student. Boston, Mass.
Edward Winslow Taylor . . . 18 . . . Philadelphia, Pa.
M.D.; Physician. Germantown, Pa.
Arthur Moxen Teschemacher. . 15 . . . San Francisco, Cal.
Stock Raising.
Joseph Herbert Towle . . . . . 14 . . . Epping.
Exeter.
Samuel Maverick Van Wyck . 16 . . . Anderson, S.C.
Merchant. " "
Richard Merriam Welton . . . 18 . . . Washington, D.C.
William Henry Wheeler . . . . 18 . . . Faribault, Minn.
Business. " "
Isaac Spaulding Whiting . . . 14 . . . Wilton.
H.U. 1882; Law Student, H.U.
James Herbert Winslow . . . . 16 . . . Portland, Me.
Robert Winsor . . . . 14 . . . Winchester, Mass.
H.U. 1880; Bankers' Clerk. Boston, Mass.
John Gerrish Wood . . . . . . 14 . . . Exeter.
H.U. 1881; Teacher. Philadelphia, Pa.

92

1874.

Henry Fisk Adams . . . . . . 17 . . . Peterborough.
M.D.; Physician. Boston, Mass.
Charles Noah Allen . . . . . . 16 . . . Burlington, Vt.
M.D.; Physician. Sheldon, Vt.
Alexander Bonnell Allen . . . 17 . . . Flemington, N.J.
Druggist. " "
Charles William Andrews . . . 15 . . . Boston, Mass.
Charles Edward Atwood . . . 16 . . . Exeter.
H.U. 1880; C.U. 1881; Teacher. "
James Woods Babcock . . . . 18 . . . Chester, S.C.
H.U. 1882; Medical Student, H.U.
Dana Chase Barber . . . . . . 15 . . . West Epping.
Dart. Coll., Civil Engineer. New York, N.Y.
William Ransom Barbour . . . 16 . . . Bangor, Me.
Yale Coll. 1880; Lawyer. New York, N.Y.
Henry Taylor Barstow . . . . 15 . . . Boston, Mass.
H.U. 1880; Medical Student, H.U. " "
Charles Hammatt Bartlett . . . 15 . . . Bangor, Me.
Law Student, H.U.
*Ellery Webster Bates . . . . . 17 . . . HinghamCenter,Mass.1876
Chas. Frederic Tiffany Beale . 17 . . . Hudson, N.Y.
H.U. 1880; Lawyer. " "
Nathaniel Maynard Brigham . 18 . . . Natick, Mass.
H.U. 1880; Govt. Service. Boston, Mass.
Charles Roscoe Brooks . . . . 17 . . . Farmington.
Farmer. New Durham.
Charles Frederic Burgess . . . 19 . . . Middleborough, Mass.
Publisher. Plainfield, Conn.
Frank Oliver Carpenter . . . . 16 . . . Milford, Mass.
H.U. 1880; Law Student. Lexington, Mass.

Edward Broadway Carter . . .	16 . . .	Henderson, Md.
Student, College of N.J.		Princeton, N.J.
Henry W. Chalfant	19 . . .	Unionville, Chester Co., Pa.
Farmer.		" " " "
William Chalfant, jr.	16 . . .	Unionville, Chester Co., Pa.
Law Student.		West Chester, Pa.
Wm. James Logan Chisholm .	16 . . .	Cleveland, O.
Manufacturer.		" "
Edwin Franklin Cloutman . . .	26 . . .	Farmington.
Lawyer.		Milton Mills.
Frederic Charles Cowper . . .	23 . . .	Buenos Ayres, S.A.
Clergyman.		Island Pond, Vt.
Dana Bradford Cram	16 . . .	Raymond.
Farmer.		"
Thomas Turpin Crittenden . .	17 . . .	San Francisco, Cal.
Charles Alfred Cross	16 . . .	Lynn, Mass.
Louis Cunningham	14 . . .	White Plains, N.Y.
Frank Moody Curtiss	18 . . .	Yonkers, N.Y.
Business.		New York, N.Y.
George Chalmers Cutler	17 . . .	Bangor, Me.
Law Student.		" "
Charles Augustus Dean	17 . . .	Le Roy, N.Y.
*George Spackman Downing . .	17 . . .	Wilmington, Del. . . 1876
Alfred Ela	16 . . .	Cambridge, Mass.
Manufacturer.		" "
William Fallon	15 . . .	San Jose, Cal.
George Nicholas Farwell . . .	16 . . .	Claremont.
Bank Cashier.		"
Charles Barrows Fletcher . . .	14 . . .	Indianapolis, Ind.
Sec. Atlas Machine Co.		" "
Jesse Fletcher	12 . . .	Indianapolis, Ind.
Student, H.U.		
Frederic Gardiner	14 . . .	Middletown, Conn.
H.U. 1880; Theological Student.		" "
Henry Parsons Garland	14 . . .	Biddeford, Me.
Business.		" "
Walter Woolfolk Greene . . .	17 . . .	Faribault, Minn.
R.R. Clerk.		New York, N.Y.
Alfred Francis Greenleaf . . .	13 . . .	Exeter.
Hotel Clerk.		Amesbury, Mass.
Ezekiel Jas. Madison Hale . .	14 . . .	Chicago, Ill.
William Dudley Hall	17 . . .	Bridgeport, Conn.
H.U. 1880; Medical Student, H.U.		
Alexander Harvey	16 . . .	Baltimore, Md.
H.U. 1881.		
Eugene Dexter Hawkins . . .	14 . . .	New York, N.Y.
H.U. 1881.		
Frederic Hayes	14 . . .	Providence, R.I.
D.U. 1881.		" "
John Joseph Hayes	20 . . .	Boston, Mass.
Elocutionist.		" "
Cyrus Foss Hill	15 . . .	Jamaica, L.I.
Lucius Henry Hobbs	21 . .	Brookfield, Mass.
Walter Granville Hodgdon . .	17 . . .	Kensington.
Business.		Haverhill, Mass.
Caspar Hopple	18 . . .	Cincinnati, O.
		" "
Frank Whitehouse Howe . . .	15 . . .	Lowell, Mass.
Business.		" "

*Frank Ahira Hoyt . . . . . 16 . . . Grafton 1874
Frank Colhoon Huidekoper . . 17 . . . Meadville, Pa.
H.U. 1880; Civil Engineer. Hofer's Gap, Va.
Homer Austin Huntington . . 17 . . . Amesbury, Mass.
M.D.
Frederic Daniel Hussey . . . 17 . . . Lowell, Mass.
Medical Student, H.U.
Thomas Parker Ivy . . . . . . 20 . . . Gainsville, Ala.
H.U. 1881; Business. Hogansville, Ga.
William Augustus Johnson . . 16 . . . Saco, Me.
M.D.; Physician. Lowell, Mass.
Emery Walter Johnson . . . 16 . . . Salem, Mass.
Charles MacVeagh . . . . . . 14 . . . Harrisburg, Pa.
H.U. 1881; Law Student. New York, N.Y.
Thomas Mahoney . . . . 14 . . . Wilton.
Walter Irving McCoy . . . . . 14 . . . Troy, N.Y.
H.U. 1882. " "
John Daniel McGann . . . . . 18 . . . Milford, Mass.
Clergyman. Millbury, Mass.
Harry Hayes Morgan . . . . . 13 . . . New Orleans, La.
Sec. Legation. Mexico.
George Frederic Morse . . . 16 . . . Clinton, Mass.
Journalist. " "
George Storer Motley . . . . . 17 . . . Lowell, Mass.
H.U. 1879; Business. " "
Albert Henry Moulton . . . . 16 . . . Kittery, Me.
Yale Coll. 1881; Real Estate Broker. New Haven, Conn.
William Gilman Pollock . . . . 25 . . . Washington,Wash.Co.,Pa.
Waldo Alton Rich . . . . . . 18 . . . Philadelphia, Pa.
Bookkeeper. Portland, Me.
Christian Henry Sampson . . 16 . . . Dorchester, Mass.
Business. Boston, Mass.
*William Gorham Sawyer . . 14 . . . Utica, N.Y. 1876
Wilhelm George Schaus . . . 15 . . . New York, N.Y.
Business. " "
William Abiel Scott . . . . . . 18 . . . Peterborough.
Lawyer. "
Charles Walter Scribner . . 16 . . . Plainfield, N.J.
Coll. N.J. 1880; Engineer. Jersey City, N.J.
Henry Sayre Scribner . . . . . 15 . . . Plainfield, N.J.
Coll. N.J. 1881; Teacher. Great Barrington, Mass.
Frederic William Sharon . . 17 . . . San Francisco, Cal.
H.U. 1881.
Samuel Wiggins Skinner . . . 16 . . . Cincinnati, O.
H.U. 1880; Electrician. " "
George Frederic Spalding . . 15 . . . Boston, Mass.
H.U. 1882; Salesman. " "
Hayward Stetson . . . . 17 . . . Bangor, Me.
H.U. 1879; Medical Student, H.U.
Frank Benjamin Swain . . . . 20 . . . Brentwood.
Henry Hillard Taylor . . . . . 14 . . . Boston, Mass.
Lumber Dealer. San Bernardino, Cal.
George Eugene Titcomb. . . . 19 . . . Exeter.
M.D.; Physician. Concord, Mass.
Clarence Constant Tucker . . . 21 . . . Pepperell, Mass.
John Samuel Warren . . . . . 15 . . . Granville, N.Y.
Lawyer. New York, N.Y.
Alfred Jerome Watson . . . 16 . . . Yonkers, N.Y.
William Livingston Watson . . 18 . . . Utica, N.Y.

Nathaniel Rowe Webster . . . 15 . . . Gloucester, Mass.
Edward Spencer Wentworth . 17 . . . Boston, Mass.
Student in Music.
Frederic Weston . . . . 17 . . . Stamford, Conn.
Timothy Lester Woodruff . . . 16 . . . New Haven, Conn.
98

1875.

David Wilson Abbott . . . . . 16 . . . Exeter.
Farmer. Raymond.
Frederic Horace Adams . . . . 15 . . . Indianapolis, Ind.
Rufus Green Angell . . . . . . 15 . . . New York, N.Y.
Columbia Coll. 1881; Business. " "
Philip Bowers Ashley . . . . . 18 . . . Dighton, Mass.
Bank Clerk. Providence, R.I.
Luther Atwood . . . . 15 . . . Exeter.
Student, H.U.
William Daniel Baker . . . . . 20 . . . Plymouth.
Farmer. Rumney.
Bruce Burley Barney . . . . . 16 . . . Toledo, O.
Business. Chicago, Ill.
William Webster Bates . . . . 16 . . . Cohasset, Mass.
Business. Beechwood, Mass.
David Nevins Baxter . . . . . 14 . . . Rutland, Vt.
Student, H.U.
George Francis Blood . . . . . 15 . . . Wilton.
Business. Nashua.
Summerfield Berry Bond . . . 14 . . . Baltimore, Md.
Student. " "
Benjamin Metcalf Borland . . 16 . . . New Castle, Me.
H.U. 1881; R.R. Clerk. Boston, Mass.
Frederic Brooks . . . . 17 . . . Boston, Mass.
Artist. Paris, France.
Frank Taylor Brown . . . . . 14 . . . Framingham, Mass.
Ranching. Laramie, Wyoming Ter.
Frederic Dennison Browning . 18 . . . Perryville, R.I.
Charles Renwick Breck . . . . 16 . . . Benicia, Cal.
Merchant. Durango, Col.
George Clifford Buell, jr. . . . 16 . . . Rochester, N.Y.
H.U. 1882.
Frederic Dent Casey . . . . . 13 . . . New Orleans, La.
Alfred Henry Cohen . . . . . 17 . . . San Francisco, Cal.
Lawyer. " "
Edgar Andrew Cohen . . . . . 16 . . . San Francisco, Cal.
Broker. " "
Henry Glidden Cushman . . . 16 . . . Brookline, Mass.
Business. Boston, Mass.
Joseph Benjamin Dimmick . . 15 . . . Honesdale, Pa.
Yale Coll. 1881; Lawyer. " "
Julian Pierce Dunn . . . . . . 18 . . . Ludlow, Vt.
Instructor, Shaw Univ. Raleigh, N.C.
Charles Edwin Dyer . . . . . . 15 . . . Exeter.
Clerk. "
Alfred Fallon . . . . 15 . . . San Jose, Cal.
James Deering Fessenden . . . 17 . . . Portland, Me.
H.U. 1880; Law Student. " "

Henry Merrill Fessenden . . . 15 . . . Portland, Me.
   Real Estate and Ins. Agent.   "   "
John Fowler . . . . 17 . . . Winchester, Mass.
   Clerk, U.S. Navy.   Washington, D.C.
William Ashen Fowler . . . . 19 . . . Agawam, Mass.
Irving Randall Fuller . . . . . 17 . . . Faribault, Minn.
   Lawyer.   Fullerton, Neb.
Robert Holmes Greene . . . . 14 . . . Brunswick, Me.
   Corporation Paymaster.   "   "
William Almus Gregg . . . . . 16 . . . Wilton.
   Business.   Nashua.
Jacob Halstead . . . . 15 . . . Harrison, N.J.
Henry Williams Harlow . . . . 16 . . . Augusta, Me.
   H.U. 1882; Medical Student.
O'Neil W. R. Hastings . . . . 16 . . . Bethel, Me.
William Gardner Hempstead . 17 . . . Chicago, Ill.
   Business.   Evanston, Ill.
Albert Andrew Howard . . . . 16 . . . Ilion, N.Y.
   H.U. 1882; Student.   Leipsic, Germany.
Thomas Marshall Huntington . 16 . . . Amesbury, Mass.
John Carter Ingersoll . . . . . 15 . . . Washington, D.C.
   Student.   "   "
James Edward Keating . . . 19 . . . Milford, Mass.
   M.D.; Physician.   Natick, Mass.
Frederic Israel Kelley . . . . . 16 . . . Milford, Mass.
                                    South Boston, Mass.
Thaddeus Davis Kenneson . . 16 . . . Andover, Mass.
   H.U. 1880; Law Student, H.U.
Chauncey Frederic Kerr . . . . 16 . . . New York, N.Y.
Alexander Johnson Kirke . . . 19 . . . Pleasant Hill, Mo.
Daniel Watson Ladd, jr. . . . 16 . . . Epping.
   Law Student.   "
*Alva Watson Ladd . . . . . . 13 . . . Epping 1881
Albert French Lane . . . . . . 15 . . . Exeter.
   H.U. 1882; Law Student, H.U.
Charles Gleason Long . . . . . 17 . . . Amesbury, Mass.
                                    "   "
Edwin Balcom Lord . . . . . . 22 . . . Tamworth.
   Lawyer.   Warsaw, Wis.
Arthur Gilman Lovering . . . 13 . . . Exeter.
   R.R. Station Master.   Springfield, Mo.
Francis Heber Dana Mason . . 16 . . . Washington, D.C.
Thomas Edward McLure . . . 17 . . . Chester, S.C.
   Lawyer.   "   "
John Francis Merrill . . . . . 16 . . . Rutland, Vt.
   Yale Coll. 1881.
Charles Mason Mitchell . . . . 16 . . . Syracuse, N.Y.
Daniel Webster Moriarty . . . 17 . . . Milford, Mass.
   Clergyman.   Lander, Wyoming Ter.
Edward Irving Morse . . . . . 19 . . . Marlborough, Mass.
   H.U. 1880; Agent Detroit Safe Co.   Louisville, Ky.
William Francis O'Callaghan . 19 . . . Milford, Mass.
   H.U. 1880; Prin. High School.   Hopkinton, Mass.
Edward William Odlin . . . . 15 . . . Exeter.
   Business.   Grand Rapids, Mich.
Frederic Alonzo Parker . . . . 17 . . . Nashua.
   Teacher.   Keene.
Francis Stuyvesant Peabody . 16 . . . Chicago, Ill.

Donald Gilbert Perkins . . . . 17 . . . Norwich, Conn.
Lawyer. " "
John Benjamin Perkins . . . . 20 . . . Woodbury, Conn.
Edgar Perry . . . . 19 . . . Rehoboth, Mass.
Editor. Attleborough, Mass.
Oscar Edward Perry . . . . . 17 . . . Rehoboth, Mass.
Manufacturer. Holyoke, Mass.
Herbert Mills Perry . . . . . . 16 . . . Boston, Mass.
H.U. 1880; Student, Johns Hopk. Univ. Baltimore, Md.
Arthur Perry . . . . 18 . . . Westerly, R.I.
H.U. 1880; Bank Clerk. " "
Ernest Henry Pillsbury . . . . 17 . . . Lewiston, Me.
H.U. 1880; Law Student. New York, N.Y.
William Pollock . . . . 16 . . . Pittsfield, Mass.
Yale Coll. 1882; Lawyer. New York, N.Y.
Walter King Purinton . . . . . 16 . . . Topsham, Me.
Business. Boston, Mass.
Ethan Allen Reynolds . . . . . 19 . . . South Bend, Ind.
Lawyer. Leadville, Col.
Walter Allen Rice . . . . 18 . . . Bangor, Me.
Elocutionist. " "
George Reed Richardson . . . 16 . . . Lowell, Mass.
Lawyer. " "
Henry Cooper Rollins . . . . . 18 . . . Exeter.
Thomas Richard Rowe . . . . 19 . . . Providence, R.I.
Business. " "
John Turner Rumsey . . . . . 16 . . . Chicago, Ill.
George Washington Savory . . 19 . . . Manchester.
Theological Student. East Liverpool, O.
William Eckart Sharpe . . . . 15 . . . Indianapolis, Ind.
Assist. U.S. Assayer. Helena, Mont.
Amos Blanchard Shattuck . . 15 . . . Manchester.
U.S. Cadet. West Point, N.Y.
William Francis Sheehan . . . 17 . . . Milford, Mass.
Bookkeeper. Lynn, Mass.
Oscar Edward Shraeder . . . . 16 . . . Evansville, Ind.
Carleton Sprague . . . . 16 . . . Buffalo, N.Y.
H.U. 1881; Business. " "
Victor Hugo Stickney . . . . . 20 . . . Tyson Furnace, Vt.
Frederic Webster Sturdivant . 21 . . . Cumberland, Me.
Dart. Coll. 1880.
Frank Overton Suire . . . . . 17 . . . Cincinnati, O.
H.U. 1880; Lawyer. " "
Jacob Sutton Sullivant . . . . 16 . . . Columbus, O.
Post Office Clerk. " "
Allen Sullivant . . . . 13 . . . Columbus, O.
Paris, France.
Leonard Herbert Swett . . . . 16 . . . Chicago, Ill.
Medical Student. " "
John Glover Thomas . . . . . 27 . . . Camden, Me.
M.D.; Physician. Worcester, Mass.
John Preston True . . . . . . 16 . . . Bethel, Me.
Christopher Carpenter Viall . . 22 . . . Rehoboth, Mass.
Farmer. " "
Paul Voorhees . . . . 16 . . . New York, N.Y.
*John Nichols Weston . . . . . 14 . . . Stamford, Conn. . . . 1880
Robert Charles Wiggin . . . . 14 . . . Boston, Mass.
Business. " "
William Pendleton Wilson . . 15 . . . Baltimore, Md.

Chas. Edward Lewis Wingate . 14 . . . Exeter.
  Student, H.U.
Arthur Woods Worthington . . 17 . . . Buffalo, N.Y.
  Insurance Agent.   Minneapolis, Minn.
William Harrison Wylie. . . . 18 . . . Chester, S.C.
  Manufacturer.   Whitinsville, Mass.
Alphonso Adelbert Wyman . . 13 . . . West Acton, Mass.
  Student, H.U.

                                              98

1876.

Robert Anderson Atherton . . 14 . . . Ludlow, Vt.
  Commercial Traveller.   "   "
William Edgar Atwater . . . . 19 . . . New York, N.Y.
Willard Shurtleff Augsbury . . 18 . . . Antwerp, N.Y.
Frank Bruce Bailey . . . . . . 18 . . . Chicago, Ill.
Arthur Eaton Baker. . . . . . 16 . . . Winchester, Mass.
  Student, B.U.
Ernest Berkeley Balch . . . 16 . . . Plymouth.
  Teacher.   "
James Merritt Bancroft . . . . 18 . . . Bradford, Mass.
  Architect.   Boston, Mass.
Clarence Bancroft . . . . . . 17 . . Hopedale, Mass.
  H.U. 1882; Student in Chemistry.   Zurich, Switzerland.
*Lewis Lawrence Bartlett . . . 14 . . . Epping 1877
Frank Clifton Bates . . . . . . 17 . . . Great Falls.
  Merchant.   "   "
Henry Bates . . . . 17 . . . Indianapolis, Ind.
  Machinist.   "   "
William Pettigrew Benedict . . 18 . . . Portsmouth.
  Bank Clerk.   "
Samuel Frederic Borland . . . 16 . . . New Castle, Me.
  Mariner.   New York, N.Y.
George Clement Bright . . . . 13 . . . New Orleans, La.
Edward Melancthon Brooks . . 16 . . . Cleveland, O.
Henry Greer Bryant . . . . . 16 . . . Philadelphia, Pa.
  Coll. N.J. 1882.   "   "
George Albert Burdett . . . . 18 . . . Brookline, Mass.
  H.U. 1881; Student.   Boston, Mass.
Francis David Chamberlain . . 17 . . . West Chester, Pa.
  Student, Yale Coll.
Charles Porter Coffin . . . . . 18 . . . Batavia, N.Y.
*William John Curry . . . . . . 20 . . . Chester, S.C. 1883
  Apothecary.   North Cambridge, Mass.
John Uriah Dale . . . . 19 . . . Weston, Mo.
  Farmer.   "   "
Henry De Ford . . . . 16 . . . Baltimore, Md.
  Business.   "   "
Oliver Dyer, jr. . . . . 15 . . . West Vernon, N.J.
Frank Britton Fay . . . . . . 17 . . . East Calais, Vt.
  Student, H.U.
George Walker Field . . . . . 17 . . . Ferrisburg, Vt.
  Farmer.   Burlington, Vt.
John McGaw Foster . . . . . 16 . . . Bangor, Me.
  H.U. 1882.

Frank Newell French . . . . . 16 . . . Exeter.
Teacher.
James Graham Gardiner . . . 14 . . . Croydon.
Student, H.U.
Clarence Getchell . . . . 16 . . . Exeter.
Student, H.U.
Edward Hooker Gilbert . . . . 16 . . . Ware, Mass.
Yale Coll. 1881; Manufacturer. " "
Milton Gray . . . . 21 . . . Shingle Creek, N.Y.
William Morton Grinnell . . . 18 . . . Greenfield, Mass.
Lawyer. Paris, France.
Richard Bradley Grinnell . . . 16 . . . Greenfield, Mass.
R.R. Clerk. Minneapolis, Minn.
Frederic Sumner Haines . . . 15 . . . Great Falls.
Student, H.U.
Frank Holmes Hall . . . . . . 15 . . . Brattleborough, Vt.
Oliver Hubbard Ham . . . . . 19 . . . Portsmouth.
Machinist. Hartford, Conn.
Abner Clarke Harding . . . . 17 . . . Chicago, Ill.
Lawyer. Peoria, Ill.
Arthur Meeks Hawkins . . . . 14 . . . New York, N.Y.
Student, H.U.
Aubrey De Vere Hiles . . . . 22 . . . Milwaukee, Wis.
Lawyer. " "
Sherman Hoar . . . . 16 . . . Concord, Mass.
H.U. 1882; Law Student, H.U.
Benjamin Blake Holmes . . . 18 . . . Bradford, Mass.
Student, H.U.
Charles Osgood Hooker . . . . 16 . . . San Francisco, Cal.
Samuel Percy Hooker . . . . . 15 . . . Le Roy, N.Y.
Bookkeeper. " "
William Turner Howard . . . 15 . . . New Orleans, La.
Willard Warren Howe . . . . 16 . . . Cincinnati, O.
Bank Clerk. " "
Jared Slocomb Howe . . . . . 17 . . . Haverhill, Mass.
H.U. 1881; Lawyer. " "
Seymour Isaac Hudgens . . . 23 . . . Sandwich, Ill.
Student, H.U.
Henry Barton Jacobs . . . . . 18 . . . South Scituate, Mass.
Student, H.U.
Albert Emerson Joab . . . . . 19 . . . Terre Haute, Ind.
Walter Stephen Johnson . . . 20 . . . Westborough, Mass.
William Winthrop Kent . . . . 16 . . . Buffalo, N.Y.
H.U. 1882; Business. " "
Moses King . . . . 22 . . . St. Louis, Mo.
H.U. 1881; Publisher. Cambridge, Mass.
James Walter Lathrop . . . . 19 . . . Worcester, Mass.
Business. " "
Levi Tisdale Lincoln . . . . . 15 . . . Barrington.
Business. Minneapolis, Minn.
William Rensselaer Lloyd . . . 16 . . . New York, N.Y.
Columbia Coll. 1881; Business. " "
Aldis Lovell . . . . 17 . . . Alstead.
George Stanley Lynde . . . . 14 . . . Skowhegan, Me.
David Ford Merrill, jr. . . . . 17 . . . Washington, D.C.
Business. " "
John Herbert Neal . . . . . . 16 . . . Epping.
Machinist. Waltham, Mass.

Alfred Cookman Oliver . . . . 20 . . . Port Carbon, Pa.
James Gillespie Orton . . . . . 16 . . . New York, N.Y.
Charles Chase Parsons . . . . 17 . . . Exeter.
Business. Boston, Mass.
Marshall Bell Peaslee . . . . . 14 . . . Plaistow.
Business. Haverhill, Mass.
Edmund Seahon Perin . . . 16 . . . Cincinnati, O.
H.U. 1882.
George William Perkins . . . . 16 . . . Topsfield, Mass.
H.U. 1882; Assist. in Biology, H.U. Cambridge, Mass.
John Edward Pickering . . . . 15 . . . Newington.
Teacher. "
Charles Ranlet . . . . 15 . . . Holyoke, Mass.
Student, H.U.
Charles Moen Rice . . . . . . 15 . . . Worcester, Mass.
H.U. 1882; Law Student. " "
George Morey Richardson . . 17 . . . Framingham Center, Mass.
H.U. 1882; Student. Jena, Germany.
Daniel Merchant Richardson . . 14 . . . Lowell, Mass.
Student, H.U.
John Samuel Richardson . . . 21 . . . East Baldwin, Me.
Law Student.
Francis James Riley . . . . . 21 . . . New Bedford, Mass.
Student, H.U.
Harry Mylinn Rohrer . . . . . 17 . . . Washington, D.C.
Lawyer. " "
Isaac Fitz Sawyer . . . . 22 . . . Exeter.
Frederic Jonathan Sawyer . . 16 . . . Dover.
Business Agent. Boston, Mass.
Charles Orlando Shaw . . . . . 16 . . . Dexter, Me.
Business. Oregon, N.Y.
James Theophilus Simpson . . 20 . . . Fremont.
Teacher. Fort Hamilton, N.Y.
Franklin Tileston Sivret . . . . 17 . . . Mattapan, Mass.
Stock Farmer. Ft. Macquirnis, Mont.
John Morrell Smith . . . . . . 21 . . . Meredith Center.
Roswell Perry Smith . . . . . 14 . . . Exeter.
Bookkeeper. Boston, Mass.
Samuel Hopkins Spalding . . . 20 . . . Wilton.
H.U. 1881.
De Witt Charles Spencer . . . 17 . . . Chicago, Ill.
Walter Edward Stearns . . . . 15 . . . Wilton.
Joseph Dalton Thyng . . . . . 16 . . . Exeter.
Clerk. Boston, Mass.
John Wheelock Titcomb . . . 15 . . . Exeter.
Business. Rutland, Vt.
Herbert Osgood True . . . . . 17 . . . Antrim.
Robert Scott Waddell . . . . . 15 . . . West Chester, Pa.
Law Student. " "
James Gould Warren . . . . . 17 . . . Buffalo, N.Y.
Lieut. U.S. Engineers.
Lewis Webb . . . . 14 . . . San Francisco, Cal.
Edward Freeman Wells . . . . 15 . . . 'Marietta, O.
Marietta Coll. 1881; R.R. Business. St. Paul, Minn.
Charles Morgan Wheeler . . . 16 . . . San Francisco, Cal.
Henry Charles White . . . . . 20 . . . Vernon, Oneida Co., N.Y.
Schuyler Sampson White . . . 15 . . . Newmarket.
Student, H.U.

Henry Lampson Wiggin . . . 15 . . . Wakefield.
Samuel Lawrence Williams . . 16 . . . Chicago, Ill.
  Real Estate Agent.   "   "
William Howard Wilmarth . . 16 . . . Attleborough, Mass.
  Instructor, Lewis Coll.   Northfield, Vt.
John Wilson . . . . 15 . . . Shrewsbury, N.J.
  Coll. N.J. 1882; Teacher State Normal School.   Indiana, Pa.
Samuel Harvey Wollerton . . . 17 . . . West Chester, Pa.
  M.D.; Physician.   "   "
Willard Everett Yager . . . . 19 . . . Oneonta, Ostego Co., N.Y.
*David Frederic Zerrahn . . . . 15 . . . Boston, Mass. 1881
  100

1877.

Harlan Page Abbott. . . . . . 16 . . . Antrim.
Charles Francis Adams . . . . 15 . . . Hooversville, Md.
Frank Oswald Adams . . . . . 16 . . . Burlington, Ia.
  Business.   "   "
Thomas Edwin Adams . . . . 15 . . . Louisville, Ky.
Fred Abbott Aldrich . . . . . 15 . . . Flint, Mich.
  Journalist.   "   "
Frank George Alger . . . . . 18 . . . Manchester.
  Student, Oberlin Coll.
John Dewitt Arnold . . . . . . 16 . . . Sacramento, Cal.
  Business.   "   "
Charles Henry Ashley . . . . . 17 . . . Ogdensburg, N.Y.
John Franklin Bailey . . . . . 18 . . . Boston, Mass.
Dana Wingate Baker . . . . . 16 . . . Exeter.
  Druggist's Clerk.   "
Ferdinand Winthrop Batchelder 15 . . . Montreal, P.Q.
Walter Cabot Baylies . . . . . 15 . . . Taunton, Mass.
  Student, H.U.
Karl Albert Bean . . . . 17 . . . Bangor, Me.
  Student, H.U.
Flavius Josephus Berry . . . . 19 . . . Barrington.
James Winchester Berry . . . 17 . . . Kensington.
Frederic Herbert Blondell . . . 21 . . . Topsham, Me.
  Bowd. Coll. 1882; Teacher.   "   "
Jeromus Rapalje Bonney . . . 18 . . . New York, N.Y.
  Paris, France.
John Eldon Bowman . . . . . 15 . . . Springfield, O.
  Law Student.   "   "
Frank Arthur Briggs . . . . . 18 . . . Amesbury, Mass.
Gilman Abraham Brown . . . 15 . . . Lowell, Mass.
  Clerk.   Boston, Mass.
Peter Burke. . . . . 19 . . . Milford, Mass.
  Law Student.   Dover.
Charles Alonzo Burns . . . . . 13 . . . Wilton.
John Willard Burns . . . . . . 17 . . . Exeter.
Joseph Charles Byron . . . . . 16 . . . Gloversville, N.Y.
Fred Eames Carpenter . . . . 18 . . . Keene.
Lucien Carr, jr. . . . . 16 . . . Cambridge, Mass.
  Business.   Boston, Mass.
Peter Julius Casey . . . . . 20 . . . Cambridge, Mass.
  Law Student, H.U.

William Cromwell Chase . . . 14 . . . Haverford College, Pa.
Student.   "   "   "
Israel Folsom Chesley . . . . . 17 . . . Salisbury, Mass.
John Henry Chesley . . . . . . 16 . . . Wakefield.
Frank Almander Churchill. . . 17 . . . Exeter.
Clerk.   Boston, Mass.
Bradbury Jenness Cilley . . . 17 . . . Manchester.
William Coombs Codman, jr. . 17 . . . Boston, Mass.
Broker.   "   "
William Herbert Crawford . . 17 . . . New York, N.Y.
Business.   "   "
Henry Laurens Dawes, jr. . . 14 . . . Pittsfield, Mass.
Student, Yale Coll.
Edgar Augustus De Witt . . . 20 . . . Rockland, Mass.
*Orlando Dyer . . . . 19 . . . Topsham, Me. . . . 1883
Zenas Hoxie Ellis . . . . 17 . . . Fairhaven, Vt.
Bank Teller.   "   "
Henry Emerson . . . . 15 . . . New York, N.Y.
     "   "
William Key Bond Emerson . . 16 . . . New York, N.Y.
Broker.   "   "
William Gordon Fellows . . . 16 . . . New York, N.Y.
H.U. 1882.
William Reynolds Fleming . . 15 . . . Harrisburg, Pa.
Apprentice, Hartford, Conn.   "   "
William Ring Gray . . . . . . 15 . . . Elizabeth, N.J.
Edward Hurd Haley . . . . . 20 . . . Dover.
     "

Addison Hamlin . . . . 14 . . . Bangor, Me.
Student, H.U.
Charles Eugene Hamlin . . . . 15 . . . Bangor, Me.
Student, H.U.
Frank Hamlin . . . . 14 . . . Bangor, Me.
Student, H.U.
*Francis Loring Hayford . . . 17 . . . Bangor, Me. 1881
George Francis Haynes . . . . 20 . . . New Hampton.
Hotel Clerk.   Exeter.
Walter Edward Hayward . . . 18 . . . Attleborough, Mass.
Student, H.U.
Benjamin Pike Hope . . . . . 17 . . . Shrewsbury, N.J.
Arthur Crockett Hull . . . . . 19 . . . Plymouth.
William Sterrett Hunnewell . . 14 . . . Exeter.
Business.   Minneapolis, Minn.
Ernest Sanford Jack . . . . . 17 . . . Portland, Me.
Student, H.U.
Fredric William Jenkins . . . 18 . . . Rochester.
Govt. Service.   Washington, D.C.
Barrett Langdon Jenness . . . 23 . . . Deerfield.
Broker's Clerk.   New York, N.Y.
Frank Elwood Jennison . . . . 16 . . . Bangor, Me.
Student, H.U.
Charles Tilton Kamm . . . . . 16 . . . Portland, Oregon.
Frederic Milbanke Kerr . . . . 14 . . . New York, N.Y.
Business.   "   "
Robert Bage Kerr . . . . 14 . . . New York, N.Y.
Student, Yale Coll.
Paul Thomas Kimball . . . . . 15 . . . Eatontown, N.J.
Stephen Strickland Kirby . . . 19 . . . Towanda, Pa.

Amos Arnold Knowlton . . . . 18 . . . Tamworth.
Student, Bowd. Coll.
*Frank Woodbury Langdon . . 18 . . . Plymouth 1880
John Washington Lewis . . . . 22 . . . Newton, Mass.
*John Willard Little . . . . . . 16 . . . Merrimac, Mass. . . 1878
Fred Messenger Lowe . . . . . 18 . . . Fitchburg, Mass.
Yale Coll. 1882; Med. Student, H.U.   No. Cambridge, Mass.
William Lyman Luther . . . . 16 . . . Brockton, Mass.
Student, H.U.
John Theodore Lyman . . . . 16 . . . Exeter.
Business.   Grinnell, Ia.
Patrick Henry Mack . . . . . 18 . . . Fitchburg, Mass.
Bookkeeper.   Lone Pine, Cal.
Ernest Homer Mariett . . . . . 20 . . . St. Armand, P.Q.
Student, Episc. Theolog. School.   Cambridge, Mass.
Henry Wheelwright Marsh . . 17 . . . Tewksbury, Mass.
Student, H.U.
Thomas Leavitt Marston . . . 18 . . . North Hampton.
Woollen Weaver.   Dover.
Henry Ely McElwain . . . . . 18 . . . Holyoke, Mass.
William Lockhart Mehle . . . 16 . . . New Orleans, La.
Dennison Burnham Merrill . . 17 . . . Ottumwa, Ia.
Alfred Eugene Miles . . . . . 17 . . . Fitchburg, Mass.
H.U. 1882.   "   "
William Norwood Needles, jr. 19 . . . West Chester, Pa.
Lawyer.   Philadelphia, Pa.
Oliver Allen Olmsted . . . . . 16 . . . Le Roy, N.Y.
H.U. 1882.
Hugh Roberts Parrish . . . . . 16 . . . Burlington, N.J.
Clerk, Pa. R.R.   Philadelphia, Pa.
Enoch William Pearson . . . . 14 . . . Epping.
Music Teacher.   "
Benjamin Whipple Pennock . . 23 . . . Rutland, Vt.
Student, Amh. Coll.   "   "
Albert Sanborn Perkins . '. . . 16 . . . Exeter.
Student, H.U.
Robert Randolph Perkins . . . 14 . . . Fort Washington, N.Y.
Howard Emerson Plimpton . . 15 . . . Walpole, Mass.
Manufacturer.   Waterford, N.Y.
Alonzo Wilder Pollard . . . . 15 . . . Boston, Mass.
Student, H.U.
Edward Learned Pollock . . . 14 . . . Pittsfield, Mass.
Robert Camp Price . . . . . . 18 . . . Cincinnati, O.
Law Student.   "   "
Jerome Comstock Read . . . . 15 . . . New York, N.Y.
Nathaniel Tucker Rhodes . . . 17 . . . Dorchester, Mass.
Business.   Boston, Mass.
Lucian Moore Robinson . . . . 17 . . . Hartford, Me.
H.U. 1882; Teacher.   Philadelphia, Pa.
William Alvah Rublee . . . . 16 . . . Madison, Wis.
Student, H.U.
Philip Leon Runkle . . . . . . 15 . . . New York, N.Y.
Business.   "   "
George Benjamin Salter . . . . 15 . . . Burlington, Ia.
Bookkeeper.   "   "
Frank Wadleigh Sargeant . . . 17 . . . Candia.
Insurance Clerk.   Manchester.

Fred Leland Sawyer. . . . . . 19 . . . Cumberland, Me.
Student, H.U.
David Whitney Scott . . . . . 22 . . . Washington, D.C.
Journalist.   "   "
Adrian Scharff . . . . 18 . . . Exeter.
Coll. of N.J. 1881; Law Student, N.Y.
Lawrence Eugene Sexton . . . 18 . . . Cleveland, O.
Student, H.U.
Edward Parsons Seymour . . . 14 . . . New Ipswich.
George Washington Simmons . 20 . . . New London, Conn.
Teacher.   Wash. Co., Miss.
Forrest Gilman Small . . . . . 16 . . . Wilton, Me.
William Whiting Spencer . . . 16 . . . Chicago, Ill.
Frank Burton Stevens . . . . 16 . . . Dover.
Law Student.   "
William Smith Stevens . . . . 13 . . . Charleston, S.C.
Frank Oswin Stewart . . . . . 13 . . . Exeter.
Charles Augustus Strong . . . 14 . . . Rochester, N.Y.
Student.   "   "
Fred Strong Tabor . . . . . . 19 . . . Aurora, Ill.
Physician.   Chicago, Ill.
Eugene Thomas . . . . 18 . . . Topsham, Me.
Student, Bowd. Coll.   "   "
Beverly Bingham Tilden . . . 17 . . . New York, N.Y.
                                       "   "
Wesley Tourtellotte . . . . . . 17 . . . Webster, Mass.
Business.   Boston, Mass.
Wheelock Veazey Towle . . . 14 . . . Exeter.
Student, Dart. Coll.
John Baldwin Walker . . . . . 16 . . . Gloversville, N.Y.
Student, H.U.
William Bernard Waring . . . 16 . . . Brooklyn, N.Y.
Edward Ingersoll Wells . . . . 17 . . . Rochester, N.Y.
Student, H.U.
John C. F. Wheelock . . . . . 19 . . . Mendon, Mass.
Law Student (Worcester, Mass.).   "   "
Benjamin Cheney White . . . . 16 . . . Concord.
                                       "
John Allison White . . . . . . 15 . . . Williamsport, Pa.
Student, H.U.
Charles Horace Wiggin . . . . 18 . . . Newmarket.
Charles Meigs Wilson . . . . . 16 . . . Philadelphia, Pa.
Physician.   "   "
Edmund Wilson . . . . 13 . . . Shrewsbury, N.J.

1878.

Charles Coleman Allen . . . . 19 . . . Troy, O.
Student, H.U.
Ethan Allen . . . . 16 . . . Mumford, N.Y.
Clerk.   Buffalo, N.Y.
Ernest Allis . . . . 19 . . . Milwaukee, Wis.
Clerk.   "   "
Randolph Morgan Appleton . . 16 . . . New York, N.Y.
Student, H.U.

Burnside Bernard Bailey ... 16 ... Montpelier, Vt.
Law Student, H.U. Chicago, Ill.
James Eliot Baker ...... 18 ... Brookline, Mass.
Student, H.U.
Sharonton Hale Baker .... 16 ... Dover.
Student, B.U.
Charles Robert Bangs ..... 17 ... Le Roy, N.Y.
Law Student. " "
Charles Sanford Barrett .... 17 ... Grafton, Vt.
Lumber Clerk. Burlington, Vt.
Walter Knox Barton ..... 14 ... Washington, D.C.
Student, H.U.
Walter Joseph Broadmeadow . 15 ... Shrewsbury, N.J.
Student, Stevens Inst. of Tech. " "
Lovine Alanson Bromley ... 21 ... Pawlet, Vt.
John Paschal Brooks ..... 16 ... Kittery, Me.
Student, Dart. Coll.
Isaac Bronson Burgess .... 20 ... Hampton Falls.
Student, B.U.
Orrin Henry Carpenter .... 17 ... Grafton, Vt.
Law Student. Bellows Falls, Vt.
Timothy William Coakley , .. 19 ... Exeter.
Theological Student, Laval Univ., Quebec.
John Codman .... 15 ... Boston, Mass.
Student, H.U.
George Antonio Cormack ... 15 ... New York, N.Y.
John Thaddeus Cressey . . .. 18 ... Dover.
Student, Dart. Coll.
Osborn Marcus Curtiss .... 18 ... Rock Island, Ill.
Teacher. " " "
Marshall Henry Cushing ... 18 ... So. Hingham, Mass.
Student, H.U.
Walter Reeves Dame ..... 17 ... Clinton, Mass.
Student, H.U.
Arthur Malcolm Dodge .... 16 ... Hampton Falls.
Manufacturer. " "
Paul Abbott Dodge ...... 19 ... Rowley, Mass.
Farmer. " "
Charles Wheelock Downing .. 13 ... Concord.
Edward Tyler Edgerly .... 14 ... Ottumwa, Ia.
Student, H.U.
Edwards Dudley Emerson ... 16 ... Underhill, Vt.
Student, Dart. Coll.
Frank Stewart Ferguson ... 17 ... Gloversville, N.Y.
Lynde Raymond Ferris .... 18 ... Brookline, Mass.
Student, H.U.
Henry Lewis Finch .... : .. 17 ... Glenn's Falls, N.Y.
Lumberman. " " "
Samuel Henry Friend ..... 16 ... Milwaukee, Wis.
Business. " "
Franklin Kent Gifford ..... 17 ... Cambridge, Mass.
Student, H.U.
Emlyn Metcalf Gill ...... 16 ... Orange, N.J.
Student, H.U.
John Richardson Gilpatrick .. 15 ... Great Falls.
Howard Robinson Goodwin . 14 ... Augusta, Me.
Student, Bowd. Coll. New York, N.Y.
William Burton Goodwin ... 14 ... Biddeford, Me.
Student, Yale Coll.

Harold Graham . . . . 14 . . . New York, N.Y.
George William Greeley . . . . 18 . . . Winchester, Mass.
Business. " "
Edward Carroll Hall . . . . . 19 . . . Topsham, Me.
William Maclay Hall, jr. . . . 14 . . . Bedford, Pa.
Student, Coll. of N.J.
Herbert Franklin Hanson . . . 16 . . . Dover.
Business. Boston, Mass.
Herbert William Harwood . . . 18 . . . Henniker.
"
Tom Dalrymple Hay . . . . . 15 . . . New Orleans, La.
David Nicholson Haynes . . . 18 . . . Whitehall, N.Y.
Lawyer. Rutland, Vt.
Henry Hobart Herrick . . . . 15 . . . New York, N.Y.
Joseph Adna Hill . . . . 18 . . . Temple.
Student, H.U.
Rodney Benjamin Hoitt . . . . 15 . . . Dover.
Business. "
John Francis Holland . . . . . 19 . . . Milford, Mass.
Student, H.U.
Harry Hubbard . . . . 18 . . . Troy.
Student, H.U. Boston, Mass.
Heber William Hull . . . . . . 16 . . . Plymouth.
Edwin Everett Jacobs . . . . . 16 . . . West Scituate, Mass.
George Jenkins . . . . 19 . . . Franklin Falls.
Teacher. Shirley, Mass.
William Scott Johnston . . . . 17 . . . Piqua, O.
Charles Dana Jones . . . . . . 15 . . . Milton.
Med. Student, H.U.
Homer Fay Jordan . . . . . . 19 . . . Dayton, O.
Lawyer. Cincinnati, O.
Samuel Hauser Kennett . . . . 17 . . . Helena, Mont.
Rensselaer Lee Kirk . . . . . 19 . . . Cambridge, Mass.
Pacific Express. Denver, Col.
Charles Berry Learoyd . . . . 18 . . . Danvers, Mass.
Student, Amh. Coll.
Charles Lindsey . . . . 17 . . . Wells, Me.
Salesman (Boston, Mass.). East Somerville, Mass.
Reuben Whittle Lovering . . . 15 . . . Hillsborough Bridge.
Student, H.U.
Frank Anthony Luques . . . . 14 . . . Biddeford, Me.
Student, H.U.
George Jeffrey Mackenzie . . . 14 . . . Wilkesbarre, Pa.
Harry Alexander Madill . . . . 18 . . . Towanda, Pa.
Frederick Hubbell Marvin . . . 13 . . . New York, N.Y.
Senior Class.
David Hunter McAlpin . . . . 16 . . . New York, N.Y.
Student, Coll. of N.J.
Harry Jackson McCoy . . . . 15 . . . Troy, N.Y.
Student, Germany.
James Henry McIntosh . . . . 19 . . . Salineville, O.
Student, H.U.
William Leander McKee . . . 15 . . . Piermont, N.Y.
Business. Rome, Ga.
George Nathaniel Plumer Mead 19 . . . Everett, Mass.
Student, H.U.
James Alfred Merrill . . . . . 15 . . . Rutland, Vt.
Student, Yale Coll.

Reuben Burnham Moffat ...	17 ...	Brooklyn, N.Y.
Student, H.U.		
Tredwell Woodbridge Moore .	14 ...	Baltimore, Md.
Henry David Nelson	16 ...	Milford, Mass.
Student, H.U.		
Joseph Willard Newman ...	19 ...	Hillsborough Bridge.
Law Student.		Chicago, Ill.
Henry Osgood.........	15 ...	Rochester, N.Y.
Business.		Chicago, Ill.
Charles Wolcott Parker	15 ...	Newark, N.J.
Student, Coll. of N.J.		
George Richmond Parsons ..	17 ...	Providence, R.I.
Student, H.U.		
Edward Eastman Pecker ...	17 ...	Boston, Mass.
Business.		" "
John Dudley Philbrick	16 ...	Candia.
Student, Dart. Coll.		
Walter Brigham Phillips....	14 ...	Chicago, Ill.
Student, H.U.		
Joseph Dexter Pierce	20 ...	Newburg, N.Y.
Charles Manice Pollock	14 ...	Pittsfield, Mass.
		" "
Edward Michael Raftery ...	21 ...	Milford, Mass.
Student, Holy Cross Coll.		
Robert Ranlet	15 ...	Holyoke, Mass.
George Reuben Raymond ...	18 ...	Boston, Mass.
Paran Flint Rice	18 ...	Syracuse, N.Y.
Law Student.		" "
Frederick Henry Richardson .	17 ...	Rutland, Vt.
Business.		" "
John Jones Roberts	18 ...	Rochester.
Student, H.U.		
James Upson Sanders	19 ...	Helena, Mont.
Law Student, Columbia Coll.		
Wilbur Edgerton Sanders ...	17 ...	Helena, Mont.
School of Mines, Columbia Coll.		
George William Sawin	18 ...	Natick, Mass.
Student, H.U.		
Harry Haskell Small	15 ...	Waterville, Me.
Student, Trinity Coll.		
*Daniel Chapman Smith	18 ...	Bedford, Pa. 1880
		" "
William Christopher Smith ..	16 ...	West Chatham, Mass.
Student, H.U.		
Augustus Burbank Stoughton .	14 ...	Washington, D.C.
William Lee Thurston	18 ...	Lancaster, Mass.
Civil Engineer.		Tampico, Mex.
George Parsons Tibbets	14 ...	Great Falls.
Student, Amh. Coll.		
Henry Trail	16 ...	Frederick, Md.
Student, H.U.		
Charles Whitcomb Tuttle ...	16 ...	Hancock.
Student, Bowd. Coll.		
Frank Hardin Walker.....	17 ...	Exeter.
Bookkeeper.		Atlanta, Ga.
Richard Ashur Ware	17 ...	Washington, D.C.
James Duncan Waring	16 ...	Brooklyn, N.Y.
Frederick Albert Weber	18 ...	Boston, Mass.

George Albert Webster . . . . 16 . . . Brooklyn, N.Y.
Student, Andover, Mass.
Frank Herbert Weed . . . . . . 18 . . . Sandwich.
Law Student.   "
Robert Means James Wells . . 14 . . . Exeter.
                                         "
Charles Brewster Wentworth . 16 . . . Dover.
Bookkeeper.   "
Frederick Livermore Wheeler . 15 . . . Boston, Mass.
Cattle Raising.   St. Clair, Ia.
John Kimball Whiting . . . . 15 . . . Wilton.
Franklin Wyman . . . . 17 . . Hillsborough Bridge.
Student, H.U.

110

1879.

Joseph Daniel Aiken, jr. . . . 17 . . . Charleston, S.C.
Manufacturer.   "   "
George Edward Bales . . . . . 16 . . . Wilton.
Senior Class.
Thomas Harris Bartlett . . . . 15 . . . Portsmouth.
Clerk.   "
John M. W. Bartol . . . . . . 15 . . . Lancaster, Mass.
Senior Class.
Louis Bell . . . . 14 . . . Chester.
Student, Dart. Coll.
Frank Everett Benjamin . . . 22 . . . Alstead.
Senior Class.
Henry de Billier . . . . 18 . . . Yonkers, N.Y.
Banker.   New York, N.Y.
Walter Levi Blossom . . . . . 17 . . . Milwaukee, Wis.
Henry Blanchard Bridge . . . 16 . . . Marblehead, Mass.
Conway Rathbone Brown . . . 16 . . . Worcester, Mass.
Senior Class.
Emanuel Gonzales Bullard . . 17 . . . Saratoga Springs, N.Y.
Law Student.   "   "   "
Harry Spencer Burrows . . . . 15 . . . Lowell, Mass.
Louis Burt . . . . 16 . . . Rutland, Vt.
Clerk.   "   "
Edward Walter Byron . . . . . 20 . . . Gloversville, N.Y.
James McCormick Cameron . . 14 . . . Harrisburgh, Pa.
Senior Class.
Charles Carroll . . . . 14 . . . Ellicott City, Md.
                                         Howard Co., Md.
Royal P. T. Carroll . . . . . . 16 . . . Ellicott City, Md.
Student, H.U.
Albert Hopkins Chadbourne . . 17 . . . Williamstown, Mass.
Student, Mass. Agric. Coll.
Allen Howard Chamberlain . . 17 . . . South Dover, Me.
Student, H.U.
Kin Kwei Chin . . . . Shanghai, China.
Charles Fish Clement . . . . . 17 . . . Rutland, Vt.
Senior Class.
Charles Edward Countryman . 19 . . . Albany, N.Y.
Law Student.   "   "
Frank Herbert Cunningham . . 23 . . . Boston, Mass.
Law Student, H.U.
Charles Warren Currier . . . . 16 . . . Canaan.

Frank Kneeland Davis . . . . 16 . . . North Andover, Mass.
Manufacturer. " " "
Albert Henry Denfeld . . . . . 19 . . . Westborough, Mass.
James Carey Evans . . . . . . 16 . . . Buffalo, N.Y.
Clerk. " "
Rush Emery Evans . . . . . . 17 . . . Hillsborough, O.
Bank Clerk. " "
John Purinton Fay . . . . . . 18 . . . Westborough, Mass.
Teacher. Upton, Mass.
George Tennant Spink Foote . 17 . . . Middletown, N.Y.
Student, Roch. Univ.
Herbert Darling Foster . . . . 16 . . . Winchendon, Mass.
Student, Dart. Coll.
Fred Fox, jr. . . . . 17 . . . Portland, Me.
Student, Mass. Inst. of Tech.
Edward Clayton Frost . . . . 19 . . . Springvale, Me.
Teacher. "
John Fox Hart . . . . 22 . . . Milton Mills.
Manufacturer. Union.
Ervin Wilbur Hodsdon . . . . 16 . . . Dover.
John Parker Holmes . . . . . 19 . . . Milford, Mass.
Student, H.U.
James Barker Hooper . . . . . 17 . . . Griggstown, N.J.
Clerk. New York, N.Y.
Charles Monroe Howard . . . 19 . . . South Newmarket.
Senior Class.
Edward Vernam Hull . . . . . 19 . . . San Francisco, Cal.
Student, H.U.
Lee Hutchins . . . . 16 . . . Washington, D.C.
Law Student, H.U. Laconia.
John Davis Kales . . . . 15 . . . Chicago, Ill.
Med. Student. " "
Pierce James Kent . . . . . . 16 . . . Exeter.
Senior Class.
Ta Ting Kin . . . . Shanghai, China.
John Kittredge . . . . 17 . . . North Andover, Mass.
Ranchman. Laramie City, Wy. Ter.
Percy Cheney Laselle . . . . . 17 . . . Goffstown.
Clerk (Manchester). "
George Hees Ledlie . . . . . . 19 . . . Utica, N.Y.
Student, H.U.
Yu Kien Li . . . . Shanghai, China.
Frank Kerr Marston . . . . . 16 . . . Clarendon, Ark.
James Lawrence McCormick . 16 . . . Bel Air, Md.
Student, Coll. of N.J.
Frank Augustus McNutt . . . 16 . . . Richmond, Ind.
Edwin Joseph Meeks . . . . . 14 . . . Mt. Vernon, N.Y.
Senior Class.
Charles Henry Merrill . . . . . 17 . . . Exeter.
Senior Class.
Nathaniel Marshall Nelson . . 15 . . . East Kingston.
Senior Class.
Shung Chow Niu . . . . 16 . . . Shanghai, China.
Edward Isaac Kimball Noyes . 17 . . . Antrim.
Student, H.U.
Albert Hilton Pike . . . . . . 15 . . . Epping.
Middle Class.
Frederic William Putnam . . . 17 . . . Waterville, N.Y.

Sheridan Pitt Read . . . . . . 17 . . . Jersey City, N.J.
James Patrick Redebean . . . 22 . . . Chelsea, Mass.
George Harlow Reed . . . . . 21 . . . Wellesley, Mass.
 Senior Class.
William Livingston Reed . . . 16 . . . Lawrence, Mass.
 Planter.   Apopka City, Fla.
Benjamin Richards . . . . . . 16 . . . East Steuben, N.Y.
 Salesman.   New York, N.Y.
Frank Henry Robinson . . . . 17 . . . Southborough, Mass.
Gustavus Adolphus Rose . . . 17 . . . La Porte, Ind.
 Banker.   " "
Thomas Parker Sanborn . . . 14 . . . Concord, Mass.
 Student, H.U.
Henry Smith, jr. . . . . 16 . . . Cobleskill, N.Y.
 Law Student.   Albany, N.Y.
Julian Alva Spafford . . . . . 18 . . . Ludlow, Vt.
 Clerk.   New York, N.Y.
Walter Ames Stebbins . . . . 16 . . . New York, N.Y.
 Student, H.U.
Hermon Weed Stevens . . . . 16 . . . Dover.
 Senior Class.
Kwoh On Tong . . . . 18 . . . Canton, China.
Gilbert Hubbard Turner . . . 17 . . . Brooklyn, N.Y.
Thomas Rice Varick . . . . . . 15 . . . Manchester.
 Senior Class.
Sherman Wentworth . . . . . 19 . . . Brookfield.
           "
Henry Hyde Whitman . . . . 17 . . . Turner Centre, Me.
 Student, Columbia Coll.
Waldo Wickham Willard . . . 14 . . . Chelsea, Mass.
 Senior Class.
Robert Thomas Wolcott . . . . 21 . . . Dover.
 Senior Class.
Tsoo Liang Woung . . . . Shanghai, China.
Gordon Woodbury . . . . . . 15 . . . New York, N.Y.
 Student, H.U.
Uriah Burdge Woolley . . . . 19 . . . Matawan, N.J.
 Druggist.   New York, N.Y.
John Stratton Wright . . . . . 17 . . . Duxbury, Mass.
 Student, H.U.

               80

1880.

Orson Adams, jr. . . . . 16 . . . Jessups, Md.
Benjamin Franklin Adler . . . 17 . . . Milwaukee, Wis.
 Clerk.   " "
Harry Allen . . . . 15 . . . Mumford, N.Y.
 Student.   " "
Edward Sawyer Bacon . . . . 17 . . . Dover.
 Student, Yale Coll.
William Woodward Baldwin . 18 . . . Baltimore, Md.
 Student, H.U.
Charles Lee Barnes . . . . . . 19 . . . Canton, Ill.
Clarence Augustus Barnes . . . 13 . . . Boston, Mass.
Frank Hurd Batchelder . . . . 17 . . . Boston, Mass.
 Clerk.   " "

John Dana Bell . . . . 14 . . . Manchester.
Middle Class.
Lewis Sherrill Bigelow . . . . 17 . . . St. Paul, Minn.
Student, Yale Coll.
William Henry Bowman. . . . 16 . . . Springfield, O.
Middle Class.
Roland William Boyden . . . . 16 . . . Beverly, Mass.
Student, H.U.
William Cowper Boyden . . . . 16 . . . Sheffield, Ill.
Student, H.U.
Arthur Preston Braisted . . . . 16 . . . Toledo, O.
Bookkeeper. " "
John Joseph Brannen . . . . . 16 . . . Milford, Mass.
Student, H.U.
Odie Patrick Brennan . . . . . 19 . . . Natick, Mass.
Student, Columbia Coll.
Walter Scott Briggs . . . . . . 26 . . . Auburn, Me.
William Allen Brooks, jr. . . . 15 . . . Haverhill, Mass.
Senior Class.
David Hanson Buffum, jr. . . . 17 . . . Great Falls.
Student, Yale Coll.
Judd Ellis Buley . . . . 20 . . . Waverly, N.Y.
Student, H.U.
Edward Fitch Bullard, jr. . . . 15 . . . Saratoga Springs, N.Y.
Business. Troy, N.Y.
Frederick Wing Burleigh . . . 17 . . . Fitchburg, Mass.
Lewis Calvin Burnes . . . . . 19 . . . St. Joseph, Mo.
Clerk. " " "
Harry Ahlborn Butler . . . . . 15 . . . Lynn, Mass.
John Christie Cate . . . . . . 18 . . . Deerfield.
Farmer.
Charles Cumston Chadbourn . 13 . . . Wilmington, N.C.
Junior Class.
William Perry Chadwick . . . 15 . . . Exeter.
Clerk. "
*Arthur Burleigh Chandler . . . 20 . . . Lebanon 1882
Law Student. "
Percy Chase . . . . 15 . . . Lynn, Mass.
Student. " "
Wayland Johnson Chase . . . 14 . . . Exeter.
Middle Class.
William Nelson Chase . . . . . 14 . . . Exeter.
Middle Class.
Yan Kung Cheong. . . . . . . 19 . . . Canton, China.
Calvin Goddard Child . . . . . 18 . . . Stamford, Conn.
Kimball Vosburg Clark . . . . 19 . . . Buffalo, N.Y.
Student. " "
Frederick Percival Clement . . 15 . . . Rutland, Vt.
Middle Class.
Willis William Colburn . . . . 18 . . . Boston, Mass.
Med. Student, H.U. " "
Maurice Wurts Cooley . . . . 19 . . . East Coldenham, N.Y.
Senior Class.
Austin Corbin . . . . 16 . . . New York, N.Y.
Timothy Currier Craig. . . . . 19 . . . Island Falls, Me.
Senior Class.
Adams Crocker . . . . 19 . . . Fitchburg, Mass.
Student, H.U.

Samuel Aldrich Crozer, jr. . . 16 . . . Upland, Pa.
Student, H.U.
Robert Woolston Cummings. . 15 . . . Toledo, O.
Student, Andover, Mass.
Charles Francis Adams Currier 18 . . . East Kingston.
Senior Class.
Henry Aaron Dexter . . . . . 19 . . . Elmira, N.Y.
Student, Germany.
Fred Drew . . . . 13 . . . Boston, Mass.
Student.   "   "
Harootune Enfiejian . . . . . . 27 . . . Harpoot, Armenia.
Student, H.U.
Mahlon Enos . . . . 19 . . . Philadelphia, N.Y.
Middle Class.
Cornelius Conway Felton . . . 16 . . . Thurlow, Pa.
Student, H.U.
Edward Fox Fessenden . . . . 14 . . . Portland, Me.
Senior Class.
Edward Dudley Floyd . . . . . 14 . . . Lynn, Mass.
Student.   "   "
Edward Elbridge Floyd, jr. . . 12 . . . Brookline, Mass.
Junior Class.
William Wakefield Gale . . . . 15 . . . Exeter.
Middle Class.
Albert Augustus Gleason . . . 16 . . . Milford, Mass.
Student, H.U.
Edwin Eldon Graham . . . . . 16 . . . Philadelphia, Pa.
Student, H.U.
Herbert Lionel Grant . . . . . 18 . . . Waterbury, Conn.
Student, Andover, Mass.
Irving Galen Greene . . . . . 16 . . . Shelburne.
Middle Class.
Luther Henry Stowell Greene . 16 . . . Dover.
Senior Class.
Charles Mather Harrington . . 18 . . . Orangeport, N.Y.
Student, H.U.
Charles Learner Harrison . . . 16 . . . Cincinnati, O.
Student, H.U.
James Mott Hartshorne, jr. . . 16 . . . New York, N.Y.
Student, H.U.
Edward James Hatch . . . . . 18 . . . Lebanon.
Student, Scientific Department, Dart. Coll.
John Wheelock Hawes . . . . 14 . . . Worcester, Mass.
Henry Brady Heywood . . . . 15 . . . Chicago, Ill.
George P. Frost Hobson . . . 19 . . . Wiscasset, Me.
Student, H.U.
Michael Joseph Holland . . . . 20 . . . Milford, Mass.
Middle Class.
William Harrison Holliday . . 16 . . . St. Louis, Mo.
Student, H.U.
William Herbert Hudnut . . . 15 . . . Orange, N.J.
Student, Coll. of N.J.
Thomas Hunt . . . . 14 . . . New Orleans, La.
Student, H.U.
John Henry Hutchings, jr. . . 16 . . . Galveston, Tex.
Student, Keene.
Henry Belden Ketcham . . . . 15 . . . Dover Plains, N.Y.
Middle Class.
George Nelson Kimball . . . . 22 . . . Hopkinton.

Ben Edward King	16	Chicago, Ill.
Kirk Kinney	20	Cincinnati, O.
Kwok Kwang Kwong		Canton, China.
Charles Garland Lane	17	Hampton.
Salesman.		Boston, Mass.
Ralph Martin Lane	17	St. Louis, Mo.
Student, H.U.		
Stanley Matthews Lawson	14	Cincinnati, O.
Student, Urbana Univ.		
John Nitsche Lewis, jr.	18	New York, N.Y.
James Law Mackey	18	Evansville, Ind.
William Mariner	17	Milwaukee, Wis.
Joseph Francis Marshall	18	Haverhill, Mass.
Middle Class.		
Charles Williston McAlpin	14	New York, N.Y.
Middle Class.		
William Truman Merrill	18	Sherman Mills, Me.
Senior Class.		
George Henry Meyers	19	Passaic, N.J.
Robert Henry Middleditch	19	Brooklyn, N.Y.
Student, N.Y. Univ.		" "
Mark Herbert Milan	19	Portsmouth, Va.
Wallace Nutting	18	Exeter.
Middle Class.		
John Amos Ordway, jr.	18	Boston, Mass.
Clerk.		" "
William Hicks Osgood	15	Rochester, N.Y.
Student, Andover, Mass.		
Chauncey Goodrich Parker	15	Newark, N.J.
Student, H.U.		
Chester Parker	18	South Lancaster, Mass.
Business.		Boston, Mass.
Robert Meade Parker	15	Newark, N.J.
Student, Coll. of N.J.		
Harry Ernest Peabody	15	Princeton, Me.
Senior Class.		
Edward Warren Peirce	18	Peabody, Mass.
Clerk.		" "
William Smith Pendleton	16	Boston, Mass.
Planter.		St. Augustine, Fla.
Charles Henry Pennypacker	13	West Chester, Pa.
Middle Class.		
Frank George Peters	19	Syracuse, N.Y.
Student, Yale Coll.		
John Matthews Peters	16	Syracuse, N.Y.
Middle Class.		
George Sawyer Pitcher	16	Portland, Me.
Middle Class.		
William Craig Powers	18	Rochester, N.Y.
Albert Richard Pritchard	16	Rochester, N.Y.
Senior Class.		
Josiah Hatch Quincy	19	Rumney Depot.
Student, Dart. Coll.		Lancaster, Mass.
John Earle Reynolds	16	Meadville, Pa.
Middle Class.		
Franklin W. Richardson	19	Milford, Mass.
Horace Ramsey Rose	17	Johnstown, Pa.

Frank Edward Sanborn . . . . 16 . . . Epping.
  Agent.   "
Frank Josiah Sanborn . . . . . 16 . . . Exeter.
  Butcher.   "
John Scammon . . . . 13 . . . Stratham.
  "
Daniel Benjamin Sheehan . . . 26 . . . Milford, Mass.
  Business.   Boston, Mass.
Herman Thyng Shepard . . . . 20 . . . West Epping.
  Middle Class.
John Wm. E. Shinnick . . . . 16 . . . Exeter.
  Middle Class.
Shirley Robinson Snow . . . . 17 . . . Auburn, N.Y.
  Student, H.U.
Frank Henry Stanyan . . . . . 18 . . . Milford.
  Senior Class.
Benjamin Alexander Stribling . 17 . . . San Antonio, Tex.
Frank Cole Sturtevant . . . . 21 . . . Keene.
  Law Student.   Lebanon.
Alfred William Taussig . . . . 18 . . . St. Louis, Mo.
  Student, H.U.
Marvin Merchant Taylor . . . 20 . . . Jefferson, N.Y.
  Law Student, Boston Univ.
Edward F. S. Titcomb . . . . 16 . . . Exeter.
  Middle Class.
Harry Forsayth Totman . . . . 14 . . . Fairfield, Me.
  Student, West Newton, Mass.
Frederick Beauchamp Ussher . 16 . . . New York, N.Y.
John Brodhead Van Schaick . 15 . . . New York, N.Y.
  Student.
Richard Abraham Varick . . . 15 . . . Manchester.
  Student in Music.   "
Joseph Walker . . . . 15 . . . Worcester, Mass.
  Middle Class.
George Edwin Wallace . . . . 16 . . . Rochester.
Fairman Warren . . . . 17 . . . New York, N.Y.
Solon Greeley Warren . . . . 15 . . . Exeter.
  Middle Class.
George Standish Weed . . . . 18 . . . Plattsburg, N.Y.
  Student, H.U.
Henry Harding Wentworth . . 21 . . . Niagara Falls, N.Y.
  Student, Will. Coll.
James Ira Weston . . . . 15 . . . Exeter.
  Clerk.   "
Frederick Shattuck Wetmore . 17 . . . Warren, Pa.
  Business.   "   "
George Redington Wilson . . . 16 . . . Waddington, N.Y.
Robert Pengilly Winters . . . . 22 . . . Boston, Mass.
  Clerk.   Albuquerque, New Mexico.
William Wisner . . . . 19 . . . Cedar Rapids, Ia.
Leung Tung Wong . . . . Shanghai, China.
Amory Trask Woodbury . . . 18 . . . Milford, Mass.
  Business.   "   "
Henry Sylvester Woodruff . . . 17 . . . Brooklyn, N.Y.
  Clerk.   "   "

1881.

John Lincoln Ames . . . . . . 18 . . . Jefferson, Me.
Senior Class.
Paul Kimball Ames . . . . . . 19 . . . Bethel, Me.
Student, Yale Coll.
Allen Harwood Babcock. . . . 16 . . . Oakland, Cal.
Middle Class.
Wakefield Baker . . . . 15 . . . San Francisco, Cal.
Senior Class.
James Gillespie Blaine, jr. . . 12 . . . Augusta, Me.
Preparatory Class.
George Pliny Buck . . . . . . 17 . . . Shrewsbury, Mass.
Student, Worcester, Mass.
Walter Prentice Butler . . . . 18 . . . Saratoga Springs, N.Y.
Junior Class.
Edward Willet Champion . . . 18 . . . Goshen, N.Y.
Student, Cornell Univ.
Fessenden Nealley Chase . . . 17 . . . Saco, Me.
Govt. Service.   "   "
Lawrence William Churchill . . 19 . . . Oswego, N.Y.
Student, Yale Coll.
Alan Cuningham . . . . 19 . . . Smyrna, Del.
Junior Class.
James Dennis Denègre . . . . 13 . . . New Orleans, La.
Junior Class.
Edward Everett Dennett . . . 23 . . . Portsmouth.
Worsted Business.   Fitchburg, Mass.
Paul Devereux . . . . 17 . . . Deposit, N.Y.
Business.   "   "
Ezra Day Dickerman . . . . . 13 . . . Bridgeport, Conn.
Student.   "   "
Edward Lacey Dickerman . . . 15 . . . Bridgeport, Conn.
Junior Class.
James Lee Doolittle . . . . . . 14 . . . Balston Spa, N.Y.
William Franklin Draper, jr. . 15 . . . Milford, Mass.
Middle Class.
Willis Reynolds Dresser . . . . 21 . . . Princeton, Me.
Teacher.   "   "
Joseph Osterman Dyer, jr. . . 17 . . . Galveston, Tex.
Senior Class.
William James Dyer. . . . . . 15 . . . Plainfield, Conn.
Junior Class.
Ephraim Howard Egolf . . . . 18 . . . Pottstown, Pa.
Charles Stanford Elgutter . . . 20 . . . Omaha, Neb.
Senior Class.
Horace Delano Everett . . . . 21 . . . Dover.
Junior Class.
Arthur Faulkner. . . . . 18 . . . Keene.
Student, H.U.   "
Edward Grinnell Faye . . . . 15 . . . New York, N.Y.
Jefferson Butler Fletcher . . . 15 . . . Brooklyn, N.Y.
Senior Class.
Albert George Follett . . . . . 16 . . . Brooklyn, N.Y.
Student, Andover, Mass.
Edward Milton Foote . . . . . 15 . . . Middletown, N.J.
Student, Rochester Univ.

158 CATALOGUE. [1881.

Leland Amory Lewis Gale . . 18 . . . West Medway, Mass.
Senior Class.
Edgar Malcolm Garnett . . . . 17 . . . San Francisco, Cal.
Senior Class.
Lindley Miller Garrison . . . . 16 . . . Camden, N. J.
Student, H.U.
John William Gerry . . . . . . 21 . . . Sherman Mills, Me.
Ward Master, City Hospital. Boston, Mass.
George Albert Giles . . . . . . 15 . . . East Kingston.
Student, Kingston.
William Francis Gleason . . . 20 . . . Milford, Mass.
Medical Student, H.U.
Leon Joseph Goetter . . . . . 16 . . . Montgomery, Ala.
Student, New York, N.Y.
*John Burnham Goldsmith . . . 17 . . . Chester 1882
George McClellan Houtz Good 18 . . . Osceola, Pa.
Claude T Griffith . . . . 15 . . . Indianapolis, Ind.
Student, Asbury Univ.
Albert Emerson Hadlock . . . 18 . . . Milford.
Middle Class.
Edward Jewett Hall . . . . . . 17 . . . Malden, Mass.
Student, H.U.
Fred Alonzo Hanson . . . . . 17 . . . Dover.
Middle Class.
Frank Lincoln Hayes . . . . . 15 . . . Dover.
Manufacturer. "
Edward Webster Herrick . . . 16 . . . Northampton, Mass.
Junior Class.
Isaac Hills, jr. . . . . 17 . . . Rochester, N.Y.
William Knowles Hobbs . . . . 19 . . . North Hampton.
Teacher. " "
Albert Fairchild Holden . . . . 13 . . . Cleveland, O.
Middle Class.
Charles Richardson Holman . . 16 . . . Worcester, Mass.
Middle Class.
Lockwood Honoré . . . . 16 . . . New York, N.Y.
Junior Class.
Timothy Howard . . . . 17 . . . North Brookfield, Mass.
Student, Amh. Coll.
Arthur Webster Howison . . . 19 . . . Milford.
Student. "
Henry Hubbard . . . . 16 . . . Chicago, Ill.
William Mann Irvine . . . . . 15 . . . Bedford, Pa.
Junior Class.
Louis Janin, jr. . . . . 15 . . . Oakland, Cal.
Edward Borden Jennings . . . 16 . . . Fall River, Mass.
Student, H.U.
Winfield Scott Jewell . . . . . 20 . . . Manchester.
Clerk. "
Frank Harrison Kelley, jr. . . 18 . . . Worcester, Mass.
Student, Yale Coll.
Edward Russell Kellogg . . . . 17 . . . San Francisco, Cal.
Student, Yale Coll.
Charles Pinckney Knapp . . . 16 . . . Deposit, N.Y.
Junior Class.
Furman Kneeland . . . . 14 . . . Brooklyn, N.Y.
Junior Class.
Benjamin Carter Lockett . . . 17 . . . New York, N.Y.

Milburn Love . . . . 16 . . . Keokuk, Ia.
Senior Class.
Samuel Cony Manley . . . . . 14 . . . Augusta, Me.
Junior Class.
Dana Giles Marble . . . . . . 17 . . . Hampstead.
Middle Class.
Harry Lowell Mason . . . . . 17 . . . Brookline, Mass.
Middle Class.
John Francis McArdel. . . . . 21 . . . Plymouth, Mass.
Business.   "   "
John McKinstry Merriam . . . 18 . . . South Framingham, Mass.
Student, H.U.
Samuel Wells Merrill . . . . . 15 . . . Rutland, Vt.
Student.   "   "
David Whipple Morison . . . . 16 . . . Minneapolis, Minn.
Junior Class.
William Nelson . . . . 15 . . . Nashville, Tenn.
Middle Class.
Luther Edgerton Newport . . . 17 . . . St. Paul, Minn.
Student.   "   "   "
Henry Warrington Ninde . . . 19 . . . Fort Wayne, Ind.
Student, H.U.
Lucien Holley Norton . . . . . 17 . . . Bridgeport, Conn.
John O'Neill . . . . 15 . . . Exeter.
Junior Class.
William Henry Paine . . . . . 18 . . . Berlin.
Junior Class.
Arthur Franklin Parrott . . . . 20 . . . Augusta, Me.
Walter Gray Parsons . . . . . 19 . . . Windham, Conn.
Bank Clerk.   Willimantic, Conn.
Giles Keeney Peck . . . . . . 19 . . . Berlin, Conn.
Farmer.   Kensington, Conn.
Frederick Wainwright Perkins . 15 . . . Burlington, Wis.
Student, Mass. Inst. of Tech.
Charles Wheeler Pierson . . . 17 . . . Florida, N.Y.
Student, Yale Coll.
Dorman Bradstreet Pike . . . . 17 . . . Sauk Centre, Minn.
Student, Dart. Coll.
Dwight Morgan Platt . . . . . 17 . . . New York, N.Y.
Clerk.   "   "   "
Joseph Parsons Prescott . . . . 15 . . . Holyoke, Mass.
Student.   "   "
Wilder Dwight Quint . . . . . 17 . . . Dover.
Middle Class.
William Henry Rand, jr. . . . 15 . . . Chicago, Ill.
· Junior Class.
Burt Henry Redfield . . . . . . 12 . . . Dover.
Student.   "
Edward Everett Rice . . . . . 17 . . . Springvale, Me.
Business.   "   "
Ellwood Jackman Ross . . . . 17 . . . Bath.
Senior Class.
William Osgood Russell . . . . 17 . . . Lawrence, Mass.
Paper Manufacturer.   "   "
Elmer Columbus Sattley . . . . 18 . . . North Ferrisburg, Vt.
Junior Class.
Edward Benjamin Schmidt . . 14 . . . Ilion, N.Y.
John Calhoun Simonds . . . . 17 . . . Charleston, S.C.
Middle Class.

Nathaniel Austin Smithwick . 17 . . . Newcastle, Me.
  Student, Worcester, Mass.
Henry Clapp Spooner . . . . . 15 . . . Bridgeport, Conn.
Mayer Marx Sterns . . . . . . 17 . . . Dover.
  Junior Class.
William Oliver Stevens . . . . 17 . . . North Andover, Mass.
Ernest Stickney . . . . 16 . . . Epping.
  Clerk.   "
Fred Lewis Storer . . . . 16 . . . Portland Me.
  Clerk.   "   "
Arthur Washington Stuart . . 21 . . . Ayer, Mass.
  Student, Amh. Coll.
Edgar James Swift . . . . . . 21 . . . Ashtabula, O.
  Student, Williams Coll.
Gilbert Bebee Taylor . . . . . 20 . . . Smyrna, Del.
  Junior Class.
John McQuaid Thompson . . . 18 . . . Webster, Mass.
  Student, H.U.
Gilbert Tompkins . . . . 18 . . . Oakland, Cal.
  Student, H.U.
Edward Joshua Vinton . . . . 14 . . . Springfield, Mass.
Edwin Ruthven Weeks . . . . 25 . . . Kansas City, Mo.
  Supt. Elec. Light Co.   "   "   "
George Perley Weeks . . . . . 18 . . . Manchester.
  Student, Dart. Coll.
Isaac Francis White . . . . . . 15 . . . Newmarket.
  Student.   "
William Kinsley Whiting . . . 16 . . . Mendon, Mass.
  Junior Class.
Samuel Austin Whitney . . . . 17 . . . Glassborough, N. J.
  Student, Mass. Inst. of Tech.
William Wallace Wilcomb . . . 16 . . . Chester.
  Middle Class.
Starling Sullivant Wilcox . . . 17 . . . Columbus, O.
  Senior Class.
Thornton Woodbury . . . . . . 14 . . . New York, N.Y.
  Junior Class.
Walter Monroe Young . . . . 18 . . . Ellsworth, Me.
                                     "   "
                                              113

1882.

Michael James Ahern . . . . . 16 . . . Milford, Mass.
  Preparatory Class.
Larz Anderson . . . . 16 . . . Washington, D.C.
  Middle Class.
Harry Eckhart Applebach . . . 18 . . . Sellersville, Pa.
  Student, Bethlehem, Pa.
Fred Jerry Arnold . . . . 16 . . . Waterville, Me.
  Preparatory Class.
John Foster Bass . . . . 16 . . . Chicago, Ill.
  Preparatory Class.
Horace Stevens Bean . . . . . 15 . . . Exeter.
  Preparatory Class.
Amos Noyes Blandin . . . . . 18 . . . Bath.
  Middle Class.
Richards Fisher Boas . . . . . 18 . . . Reading, Pa.
  Student, Will. Coll.

Walter Lincoln Boyden	17 . . .	Beverly, Mass.
Senior Class.		
Edward Knight Boynton . . .	18 . . .	Winchester, Mass.
Preparatory Class.		
Fred Thompson Brooks	15 . . .	Kittery, Me.
Preparatory Class.		
Walter Atwood Brown	17 . . .	Salmon Falls.
Preparatory Class.		
Arthur Sumner Burrill.	14 . . .	Wellesley, Mass.
Preparatory Class.		
Clark Magwire Carr	16 . . .	Fort Apache, Arizona.
Preparatory Class.		
Frank Morris Cilley	15 . . .	Exeter.
Preparatory Class.		
Harry Wood Clement	16 . . .	Rutland, Vt.
Preparatory Class.		
James Bell Coffin	15 . . .	Alton.
Student.		Meredith.
George Augustus Colby	17 . . .	Pittsfield, Mass.
Student, Stockbridge, Mass.		
John Langdon Colby, jr. . . .	18 . . .	Pittsfield, Mass.
Student, Stockbridge, Mass.		
Harry Hawkins Colony	17 . . .	Keene.
Preparatory Class.		
Guy Cunningham	15 . . .	Gloucester, Mass.
Senior Class.		
John Lysander Cutler, jr. . . .	15 . . .	Bangor, Me.
Middle Class.		" "
Charles Henry Deetz	18 . . .	Sellersville, Pa.
Preparatory Class.		
Frank Lyle Dickey	19 . . .	Carthage, Mo.
Middle Class.		
Edward Warberton Durant . .	18 . . .	Stillwater, Minn.
Middle Class.		
Henry Clinton Fay, jr.	16 . . .	Northwood.
Preparatory Class.		
Edmund Franklin Folsom . . .	16 . . .	Philadelphia, Pa.
Junior Class.		
Hervey Richards Franklin . . .	15 . . .	North Attleborough, Mass.
Middle Class.		
Tracy Barton Fuller	15 . . .	Binghampton, N.Y.
Student, Newburg, N.Y.		
William Stebbins Gage, jr. . .	19 . . .	San Francisco, Cal.
Student.		
Alfred Gaither	19 . . .	Cincinnati, O.
Senior Class.		
Fritz Maurice Gamble	16 . . .	New York, N.Y.
Nathan Richard George, jr. . .	17 . . .	Mendon, Mass.
Junior Class.		
John Shackford Grouard . . .	15 . . .	Exeter.
Preparatory Class.		
William Albert Guild	20 . . .	Milford.
Junior Class.		
Victor Harding	16 . . .	Chicago, Ill.
Preparatory Class.		
Francis Grant Higgins	18 . . .	Missoula, Montana.
Middle Class.		
John Richard Higgins	16 . . .	Missoula, Montana.
Junior Class.		

John Hill . . . . 14 . . . Saratoga Springs, N.Y.
   Junior Class.
John Howard Hume . . . . . . 16 . . . Poughkeepsie, N.Y.
   Senior Class.
Allston Fróst Hunt . . . . . . 20 . . . Portland, Me.
   Middle Class.
Harry Wilbur Hurd . . . . . . 15 . . . Grantham.
   Preparatory Class.
Charles Milton Jackson . . . . 15 . . . Newport.
   Junior Class.
James Craik Jackson . . . . . 16 . . . Frankfort, Ky.
   Preparatory Class.
Robert William Jennings, jr. . 17 . . . Nashville, Tenn.
   Student, H.U.
Olin Coit Joline . . . . 20 . . . Tottenville, N.Y.
   Junior Class.
Arthur Russell Jones . . . . . 16 . . . Merrimac, Mass.
   Middle Class.
Charles Walker Jones . . . . . 16 . . . Exeter.
   Preparatory Class.
Walter Reuben Kaharl . . . 14 . . . Exeter.
   Preparatory Class.
Franklin John Kaufman . . . . 19 . . . Syracuse, N.Y.
   Preparatory Class.
George Draper Kelley . . . . . 16 . . . Worcester, Mass.
   Junior Class.
William Josiah Kingsbury . . . 15 . . . Exeter.
   Preparatory Class.
Albert John Küssner . . . . . 21 . . . Terre Haute, Ind.
   Junior Class.
Albert Eveleth Kyte . . . . . . 18 . . . North Haverhill, Mass.
   Junior Class.
Henry Haddock Lawrence . . . 15 . . . Saratoga Springs, N.Y.
   Junior Class.
Samuel De Wolf Lewis . . . . 15 . . . Newport.
   Preparatory Class.
Albert Lilienthal . . . . 17 . . . Saratoga Springs, N.Y.
   Junior Class.
Linn Luce . . . . 16 . . . Waltham, Mass.
   Senior Class.
James Thomas Malone . . . . 17 . . . Fitchburg, Mass.
   Preparatory Class.
John Francis McGuire . . . . 16 . . . Hopkinton, Mass.
   Preparatory Class.
Arthur Lucius Merrick . . . . 15 . . . East Hampton, Conn.
   Preparatory Class.
Frank Abner Merrill . . . . . 16 . . . Exeter.
   Middle Class.
Edgar Ormsby Mitchell . . . . 17 . . . Newburg, N.Y.
   Junior Class.
Samuel Benjamin Morison . . . 14 . . . Minneapolis, Minn.
   Preparatory Class.
Patrick William O'Brien . . . . 23 . . . Hopkinton, Mass.
   Clerk.   "   ".
Cornelius Morris O'Connor . . 19 . . . Boston, Mass.
   Preparatory Class.
Frank Lincoln Olmsted . . . . 17 . . . Saratoga Springs, N.Y.
   Junior Class.
Jesse Maxwell Overton . . . . 18 . . . Nashville, Tenn.
   Student, H.U.

Robert Edmund Lee Overton . 16 . . . Nashville, Tenn.
Junior Class.
Bradley Webster Palmer . . . 16 . . . Wilkesbarre, Pa.
Middle Class.
Frank Dixon Peale . . . . . . 17 . . . Lock Haven, Pa.
Middle Class.
Gifford Pinchot . . . . 16 . . . New York, N.Y.
Middle Class.
Rufus King Porter. . . . . . . 14 . . . Calais, Me.
Preparatory Class.
Thomas Fletcher Poynter . . . 16 . . . Shelbyville, Ky.
Junior Class.
Edward Watson Rand . . . . . . 18 . . . Baltimore, Md.
Junior Class.
Mervyn Ap Rice . . . . 14 . . . Rockland, Me.
Preparatory Class.
George Rublee . . . . 14 . . . Milwaukee, Wis.
Junior Class.
John Sanborn . . . . 18 . . . Stirling, Ill.
Junior Class.
Francis Seward Scharff . . . . 18 . . . Exeter.
Middle Class.
Joseph Henry Scharff . . . . . 16 . . . Exeter.
Junior Class.
Charles Edward Shattuck . . . 16 . . . Lawrence, Mass.
Senior Class.
Timothy James Shinnick . . . 14 . . . Exeter.
Preparatory Class.
Frank French Shute . . . . . . 17 . . . Exeter.
Junior Class.
Frank Chester Southworth . . 18 . . . Forestville, N.Y.
Middle Class.
Charles F Spalding . . . . . . 16 . . . Chicago, Ill.
Lumber Clerk.   "   "
Frederick Orlester Swain . . . 18 . . . New York, N.Y.
John Jacob Tilton . . . . 15 . . . East Epping.
Preparatory Class.
Joseph Brown Thomas Tuthill . 19 . . . Santa Cruz, Cal.
Senior Class.
Edwin Jenkins Van Schaick . . 14 . . . New York, N.Y.
Preparatory Class.
Howard Baldy Waldron . . . . 16 . . . Hillsdale, Mich.
Junior Class.
George Walker . . . . 15 . . . Worcester, Mass.
Preparatory Class.
Russell Tyng Walker . . . . . 15 . . . Exeter.
Preparatory Class.
George Wentworth . . . . . . 14 . . . Exeter.
Preparatory Class.
John Burleigh Wentworth . . . 18 . . . Le Roy, N.Y.
Middle Class.
George Waterbury Wheeler . . 19 . . . Deposit, N.Y.
Junior Class.
Morris Whitridge . . . . 17 . . . Baltimore, Md.
Junior Class.
Hallam Gregory Williamson . . 18 . . . Washington, D.C.
Middle Class.
Frank Gregory Wood . . . . . 18 . . . Washington, D.C.
Student, Cheshire, Conn.

1883.

Louis Springer Delaplaine . . . 15 . . . Wheeling, W. Va.
  Preparatory Class.
John Powell Hunter . . . . . . 17 . . . Lewistown, Pa.
  Junior Class.
Mark Baldwin Lewis . . . . . 16 . . . Talladega, Ala.
  Student, Dummer Acad.
Elmer Hoff Oulton . . . . . . 14 . . . San Francisco, Cal.
  Junior Class.
Warren Edmund Raymond . . 14 . . . Fargo, D.T.
  Preparatory Class.
Daniel Marcy Ross . . . . . . 15 . . . Portsmouth.
  Preparatory Class.
Herbert Augustine Smith . . . 16 . . . Middletown, Conn.
  Junior Class.
Joshua Wright Stedman . . . . 15 . . . Wilmington, N.C.
  Junior Class.
Horatio Nelson Strait . . . . . 16 . . . Troy, N.Y.
  Junior Class.
Arthur Henry Wilcomb . . . . 15 . . . Chester.
  Preparatory Class.

10

INDEX.

Abbot
1800 Ephraim
1803 John E.
1812 Abiel
1814 Charles B.
1822 John S.
1822 Theodore T.
1823 Ezra
1824 Charles
1824 William E.
1825 Abiel
1826 William P.
1827 Ezra
1827 Josiah
1828 George J.
1828 Rufus
1830 Harris
1835 Ezra
1839 Francis P.
1846 Oscar D.
1849 John W.
1854 George E. H.
1855 Luther C.
1859 Edward S.
1867 Abiel J.

Abbott
1875 David W.
1877 Harlan P.

Adams
1784 Nathaniel
1788 Thomas
1792 Nathaniel F.
1793 William
1794 William P.
1802 Caleb
1804 Jeremiah P.
1808 John
1814 Joseph
1816 Nathaniel S.
1823 Obed E.
1827 Ebenezer
1830 John Q.
1843 Henry Q.
1856 George E.
1859 George H.
1862 Frederick M.
1866 Herbert B.
1867 Charles W. S.
1870 George B.
1873 Joseph T.
1874 Henry F.
1875 Frederick H.

1877 Charles F.
1877 Frank O.
1877 Thomas E.
1880 Orson, jr.

Adler
1880 Benjamin F.

Ager
1841 George B.

Ahern
1882 Michael J.

Aiken
1804 Peter
1825 Charles
1879 Joseph D., jr.

Akerman
1836 Amos T.

Aldrich
1877 Fred A.

Alexander
1860 Morison
1863 William P.

Alger
1864 Edwin A.
1877 Frank G.

Allen
1807 Henry
1807 Zachariah
1809 Crawford
1816 Benjamin
1831 William
1832 Ebenezer
1846 William F.
1851 Roger N.
1867 Lowell D.
1871 John H.
1871 William H.
1873 Charles W.
1874 Alexander B.
1874 Charles N.
1878 Charles C.
1878 Ethan
1880 Harry

Alley
1848 John H.
1861 Richard F.

Allis
1878 Ernest

Allison
1848 John P.

Allyn
1856 John

Alton
1863 Charles De L.

Alvord
1832 Daniel W.

Ambrose
1789 Nathaniel

Amen
1872 Harlan P.

Ames
1813 Stephen
1849 Frederick L.
1856 Timothy K.
1859 Charles A.
1862 Willis L.
1881 John L.
1881 Paul K.

Ammidown
1862 Albert H.
1869 Lucius E.

Amory
1821 George F.

Anderson
1860 Edward L.
1866 Joseph L.
1882 Larz.

Andrew
1857 Forrester

Andrews
1807 Abraham
1870 Clifford
1870 Frank V.
1874 Charles W.

Angell
1875 Rufus G.

Anthony
1870 Arthur

Applebach
1882 Harry E.

Appleton
1824 Charles T.
1824 William C.
1857 Edward L.
1878 Randolph M.

Apthorp
1808 Charles W.
1810 George K.
1810 Thomas
1810 William
1815 John T.

Archer
1821 Samuel W.

Arnold
1861 Frank B.
1862 Charles H.
1877 John D.
1882 Fred J.

Ashbrook
1873 Thomas R.

Ashley
1875 Philip B.
1877 Charles H.

Atherton
1856 George W.
1876 Robert A.

Atkinson
1800 Charles
1806 Amos
1815 John P.
1821 William K.

Attrill
1870 James B.

Atwater
1863 Henry G.
1876 William E.

Atwood
1862 Thomas I.
1864 Francis
1874 Charles E.
1875 Luther

INDEX.

Augsbury
1876 Willard S.

Austin
1825 William
1831 Henry D.
1854 Elijah H.

Averill
1864 James K.

Avery
1805 Samuel
1812 Charles E.
1866 John
1866 John C.

Ayer
1843 Adams
1847 Day F.
1855 George

Ayers
1861 George W.

Babcock
1842 George W.
1874 James W.
1881 Allen H.

Babson
1847 William
1850 Robert E.

Bachelder.
1817 Nathan
1832 Joseph W.

Bacon
1835 William B.
1841 Ebenezer
1843 Horace C.
1863 Edward R.
1871 Charles G.
1873 Charles W.
1873 Edward R.
1880 Edward S.

Badger
1824 Charles H.
1837 Samuel A.
1840 George W.
1864 George A.

Bagley
1794 William

Bailey
1855 Marcellus
1872 Benjamin F.
1876 Frank B.
1877 John F.
1878 Burnside B.

Bainbridge
1819 William

Baker
1825 Otis
1834 Nathaniel B.
1859 Daniel
1868 Walter

1873 Frank W.
1875 William D.
1876 Arthur E.
1877 Dana W.
1878 James E.
1878 Sharonton H.
1881 Wakefield

Balch
1791 William
1794 Horatio G.
1795 Joseph
1831 William C.
1839 George E.
1840 Leonidas
1876 Ernest B.

Baldwin
1867 Thomas W.
1868 Henry
1870 Edward D.
1880 William W.

Bales
1879 George E.

Balestier
1859 John A.

Ball
1837 John B.

Bancroft
1811 George
1872 William A.
1876 Clarence
1876 James M.

Banfield
1845 Everett C.
1872 Richard

Bangs
1878 Charles R.

Barber
1817 Charles
1839 Daniel W.
1854 George W.
1874 Dana C.

Barbottiau
1798 Nicholas R.

Barbour
1874 William R.

Barker
1790 William
1808 David
1808 Noah
1811 Mark
1812 George
1815 Benjamin
1834 David A.
1837 Jeremy B.
1837 William
1840 Ezra
1851 Stephen
1851 George F.
1858 Augustus

1863 Fordyce D.
1865 Wallace C.
1871 Alfred Y.

Barnard
1871 William M.

Barnes
1822 Lewis G.
1852 James B.
1853 Benjamin
1859 Alfred W.
1859 Francis
1868 Cecil
1880 Charles L.
1880 Clarence A.

Barney
1864 Albert C.
1875 Bruce B.

Barnum
1864 Leslie P.

Barrett
1848 Richard A.
1867 Henry H.
1870 Richard S.
1878 Charles S.

Barstow
1838 Henry H.
1874 Henry T.

Bartlett
1784 Josiah
1785 Ezra
1789 Israel
1800 Joseph
1800 Richard
1812 Jacob
1817 John M.
1827 Levi S.
1843 Josiah
1847 Ezra
1862 Franklin
1862 Josiah C.
1870 Horace I.
1874 Charles H.
1876 Lewis L.
1879 Thomas H.

Bartol
1822 William
1823 Horace
1835 George M.
1879 John M. W.

Barton
1862 George L.
1878 Walter K.

Bass
1848 William H.
1882 John F.

Bassett
1817 Christopher

Batchelder
1846 Hendrick D.
1856 William N.

1861 Josiah B.
1862 Edward S.
1866 Charles E.
1877 Ferdinand W.
1880 Frank H.

Bates
1807 Barnabas
1857 James E.
1866 George S.
1868 George
1870 William E.
1871 William C.
1874 Ellery W.
1875 William W.
1876 Frank C.
1876 Harry

Baum
1803 David A.

Baxter
1808 Joseph
1821 Henry V.
1822 Robert A.
1826 Benjamin D.
1875 David N.

Baylies
1872 Edmund L.
1877 Walter C.

Bazin
1807 Peter
1810 Abraham

Beach
1813 Aaron
1860 Charles A.

Beale
1788 Benjamin
1830 George W.
1837 John B.
1874 Charles F. T.

Beals
1868 Gorham

Bean
1787 Elisha
1793 Stephen
1829 James
1844 Curtis C.
1862 Jeremiah S.
1865 Frank J.
1877 Karl A.
1882 Horace S.

Becker
1863 Washington

Beckett
1827 Joseph L.

Beckwith
1859 Sidney K.

Beede
1791 Thomas
1851 Joshua W.
1862 Samuel F.
1864 James R.

Bell
1787 William
1817 Andrew W.
1837 Charles H.
1857 Charles U.
1857 James D.
1866 William A.
1869 Charles J.
1879 Louis
1880 John D.

Bellows
1822 Thomas
1836 Stephen R.
1837 Abel H.

Belmont
1868 August

Bemis
1827 Seth
1828 Charles V.

Benedict
1876 William P.

Benjamin
1825 James
1879 Frank E.

Bennett
1859 William P.
1861 William H.
1868 Ellery J.
1870 George W.

Benson
1845 George F.

Benton
1864 John C.

Bergeron
1791 Pierre

Bernadent
1790 Gabriel

Berry
1831 Joshua
1865 Horace
1871 John J.
1877 Flavius J.
1877 James W.

Bevin
1864 Leander A.

Bickford
1812 Thomas
1861 Charles W.

Bidau
1807 Thomas P.

Bigelow
1805 Horatio
1819 Francis R.
1880 Lewis S.

De Billier
1873 Frederick O.
1879 Henry

Billings
1865 Henry O.

Bingham.
1796 James H.
1859 Egbert B.

Binney
1834 Amos R.

Bishop
1802 John

Bixby
1789 Luke

Blackmar
1861 Wilmon W.

Blaine
1881 James G., jr.

Blair
1802 James
1859 Albert
1866 Woodbury
1871 Lafayette G.

Blaisdell
1853 Isaac I.
1857 Clark

Blake
1790 Joshua
1806 John L.
1828 Lyman
1838 Sherburne P.
1840 George A.
1854 William B.
1857 Charles E.
1857 Marshall W.
1862 Christopher C.

Blanchard
1804 Amos
1805 Eleazer
1806 Levi
1807 Elias

Blandin
1882 Amos N.

Bliss
1800 John
1850 Willard F.

Blodget
1792 Charles F.
1792 Samuel G.
1792 William H.
1822 William P.
1836 James

Blodgett
1866 Nathaniel H.
1869 Samuel F.
1870 Robert B.
1871 George W.
1872 John A.

Blondell
1877 Frederic H.

Blood
1875 George F.

Blossom
1879 Walter L.

Blunt
1807 Joseph

Blymyer
1870 Charles A.
1870 George G.

Boardman
1784 Nathaniel
1792 Thomas
1796 Benjamin G.
1797 Joseph
1798 William
1800 Francis
1800 Thomas J.
1808 Thomas
1858 William E.
1864 William R.

Boas
1882 Richards F.

Boit
1873 John

Bolton
1855 Thomas K.
1871 Charles C.

Bond
1803 Samuel
1805 John
1848 John G.
1869 William L.
1873 Benjamin D.
1873 Hugh L.
1873 Nicholas P.
1875 Summerfield B.

Bonhomme
1808 Achille

Bonney
1877 Jeromus R.

Boott
1818 William

Borden
1862 Nathaniel B.

Borland
1875 Benjamin M.
1876 Samuel F.

Bosson
1869 Albert D.

Boutelle
1825 Timothy

Boutwell
1822 William T.
1861 Henry T.

Bowden
1813 John

Bowen
1814 George
1820 Francis

Bowers
1810 William C.
1811 Charles E.

Bowler
1871 Frank

Bowles
1844 Robert C. M.

Bowman
1877 John E.
1880 William H.

Boyd
1792 George
1802 George W.
1809 Ebenezer L.
1812 Cleopas
1812 Theophilus
1821 Samuel S.
1852 William A.
1857 Charles M.

Boyden
1829 Joseph
1853 Dwight
1853 Frederick
1856 Benjamin F.
1880 Roland W.
1880 William C.
1882 Walter L.

Boynton
1848 George
1869 William E.
1882 Edward K.

Brackett
1790 Thomas
1791 Joshua
1820 Joshua
1837 Adino N.
1857 Solomon H.
1860 Frank A.

Bradbury
1798 Jeremiah
1824 Elbridge

Bradford
1810 William
1857 Francis E.
1870 Edward F.

Bradley
1827 Alexander R.
1828 Cyrus P.
1828 John J.

1828 Thomas S.
1835 Charles T.
1837 Joseph H.
1858 Samuel H.
1869 William M.
1870 Robert S.

Bradshaw
1828 Peyton

Bragdon
1866 George H.

Bragg
1871 Charles F.

Brainard
1869 Erastus
1870 Frank

Braisted
1880 Arthur P.

Brannen
1880 John J.

Branscomb
1839 Charles H.

Brashear
1866 Osborn F.

Bray
1827 Daniel

Breck
1875 Charles R.

Brennan
1880 Odie P.

Brewer
1869 George E.

Brewster
1784 William
1820 Stephen C.
1855 Alfred

Briard
1816 George

Brickett
1861 Benjamin F.
1865 Charles R.
1866 Henry J.

Bridge
1862 Charles L. F.
1863 Joseph H.
1879 Henry B.

Bridgman
1869 George H.

Briggs
1807 Charles
1813 John K.
1814 Henry
1830 John A.
1861 Joseph E.
1866 Frank O.

1870 Charles
1870 John
1877 Frank A.
1880 Walter S.

Brigham
1830 Abijah
1859 William F.
1874 Nathaniel M.

Bright
1876 George C.

Bristol
1873 Graham B.

Broadmeadow
1878 Walter J.

Brodhead
1827 George H.
1833 Thornton F.

Bromley
1878 Lovine A.

Brooks
1783 William
1784 Samuel
1796 Edward
1806 Oliver
1812 James E.
1813 Peter C.
1813 Sidney
1815 Ward C.
1818 Henry
1825 Horatio
1828 Isaac A.
1834 John
1848 Stephen H.
1862 Luke S.
1873 Edward
1873 Henry
1874 Charles R.
1875 Frederick
1876 Edward M.
1878 John P.
1880 William A., jr.
1882 Frederick T.

Brown
1791 William
1792 Samuel
1794 Joseph
1795 Daniel
1796 Stewart
1797 Jonathan
1802 Thomas
1802 William
1805 Charles
1808 Americus
1812 Abel
1815 Lawrence
1816 Nathan
1821 Washington
1825 Robert J.
1827 John S.
1834 James W.
1839 Charles H.
1842 Nathaniel P.
1843 James F.
1850 Edward J.

1850 Langley B.
1854 Henry F.
1856 Charles H.
1856 Cyrus O.
1856 William R.
1857 Addison R.
1860 Albert L.
1860 William G.
1863 Charles R.
1863 Samuel E.
1864 George C.
1864 John K.
1865 Edward B.
1865 Horace
1868 Charles G.
1868 George W.
1869 Henry R.
1871 Arthur H.
1871 Henry H.
1872 Henry A.
1872 John A.
1875 Frank T.
1877 Gilman A.
1879 Conway R.
1882 Walter A.

Browning
1875 Frederick D.

Bruce
1785 Stephen

Bryant
1791 Benjamin D.
1794 Charles S.
1812 Cushing
1855 Perley B.
1864 Walter H.
1876 Henry G.

Buck
1842 Edwin A.
1856 William E.
1860 Clarence C.
1881 George P.

Buckminster
1795 Joseph S.
1808 Isaac L.

Buckner
1856 James H.

Buell
1875 George C., jr.

Buffum
1872 Edgar S.
1873 Harry A.
1880 David H., jr.

Buley
1880 Judd E.

Bulfinch
1809 Charles
1809 Thomas

Bull
1872 Melville

Bullard
1811 Otis
1835 Enoch P.
1837 George H.
1863 Edward C.
1879 Emanuel G.
1880 Edward F., jr.

Bunker
1858 Charles A.

Burdett
1869 Henry M.
1876 George A.

Burges
1815 Welcome A.

Burgess
1863 James H.
1874 Charles F.
1878 Isaac B.

Burgin
1790 John
1791 Joseph Y.

Burke
1877 Peter

Burleigh
1806 Henry
1845 George W.
1866 William R.
1871 Edward S.
1872 John M.
1873 Francis M.
1873 Walter A.
1880 Frederick W.

Burley
1791 Samuel
1795 James
1814 Joseph
1826 Arthur
1834 Augustus
1834 Charles
1858 Elbridge T.
1867 Frank E.

Burnes
1880 Lewis C.

Burnham
1792 John

Burns
1877 Charles A.
1877 John W.

Burrill
1872 George H.
1882 Arthur S.

Burrows
1879 Harry S.

Burt
1879 Louis

Busiel
1862 John T.

INDEX.

Butler
1811 Isaac
1829 Benjamin F.
1830 Horace
1830 Josiah
1856 James D.
1861 Francis W.
1869 John A.
1870 Henry S.
1872 George M.
1872 Harry
1880 Harry A.
1881 Walter P.

Buxton
1830 Edward

Buzell
1819 George W.
1819 Samuel B.
1819 Solomon C.
1856 Albert C.

Byington
1873 Charles E.

Byne
1856 Joseph H.

Byron
1877 Joseph C.
1879 Edward W.

Cain
1857 William J.

Caldwell
1824 William S.
1860 Francis M.
1860 Leonard H.

Calef
1800 Josiah

Call
1789 Samuel

Callender
1865 William N.

Cameron
1879 James McC.

Campbell
1859 Augustus S.
1867 George H.

Canfield
1870 George F.

Canerdy
1873 John D.

Canney
1791 Ichabod

Capron
1808 Effingham

Carleton
1857 Charles M.
1868 Frederick W.

Carlisle
1861 James W.

Carlton
1826 John L.

Carpenter
1861 Frank A.
1870 William D.
1874 Frank O.
1877 Fred E.
1878 Orrin H.

Carr
1841 Jeremiah O.
1877 Lucien, jr.
1882 Clark M.

Carroll
1805 William
1879 Charles
1879 Royal P. T.

Carter
1799 Nathaniel
1806 Nathaniel H.
1815 Galen C.
1816 James F.
1842 Charles P.
1849 Joseph A.
1851 Daniel R.
1855 Buel C.
1859 Henry C.
1874 Edward B.

Cartland
1810 Samuel

Casey
1875 Frederick D.
1877 Peter J.

Cass
1792 Lewis
1797 Charles L.
1797 George W.

Cate
1858 Henry S.
1870 Martin L.
1880 John C.

Cavender
1840 John S.

Caverno
1826 Sullivan

Cenas
1850 James S.

Chadbourn
1880 Charles C.

Chadbourne
1807 Alexander S.
1842 Paul A.
1850 Sylvester W.
1879 Albert H.

Chadwick
1797 Peter
1820 Alfred
1823 Joseph M.
1827 Edmund
1829 Edmund
1832 Coffin M.
1832 John
1851 Ward
1859 John W.
1873 Austin K.
1880 William P.

Chalfant
1874 Henry W.
1874 William, jr.

Chamberlain
1794 Samuel P.
1803 Jacob T.
1810 William F. R.
1814 Charles
1820 Edward G.
1825 Henry P.
1842 James L.
1847 David T.
1860 Maro J.
1860 William E.
1876 Francis D.
1879 Allen H.

Chambers
1850 Benjamin G.

Champion
1881 Edward W.

Chandler
1800 Abiel
1805 John A.
1813 Alpheus S.
1817 Gardiner G.
1828 George
1832 William H.
1861 Josiah A.
1880 Arthur B.

Channing
1811 Edwin
1811 William
1812 John M.

Chapin
1829 Moses T.
1803 Frederick W.
1863 Leander
1864 Edward F.

Chaplin
1837 Daniel

Chapman
1792 Andrew McC.
1805 Isaac
1817 Jonathan

1818 Dummer R.
1819 George
1827 Jacob
1838 Ozias G.
1849 Jonathan
1853 Augustus W.
1855 Simon L.
1866 Alonzo
1871 Charles H.
1872 George B.

Chase
1801 Theodore
1816 George
1829 Heber
1840 Hiram
1844 Robert W.
1854 Philo
1855 Howard M.
1860 Albro E.
1867 Ezra B.
1872 Edward F.
1877 William C.
1880 Percy
1880 Wayland J.
1880 William N.
1881 Fessenden N.

Chauncy
1785 Andrew
1813 Charles W.

Cheney
1849 Elias H.
1857 Charles A.
1863 James R.
1873 George L.

Cheong
1880 Yan K.

Chesley
1872 John E.
1877 Israel F.
1877 John H.

Cheswell
1784 Thomas

Chichester
1867 James H.

Child
1880 Calvin G.

Childs
1823 Lowell
1865 Frank L.

Chin
1879 Kin K.

Chisholm
1868 Henry A.
1874 William J. L.

Chittenden
1868 Charles B.
1868 Daniel G.

Choate
1863 Washington.

Churchill
1877 Frank A.
1881 Lawrence W

Cilley
1818 Horatio G.
1820 Joseph L.
1834 Bradbury P.
1842 Nathaniel W.
1851 Bradbury L.
1852 John K.
1857 Joseph L.
1865 George E.
1870 Edward H.
1870 Moses H.
1877 Bradbury J.
1882 Frank M.

Claflin
1854 William W.

Clapp
1783 Mele
1864 Henry L.

Clark
1785 Ebenezer
1785 Thomas M.
1786 Enoch
1789 Benjamin
1791 Moses
1795 Benjamin
1795 George
1795 Greenleaf
1797 James
1798 David
1800 Samuel
1803 Jonathan
1811 Samuel
1828 Elias M.
1828 Rufus W.
1830 David J.
1831 Nicholas A.
1837 George F.
1840 John Q. A.
1841 Charles E.
1841 Samuel F.
1845 George W.
1846 John W.
1846 Lester
1864 Galen A.
1865 Benjamin F.
1868 Chester W.
1880 Kimball V.

Clarke
1844 Samuel G.
1846 Albee C.
1850 Gardiner H.
1851 John T.
1851 William T.
1854 Ellery C.
1854 Stephen W.
1863 Arthur D.

Clement
1843 John W.
1869 Frank
1879 Charles F.
1880 Frederick P.
1882 Harry W.

Clements
1834 Thomas

Cleaveland
1840 George N.
1840 Joseph M.
1841 Henry W.

Cleveland
1822 Charles D.
1860 Clement

Clifford
1794 George
1847 Nathan
1860 John F.
1865 Walter
1867 Arthur

Clifton
1865 Charles R.

Clough
1785 Jeremiah
1833 William
1870 Arthur J.

Cloughtman.
1874 Edwin F.

Cloyes
1819 Joseph

Cluck
1872 Alva H.

Cluskey
1859 Henry

Coakley
1878 Timothy W.

Cobb
1799 Richard
1814 Frederick A.
1861 George W.
1868 Melville L.

Cobbs
1837 William H.
1844 George S.
1847 John M.

Coburn
1861 Samuel A.

Cochrane
1873 William G.

Cockey
1869 Frank C.

Codman
1801 Henry
1802 Edward
1877 William C., jr.
1878 John

Coe
1838 John

Coelho
1849 William H.

Coffin
1783 Peter
1784 Enoch
1786 John T.
1789 Tristram
1790 Amos
1790 David
1792 Charles
1795 Hector
1796 David
1799 Isaac F.
1800 Nathaniel
1803 David
1812 Arthur G.
1812 Francis A.
1814 Rufus
1816 John P.
1817 Thomas S.
1821 Charles P.
1828 Horatio
1876 Charles P.
1882 James B.

Cogswell
1784 Nathaniel
1801 Joseph G.
1843 George W.

Cohen
1875 Alfred H.
1875 Edgar A.

Coit
1867 Frank S.

Coker
1825 Robert A.

Colburn
1817 Elijah
1848 Theodore E.
1880 Willis W.

Colby
1803 Moses
1871 Frank A.
1882 George A.
1882 John L., jr.

Colcord
1789 Benjamin
1793 Edward

Cole
1847 Edward C.
1849 Thomas P.
1856 John T.
1858 Harrison
1862 Rollo M.
1871 George W.
1872 Frederic F.

Collamore
1841 George W.

Colley
1871 Percival C.

Collins
1868 Everett T.
1870 Walter S.

Colony
1872 Edward
1882 Harry H.

Colton
1844 Willis S.

Comey
1859 Henry N.

Conner
1785 Daniel
1786 Jesse
1789 Nathaniel
1794 Samuel S.
1796 Joseph
1815 Oliver W.
1823 William
1826 Phineas
1826 Thomas
1828 Phineas S.
1829 Alfred
1833 John P.
1845 Charles G.
1847 Edward J.
1855 Daniel G.
1856 George T.

Connor
1865 Virgil R.
1867 John E.

Cook
1798 Jonathan
1829 Horatio S.
1867 Louis A.

Cooke
1862 Herbert J.
1864 Francis E.

Cooley
1880 Maurice W.

Coolidge
1821 John T.
1828 Edwin

Cooper
1796 William S.

Copeland
1855 William E.
1870 Charles W.

Copp
1784 David
1812 John M.
1827 John
1837 George W.
1841 Frederick A.

Corbin
1880 Austin

Corey
1858 Henry C.

Cormack
1878 George A.

Corthell
1858 Ellmer L.

Corwin
1868 Oliver G.

Countryman
1879 Charles E.

Cowper
1874 Frederick C.

Cox
1825 Ebenezer E.
1859 Lucien A.

Crafts
1803 Thomas P.

Craig
1880 Timothy C.

Craige
1797 John
1797 Samuel
1797 Thomas

Cram
1790 Jonathan
1792 Benjamin
1793 Jacob
1804 Benjamin
1853 Jacob A.
1857 William A.
1874 Dana B.

Cranch
1871 Quincy A.

Crane
1840 Henry M.

Craven
1821 Alfred W.
1821 Thomas T.

Crawford
1877 William H.

Creighton
1790 John S.

Cressey
1878 John T.

Cressy
1848 Oliver S.

Crittenden
1859 James L.
1874 Thomas T.

Crocker
1851 Samuel R.
1880 Adams

Crockett
1848 Charles B.
1853 James A.

Crooker
1809 Stephen

Crosby
1798 Jnazaniah
1822 Alpheus
1822 William
1842 John H. R.
1862 John S.

Cross
1805 William
1810 Henry
1830 Robert A.
1874 Charles A.

Crow
1869 Wayman, jr.

Crowell
1865 Edwin D.

Crown
1824 William B.

Crowninshield
1826 George C.

Crozer
1880 Samuel A., jr.

Cruft
1839 James J.

Culbertson
1871 Frank

Cullum
1859 George S.

Culver
1870 Andrew R.

Cumming
1871 George M.

Cummings
1841 Isaac I.
1856 Horace S.
1859 Prentiss
1864 Lowell M.
1872 Samuel W.
1880 Robert W.

Cummins
1843 Thomas K.

Cuningham
1881 Alan

Cunningham
1868 Charles G.
1874 Louis
1879 Frank H.
1882 Guy

Curley
1856 Edmund J.

Currier
1780 William
1794 Ebenezer
1814 John
1814 Thomas
1827 John M.
1832 Jacob M.
1846 John
1846 Thomas
1865 Dorrance B.
1879 Charles W.
1880 Charles F. A.

Curry
1876 William J.

Curtin
1859 Jeremiah

Curtis
1842 Francis
1843 Henry

Curtiss
1874 Frank M.
1878 Osborn M.

Cushing
1799 John P.
1811 Jonathan P.
1851 Thomas A.
1854 Edmund H.
1868 Charles J.
1878 Marshall H.

Cushman
1856 Charles S.
1866 Charles H.
1875 Harry G.

Cutler
1861 Elbridge G.
1861 Nathan
1863 William B.
1869 Walter S.
1874 George C.
1882 John L., jr.

Cutter
1823 Ralph
1867 Ammi

Cutts
1807 Joseph
1818 Hampden
1830 Thomas

Dabney
1803 Jonathan P.

Daland
1856 John

Dale
1876 John U.

Dalton
1852 Francellus G.
1856 Elleus G.

Dam
1813 Leader

Dame
1854 Samuel P.
1878 Walter R.

Damon
1841 Henry
1865 George W.

Dana
1799 James G.
1805 Jonathan F.
1806 Samuel L.
1808 Nathaniel G.
1813 Charles

Dane
1794 John
1827 Gilman

Danforth
1817 Samuel
1821 Blowers
1871 Henry G.

Darley
1866 George B.

Darling
1790 John
1816 Jonathan P.
1816 Timothy

Darlington
1864 Ellwood H.

Dart
1870 Joseph W.

Davenport
1849 George L.
1871 William C.

Davidge
1869 Richard W.

Davidson
1811 Loammi
1829 Herman E.

Davies
1829 John T. G.
1832 Edward H.
1860 Ira L.

Davis
1799 Isaac S.
1800 John
1804 Israel W.
1807 John
1810 John B.
1812 George
1833 James
1836 Joseph D. L.
1839 John L.
1852 Wendell
1853 James C.
1856 Nathaniel R.
1857 David F.

INDEX.

1859 Benjamin P.
1859 George W.
1860 George H.
1860 George W.
1860 William C.
1861 William F.
1864 Frank D.
1867 Frank M.
1867 Thomas A.
1870 William
1879 Frank K.

Davison
1839 Benjamin R.

Dawes
1877 Henry L., jr.

Deal
1819 Augustus G.

Dean
1783 John
1792 Charles
1792 Thomas
1795 Jeremiah
1800 Henry
1802 Clarke
1868 Charles F.
1874 Charles A.

Deane
1858 Frederick B.

Dearborn
1784 Benjamin
1790 Luther
1792 John H.
1793 Trueworthy
1794 Freeze
1797 Levi
1808 John
1815 Abraham D.
1816 Daniel
1822 Samuel F.
1827 George W.
1827 John A.
1846 Josiah H.
1847 John L.
1853 James S.
1855 Frederick M.
1855 Samuel Q.
1857 Clarkson
1858 Brainerd
1859 Cyrus W.
1864 Joseph H.

Deblois
1806 Thomas A.
1809 John A.

Deering
1803 Nathaniel
1810 George
1810 James F.

Deetz
1882 Charles H.

De Ford
1876 Henry

Delaplaine
1883 Louis S.

Delorm
1806 Godfrey

Demeritt
1823 Oliver C.
1857 Addison L.
1862 Charles J.
1862 Edwin
1863 Frank

Denègre
1881 James D.

Denfeld
1879 Albert H.

Dennett
1881 Edward E.

Denny
1863 St. Clair

Derby
1810 Elias H.

Devens
1824 David S.

Devereux
1881 Paul

Dewhurst
1854 George W.
1868 William W.

De Witt
1877 Edgar A.

Dexter
1783 Samuel L.
1870 Orrando P.
1880 Henry A.

Dickerman
1850 Albert
1881 Edward L.
1881 Ezra D.

Dickey
1882 Frank L.

Dillaye
1872 Henri D.

Dillingham
1862 Moses B.
1866 Thomas M.

Dimmick
1875 Joseph B.

Dinsmoor
1860 Frank F.
1862 Samuel

Dix
1807 Henry E.
1809 John A.
1827 John H.

Doak
1822 William A.

Dodge
1785 Benjamin
1785 Oliver
1789 Joseph
1790 Jabez
1793 John
1809 Isaac
1816 Samuel
1817 Allen W.
1828 Samuel
1852 John E.
1856 Timothy S.
1861 William H.
1878 Arthur M.
1878 Paul A.

Doe
1803 Nicholas B.
1834 Thomas B.
1844 Charles

Doggett
1842 John L.
1869 Frederick F.

Dolby
1862 William H.

Dole
1794 Benjamin
1814 Carlton
1869 Nathan H.

Dolloff
1784 Jesse
1872 George L.

Doolittle
1881 James L.

Dorr
1812 Ebenezer R.
1812 Edward
1812 John
1816 William
1816 William B.
1817 Samuel F.
1817 Thomas W.
1820 Allen
1823 Francis F.
1826 James A.

Dorsheimer
1847 William E.

Doubleday
1800 Thomas P.

Douglas
1810 John A.

Douglass
1853 Richard D.

Dow
1783 Benjamin
1784 Benjamin
1796 Joseph W.

1800 Warren
1814 Jeremiah
1814 Retier P.
1816 John
1818 Samuel W.
1820 Jeremiah
1821 Frederick H.
1821 Henry
1831 John M.
1832 Charles G.

Downing
1874 George S.
1878 Charles W.

Downs
1862 Horace P.

Drake
1872 Herbert H.

Draper
1881 William F., jr.

Dresser
1881 Willis R.

Drew
1822 Valorous
1836 David F.
1837 Stephen W.
1848 William P.
1853 William B.
1856 Horace
1859 Moses A.
1880 Fred

Droun
1856 Charles

Du Bois
1860 Pierre C.

Dudley
1798 John
1812 James
1838 Charles D.

Dumesnil
1790 Peter

Dunbar
1844 Charles F.

Duncan
1803 Samuel W.
1806 James H.
1826 William H.

Duncklee
1872 William R.

Dunham
1820 Alfred F.

Dunlap
1843 James B.
1862 Charles H.

Dunn
1872 Frank D.
1875 Julian P.

INDEX. 173

Dupee
1861 Lewis F.

Duquery
1790 William

Durant
1882 Edward W.

Durell
1789 Daniel M.
1794 John S.
1815 John S. H.
1821 Charles J. F.
1821 St. John
1826 Edward H.
1829 George C.
1834 George O. J.

Durgin
1845 Daniel H.

Dutton
1864 Henry J.

Dwight
1817 William
1821 Francis
1821 Thomas
1846 Wilder
1850 Daniel A.
1850 Howard
1863 John F.

Dwinel
1834 Charles

Dyer
1873 Franklin
1875 Charles E.
1876 Oliver, jr.
1877 Orlando
1881 Joseph O., jr.
1881 William J.

Eames
1803 Theodore

Earley
1861 John E.

Eastham
1803 Henry L.

Eastman
1833 George N.
1865 Edwin C.

Eaton
1822 John H.
1847 Edward F.
1848 Russell P.
1853 Charles W.
1855 Sherburne B.
1858 Warren E.
1866 Eldridge M.

Edes
1815 Edward H.

Edgerly
1853 Samuel J.
1858 George P.
1865 Winfield S.
1878 Edward T.

Edwards
1799 William
1851 Presley J.
1860 Thomas C.
1862 Amos S.
1869 Frank

Egerton
1850 Raymond

Egolf
1881 Ephraim H.

Ela
1865 Richard
1865 Walter
1874 Alfred

Elder
1856 Frederick H.

Eldredge
1864 Henry W.

Eldridge
1858 John M., jr.

Elgutter
1881 Charles S.

Eliot
1870 Amory

Elkins
1791 David
1847 Joseph L.

Ellery
1811 Epes

Elliot
1813 John
1820 William
1832 James M.
1835 Gardner
1836 Walter M.
1845 Jacob E.
1858 James H.
1865 William H.
1867 John W.

Elliott
1865 Lewis J.

Ellis
1827 Joseph W.
1849 Payson P.
1855 William C.
1877 Zenas H.

Elwyn
1816 Alfred W. L.
1817 Charles H. L.

Ely
1867 Addison

Emerson
1789 Andrew
1794 Rufus
1804 George L.
1806 Edward A.
1812 Charles O.
1814 Andrew L.
1847 John B.
1863 Theodore H.
1867 George
1877 Henry
1877 William K. B.
1878 Edwards D.

Emery
1784 Richard
1788 Nicholas
1789 John
1792 Noah
1798 Caleb
1814 Moses J.
1824 Samuel M.
1835 Nicholas
1836 John A.
1860 Manning
1861 George F.

Enflejian
1880 Harootune

Enos
1880 Mahlon

Esty
1860 Willard F.

Etheridge
1815 John

Evans
1789 Daniel
1827 John N.
1879 James C.
1879 Rush E.

Eveleth
1859 Edward S.
1863 Philemon

Everett
1807 Edward
1810 Thomas H.
1841 William A.
1881 Horace D.

Eyre
1871 Lincoln L.

Fairbrother
1865 Joseph A.

Fales
1827 Edward G.

Fall
1861 Charles G.

Fallon
1874 William
1875 Alfred

Farley
1815 Ebenezer
1815 Joseph H.
1815 William J.
1817 Charles A.
1820 Francis D.
1820 Joseph
1838 Caleb E.
1840 Frederick

Farnsworth
1847 Billings

Farnum
1834 James E.

Farquhar
1860 David W.

Farrar
1854 Henry W.

Farrington
1847 James B.

Farwell
1842 Levi
1870 Levi A.
1874 George N.

Faulkner
1839 George
1841 Francis A.
1847 William F.
1868 Francis C.
1872 Frederick A.
1881 Arthur

Faunce
1863 Sewall A.

Favor
1833 Bagley

Fay
1825 Samuel
1861 Joseph A.
1876 Frank B.
1879 John P.
1882 Henry C., jr.

Faye
1881 Edward G.

Felch
1821 Alpheus
1873 Daniel H.

Fellows
1803 Jeremiah
1805 Samuel
1809 Ephraim
1877 William G.

Felter
1869 William G.

INDEX.

Felton
1880 Cornelius C.

Ferguson
1873 William P.
1878 Frank S.

Fernald
1856 Orlando M.
1864 Benjamin M.

Ferris
1863 William N.
1878 Lynde R.

Fessenden
1855 Samuel
1866 Charles N.
1875 Henry M.
1875 James D.
1880 Edward F.

Fevea
1790 Alexander

Ffrost
1784 George
1790 John
1815 George
1818 William
1850 George S.

Field
1851 Artemas C.
1866 Roswell M.
1876 George W.

Fifield
1812 John
1841 William C. B.
1843 Lebeus B.
1856 Charles W.

Fillebrown
1862 Charles B.

Finch
1878 Henry L.

Fish
1835 Benjamin F.

Fisher
1850 Edward T.
1860 George A.
1865 Gilman C.

Fisk
1797 Abel
1817 Samuel P.
1830 Robert F.
1830 Samuel A.

Fiske
1813 Robert T. P.
1849 Cornelius
1862 Arthur I.
1867 Frank W.
1868 Frank W.

1869 Andrew
1869 Lewellyn E.
1872 John W.

Fitts
1827 Moses H.
1854 Daniel B.

Flagg
1859 William A.
1860 George A.
1861 Charles C.

Flanders
1841 Abraham H.
1860 James G.

Fleming
1877 William R.

Fletcher
1799 Robert
1822 Abel
1830 James C.
1862 Taylor B.
1865 Edgar A.
1874 Charles B.
1874 Jesse
1881 Jefferson B.

Flint
1863 Omar A.

Floyd
1880 Edward D.
1880 Edward E., jr.

Fogg
1792 Peter
1803 Jeremiah P.
1825 James P.
1832 Josiah
1838 William P.
1848 Amasa
1851 Francis F.
1873 Frank M.

Folensbee
1792 George

Follett
1881 Albert G.

Folsom
1783 Nathaniel
1783 Thomas
1787 Dudley
1789 Peter
1789 Peter
1789 Thomas
1790 John
1791 James
1791 Joseph S.
1791 Peter L.
1792 Nathan B.
1792 Samuel
1793 John
1796 Simeon
1799 Jacob
1799 Joseph G.
1804 Henry

1806 Charles
1809 Nathaniel
1813 Charles L.
1813 George W.
1816 Isaac L.
1824 Nathaniel S.
1826 Josiah H.
1838 William N.
1841 Ira F.
1841 Josiah J.
1842 Ebenezer
1844 Benjamin F.
1845 Charles F.
1846 Robert W.
1853 Simeon B.
1856 Charles H.
1857 Charles F.
1861 John H.
1864 Channing
1865 Herbert
1867 John D.
1873 William H.
1882 Edmund F.

Foote
1850 Cleaveland
1870 George T. S.
1861 Edward M.

Footman
1797 Jonathan
1866 Frederick N.

Fosdick
1798 Benjamin H.

Foskett
1863 George F.

Foss
1791 David
1797 Job
1857 Robert P.

Foster
1791 David
1824 William E.
1852 John
1863 William R.
1870 William R.
1876 John McG.
1879 Herbert D.

Foulkes
1870 Franklin P.

Fowle
1834 George D.

Fowler
1867 William P.
1875 John
1875 William A.

Fox
1829 Edward
1836 Marcus
1879 Fred, jr.

Francis
1836 Philemon B.

Franklin
1882 Hervey R.

Freeman
1842 Watson

French
1786 Frederick
1789 Daniel
1792 Benjamin
1794 Jonathan
1797 John
1803 Henry
1812 Tilton
1827 Henry
1841 Jonathan F.
1847 John H.
1852 Francis O.
1852 James P.
1856 William M. R.
1857 Jonathan J.
1858 Benjamin B.
1860 Robert H.
1862 William H.
1866 Solon T.
1868 Frank W.
1876 Frank N.

Friend
1878 Samuel H.

Frisbie
1856 Jesse F.

Frost
1806 Jacob
1824 Barzillai
1825 George A.
1844 William W.
1864 Thomas B.
1879 Edward C.

Frothingham
1835 Robert I.
1842 John B.
1869 Nathaniel L.

Fuller
1842 Robert H.
1852 William D.
1854 Frederick A.
1859 Charles
1861 William H.
1873 Gideon S.
1875 Irving R.
1882 Tracy B.

Fullington
1788 David

Furber
1792 John
1837 Joel S.

Fyler
1861 Carlton C.

Gaff
1870 James W.
1870 Thomas T.

INDEX. 175

Gage
1797 Joseph H.
1861 Charles S.
1882 William S., jr.

Gaither
1882 Alfred

Gale
1787 Amos
1787 Gilman
1789 Benjamin
1790 Benjamin
1795 Israel
1807 John
1812 George
1819 Charles C. P.
1837 Andrew B.
1838 Ezra W.
1841 Charles S.
1843 John P.
1847 Charles W.
1850 George W.
1851 John H.
1853 Walter
1861 Edward F.
1861 Justin E.
1880 William W.
1881 Leland A. L.

Gamble
1882 Fritz M.

Gambrill
1867 Charles A.
1867 Richard A.

Gardiner
1874 Frederic
1876 James G.

Gardner
1811 John
1811 John D.
1813 George
1816 Ebenezer F.
1819 Joseph C.
1820 William H.
1822 Joseph B.
1828 Henry J.
1835 Augustus K.
1842 George L.
1848 John E.
1866 Walter R.
1869 Henry

Garland
1794 William
1872 Otis W.
1874 Henry P.

Garnett
1881 Edgar M.

Garrison
1881 Lindley M.

Garvin
1856 Paul C.
1863 Samuel H.

Gassett
1832 Albert
1845 Walter

Geer
1868 Frank C.

Gellineau
1812 Peter

Genet
1790 Gabriel J.
1791 Pierre G. D.

George
1882 Nathan R., jr.

Gerrish
1814 James
1858 William
1860 Orville K.
1865 John B.

Gerry
1814 Hollis
1869 Elbridge, jr.
1881 John W.

Getchell
1843 John W.
1876 Clarence

Gibbs
1800 Charles L.

Gibson
1850 Charles H.
1850 John G.

Giddings
1794 Eliphalet
1797 Nathaniel
1803 Nathaniel

Gifford
1878 Franklin K.

Gilbert
1866 William T.
1876 Edward H.

Gilchrist
1813 John
1835 Daniel S.
1854 James

Giles
1881 George A.

Gill
1854 Charles S.
1855 George F.
1861 Clifford B.
1878 Emlyn M.

Gilman
1783 Benjamin I.
1783 Daniel
1783 John S.
1783 Samuel
1783 Thomas
1783 William
1784 Bartholomew
1784 Bartholomew, jr.
1784 Joseph
1784 Samuel
1785 Allen
1785 Ephraim D.
1786 Stephen
1787 Ebenezer
1787 John T., jr.
1787 Josiah
1792 Nathaniel
1792 Nathaniel C.
1792 Samuel K
1792 Warren
1794 Joseph
1794 Tristram
1795 Broadstreet
1796 John
1797 Charles
1797 Jonathan
1797 Nicholas
1797 Samuel
1799 Phillips
1803 Charles W.
1806 Nathaniel
1806 William C.
1807 Benjamin I.
1810 Nicholas
1810 Samuel K.
1811 George
1811 Samuel T.
1813 Charles
1813 Joseph
1814 Daniel
1816 John T.
1817 Daniel
1818 Lyman
1819 Charles
1821 Charles E.
1822 Joseph T.
1824 Samuel C.
1830 Nathaniel G.
1831 Ezekiel
1831 John
1832 John G.
1835 Charles J.
1836 Benjamin F.
1838 William H.
1843 Gardiner
1847 Nicholas
1859 Charles A.
1866 Daniel
1871 David D.

Gilmore
1869 Addison

Gilpatrick
1878 John R.

Gleason
1857 Samuel H.
1873 Zebina A.
1880 Albert A.
1881 William F.

Glidden
1790 Samuel

Glover
1784 Jonathan

Goddard
1797 John H.
1798 Henry
1800 Samuel
1807 John
1811 Thatcher
1820 John T.

Godfrey
1862 Charles B.
1864 Charles B.

Goetter
1881 Leon J.

Gold
1802 Sydney K.

Goldsmith
1881 John B.

Gooch
1863 Lyman F.

Good
1881 George McC. H.

Goodall
1830 David G.
1838 Samuel H.

Goodhue
1793 Stephen

Goodsoe
1868 George W.

Goodrich
1857 Mercer
1867 Arthur L.

Goodwin
1828 Elisha
1828 James M.
1843 Charles H.
1878 Howard R.
1878 William B.

Gookin
1792 Daniel
1802 John

Gordon
1798 William
1799 William
1803 Charles
1806 John T.
1806 Nathaniel B.
1808 Robert
1810 Stephen L.
1817 George W.
1829 William F.
1833 Nathaniel
1847 George
1847 Joseph G.
1856 John
1859 William L.
1863 Joseph F.
1868 Moses S.
1873 Nathaniel, jr.

Gore
1800 Christopher

Gorham
1815 David W.
1837 William H.
1844 Nathaniel., jr.
1852 George
1873 Arthur

Gorman
1859 Francis

Gould
1789 Nathaniel
1809 Josiah
1838 Charles H.
1843 Francis J.
1856 Henry F.
1859 John F.
1859 Samuel L.
1865 Moses B.

Gourgas
1818 John M.

Gove
1828 Samuel T.
1848 Walter S.
1857 Richard L.
1858 La Roy S.

Goward
1865 Gustavus

Gowdey
1859 Henry C.

Grafton
1803 George

Graham
1878 Harold
1880 Edward E.

Grant
1797 John
1797 Joseph
1798 Moses
1800 George
1841 Daniel F.
1852 Edward D.
1855 Gasper S.
1855 William H.
1869 Ulysses S., jr.
1880 Herbert L.

Graves
1825 John W.
1834 William

Gray
1784 Salmon
1812 Sylvanus
1815 Winthrop
1830 James H.
1847 Charles W.
1859 William H.
1861 Thomas H.
1864 Francis I.
1876 Milton
1877 William R.

Greeley
1878 George W.

Greely
1805 Joseph

Green
1840 James W.
1857 Charles E.
1857 John P. M.
1858 John O.
1869 George R.
1869 Henry H.
1869 John A.
1870 George W.
1870 Herbert

Greene
1797 David
1799 Reuben H.
1800 Jonathan
1802 Charles
1814 Ezra
1815 Walter C.
1815 William R.
1822 Albert G.
1827 Christopher G.
1835 James W.
1836 Moses F.
1855 Charles W.
1855 George S.
1874 Walter W.
1875 Robert H.
1880 Irving G.
1880 Luther H. S.

Greenfield
1866 John

Greenleaf
1818 Samuel
1822 Alfred
1825 Charles H.
1874 Alfred F.

Greenough
1864 Henry

Gregg
1875 William A.

Gregory
1844 William B.
1863 Friend H.

Gremmels
1858 Henry

Gridley
1824 Albert G.
1827 Timothy
1833 Oliver L.

Griffin
1860 La Roy F.
1867 Luther W.

Griffith
1881 Claude T.

Grinnell
1876 Richard B.
1876 William M.

Griswold
1868 William McC.

Groom
1849 Thomas

Grouard
1882 John S.

Grover
1861 George W.
1871 Ralph W.

Guild
1801 Josiah Q.
1882 William A.

Gunn
1866 Elisha

Gunning
1871 Revere C.
1873 Thomas B.

Gunter
1860 Leverett D.

Guptill
1870 Albert B.

Gurney
1836 Elbridge
1859 Preston

Hackett
1784 John
1856 Frank W.
1870 Allan J.

Hadlock
1881 Albert E.

Hadsell
1856 William H.

Haggin
1870 James B.

Haight
1866 Ogden

Haines
1854 Charles G.
1876 Frederick S.

Halberstadt
1873 George H.

Hale
1783 William
1805 Ebenezer
1805 Samuel
1814 Thomas W.
1815 William P.
1817 William
1820 John P.
1839 George S.
1841 Samuel
1862 Henry H.
1863 Charles G.
1863 William G.

Haley
1863 John
1877 Edward H.

Hall
1795 Leonard
1824 Henry R.
1827 James
1838 Benjamin E.
1857 John D.
1858 Moses U.
1863 Joseph W.
1864 Lewis B.
1867 John K.
1871 Edward C.
1874 William D.
1876 Frank H.
1878 Edward C.
1878 William M., jr.
1881 Edward J.

Hallet
1854 Frederic

Halsey
1814 Charles B.
1863 Frederick R.

Halstead
1873 John C.
1875 Jacob

Ham
1791 John
1876 Oliver H.

Hamilton
1791 John
1802 Joseph
1802 Oliver

Hamlin
1877 Addison
1877 Charles E.
1877 Frank

Hammett
1869 Chauncey

Hammond
1813 Samuel
1816 William D.
1837 Charles
1861 William P.

Hanaford
1794 Levi

Handiboe
1853 Edward J.

1869 Arthur D.
1869 Charles K.
1870 Harry S.
1870 Philip
1871 Henry
1871 Joseph C.
1871 Roderick F.
1872 Edward
1874 Ezekiel J. M.

INDEX. 177

Handley
1870 Thomas

Hankins
1871 Henry

Hanscom
1815 Alpheus
1860 Meldon L.

Hanson
1805 Benaiah
1828 Albert F.
1857 James W.
1878 Herbert F.
1881 Fred A.

Hapgood
1852 Charles H.
1869 William W.
1870 William F.

Harding
1843 Chester
1843 Horace
1844 James
1870 Emor H.
1872 John B.
1876 Abner C.
1882 Victor

Hardy
1811 Charles
1867 George H.
1867 George P.

Harlow
1875 Henry W.

Harper
1794 John A.

Harriman
1854 James L.
1864 Hiram P.

Harrington
1827 Joseph
1828 Henry F.
1880 Charles M.

Harris
1816 Robert
1817 Robert L.
1818 Edward P.
1818 Herman B.
1818 Joseph W.
1821 James W.
1821 John A.
1823 George O.
1824 Charles
1825 Charles
1825 George
1870 Azariah B.
1872 Robert O.

Harrison
1855 George W.
1880 Charles L.

Hart
1879 John F.

Hartness
1853 James A.

Hartshorne
1880 James M., jr.

Hartwell
1822 George H.
1825 Jonathan W.
1827 John W.
1828 James L.
1830 Augustus C. L.
1840 Seth W.
1844 George W.
1870 Walker

Hartzell
1872 Melvin G.

Harvey
1815 Charles
1869 John T.
1874 Alexander

Harwood
1844 Joseph A.
1870 Herbert J.
1878 Herbert W.

Hasbrouck
1871 Roe

Haskell
1806 Ezra
1821 George

Hastings
1840 John A.
1870 Edmund T.
1871 Robert P.
1873 Edward H.
1875 O'Neil W. R.

Hatch
1810 Daniel G.
1811 Joseph
1814 Samuel
1818 William
1822 Johnson
1823 Charles
1833 Edward W.
1837 William S.
1843 John L.
1863 Frank E.
1880 Edward J.

Hathaway
1852 William F.

Haven
1800 Nathaniel A.
1821 Samuel F.
1823 Thomas A.
1829 Joshua P.
1832 Edward St. L.
1852 Alfred H.
1856 Samuel C.

Hawes
1855 William
1880 John W.

Hawkes
1808 Micajah

Hawkins
1874 Eugene D.
1876 Arthur M.

Hay
1873 Henry C.
1878 Tom D.

Hayden
1814 John
1818 William A.

Hayes
1831 Seth
1833 Francis B.
1837 Henry Y.
1839 Moses W.
1844 Augustus L.
1853 Edward A.
1858 John S.
1860 Charles
1861 William A.
1874 Frederick B.
1874 John J.
1881 Frank L.

Hayford
1877 Francis L.

Haynes
1869 John M.
1877 George F.
1878 David N.

Hayward
1817 William
1877 Walter E.

Haywood
1854 Jedediah K.

Hazeltine
1855 Mayo W.

Hazelton
1822 Horace L.

Hazen
1859 Elijah B.

Head
1801 Charles
1804 George E.
1847 Orin McC.

Heald
1866 John O.

Healey
1803 Wells
1812 Joseph
1836 Wells
1840 Charles N.
1845 William P.
1849 George W.

Heard
1799 Augustine
1801 Charles

Heath
1807 John
1856 William B.

Heaton
1862 William W.

Hedden
1865 David C.

Hedge
1813 John

Hellen
1823 Thomas T.

Hemenway
1873 Charles P.

Heminway
1871 Truman

Hempstead
1859 Louis R.
1875 William G.

Henderson
1823 Howard M.
1831 J. M.
1834 William
1844 Alexander
1873 George A.
1873 George H.

Henry
1828 Hugh H.

Herbert
1842 John

Herman
1843 Cornelius H.

Herrick
1878 Henry H.
1881 Edward W.

Hervey
1865 Louis P.

Hewett
1846 James D.
1846 William W.

Hewitt
1867 Roscoe E.

Heywood
1880 Henry B.

Hibbard
1872 Charles B.

Hickey
1868 Charles M.

INDEX.

Hickok
1855 Gilman C.
Hidden
1830 Ephraim N.
Higgins
1860 Orville P.
1883 Francis G.
1882 John R.
Higginson
1801 James P.
Higinbotham
1866 Henry C.
Hilbourne
1872 Jerome
Hildreth
1811 Abel F.
1811 Richard
1816 Richard
1830 Samuel T.
1838 Charles H.
1862 William H.
Hiles
1876 Aubrey De V
Hill
1786 Samuel
1794 John
1795 William
1810 John L.
1810 Mark L.
1827 Silas H.
1833 William P.
1843 David C.
1852 Edward L.
1853 Charles E.
1858 Laban M.
1859 George A.
1863 George
1863 John E.
1866 Walter C.
1869 Edward W.
1872 William B.
1873 William B.
1873 William P.
1874 Cyrus F.
1878 Joseph A.
1882 John
Hilliard
1796 Abraham
1803 Timothy
1800 Joseph C.
1835 Rufus K.
1838 Joseph C.
1864 Rufus E.
Hillis
1863 John
Hills
1825 Nathaniel
1864 William B.
1881 Isaac, jr.
Hilton
1789 Andrew
1791 Nathan
1807 Winthrop
1816 George O.

Hinkley
1860 Otis
Hitchings
1872 Hector M.
1873 Henry
Hoa
1869 Albert
Hoag
1862 William H.
Hoague
1862 Izaak T.
Hoar
1864 Charles E.
1876 Sherman
Hobart
1783 Dudley
1783 Samuel
1831 Aaron
1834 George
1845 Joseph
1870 George B.
Hobbs
1791 Morris
1818 Hiram H.
1825 Robert G.
1841 Augier M.
1848 David L.
1852 Isaac W.
1852 Lewis F.
1855 George F.
1864 John O.
1868 George La F.
1868 Isaac H.
1870 Willis F.
1873 Charles A.
1874 Lucius H.
1881 William K.
Hobson
1880 George P. F.
Hodgdon
1814 John
1821 John
1872 Oscar W.
1874 Walter G.
Hodges
1864 Edward F.
1871 Charles F.
Hodsdon
1879 Ervin W.
Hogins
1816 Asa B.
Hoit
1793 Benjamin
1793 Joseph
1793 Joseph
1793 Joseph J.
1793 William

1795 Benjamin
1798 Richard
1812 Joseph
1826 Moses F.
Hoitt
1841 John S.
1842 Gardner J.
1854 Ira G.
1856 Leander M.
1858 George I.
1878 Rodney B.
Holbrook
1872 George A.
Holden
1864 Henry P.
1881 Albert F.
Holland
1878 John F.
1880 Michael J.
Holliday
1880 William H.
Hollis
1855 Abijah
Holman
1796 Silas
1810 Silas
1841 Henry W.
1869 John C.
1873 Walter A.
1881 Charles R.
Holmes
1822 Cyrus
1824 Charles H.
1831 Nathaniel
1836 Howland
1838 Samuel A.
1864 Artemas H.
1867 Joseph C.
1869 Robert B.
1876 Benjamin B.
1879 John P.
Holt
1816 Jeremiah
1816 Peter
1821 Joshua
1862 George A.
Holway
1863 Joseph H.
Holyoke
1871 Frank
Honoré
1881 Lockwood
Hook
1791 Josiah
1791 Moses
1798 Josiah
1817 Josiah S.
1819 Edward W.

Hooker
1810 Horace
1876 Charles O.
1876 Samuel P.
Hooper
1813 John H.
1851 Henry O.
1870 Henry M.
1879 James B.
Hoover
1855 George W.
Hope
1877 Benjamin P.
Hopkinson
1783 Parker
1790 John
1842 Israel S.
Hopper
1872 Isaac T.
Hopple
1874 Caspar
Horne
1853 Charles A.
1873 Frederick E.
Hosmer
1870 Arthur B.
Hotchkiss
1870 William H.
Houghton
1854 Jesse H.
Houlton
1847 Amos
Hovey
1784 Temple
How
1796 Eliphalet
Howard
1834 Samuel E.
1835 Edward F.
1851 Selah B.
1860 William C.
1872 William D.
1875 Albert A.
1876 William T.
1879 Charles M.
1881 Timothy
Howe
1858 Edward R.
1869 James M.
1874 Frank W.
1876 Jared S.
1876 Willard W.
Howell
1873 Rufus K., jr.

INDEX.

Howison
1881 Arthur W.

Hoxie
1863 Henry N.

Hoyt
1816 Aaron B.
1860 James O.
1863 William E.
1865 Joseph G.
1866 Samuel
1868 Edward H.
1870 Louis G.
1873 James K.
1874 Frank A.

Hubbard
1823 John
1825 Nathaniel H.
1826 Calvin
1834 Aaron M.
1835 Nathaniel D.
1836 Aaron D.
1836 Richard
1860 Sanford B.
1861 George F.
1864 John
1866 Lucius L.
1873 Rufus P.
1878 Harry
1881 Henry

Hudgens
1876 Seymour I.

Hudnut
1880 William H.

Hughes
1863 Joseph A. D.

Huidekoper
1862 Edgar
1863 Arthur C.
1871 Rush S.
1874 Frank C.

Hull
1811 Elias
1877 Arthur C.
1878 Heber W.
1879 Edward V.

Hume
1882 John H.

Humphrey
1804 James L.
1871 Friend

Hundley
1871 Oscar R.

Hunnewell
1800 Leonard
1810 Henry
1861 Arthur
1877 William S.

Hunking
1866 Charles D.

Hunt
1804 Richard T.
1810 Samuel
1841 Peter T.
1861 Samuel C.
1865 Frank W.
1869 Henry McG.
1880 Thomas
1882 Allston F.

Hunter
1883 John P.

Huntington
1872 Edward W.
1874 Homer A.
1875 Thomas M.

Huntoon
1857 Daniel T. V.

Hurd
1810 Josiah S.
1830 Francis P.
1842 John A.
1882 Harry W.

Hurry
1813 John

Hussey
1874 Frederick D.

Hutchings
1810 William
1873 Samuel
1880 John H., jr.

Hutchins
1799 Charles
1804 Fitz E.
1826 George
1830 Horace G.
1879 Lee

Hutchinson
1825 Samuel R.
1866 Oliver A.

Hyde
1830 Ephraim A.
1866 Daniel B.
1872 William De W.

Ingalls
1823 Charles C.
1823 John

Ingersoll
1810 George G.
1875 John C.

Ingraham
1802 William S.
1805 John H.

Ireland
1861 Frederick G.

Irons
1861 Alfred B.

Irvine
1881 William M.

Ivy
1874 Thomas P.

Jack
1877 Ernest S.

Jackman
1871 David K., jr.

Jackson
1798 John
1816 Amasa
1827 Charles D.
1852 William F. B.
1856 John McK.
1856 Richard H.
1864 Charles G.
1873 Ernest H.
1882 Charles M.
1882 James C.

Jacobs
1870 John T.
1876 Henry B.
1878 Edwin E.

James
1785 Caleb
1786 Joshua
1859 Charles E.

Jamieson
1843 Thomas S.
1846 Robert
1872 Alexander F.

Janes
1865 William M.

Janin
1881 Louis, jr.

Jauvrin
1852 Joseph E.

Jaques
1824 Samuel

Jaquith
1838 Abram

Jarvis
1832 Charles
1836 Leonard F. E.
1836 William

Jefferds
1802 George
1814 Ivory

Jenckes
1818 Francis C.
1819 Jerathmel B.
1819 Joseph S.

Jenkins
1796 Robert D.
1816 Robert
1817 Gilbert T.
1817 John C.
1818 Francis W.
1846 John H.
1877 Fredric W.
1878 George

Jenness
1877 Barrett L.

Jennings
1881 Edward B.
1882 Robert W., jr.

Jennison
1877 Frank E.

Jerome
1869 Lawrence R.

Jewell
1828 John L.
1849 William E.
1862 Hiram
1863 Joseph H.
1881 Winfield S.

Jewett
1785 Enoch
1789 Gilman
1798 Paul
1799 Joseph
1811 George
1851 Horace
1859 Nathaniel M.

Joab
1876 Albert E.

Joachinson
1865 Edward A.

Johnson
1785 Caleb
1796 Haynes
1797 James
1797 William
1798 William S.
1799 James
1804 Ralph
1805 Caleb
1847 James M.
1849 George H.
1852 Richard M.
1860 John W.
1864 Charles W.
1868 Oliver T.
1872 Benjamin N.
1874 Emery W.
1874 William A.
1876 Walter S.

Johnston
1815 George C.
1832 Edward R.
1878 William S.

INDEX.

Joline
1882 Olin C.

Jones
1783 Daniel
1789 Theophilus
1793 George
1807 Stephen F.
1826 William P.
1831 Frederick
1860 Frank W.
1860 Ludlow A.
1866 George I.
1869 Alfred H.
1871 Edward A.
1878 Charles D.
1882 Arthur R.
1882 Charles W.

Jordan
1872 Herbert S.
1878 Homer F.

Judkins
1789 Hill
1791 Amos
1799 Moses

Judson
1873 William H.

Julian
1852 John A. L.
1853 George N.

Junkins
1819 Samuel

Kaharl
1882 Walter R.

Kales
1879 John D.

Kamm
1877 Charles T.

Kaufman
1882 Franklin J.

Keating
1808 Charles
1808 Oliver
1812 Theodore
1831 Edward M. E.
1875 James E.

Keenan
1868 James

Keith
1853 Henry M.

Kelley
1875 Frederick I.
1881 Frank H., jr.
1882 George D.

Kelly
1813 Henry T.
1817 John
1829 James B.
1836 John P. P.
1854 John S. C.

Kellogg
1870 William C.
1881 Edward R.

Kelsey
1871 Charles S.
1871 Herbert S.

Kendall
1814 Payson
1844 James W.

Kennard
1854 Albert E.

Kenner
1824 Minor

Kenneson
1875 Thaddeus D.

Kennett
1878 Samuel H.

Kent
1805 Joseph
1808 George
1867 George R.
1868 Sheldon L.
1871 Frederick C.
1876 William W.
1879 Pierce J.

Kerr
1827 Robert T.
1868 Robert
1875 Chauncey F.
1877 Frederic M.
1877 Robert B.

Ketcham
1880 Henry B.

Kettell
1822 Jacob K.

Kews
1810 Jeremiah

Kibling
1873 Curtis A.

Kidder
1851 Chauncey H.
1866 Camillus G.

Kilbourn
1854 William A.

Kilham
1830 Austin D.

Kilner
1849 Frederick B.

Kimball
1783 John
1786 Bartholomew
1789 Thomas
1806 Edmund
1821 Richard
1822 Gilman
1822 Jeremiah
1824 Increase S.
1826 John
1835 William A.
1836 Samuel
1837 Charles E.
1841 Charles
1843 John H.
1848 Robert P.
1870 Edward W.
1873 John C.
1877 Paul T.
1880 George N.

Kin
1879 Ta Ting

King
1848 Henry L. P.
1860 William H.
1865 John L.
1865 William N.
1867 Thomas W.
1873 Henry W.
1876 Moses
1880 Ben E.

Kingman
1837 John W.
1846 Charles H.

Kingsbury
1856 Josiah W.
1857 Harlan P.
1857 James M.
1871 Herbert D.
1882 William J.

Kinney
1860 Kirk

Kip
1871 William F.

Kirby
1877 Stephen S.

Kirk
1875 Alexander J.
1878 Rensselaer L.

Kittredge
1816 Theodore
1841 John
1858 George W.
1879 John

Knapp
1861 Thomas L.
1881 Charles P.

Kneeland
1881 Furman

Knight
1822 Isaac
1825 Jeremiah
1826 John McD.
1847 Elias D.
1870 Joseph E.

Knowlton
1877 Amos A.

Kollock
1816 Phineas M.

Küssner
1882 Albert J.

Kwong
1880 Kwok Kwang

Kyte
1882 Albert E.

Lackey
1795 Joseph
1841 William H.

Ladd
1783 Eliphalet
1787 William
1796 John
1796 Isaac
1797 Alexander
1799 John
1803 Eliphalet
1806 Samuel
1823 Haven
1823 Henry
1828 Alexander H
1830 John S.
1834 Joseph H.
1843 Samuel P.
1856 Abraham G.
1860 William J.
1861 William F.
1875 Alva W.
1875 Daniel W., jr.

Laine.
1823 Lewis F.

Lakeman
1786 Nathaniel
1795 John
1805 Israel

Lamprey
1848 Jonathan M.

Lamson
1783 Joseph
1783 Stephen
1797 Henry
1801 Charles
1805 George
1807 Ephraim K.
1810 John
1824 George D.
1844 Caleb

INDEX.

Lane
1784 Joshua
1789 James
1790 Ebenezer
1793 Joshua
1797 Josiah
1801 John
1803 Daniel
1805 Mark
1806 Joshua
1813 William F.
1827 Thomas C.
1838 Franklin
1839 Jonathan H.
1842 William F.
1861 Charles E.
1875 Albert F.
1880 Charles G.
1880 Ralph M.

Lang
1805 William

Langdell
1845 Christopher C.

Langdon
1784 Woodbury
1795 Joshua B.
1799 Walter
1810 John W.
1877 Frank W.

Lanoirolx
1791 Huard

Lapish
1798 Benjamin U.
1799 John

Larrabee
1853 James M.

Laselle
1879 Percy C.

Latham
1859 George C.
1860 George H.
1861 Edward H.
1872 Aaron H.

Lathrop
1876 James W.

Latimer
1861 William

Lawrence
1793 Jotham
1814 William F.
1815 Prescott
1823 Alexander H.
1830 Fitz H.
1836 Samuel C.
1859 Edward N.
1860 Anson H.
1863 George H.
1882 Henry H.

Lawson
1880 Stanley M.

Lawton
1849 Lewis C.

Leach
1812 Andrew T.
1834 Joseph L.
1856 Roscius H.
1863 Joshua H.

Learned
1873 Frank
1873 William P.

Learoyd
1878 Charles B.

Leath
1785 James

Leaver
1853 Henry K.

Leavitt
1783 Gilman
1789 Benjamin
1789 Isaac
1789 James
1789 Joseph
1790 Dudley
1791 Thomas
1793 Ephraim
1794 Thomas
1797 John T.
1798 John
1798 Moses
1801 Benjamin
1801 Gilman
1806 Bradstreet G.
1806 Nathaniel
1808 Thomas
1854 Simeon S.

Ledlie
1879 George H.

Lee
1784 Samuel
1796 Cassius
1796 Francis L.
1802 John
1814 George
1859 Douglass
1859 Heywood
1867 Francis W.

Leggett
1863 Leverett L.

Leighton
1804 John

Leland
1861 Irving

Lemon
1846 William H.

Lent
1863 Edwin B.

Leonard
1808 Nathan
1849 William S.
1857 Otis L.
1860 John E.

Leslie
1870 Charles F.

Leverett
1804 William A.

Lewis
1861 James P.
1865 Elijah H.
1877 John W.
1880 John N., jr.
1882 Samuel De W.
1883 Mark B.

Li
1879 Yu Kien

Libby
1857 James L.

Liddle
1825 Thomas H.

Lighthipe
1868 Charles F.

Lilienthal
1882 Albert

Lillibridge
1869 Edward L.

Lincoln
1857 Rufus P.
1859 Robert T.
1876 Levi T.

Lindsey
1878 Charles

Lippincott
1862 Daniel P.

Little
1793 Edward
1798 Charles
1799 Ebenezer
1799 Moses
1799 Timothy
1802 Dudley
1806 Josiah
1819 Timothy W.
1820 Josiah S.
1843 Charles W.
1877 John W.

Littlefield
1851 Joseph D.
1856 Newton

Livermore
1799 Samuel
1826 Abiel A.
1830 Thomas A.
1832 Samuel

Lloyd
1876 William R.

Locke
1796 Hall J.
1827 Frederick A.
1836 James W.
1836 Samuel B.
1840 John
1855 Joseph A.
1858 William N.

Lockett
1881 Benjamin C.

Lockwood
1845 John E.

Lombard
1828 Nathaniel K.

Long
1805 George
1813 Joseph
1875 Charles G.

Longfellow
1792 Jonathan
1798 Jacob

Longley
1856 Timothy M.

Lord
1790 Isaac
1814 James
1825 Nathaniel
1830 Abram B.
1875 Edwin B.

Loring
1802 Charles
1847 James L.
1865 David
1866 Francis B.

Lothrop
1852 John A. P.
1863 George L.

Loud
1860 Arthur J.

Lougee
1803 John

Love
1881 Milburn

Lovejoy
1784 Phineas

Lovell
1876 Aldis

Lovering
1791 John
1792 Benjamin
1802 Richard
1813 John
1830 John G.
1830 Nathaniel
1832 John L.

INDEX.

1833 Richard
1836 Albert W.
1875 Arthur G.
1878 Reuben W.

Low
1798 William
1831 Henry L.
1832 William H.
1846 Alexander C.
1853 Nathaniel, jr.

Lowe
1840 Charles
1877 Fred M.

Lowell
1801 Jonathan
1811 Reuben B.
1868 James D.

Luce
1882 Linn

Lufkin
1870 Walter E.

Lunt
1818 George
1858 Henry

Luques
1878 Frank A.

Luther
1877 William L.

Luzenberg
1852 Charles H.

Lyford
1789 Theophilus
1811 Gideon C.
1857 Joshua E. G.

Lyman
1783 William
1796 Isaac
1804 Theodore
1846 James F.
1851 Benjamin S.
1862 John P.
1865 Francis O.
1877 John T.

Lynde
1865 Tilly
1876 George S.

Lyon
1864 Edward
1870 George, jr.

Macauley
1871 Thomas

Mack
1872 Charles S.
1877 Patrick H.

Mackay
1787 William

Mackenzie
1870 James C.
1878 George J.

Mackey
1880 James L.

Mackintosh
1844 James W.

MacVeagh
1874 Charles

Madill
1878 Harry A.

Madison
1806 John

Magee
1806 Augustus

Magoun
1816 Calvin B.
1820 George W.
1827 Benjamin F.

Mahoney
1874 Thomas

Main
1862 Herschel

Maine
1794 Jacob

Makepeace
1819 George R.

Malone
1882 James T.

Malony
1827 Richard S.

Manker
1873 James L.

Manley
1881 Samuel C.

Mann
1863 George W.

Manning
1799 Thomas
1802 Joseph B.
1805 John
1808 Edward S.
1855 Jerome F.
1866 Henry L.

Mansfield
1785 Theodore
1799 Isaac

Manson
1857 Albert G.

Marble
1881 Dana G.

, **March**
1795 John H.
1805 John H.
1815 Jonas C.

Marden
1856 Francis A.

Mariett
1877 Ernest H.

Mariner
1880 William

Marrett
1822 William

Marseilles
1862 Charles

Marsh
1822 Jeremiah W.
1823 William B.
1825 Ezekiel
1854 Washington
1858 Charles B.
1858 William H.
1870 Edward B.
1877 Henry W.

Marshall
1783 Hawley
1852 Jesse P.
1869 Herbert W.
1880 Joseph F.

Marston
1800 James C.
1807 Henry
1856 Elias H.
1865 John D.
1877 Thomas L.
1879 Frank K.

Martin
1796 Edward
1813 Enoch
1871 Daniel

Martinez
1850 Michael C.

Marvin
1878 Frederick H.

Mason
1818 Alfred
1818 James J.
1820 Charles
1862 Allison Z.
1871 William, jr.
1875 Francis H. D.
1881 Harry L.

Masten
1872 Joseph G.

Mathes
1852 George
1852 Henry

Mathews
1855 John B.

May
1856 James R.

Maynard
1862 Elisha B.

McAlpin
1878 David H.
1880 Charles W.

McArdel
1881 John F.

McCaleb
1825 Theodore H.

McCandless
1864 Gardiner F.

McClary
1784 John
1796 John
1799 Andrew

McClelland
1864 William S.

McClintock
1818 Samuel

McClure
1788 James
1797 John

McCobb
1865 James

McCord
1873 William H.

McCormick
1879 James L.

McCoy
1874 Walter I.
1878 Harry J.

McCreary
1860 Henry C.

McCrillis
1830 William H.

McCulloch
1823 Alexander

McDaniel
1853 Virgil H.

McDonald
1818 John
1865 Herbert J.

McDuffee
1826 Franklin
1830 Jarvis

McElwain
1877 Henry E.

INDEX. 183

McGann
1874 John D.

McGregor
1865 William

McGuire
1882 John F.

McIntire
1852 Malcolm

McIntosh
1878 James H.

McKaye
1871 Henry G.

McKee
1878 William L.

McKenzie
1856 Collin S.

McKinney
1855 Edward P.

McLaughlin
1855 Henry
1865 George A.

McLellan
1803 Joseph

McLennan
1873 Francis

McLure
1875 Thomas E.

McMartin
1870 Daniel C.

McMillan
1869 George F.

McNeal
1853 Benjamin B.

McNutt
1879 Frank A.

McPhail
1803 Archibald

Mead
1784 John
1785 Jeremiah
1790 Stephen
1812 Samuel
1814 Levi H.
1859 Henry B.
1861 Charles S.
1871 Julian A.
1871 Martin H.
1878 George N. P.

Means
1799 Robert

Meconkey
1859 Richard J.

Medbery
1857 James K.

Meeks
1879 Edwin J.

Megregory
1815 Elias

Mehle
1877 William L.

Melcher
1800 Daniel
1802 Sylvester
1838 Daniel F.
1861 Edwin F.
1861 Lewis C.

Mellen
1814 John P.
1815 George F.
1818 William P.

Meloon
1851 Horace H.

Merriam
1881 John McK.

Mercur
1870 John D.
1870 Rodney A.
1871 James W.

Merrick
1859 Charles S.
1882 Arthur L.

Merrihew
1847 Stephen E.

Merrill
1789 Phineas
1797 Benjamin
1797 John
1798 Joseph
1801 James C.
1801 Samuel
1815 Gilman
1815 Nathan
1817 John G.
1826 Samuel H.
1829 Leonard W.
1834 Horatio
1837 Benjamin H.
1838 Abner L.
1840 Henry R.
1844 David W.
1851 Edward B.
1853 Hiram A.
1855 Joseph W.
1857 Payson
1862 Henry P.
1864 Royal W.
1867 George F.
1868 Charles A.
1872 Frederick T.
1875 John F.

1876 David F., jr.
1877 Dennison B.
1878 James A.
1879 Charles H.
1880 William T.
1881 Samuel W.
1882 Frank A.

Merritt
1851 Washington H.

Métivier
1869 James

Meyers
1880 George H.

Middleditch
1880 Robert H.

Milan
1880 Mark H.

Miles
1877 Alfred E.

Miller
1860 Franklin
1872 Charles E.
1872 Frank W.

Millett
1869 Josiah B.

Mills
1820 George
1847 William C.
1873 Ogden

Milne
1871 Joseph D.

Miltimore
1802 James
1807 Andrew W.

Minor
1822 Stephen

Minot
1831 George
1861 George S.

Mitchell
1828 James H.
1832 Asa
1833 Charles H.
1860 John A.
1862 Henry
1865 Gordon
1867 Eugene U.
1875 Charles M.
1882 Edgar O.

Moffat
1784 Robert
1784 Thomas P.
1878 Reuben B.

Molloy
1799 John M.

Monroe
1825 Nathan W.
1865 Alfred J.

Montague
1870 Richard

Montgomery
1864 John C.

Moody
1817 Samuel
1820 Isaiah P.

Mooney
1815 John

Moor
1867 Charles F. C.

Moore
1786 Robert
1817 Abraham
1844 John
1840 George P.
1859 James C.
1863 Lo P.
1869 Martin
1872 William E.
1878 Tredwell W.

Mordough
1830 John H.
1859 John C.

Morgan
1860 Charles C.
1871 Frank H.
1872 Hickey H.
1874 Harry H.

Moriarty
1875 Daniel W.

Morison
1784 John
1825 John H.
1831 Horace
1834 Nathaniel H.
1836 James
1836 Samuel A.
1857 George S.
1862 Robert S.
1864 Ernest N.
1865 Robert B.
1866 Samuel L.
1868 William G.
1881 Daniel W.
1882 Samuel B.

Morrill
1784 Abraham
1790 David L.
1793 John
1796 Samuel
1814 Samuel
1815 Moses
1823 Nahum
1833 Frederick
1857 William H.
1860 Clinton
1863 Charles A.

INDEX.

Morris
1870 William R.

Morrison
1780 Charles

Morse
1797 Ezekiel W.
1852 John B.
1857 Wareham
1858 George H.
1860 George L.
1861 James F.
1862 Francis A.
1862 John H.
1869 William L.
1871 Alonzo S.
1871 William S.
1873 Edwin W.
1874 George F.
1875 Edward I.

Morton
1825 William S.
1828 Christopher

Moseley
1799 Emperor
1829 William O.
1864 Charles W.

Moses
1804 Theodore B.
1811 Samuel T.
1816 William P.
1830 Theodore B.
1831 James C.
1834 John L.
1841 Howard M.
1841 Samuel D.
1856 John F.
1864 Charles H.
1867 Theodore W.
1871 Herbert H.

Motley
1874 George S.

Moulton
1783 Jacob
1783 Joseph
1832 William P.
1836 Nathan A.
1852 William
1866 Andrew M.
1874 Albert H.

Movius
1864 Edward H.

Mulholland
1853 James H.

Munroe
1843 John A.
1857 William F.

Munson
1821 Joseph W.

Murdoch
1819 Charles T.
1819 James
1823 Joseph
1826 John
1826 William

Murray
1790 William
1835 Timothy J.
1871 John H.

Mussey
1830 John F. H.

Myers
1864 James J.

Nagle
1868 James

Nairn
1872 John J.

Nason
1863 William W.
1866 Rufus W.

Nasson
1798 Thomas

Neal
1784 John
1855 Daniel G.
1858 Samuel B.
1860 George W.
1876 John H.

Needles
1877 William N., jr.

Neil
1806 Robert
1814 Ebenezer H.
1846 John G.

Nielsen
1872 Mikkel

Nelson
1796 John
1799 John
1816 Horatio G.
1862 George P.
1867 Edward B.
1872 Edwin J.
1873 Samuel N.
1878 Henry D.
1879 Nathaniel M.
1881 William

Nesmith
1864 Thomas
1871 James E.

Newbury
1870 Arthur St. J.

Newcomb
1799 Daniel
1799 Henry S.
1799 Seth

Newell
1867 Francis A.

Newhall
1849 Wilbur F.
1853 Horatio C.

Newman
1789 Mark
1799 Thomas
1878 Joseph W.

Newport
1881 Luther E.

Newton
1863 William M.
1872 William T.

Nichols
1791 George
1812 David L.
1826 George H.
1829 John T. G.
1850 Ralph K.
1869 Frederic McC.
1871 Henry G.

Ninde
1881 Henry W.

Nisbet
1873 Charles S.

Niu
1879 Shung Chow

Noble
1844 John
1853 George W. C.

Noonan
1863 Frederic G.

Noone
1859 Joseph F.

Norcross
1868 Walter S.

Norris
1793 Thomas C.
1855 Albert L.
1855 Rufus G.
1857 James W.

Norton
1868 Carmi A.
1881 Lucien H.

Nourse
1836 John C.

Noyes
1791 John
1831 Nathaniel
1834 David M.
1879 Edward I. K.

Nudd
1836 William

Nutter
1798 Henry

Nutting
1880 Wallace.

Nye
1846 Charles H.
1852 Edwin A.
1857 Francis C.
1865 Charles F.
1871 George H.

Oakes
1873 Frederic B.

O'Brien
1799 John
1800 Dennis
1882 Patrick W.

O'Callaghan
1875 William F.

O'Callogan
1829 Hezekiah

O'Connor
1873 John
1882 Cornelius M.

Odell
1805 James
1811 George
1857 William A.

Odiorne
1783 Ebenezer
1783 George
1783 John
1783 Thomas
1798 John
1834 George G.

Odlin
1784 John
1797 Peter
1797 Woodbridge
1817 Woodbridge
1830 James W.
1837 George O.
1863 Charles C.
1875 Edward W.

O'Farrell
1871 Frank

Ogden
1862 William M.

Ogle
1808 Benjamin

Olcott
1800 George
1800 Henry

Oliver
1802 Nathaniel K. G.
1876 Alfred C.

INDEX. 185

Olmsted
1871 John B.
1877 Oliver A.
1882 Frank L.

O'Neill
1881 John

Ordway
1789 John
1790 Nehemiah
1826 Merrill
1860 David L.
1869 George L.
1880 John A., jr.

Orne
1793 Azor
1798 William B.
1808 Richard E.
1815 Frederick F.
1815 Woodbury L.
1824 William W.
1840 Charles W.

Orr
1820 Samuel

Orton
1876 James G.

Osborne
1797 Joseph D.
1800 Henry
1804 George W.
1810 Joseph
1811 Oliver W.
1816 Oliver W.

Osgood
1793 Daniel
1795 Joseph
1799 Moses
1800 John
1812 Nathaniel W.
1827 Henry B.
1832 Edward S.
1834 Joseph
1836 George
1838 Samuel B.
1843 William
1859 Josiah A.
1870 George
1872 Abner M.
1878 Henry
1880 William H.

Otis
1852 Charles P.
1861 Robert M.
1862 Edward O.
1869 Walter J.
1871 Henry S.

Oulton
1883 Elmer H.

Overton
1882 Jesse M.
1882 Robert E. L.

Packard
1811 Alpheus S.

Packer
1859 Boyd C.
1864 William F.

Page
1783 Benjamin
1786 John
1789 Joseph C.
1793 Daniel
1794 Samuel
1794 William H.
1797 Rufus
1797 Samuel
1806 Elijah F.
1817 John H. W.
1831 Edwin A. C.
1839 Rolla O.
1846 William H.
1846 Kingman F.
1850 James P.
1850 Daniel H.
1855 John S.
1860 Calvin
1861 Thomas M.
1862 Walter
1872 Harrison P.

Paine
1798 John
1806 Nathaniel A.
1812 Gardner
1813 Charles
1821 George
1828 Nicholas E.
1881 William H.

Palfrey
1809 John G.
1848 George
1851 Edward
1855 Hersey G.

Palmer
1800 John C. R.
1842 Mark S.
1864 Charles L.
1866 Joseph B.
1866 Joseph W.
1882 Bradley W.

Parker
1783 John J.
1783 Samuel
1791 Nathaniel A.
1802 George
1828 Lucius
1828 Grenville
1828 Daniel
1834 Francis E.
1839 Horace
1855 Retire H.
1857 John McC.
1858 Edward G.
1859 John D.
1859 Edward E.
1868 Harold
1870 John P.
1873 Walter H.

1875 Frederick A.
1878 Charles W.
1880 Chauncey G.
1880 Chester
1880 Robert M.

Parkinson
1868 Charles E.

Parks
1865 Edward L.

Parrish
1862 Thomas C.
1863 Samuel L.
1877 Hugh R.

Parrott
1793 Enoch G.
1881 Arthur F.

Parsons
1783 Joseph
1783 John W.
1786 Stephen
1786 John U.
1796 John W.
1796 Joseph
1797 John
1816 Isaac D.
1819 Thomas J.
1822 Charles G.
1827 William H.
1829 John
1846 John S.
1850 Daniel D.
1857 John W.
1866 Frank M.
1869 Henry
1876 Charles C.
1878 George R.
1881 Walter G.

Pattee
1861 Elbridge J.

Patton
1869 John S.
1870 Robert L.
1872 Jacob C.

Paul
1786 Alexander
1853 Amos M.

Payne
1818 Edward W.
1818 William E.
1855 Arthur L.

Peabody
1808 William B. O.
1808 Oliver W. B.
1808 Aaron
1812 Edward B.
1821 Ephraim
1847 Oliver W.
1847 William B.
1864 Asa L.
1875 Francis S.
1880 Harry E.

Peak
1801 Samuel

Peale
1882 Frank D.

Pearce
1804 George
1806 Benjamin
1864 Charles
1864 John O.
1864 Lewis E.

Pearse
1820 Oliver P.

Pearson
1792 Jacob
1794 Charles
1794 James
1800 Jeremiah
1800 Edmund
1804 John
1813 William B.
1814 Nathaniel
1825 James
1840 George H.
1860 Henry H.
1877 Enoch W.

Pease
1791 Nathaniel

Peaslee
1862 Joab
1862 Willetts
1876 Marshall B.

Peasley
1811 Isaac

Peavey
1795 Chandler
1838 George C.

Peck
1872 George R.
1873 Charles B.
1881 Giles K.

Pecker
1878 Edward B.

Pedrick
1814 John

Peele
1865 Willard S.

Peet
1870 Anson W.

Peirce
1798 Mark W.
1803 Joshua W.
1812 Daniel H.
1828 Charles H.
1842 Silas F.
1843 George H.
1844 Joseph W.
1844 Joshua R.

INDEX.

1845 James
1852 Robert C.
1864 Herbert H. D.
1868 William
1870 Palo A.
1880 Edward W.

Peirson
1797 Samuel P.

Pendergast
1848 William W.

Pendery
1860 Henry R.

Pendexter
1830 George W.
1832 Samuel H.
1835 Frederick O.

Pendleton
1880 William S.

Pennell
1864 Robert F.

Penniman
1851 Edward A.

Pennock
1877 Benjamin W.

Pennypacker
1861 Charles H.
1880 Charles H.

Perham
1847 Samuel

Perin
1876 Edmund S.

Perkins
1807 Thomas H., jr.
1815 Isaac H.
1818 Henry
1822 James H.
1826 Hamilton E.
1827 Benjamin
1837 John Q. A.
1841 Thomas K.
1843 Woodbridge O.
1852 John McC.
1853 Edwin R.
1854 Charles E.
1857 Edward C.
1857 Benjamin J.
1863 David W.
1863 James H.
1875 Donald G.
1875 John B.
1876 George W.
1877 Albert S.
1877 Robert R.
1881 Frederick W.

Perley
1812 Enoch

Perry
1833 William G.
1838 Nathaniel G.
1843 John T.
1847 Henry
1869 Nelson W.
1873 Chester M.
1875 Arthur
1875 Edgar
1875 Herbert M.
1875 Oscar E.

Peters
1859 William
1866 Richard
1880 Frank G.
1880 John M.

Pettengill
1799 Amos
1873 John Q. A.

Phelps
1865 John H.
1867 Jesse B.

Philbrick
1791 Edward
1797 Samuel
1809 Benjamin
1811 Joseph
1878 John D.

Philbrook
1861 Charles E.

Phillips
1816 Jonathan
1830 Nathaniel G.
1846 Ivers C.
1850 Willard Q.
1878 Walter B.

Phinney
1863 Robert J. W.
1872 Guy C.

Phipps
1865 Vincent E.
1871 Walter A.

Pickering
1786 Benjamin
1790 William
1802 George
1812 Richard
1813 Daniel
1820 William L.
1839 John J.
1876 John E.

Pickett
1842 John S.

Pickman
1804 Clark G.
1805 Benjamin

Pidgeon
1780 William

Pierce
1867 William F.
1878 Joseph D.

Pierson
1805 John
1881 Charles W.

Pike
1830 John T. G.
1831 Daniel P.
1832 Matthew
1835 Elvin J.
1858 Benjamin S.
1862 Albert F.
1873 John Q.
1870 Albert H.
1881 Dorman B.

Pillsbury
1795 John N.
1795 William
1806 Moses
1822 David
1860 Leonard H.
1875 Ernest H.

Pinchot
1882 Gifford

Pinkham
1787 Eliphalet
1790 Isaac

Piper
1793 John L.
1806 Edward C.
1812 Ebenezer S.
1828 Sherburne B.

Pitcher
1880 George S.

Pitman
1820 Isaac

Place
1860 Charles A.

Platt
1881 Dwight M.

Plimpton
1868 Arthur W.
1860 Lewis H.
1870 George A.
1871 James E.
1873 Arthur S.
1877 Howard E.

Plumer
1802 William
1836 William
1839 William L.
1843 George W.

Plummer
1839 Joseph
1863 Bard B.

Pollard
1809 George
1877 Alonzo W.

Pollock
1874 William G.
1875 William
1877 Edward L.
1878 Charles M.

Poole
1820 Romulus
1853 Lawrence V.
1853 Marcus M.
1862 Jerome B.

Poor
1865 George A.

Pope
1859 John T.
1869 Frank H.

Porter
1795 Moses
1797 Richard K.
1800 Samuel H.
1807 William K.
1810 Daniel
1814 John
1816 John
1819 Oliver
1826 Huntington
1831 William B.
1835 Charles H.
1835 Fitz J.
1840 William C.
1851 John D.
1854 Warren W.
1860 Almon
1864 Thomas M.
1882 Rufus K.

Potter
1832 John F.
1835 Barrett E.
1835 Daniel F.
1852 Treat W.
1873 Barrett

Powers
1809 Lucius
1856 James F.
1858 Henry W.
1880 William C.

Poynter
1882 Thomas F.

Pratt
1804 John
1809 William
1810 Edward
1858 Gustavus P.
1863 David G.
1864 John M. W.
1870 Jonathan W.

Pray
1857 Ezra

Preble
1810 Charles
1831 William P.

INDEX. 187

Prentiss
1795 John
1818 William
1856 Nathaniel A.
1858 William S.
1867 Samuel R.

Prescott
1790 George W.
1797 Levi
1803 Joseph
1808 George W.
1815 Plumer
1815 Ebenezer
1816 Charles
1850 Benjamin F.
1855 Henry E.
1860 Samuel P.
1881 Joseph P.

Prevaux
1842 Francis E.

Price
1873 William C.
1877 Robert C.

Prichard
1867 Joseph V.

Primer
1868 Sylvester

Prince
1801 Benjamin
1807 George

Pritchard
1880 Albert R.

Proctor
1860 George N.

Purdy
1846 Alexander W.
1848 Edward J.

Purinton
1875 Walter K.

Pushee
1865 George A.

Putnam
1799 Thorndike
1822 Roman L.
1833 Edward W.
1856 Granville B.
1865 Dwight R.
1872 Earl D.
1879 Frederick W.

Quarles
1855 Samuel D.

Quimby
1799 Moses
1870 Thomas F.

Quinby
1858 Hosea M.

Quincy
1880 Josiah H.

Quinn
1854 William J.

Quint
1881 Wilder D.

Raftery
1878 Edward M.

Ramsdell
1867 Alphonso B.

Rand
1810 Caleb
1810 Isaac H.
1837 Oliver J.
1854 Edward M.
1881 William H., jr.
1882 Edward W.

Randall
1815 Benjamin J.

Randolph
1872 George

Ranlet
1784 Henry
1806 Henry A.
1855 Daniel W.
1876 Charles
1878 Robert

Ranney
1860 Henry F.
1868 John R.

Ransom
1872 Frank T.

Rawle
1863 Francis

Rawlings
1783 Paul

Ray
1811 Joseph

Raymond
1878 George R.
1883 Warren E.

Read
1877 Jerome C.
1879 Sheridan P.

Redehean
1879 James P.

Redfield
1881 Burt H.

Reed
1799 Robert
1805 William
1835 Edward
1848 Lucius J.

1858 Edwin S.
1859 Seth G.
1862 Joseph W.
1872 Edward P.
1879 George H.
1879 William L.

Reeves
1799 Daniel

Reid
1865 John E.
1866 Newton W.

Reynolds
1847 John R.
1856 Edward J.
1875 Ethan A.
1880 John E.

Rhoades
1829 Benjamin H.

Rhodes
1877 Nathaniel T.

Rice
1812 William
1815 Alexander
1831 George W.
1848 Alphonso A.
1855 George
1859 John M.
1865 John H.
1865 Sylvester W.
1869 Edward F.
1875 Walter A.
1876 Charles M.
1878 Paran F.
1881 Edward E.
1882 Mervyn A.

Rich
1874 Waldo A.

Richards
1815 Amos A.
1816 Charles
1830 Joseph H.
1841 Joseph
1862 William W.
1863 Robert H.
1871 Edward O.
1879 Benjamin

Richardson
1785 Phineas
1810 John A.
1820 Augustus L.
1844 George F.
1853 Henry A.
1855 Samuel C.
1863 Henry B.
1865 Homer
1866 John F.
1873 Henry K.
1875 George R.
1876 Daniel M.
1876 George M.
1876 John S.
1878 Frederick H.
1880 Franklin W.

Richmond
1822 George M.
1823 James C.
1823 Thomas A.
1832 George A.
1865 Charles E.

Riddle
1813 David

Ridgway
1819 Benjamin

Riley
1830 John
1876 Francis J.

Rindge
1827 John L.

Ripley
1787 John P.

Robbins
1783 Isaac
1807 William H.

Roberts
1795 Thomas
1857 Garland
1861 Charles T.
1873 Edwards
1878 John J.

Robertson
1844 Charles A.
1871 William D.

Robeson
1857 William R.

Robinson
1783 Ephraim
1784 James
1789 John
1792 Josiah
1792 Paul
1793 Noah
1796 Ede
1807 William
1810 Charles
1813 Charles
1813 Josiah
1813 Trueworthy
1818 John P.
1821 Frederick
1830 Abraham H.
1834 Nathaniel G.
1840 Eliphalet P.
1841 Robert L.
1843 Jonathan
1854 Wilson W.
1855 George W.
1867 Charles C.
1867 Edgar W.
1872 Gilman P.
1872 Herbert J.
1872 Warren M.
1873 John W.
1877 Lucian M.
1879 Frank H.

INDEX.

Roby
1805 Charles
1848 James S.

Roddin
1850 Charles O.

Rodman
1837 Alfred

Rogers
1790 Nathaniel
1797 George
1800 John W.
1800 Nathaniel L.
1800 Richard S.
1804 John
1804 Richard W.
1805 William A.
1831 John F.
1831 Nathaniel G.
1840 Jacob
1840 William
1865 George W.

Rohrer
1876 Harry M.

Rollins
1804 Ichabod
1805 Richard
1806 John
1809 Jonathan
1810 William
1812 John
1857 George F.
1875 Henry C.

Roman
1871 James D.

Ropes
1814 John H.

Rose
1855 Rufus P.
1879 Gustavus A.
1880 Horace R.

Ross
1854 Frederick A.
1881 Ellwood J.
1883 Daniel M.

Rotch
1865 Morgan

Rowe
1790 Joseph F.
1810 Frederic
1815 Edward
1818 James S.
1818 Rufus
1824 Augustus J.
1852 Joseph W.
1859 George H. M.
1875 Thomas R.

Rowell
1792 Thomas

Rowland
1817 William F.
1831 William S.
1852 Edmund

Rublee
1877 William A.
1882 George

Ruddock
1865 Walter R.

Ruggles
1873 Henry E.

Ruker
1797 Pelatiah

Rumsey
1872 Bronson
1875 John T.

Rundlett
1785 James
1787 Edward
1793 John
1793 Samuel
1795 Charles
1799 Daniel
1801 Josiah
1806 Nathaniel
1815 Edward
1820 Daniel H.
1840 James H.
1855 Charles E.

Runkle
1877 Philip L.

Rusk
1870 William D.
1872 Frank T.

Russ
1818 John D.

Russell
1810 Charles
1812 David M.
1813 Edward B.
1817 George R.
1823 Charles
1829 Benjamin F.
1839 Jonathan
1848 Robert
1850 Edward G.
1859 George B.
1860 Samuel A.
1863 Andrew H.
1863 Edward
1881 William O.

Rust
1869 Alfred L.

Ryan
1845 Thomas

Sabine
1854 Francis W.

Sackett
1858 Frederick M.
1857 Charles A.
1866 Eugene K.

Sadler
1814 Henry R.

Safford
1785 Joseph
1794 Samuel
1799 Joshua
1820 Charles G.
1862 Nathaniel M.

Salter
1799 William F.
1801 John
1808 Benjamin F.
1816 Henry P.
1855 Charles C.
1872 George W.
1877 George B.

Saltonstall
1796 Leverett
1838 Richard
1842 Henry

Sampson
1873 Charles F.
1874 Christian H.

Sanborn
1785 Peter
1789 Isaiah
1789 Josiah
1795 Nathan
1796 Benjamin
1821 John J.
1830 Benning W.
1837 John E.
1838 Charles H.
1851 Franklin B.
1852 John W.
1853 Daniel W.
1855 Noah
1855 Hiram M.
1863 Joseph L.
1866 Charles W.
1866 John W.
1870 George H.
1870 George H.
1879 Thomas P.
1880 Frank E.
1880 Frank J.
1882 John

Sanders
1861 Lewis C.
1878 James U.
1878 Wilbur E.

Sands
1862 Albert I.

Sargeant
1877 Frank W.

Sargent
1791 Christopher
1791 Orlando
1800 James H.
1801 Lucius M.
1802 Winthrop
1812 Fitz W.
1836 Henry
1868 George A.

Sattley
1881 Elmer C.

Saul
1822 Benjamin M.

Saulsbury
1871 John P.

Saunders
1831 James M.

Savage
1816 John

Saville
1860 Clifford

Savory
1875 George W.

Sawin
1859 Henry C.
1859 James M.
1878 George W.

Sawyer
1783 Joseph
1783 William
1792 Joseph
1799 Thomas
1822 George Y.
1822 Luther D.
1822 John
1843 Nathaniel I.
1848 George W.
1853 Charles H.
1857 Ira O.
1861 James E. C.
1866 Frank H.
1867 Robert W.
1867 Edwin F.
1874 William G.
1876 Frederick J.
1876 Isaac F.
1877 Fred L.

Sayles
1858 Daniel S.

Scammon
1862 James
1863 Hezekiah
1880 John

Scates
1829 Charles W.

INDEX. 189

Scharff
1877 Adrian
1882 Francis S.
1882 Joseph H.

Schaus
1874 Wilhelm G.

Schenck
1850 Allen

Schmidt
1881 Edward B.

Scott
1841 Albert S.
1859 Andrew H.
1867 Charles O.
1867 James P.
1870 John W.
1874 William A.
1877 David W.

Scoville
1857 Nathaniel C.

Scribner
1874 Charles W.
1874 Henry S.

Scrimgeour
1853 William

Seamans
1870 William S.

Searle
1792 Jethro S.

Sears
1852 Richard W.
1869 Alfred F.

Seaver
1808 William J.
1860 Edwin P.
1861 Walter H.

Seavey
1867 Amos W.

Secor
1867 Thomas E.

Seligman
1870 David T.

Senter
1857 Joseph H.

Severance
1853 Jonathan A.

Sevey
1813 John

Sewall
1795 Joseph
1804 Thomas R.
1811 Samuel E.
1813 Edward B.
1814 Charles C.
1852 Walter D.

Seward
1861 Josiah L.

Sexton
1877 Lawrence E.

Seymour
1871 Digby G.
1877 Edward P.

Shackford
1831 William H.
1831 Charles C.
1838 John E.
1840 George W.
1852 William G.

Shade
1786 Peter

Shannon
1797 William
1799 Thomas
1810 Thomas W.

Shapleigh
1864 Horace S.

Sharon
1874 Frederick W.

Sharpe
1875 William E.

Shattuck
1875 Amos B.
1882 Charles E.

Shaw
1789 Caleb
1793 Benjamin
1793 Nathaniel
1820 Francis G.
1833 Edward
1845 Elijah M.
1853 Joseph A.
1854 Winborne A.
1858 John B.
1870 Herbert
1876 Charles O.

Sheafe
1791 Henry
1795 George M.
1796 Thomas, jr.
1798 Jacob
1799 Samuel
1800 Daniel R.
1800 Francis
1802 James
1803 Edmund Q.
1805 John L.
1807 Charles
1808 Theodore
1809 John H.
1812 Oliver
1820 George
1820 John F.
1821 James E.
1844 William

Sheehan
1875 William F.
1880 Daniel B.

Shepard
1784 Joseph
1789 Benjamin
1842 Luther E.
1880 Herman T.

Shepherd
1821 Forrest

Shepley
1866 Charles H.

Sherburne
1783 John
1783 Samuel
1799 Henry
1805 William
1809 John H.

Sherman
1871 Franklin B.

Sherriff
1823 John L.

Shillito
1873 Stewart

Shinnick
1880 John W. E.
1882 Timothy J.

Shores
1831 James F.

Shorey
1867 George L.

Shortlidge
1861 Swithin C.

Shraeder
1875 Oscar E.

Shumway
1868 Milton A.

Shute
1821 Alfred R.
1831 Henry A.
1831 Isaac S.
1838 George S.
1845 Nathaniel A.
1872 Henry A.
1882 Frank F.

Sibley
1819 John L.

Signorette
1804 John

Sigourney
1800 William P.

Sill
1853 Edward R.

Silsbee
1863 Joseph L.

Silsby
1808 Jonathan
1870 Arthur W.

Simes
1809 George

Simmons
1863 William C.
1868 John F.
1877 George W.

Simonds
1881 John C.

Simons
1859 Charles J.

Simpkins
1850 Nathaniel S.

Simpson
1788 Joseph
1805 William B.
1816 Thomas
1872 James T.

Sinclair
1844 William H.
1852 John E.
1866 Charles A.

Sivret
1876 Franklin T.

Skinner
1820 John F.
1874 Samuel W.

Sleeper
1800 Sherburne
1807 John S.
1845 Howard
1845 William T.
1871 William W.

Sloan
1831 David S.

Sloane
1870 Thomas M.

Slocum
1841 William H.

Small
1868 Edwin F.
1877 Forrest G.
1878 Harry H.

Smallcorn
1785 John

190 INDEX.

Smart
1814 Burley
1848 James N.

Smith
1783 Benjamin
1784 John
1784 John
1784 Samuel
1787 Zebulon
1788 Ezra
1788 Joseph
1789 Samuel
1791 Walter
1792 William
1793 William T.
1794 Elisha
1796 Jonathan
1798 Ebenezer
1799 Jacob S.
1799 Valentine
1800 Daniel
1800 John
1801 Ebenezer
1804 George
1804 Henry
1806 Josiah G.
1807 Alfred
1807 Edwin
1807 James
1810 William
1811 James
1811 Lyndon A.
1812 Charles
1814 Henry
1814 Jonathan
1817 Francis O. J.
1817 Jonathan A.
1818 John
1819 Josiah
1821 William
1822 Hamilton
1825 Robert
1827 William G.
1830 John
1834 William B.
1835 James
1836 Samuel
1840 Charles C.
1842 James C.
1842 Walter D.
1843 Samuel A.
1845 George W.
1846 George O.
1846 George W.
1847 Charles C.
1848 Uriah
1849 Jeremiah
1854 Francis B.
1854 John D.
1855 Alvah A.
1855 Charles E.
1856 Charles A.
1856 Lucius
1857 Frederic W.
1859 Job R.
1861 George E.
1862 Charles F.
1863 Charles H.
1863 Elliot
1863 Sandford S.
1863 Thomas H.
1864 Nathaniel S.
1866 Andrew G.
1866 William C.
1867 Henry St. J.
1867 Jeremiah
1868 Howard A.
1871 Augustus D.
1871 Franklin A.
1872 Forrest S.
1872 Gerardus
1872 Willard E.
1876 John M.
1876 Roswell P.
1878 Daniel C.
1878 William C.
1879 Henry, jr.
1883 Herbert A.

Smithwick
1881 Nathaniel A.

Snitcher
1869 Elijah J.

Snow
1800 Ichabod
1839 Charles H. B.
1851 Henry F.
1858 Marshall S.
1880 Shirley R.

Snyder
1868 Benjamin C.

Solomon
1847 Washington

Soule
1813 Gideon L.
1815 Charles
1822 Moses
1833 Charles E.
1834 John B. L.
1835 Nicholas E.
1837 Augustus L.

Southgate
1794 Horatio
1805 Frederick

Southworth
1882 Frank C.

Spafford
1879 Julian A.

Spalding
1874 George F.
1876 Samuel H.
1882 Charles F.

Sparhawk
1786 Thomas
1824 Thomas
1872 Edward E.

Sparks
1809 Jared
1863 William E.

Spaulding
1872 Albert E.

Spence
1798 William

Spencer
1866 James D.
1876 Dewitt C.
1877 William W.

Spofford
1850 George W.

Spooner
1861 John W.
1864 George P.
1881 Henry C.

Sprague
1837 Ebenezer C.
1875 Carleton

Spring
1802 Samuel
1868 Edward E.

Staats
1844 Nicholas J.

Stackpole
1826 Thomas
1861 George

Stacy
1826 John B.

Stanley
1862 John L.

Stanton
1839 Samuel

Stanwood
1812 Daniel R.
1862 James R.

Stanyan
1880 Frank H.

Starbuck
1866 Henry P.

Stark
1808 Henry

Starr
1798 James
1869 Benjamin C.

Stearns
1780 Samuel
1804 William
1819 Richard S.
1826 Henry
1862 Charles O.
1865 John O.
1867 William H.
1868 Richard S.
1876 Walter E.

Stebbins
1844 Horatio
1854 Alfred
1854 Calvin
1879 Walter A.

Stedman
1813 Francis D.
1815 Charles H.
1883 Joshua W.

Steele
1784 John
1808 Richard

Stelle
1862 Morton B.

Stephenson
1853 James W.

Sterns
1881 Mayer M.

Stetson
1850 Charles E.
1856 Edward G.
1857 Albert
1869 Edward
1874 Hayward

Stevens
1799 James
1803 Samuel
1804 Thomas
1814 Charles
1822 Samuel F.
1846 Moody A.
1848 James H.
1850 George H.
1852 Henry J.
1852 Horace N.
1853 Warren C.
1855 George W.
1857 Chester C.
1862 Calvin A.
1863 Winthrop F.
1865 Daniel A.
1870 William H.
1873 Joseph T.
1877 Frank B.
1877 William S.
1879 Hermon W.
1881 William O.

Stewart
1851 Robert K.
1877 Frank O.

Stickney
1846 Joseph A.
1849 George
1873 William W.
1875 Victor H.
1881 Ernest

Stiles
1870 Maynard F.

Stillings
1871 Vinton

INDEX. 191

Stimson
1842 Rodney M.
1872 James P.

Stocker
1796 William

Stoddard
1841 Elijah B.
1857 Charles B.
1859 Frank R.
1860 William P.
1870 Edwin D.

Stone
1840 Jonathan C.
1860 Andrew C.
1865 Josiah E.
1865 Ralph
1867 Henry B.
1868 Charles W.
1868 Cyrus A.

Storer
1798 Seth
1798 Woodbury
1801 John
1803 George W.
1804 George L.
1806 Tristram
1827 Henry G.
1830 Charles W.
1835 Samuel
1881 Fred L.

Storrs
1870 George M.

Story
1831 John M.
1849 Benjamin S.
1856 Norman

Stoughton
1878 Augustus B.

Strahan
1863 Thomas

Strait
1883 Horatio N.

Strang
1868 Eugene E.

Stratton
1828 Charles E.

Straw
1815 David R.

Streeter
1862 Solomon T.

Stribling
1880 Benjamin A.

Strong
1805 George
1868 Henry A.
1871 Charles P.
1877 Charles A.

Stuart
1855 Charles C.
1864 Frank N.
1868 John B.
1881 Arthur W.

Stubbs
1870 Robert N.

Sturdivant
1875 Frederick W.

Sturgis
1700 Henry
1801 James P.
1806 George W.
1817 Russell
1817 Henry P.
1827 George
1846 Russell, jr.

Sturtevant
1856 Edwin A.
1858 Edward L.
1880 Frank C.

Suire
1875 Frank O.

Sullavou
1864 Emanuel

Sullivan
1783 John
1783 James
1783 George
1813 John
1822 James
1824 William H.
1832 Edward
1845 George S.
1855 John

Sullivant
1875 Allen
1875 Jacob S.

Sumner
1859 James B.
1865 George S.

Sutliff
1869 William E.

Sutro
1863 Theodore

Swain
1830 Robert
1854 Arthur J.
1874 Frank B.
1882 Frederick O.

Swan
1836 Richard W.
1854 Charles L.

Swasey
1784 Joseph
1789 William
1800 Rufus
1801 John
1816 Charles A.
1852 Benjamin F.

Sweetser
1860 Ezra K.

Swett
1798 John B.
1801 William B.
1807 Tasker H.
1854 Warren L.
1860 Samuel
1863 Charles F.
1870 William L.
1875 Leonard H.

Swift
1856 Stephen T.
1865 Henry W.
1867 Frederick
1870 William N.
1881 Edgar J.

Swinerton
1858 John R.

Sykes
1872 Gerritt S.

Sylvester
1845 Richard H.

Symmes
1856 Algernon S.

Tabor
1877 Fred S.

Taft
1863 Stephen S.

Talbot
1867 Josiah R.
1873 Ambrose

Tappan
1785 James
1785 John
1803 Weare
1814 James
1824 James M.
1853 Edward S.
1860 James M.
1872 George P.

Tarbell
1829 William F.
1856 George G.
1867 Charles F.

Tash
1802 James

Taussig
1880 Albert W.

Tayloe
1807 Benjamin O.
1807 John
1808 William H.

Taylor
1793 Samuel
1810 David
1843 Samuel
1849 David H.
1854 John L.
1859 George M.
1860 John H.
1861 John W.
1868 Nelson, jr.
1872 Frederick W.
1872 William R.
1873 Edward W.
1874 Henry H.
1880 Marvin M.
1881 Gilbert B.

Tebbets
1835 Jonas M.
1845 Theodore
1854 Pearson C.
1855 Jeremiah H. W.

Ten Broeck
1856 Edward P.

Tenney
1806 Samuel
1833 William C.
1834 Walter H.

Terry
1871 Albert S.

Teschemacher
1872 Hubert E.
1873 Arthur M.

Tevis
1869 Carter

Thaler
1860 Godfrey S.

Thatcher
1804 Josiah
1854 Charles C.
1869 Henry K.

Thayer
1783 Nathaniel
1794 Andrew E.
1869 Frederic W.

Thing
1784 Samuel
1802 Thomas S.

Thomas
1816 Frederick
1866 Charles N.
1871 Isaiah
1875 John G.
1877 Eugene

Thomes
1841 George D.

Thompson
1794 William
1801 John
1801 William
1800 Ebenezer
1815 John
1820 Charles A.
1824 Abraham R.
1830 Benjamin A.
1832 Andrew W.
1851 Charles A. C.
1851 Peter S.
1851 William H.
1854 Jacob H.
1857 Stephen M.
1859 Frederick H.
1859 George W.
1859 John B.
1861 Daniel G.
1863 Frederick
1866 Frank E.
1868 Henry G.
1868 William E.
1871 Henry B.
1872 Roswell P.
1881 John McQ.

Thomsen
1870 Alonzo L.

Thorndike
1800 George
1800 Israel
1801 Andrew
1803 Timothy
1806 Charles
1806 Edward
1807 Augustus
1807 William
1813 Albert

Thornton
1784 James
1828 Albert G.
1865 William

Thurrell
1855 Charles E.

Thurston
1783 James
1783 William
1792 John P.
1798 Benjamin
1820 James
1820 John R.
1855 George C.
1878 William L.

Thwing
1816 Supply C.

Thyng
1830 Joseph D.
1837 Samuel S.
1841 Charles H.
1843 John H.
1862 Charles H.
1876 Joseph D.

Tibbets
1794 Samuel
1803 John
1869 William S.
1878 George P.

Tibbetts
1851 Newell

Tilden
1862 George T.
1877 Beverly B.

Tilton
1783 Daniel
1783 Henry
1783 John S.
1791 Joseph
1791 Nathan
1812 John
1829 John L. W.
1842 Nathan B.
1868 Lucian S.
1882 John J.

Tink
1824 Richard T.

Tirrell
1854 Minot

Tisdale
1850 Edward S.

Titcomb
1797 Moses
1799 Benjamin
1849 John S.
1866 Jeremy W.
1874 George E.
1876 John W.
1880 Edward F. S.

Todd
1817 Francis B.

Todhunter
1863 John

Tompkins
1881 Gilbert

Tompson
1833 Charles

Tong
1879 Kwoh On

Topliff
1855 Orestes

Toppan
1788 Edmund

Torr
1841 George H.

Torrey
1799 Samuel
1828 Charles T.

Totman
1866 Everett
1880 Harry F.

Tourtellotte
1877 Wesley

Tower
1845 Reuben
1847 George B. N.
1850 Charles W.
1865 Charlemagne

Towle
1789 Joseph
1792 Daniel
1825 George W.
1838 Amos
1840 Joseph W.
1842 John F.
1847 Hamilton E.
1856 Amos
1860 Alonzo
1861 James M.
1864 Frank H.
1873 Joseph H.
1877 Wheelock V.

Towne
1801 Joseph B.
1801 Thomas
1863 Everett A.

Townsend
1845 Patrick H.
1859 Henry H.
1863 Elijah V. S.

Tracy
1835 Nathaniel

Trail
1878 Henry

Train
1860 Charles J.

Trask
1814 John E.
1815 Isaac
1815 Israel
1830 Ebenezer
1856 Jabez N.

Travers
1868 Charles E.

Travis
1862 George C.
1860 Benjamin C.
1869 Louis K.

Treadwell
1852 John P.
1865 Eugene

Treat
1853 James O.
1853 John H.
1854 John S.

Tredick
1815 Jonathan M.
1849 Titus S.
1852 John

Trevett
1794 Samuel R.

Trickey
1872 Edward K.

True
1875 John P.
1876 Herbert O.

Trumbull
1804 George A.
1843 Joseph

Tubbs
1842 Elijah M.
1858 Daniel L.
1858 Ransom T.

Tuck
1790 Richard
1815 Enos
1827 Henry
1831 Jeremiah W.
1854 Edward.

Tucke
1831 Samuel P.
1837 Ebenezer F.
1839 Edward P.

Tucker
1827 Nathaniel S.
1828 True
1870 Frederick M.
1874 Clarence C.

Tudor
1819 Samuel H.

Tufts
1872 James A.

Tukesbury
1807 David
1833 Munroe G. I.

Tullock
1860 Thomas L.

Turner
1817 Harris
1865 Samuel E.
1870 Gilbert H.

Tuthill
1882 Joseph B. T.

INDEX. 193

Tuttle
1795 Elijah
1830 Erastus S.
1859 Jay
1872 Charles
1878 Charles W.

Tuxbury
1839 George W.
1844 Franklin
1849 Warren V. B.
1863 Willis
1865 George A.

Tweedy
1864 James F.

Twilight
1859 William H.

Tyler
1810 Thomas
1823 Joseph D.
1829 Royal
1867 Rolla A.

Tytus
1864 John B.

Underwood
1808 Jonas
1810 James
1864 Charles M.

Upham
1793 Nathaniel
1816 Nathaniel G.
1830 Francis W.
1832 Albert G.
1834 George T.
1856 Joseph B.

Ussher
1880 Frederick B.

Van Buren
1862 William A.

Van Duzer
1870 William Van A.

Van Schaick
1880 John B.
1882 Edwin J.

Van Wyck
1860 Augustus
1869 Benjamin S.
1873 Samuel M.

Varick
1879 Thomas R.
1880 Richard A.

Varnum
1833 Richard S.

Veazey
1831 Daniel A.
1834 John M. C.
1852 Wheelock G.
1856 Daniel B.

Verplanck
1870 William E.

Viall
1875 Christopher C.

Vinal
1860 Frank T.

Vinton
1823 John A.
1871 Charles H.
1881 Edward J.

Voorhees
1875 Paul

Waddell
1876 Robert S.

Wade
1846 Edward

Wadleigh
1837 John C.
1856 George A.

Wadsworth
1798 Henry
1856 Joseph D.

Wainwright
1817 Benjamin G.

Wait
1805 Lucien A.
1869 Horace C.

Walden
1847 Edward

Waldo
1816 Daniel

Waldorf
1870 George P.

Waldron
1790 Isaac
1791 John
1821 Charles
1824 John
1825 Henry
1882 Howard B.

Walker
1784 Charles
1797 Samuel
1797 Seth S.
1797 William
1812 Charles
1814 Charles
1815 Augustus W.
1824 Henry A.
1833 James S.
1836 George
1838 Joseph B.
1838 Joseph H.
1847 William H.
1865 William B.
1867 Charles R.
1870 James S.

1877 John B.
1878 Frank H.
1880 Joseph
1882 George
1882 Russell T.

Wallace
1806 Elisha F.
1844 Ebenezer G.
1844 Edwin
1880 George E.

Walsh
1799 John

Walter
1810 William B.

Ward
1810 Henry A.
1816 Jonathan
1816 Wilson
1820 Charles T.
1865 Raymond L.

Ware
1836 John S.
1847 William R.
1860 Henry
1864 William R.
1872 Joseph W.
1878 Richard A.

Warfield
1862 Frank A.

Waring
1877 William B.
1878 James D.

Warland
1822 John H.

Warren
1832 John W.
1840 Nathaniel
1847 Marquis D.
1858 Charles H.
1863 George A.
1866 Joseph W.
1866 Thomas B.
1874 John S.
1876 James G.
1880 Fairman
1880 Solon G.

Warrington
1833 Lewis

Washburn
1858 Thomas J.
1865 Eli

Washington
1796 Augustine
1796 Bushrod

Waterhouse
1847 Sylvester

Waterman
1861 Byron H.

Waters
1863 William J.

Watson
1804 Winthrop
1826 Winslow M.
1839 John S.
1871 Donald R.
1874 William L.

Webb
1837 Seth
1876 Louis

Weber
1878 Frederick A.

Webster
1785 Ebenezer
1785 William
1794 Samuel H.
1796 Daniel
1806 Richard
1817 Eliphalet K.
1830 George B.
1832 Francis B.
1834 Edward
1839 William
1847 John B.
1849 Joseph R.
1860 Charles E.
1874 Nathaniel R.
1878 George A.

Wedgewood
1793 Dearborn
1827 David D.

Weed
1792 Samuel
1878 Frank H.
1880 George S.

Weeks
1790 Jacob
1794 John
1795 John
1802 James
1807 George W.
1823 Charles M.
1838 Augustus H.
1839 Albert G.
1871 Charles W.
1881 Edwin R.
1881 George P.

Weidman
1871 Barge C.

Welch
1808 Deshler

Weld
1805 Joseph

Welles
1869 James H.

INDEX.

Wellington
1843 Elbridge G.

Wells
1783 Moses
1788 Titus
1798 Elijah
1819 William E.
1822 David
1825 Nathaniel
1825 Nathaniel
1827 Theodore
1847 Henry B.
1856 Daniel F.
1876 Edward F.
1877 Edward I.
1878 Robert M. J.

Welton
1873 Richard M.

Wentworth
1795 Charles
1795 Paul
1827 John B.
1830 Jacob S.
1851 Samuel H.
1852 George A.
1858 Alonzo B.
1860 Charles E.
1862 Thomas F.
1874 Edward S.
1878 Charles B.
1879 Sherman
1880 Henry H.
1882 George
1882 John B.

Wescott
1856 William H.

West
1797 Thomas
1840 Charles H.
1872 Edward G.

Weston
1821 William N.
1847 Ephraim
1864 Arthur H.
1864 Mandell W.
1874 Alfred J.
1874 Frederic
1875 John N.
1880 James I.

Wetherbee
1847 Henry K.

Wetmore
1880 Frederick S.

Wheeler
1815 Benjamin
1847 James H.
1848 Frederick
1856 Alexander W.
1857 John W.
1858 Allen B.
1861 Leonard
1871 William L.
1872 John C.

1873 William H.
1876 Charles M.
1878 Frederick L.
1882 George W.

Wheelock
1877 John C. F.

Whidden
1871 John W.

Whitaker
1792 Jonathan

White
1796 David
1799 John C.
1806 Ebenezer
1807 Warren
1824 Edward
1827 Oramel
1831 Ashton S. H.
1835 Joseph A.
1835 William O.
1841 Ephraim
1841 George
1856 Heber M.
1856 Russell H.
1859 Alphonso
1863 Berlin
1866 Clarence M.
1866 John B.
1866 Moses P.
1868 Hugh L.
1868 John B.
1872 Joseph
1876 Henry C.
1876 Schyler S.
1877 Benjamin C.
1877 John A.
1881 Isaac F.

Whitehouse
1843 Charles S.
1863 Arthur D.

Whiting
1843 John S.
1862 Arthur N.
1865 Elliott B.
1868 William H.
1873 Isaac S.
1878 John K.
1881 William K.

Whitman
1815 Bernard
1818 Jason
1820 Jonas
1833 Edmund B.
1834 Henry C.
1835 Augustus
1841 Bernard C.
1841 Rufus A.
1842 John
1862 Channing W.
1862 Henry M.
1879 Henry H.

Whitney
1812 Israel
1863 Eli

1865 Francis E.
1881 Samuel A.

Whitridge
1854 Alonzo C.
1882 Morris

Whittemore
1832 Bernard B.
1835 Joseph P.
1846 Henry C.
1846 Horatio H. F.
1869 Jacob B.

Whittier
1861 Joseph W.

Whitwell
1815 Frederick H.
1815 William A.
1819 Charles E.
1863 William S.

Wiggin
1786 Joshua
1790 Chase
1791 Permot
1793 Edmund
1795 Bradstreet
1796 Benjamin
1796 Samuel
1805 Thomas
1806 Andrew P.
1807 Samuel
1810 Peter
1810 William T.
1813 Noah P.
1814 Caleb
1843 George H.
1845 Norris J.
1854 Augustus W.
1856 George W.
1856 Joseph F.
1859 Charles E.
1862 Charles D.
1862 Charles I.
1862 George W.
1862 Samuel B.
1875 Robert C.
1876 Henry L.
1877 Charles H.

Wiggins
1869 John

Wilby
1865 Richard C.

Wilcomb
1881 William W.
1883 Arthur H.

Wilcox
1869 Frank H.
1881 Starling S.

Wilder
1842 Charles W.
1859 Charles S.
1859 Joseph H.
1860 Joseph W.
1860 Rufus L.

Wildes
1835 George D.
1866 George D.

Wilds
1864 Judson B.

Wilkins
1852 Jesse A.

Willard
1810 Henry
1856 Joseph H.
1872 John H.
1879 Waldo W.

Willey
1796 Samuel
1829 Worcester
1830 Hollis
1830 Tolman
1857 James
1861 Henry

Williams
1783 Daniel
1784 Isaac
1785 Samuel
1788 Nathaniel
1790 George
1799 John
1801 David
1801 James C.
1812 John P.
1822 Lemuel S.
1834 John M.
1839 George H.
1842 Frederick W.
1842 William F.
1860 Gorham D.
1876 Samuel L.

Williamson
1882 Hallam G.

Willis
1797 Robert B.
1808 William
1830 Carlos

Wills
1831 George H.

Willson
1867 Hiram

Wilmarth
1876 William H.

Wilson
1786 John
1788 Philip
1813 Benjamin
1813 James
1818 John
1822 Luther T.
1822 Robert
1838 James
1860 George W.
1862 Joseph C.
1863 James C.

INDEX. 195

1865 Arno S.
1865 Ellwood
1871 Edgar A.
1875 William P.
1876 John
1877 Charles M.
1877 Edmund
1880 George R.

Winchester
1851 Wilbur
1870 Frank W.

Windle
1802 William S.

Windship
1802 John C. M.
1803 Letsom

Wing
1859 Henry T.

Wingate
1788 George
1792 John
1843 Joseph C. A.
1875 Charles E. L.

Winkley
1811 Daniel
1830 John F.

Winslow
1791 Samuel
1854 John
1871 John F.
1873 James H.

Winsor
1864 Walter T.
1867 Ernest
1873 Robert

Winter
1841 Samuel W.

Winters
1880 Robert P.

Wirgman
1820 Charles

Wise
1835 William G.
1851 George L.

Wisner
1860 William

Wistar
1864 Dillwyn

Wiswall
1829 William
1831 Henry L.
1838 Augustus
1840 Henry T.
1870 Frederick P.

Wiswell
1871 Charles H.

Witcher
1793 Jedediah

Wolcott
1863 Douglas D.
1879 Robert T.

Wolfe
1865 Leon B.

Wollerton
1876 Samuel H.

Wong
1879 Tsoo Liang
1880 Leung Tung

Wood
1811 Wilmot
1813 Abner
1832 George A.
1856 William A.
1862 Edward L.
1862 George A.
1872 Henry A.
1873 John G.
1882 Frank G.

Woodard
1865 Charles F.

Woodberry
1871 George E.

Woodbridge
1790 William

Woodbury
1806 Samuel
1811 Jonathan
1813 Benjamin
1827 Asa
1842 Augustus A.
1844 Augustus
1879 Gordon
1880 Amory T.
1881 Thornton

Woodman
1801 Daniel
1802 Joseph
1820 Moses E.
1824 Charles W.
1827 Jeremiah H.
1830 Theodore C.
1836 Horatio
1839 Levi T.
1863 Frank
1870 Francis J.

Woodruff
1874 Timothy L.
1880 Henry S.

Woods
1851 Edward

Woolley
1879 Uriah B.

Wooster
1865 Augustus G.

Worcester
1828 Noah

Worthington
1875 Arthur W.

Wright
1861 Frank
1867 Frank H.
1872 James A.
1879 John S.

Wyatt
1789 Josiah
1793 Samuel

Wyeth
1854 Charles J.

Wylie
1875 William H.

Wyman
1817 Oliver C.
1826 Jeffries
1826 Morrill
1850 Samuel B.
1875 Alphonso A.
1878 Franklin

Yager
1876 Willard E.

York
1838 Jasper H.
1854 George S.

Young
1791 Jonathan
1791 William H.
1797 Eleazer
1798 Edmund S.
1805 William
1816 George M.
1829 Timothy R.
1832 Lewis
1838 William
1843 George W.
1852 Solomon W.
1859 James L.
1868 Daniel B.
1881 Walter M.

Zerrahn
1876 David F.

SUMMARY.

Number of students who entered before 1800				. . . . .	647
"	"	"	from 1800 to 1810	. . . .	307
"	"	"	" 1810 " 1820	. . . .	441
"	"	"	" 1820 " 1830	. . . .	378
"	"	"	" 1830 " 1840	. . .	365
"	"	"	" 1840 " 1850	. . . .	357
"	"	"	" 1850 " 1860	. . . .	567
"	"	"	" 1860 " 1870	. . . .	807
"	"	"	" 1870 " 1880	. . . .	902
"	"	"	" 1880 " May 1, 1883	. .	357
	Whole number of students		. . . . . .		5,278

ADDITIONS AND CORRECTIONS

RECEIVED TOO LATE FOR INSERTION IN THEIR PROPER PLACES.

ADDITIONS.

1784 Salmon Gray. Died at Saco, Me.
1784 John Mead, farmer and trader, Newmarket.
1785 Jeremiah Mead, farmer and trader, Newmarket.
1794 George Clifford, mechanic, Cuba.
1797 John H. Goddard, merchant, Boston, Mass. Died at Groton, Mass.
1797 Samuel P. Peirson, merchant. Died in Africa.
1805 John Pierson, shipmaster.
1807 John Goddard. Died in Lisbon, Portugal, 1823.
1811 Richard Hildreth, farmer, Andrew, Ia.
1811 George Jewett, lawyer, Portland, Me.
1813 John Hedge. Died in Massachusetts.
1813 John Sevey, lawyer, New Orleans, La.
1815 Alpheus Hanscom, farmer and teacher. Died 1847.
1825 Nathaniel Hills, lawyer, Newburyport, Mass.
1827 Joseph W. Ellis, printer and teacher, Mt. Vernon, Mo.
1827 Christopher Gore Green. Died at Winslow, Me.
1828 John J. Bradley, Fryeburg, Me.
1828 Albert G. Thornton, lawyer, Biddeford, Me.
1829 George C. Durell. Died in Texas.
1829 John Parsons, merchant, Bay Port, Fla.
1830 Thomas Cutts, lumber dealer, Chicago, Ill. Died at Leavenworth, Kan.
1830 Thomas A. Livermore. Died at Galena, Ill., 1862.
1830 Nathaniel G. Phillips. Died at Griffin, Ga.
1832 William H. Chandler, lawyer and farmer, Thompson, Canada.
1833 Munroe G. I. Tukesbury, M.D., physician, Manchester.
1838 Ozias G. Chapman. Died at St. Louis, Mo., 1866.
1841 *George W. Collamore, lawyer, killed at Lawrence, Kan., 1863.
1852 *Francellus G. Dalton, M.D. Died 1861.
1853 Richard D. Douglass, Amherst Coll., 1860, general superintendent of Children's Aid Society, Brooklyn, N.Y.
1853 Virgil H. McDaniel, auctioneer, Dover.
1853 Benjamin B. McNeal, Government service.
1856 *Elleus G. Dalton, M.D., physician, Philadelphia, Pa. Died 1881.
1860 Morison Alexander, dentist, Lisbon, Portugal.

ADDITIONS AND CORRECTIONS.

1863   Sewall A. Faunce, lawyer.
1863   Samuel H. Garvin, farmer, Acton, Me.
1863   Frederick Thompson, M.A., rector and principal, St. John's School, Faulkland, Del.
1869   John T. Harvey, farmer.
1870   James Ben-Ali Haggin, business, New York, N.Y.
1871   David K. Jackman, business, Poughkeepsie, N.Y.
1871   Henry B. Thompson, banker, Gunnison, Col.
1872   Hickey Hunt Morgan, student, Harvard University.
1872   John J. Nairn, business, Washington, D.C.
1874   Emery W. Johnson, mining and stock broker, Denver, Col.
1875   Paul Voorhees, student, Polytechnic Institute, Troy, N.Y.
1877   Bradbury J. Cilley, business, Buffalo, N.Y.

CORRECTIONS.

1785   For James Toppan read James Tappan.
1785   For John Toppan read John Tappan.
1788   After Nicholas Emery, Dart. Coll., 1795, read A.M.
1790   For *Daniel L. Morrill* read *David L. Morrill.*
1791   After Morris Hobbs, for Northampton, Mass., read North Hampton.
1803   After Joseph Prescott read H.U. 1809.
1803   For Letsom Winship read Letsom Windship.
1807   For David Tukesbury read *David Tukesbury.*
1819   For James Murdock read James Murdoch.
1819   For Charles T. Murdock read Charles T. Murdoch.
1828   After Henry J. Gardner read A.M., LL.D.
1830   For *John H. Murdough* read *John H. Mordough.*
1830   For John F. H. Muzzey read John F. H. Mussey.
1830   For Carlos Willey read Carlos Willis.
1831   For Samuel P. Tuck read Samuel P. Tucke.
1831   After Ezekiel Gilman, for New York, N.Y., read Coinjock, Carrituck Co., N.C.
1834   After Nathaniel H. Morison, for Teacher read Provost, Peabody Institute.
1834   After *John B. L. Soule* read D.D., Prof. Lit. and Greek, Blackburn Univ.
1835   For Rufus H. Hilliard read Rufus Kitridge Hilliard.
1835   After *Geo. D. Wildes* read A.M., D.D.
1836   For Joseph D. L. Davis read Joseph De Lacroix Davis.
1836   For George Osgood read *George Osgood.*
1837   After Charles H. Bell, before LL.D., read A.M.
1839   After Charles H. Branscomb, for Business, Birmingham, Eng., read U.S. Consul, Manchester, Eng., 1869 to 1874. Lawrence, Kan.

ADDITIONS AND CORRECTIONS. 199

1843 For Daniel C. Hill read David C. Hill.
1844 For *Joseph W. Peirce* read Joseph W. Peirce.
1845 After Geo. W. Clark, for Business, Boston, Mass., read Business, Exeter.
1845 After Richard H. Sylvester, for St. Louis, Mo., read Washington, D.C.
1848 For William Pitt Drew read William Paley Drew, Bowd. Coll., 1853, Prof. Anc. Lang., Tufts Coll. Bank Examiner, N.J. and Pa.
1852 After Charles H. Hapgood, for Chicago, Ill., read Alton, Ill.
1854 After Stephen W. Clarke, for Teacher, Portsmouth, read Business, Manchester.
1854 After Alfred Stebbins, for Farmer, San Buenaventura, Cal., read Business, Dubuque, Ia.
1854 After *Calvin Stebbins,* for Detroit, Mich., read Lebanon.
1854 For Jacob Hall Thompson read Jacob Hale Thompson.
1854 After George S. York, for Exeter read Boston, Mass.
1855 After Abijah Hollis, for Concord, Mass., read Concord.
1855 After Noah Sanborn read Bayonne City, N.J.
1863 After Charles R. Brown read H.U. 1877.
1863 After George W. Mann, for Hanover read Hanover, Mass., Lawyer. Bay City, Mich.
1870 After Alonzo L. Thompsen read H.U. 1876.
1870 For Maynard F. Styles read Maynard F. Stiles.

1829 Royal Tyler, formerly Chas. T. Tyler.
1830 Joseph D. Thyng, afterwards Joseph T. Porter.

NOTE.

ALUMNI and others who can supply information which will make future editions of this Catalogue more accurate are requested to communicate the same to

PROF. B. L. CILLEY.

WM. H. GORHAM,
B. L. CILLEY,   } *Committee.*
J. A. TUFTS,

EXETER, N.H., May 25, 1883.

www.ingramcontent.com/pod-product-compliance
Lightning Source LLC
Chambersburg PA
CBHW030817230426
43667CB00008B/1263